CEREMONIAL VIOLENCE

CEREMONIAL VIOLENCE

UNDERSTANDING COLUMBINE AND OTHER SCHOOL RAMPAGE SHOOTINGS

JONATHAN FAST, PH.D.

THE OVERLOOK PRESS
New York

This edition first published in paperback in the United States in 2009 by

The Overlook Press, Peter Mayer Publishers, Inc.
141 Wooster Street
New York, NY 10012

Cataloging-in-Publication Data is available from the Library of Congress

Book design and type formatting by Bernard Schleifer
Manufactured in the United States of America
ISBN 978-1-59020-253-1
10 9 8 7 6 5 4 3 2 1

Du auf dem Schulhof
ich zum Töten bereit
und keiner hier weiss
von meiner Einsamkeit
You, in the schoolyard
I am ready to kill
and no one here knows
of my loneliness

—RAMMSTEIN, "White Flesh," from the album,
Herzeleid (among Eric Harris's favorite bands

When somebody has so little to lose, so that it all seems meaningless to them, then they're likely to consider revenge as having considerable value. They may think of suicide as an escape from it all. That's a terrible combination, being suicidal and wanting revenge. That's at the heart of most of the workplace and school mass murders of the last 20 years.

—DR. PARK DIETZ, as quoted in *The Hook*, 12/4/03

This is a wound that is so deep, you can't measure it in terms of weeks, months, or even years to heal. It is something I will never be over, and I don't think many who were there will.

—FRANK CRAWFORD, a teacher at Lindhurst High,
quoted following the Eric Houston shooting in 1992

CONTENTS

INTRODUCTION

WHY STUDY SCHOOL RAMPAGE SHOOTING?

SCHOOL RAMPAGE (SR) SHOOTINGS are acts of terrorism without an ideological core. At best there is a sham of an ideology cobbled together from books like *Mien Kampf*, Ayn Rand's *Atlas Shrugged*, the writings of Nietzsche, the glamorized pop-culture accounts of Charles Manson and his followers, and movies such as *Natural Born Killers*; it is a hazy, poorly-wrought chain of reasoning that justifies the killing of the innocent by those who have convinced themselves that they are somehow superior. Like other acts of terrorism, SR shootings throw people's lives out of kilter and convince them that the world is a menacing place. They crush the spirit of the community and generate waves of despair across the nation. Names of high schools and communities are stripped, in an instant, of reputations built over decades, as was the case with Columbine, which, during the course of a day— April 20, 1999—was transformed from a better-than-average suburban high school to an evocation of horror and bloodshed. People come to believe that schools are no longer safe, that murderous children have become commonplace, and that American culture has slipped another rung in its descent into barbarity.

In fact, government studies show that school remains among the safest places a child can be. Most injuries that occur in a school are sports-related sprains; most crimes involve petty thievery of items from classrooms and lockers. Regarding the deaths of teenagers, accidents are the primary cause (33 deaths per hundred thousand teens), then homicides (9.5 deaths per hundred thousand), and suicides (7.3 deaths per hundred thousand). The number of adolescent deaths attributable to SR shootings is less than a hundredth of a single percent. Yet in a national poll of 409 teenagers conducted following the Columbine High School shootings, a third believed that a similar incident would occur in their own high school.

So what can be learned by this study has less to do with reducing adolescent deaths than with understanding aspects of certain types of terrorism; that which is constructed on a sham ideology, rather than the terrorism of, for example, a vulnerable people fighting off a tyrannical oppressor. What experiences transform the "normal" elementary school student into a murderous teen? Many school rampage shooters appear to be middle-class teens, healthy, intelligent, apparently well-treated, and provided with opportunities to grow and learn. Yet they become brooding adolescents, plan and execute apparently pointless multiple murders, and then commit suicide or give themselves up to the law and idle away the rest of their lives in a prison cell, in the company of other violent criminals.

Though the victims of SR shootings are few compared with those claimed by the more common hazards of adolescence, their passing is unusually tragic as it is with all victims of human violence. Their parents grieve their lost children in one way or another for the rest of their lives. And what of the wounded? Exposure to cinematic gun fights, where the just-shot engage in strenuous activity, scaling walls and performing acrobatic leaps from rooftops as though they have suffered nothing worse than an insect bite, has desensitized us all to the havoc a bullet creates in human tissue and bone. While a few lucky victims may leave the hospital the same day, more endure dozens of operations and years of occupational therapy before they recover the use of an arm or a leg. Some who avoided the bullets but witnessed the shooting are too traumatized to ever set foot in a school again, and suffer from panic attacks and flashbacks; over time, untreated, many victims become substance abusers or engage in self-destructive behaviors such as self-mutilation or promiscuous, unprotected sex.

Often the community itself becomes a victim. In cases where the killer commits suicide, the community feels cheated of their opportunity to learn his motivation for the crime and the chance to see justice served. Where the killer survives, his slow progress through the legal system repeatedly retraumatizes the community as well as those communities that have been the sites of prior shootings. The period of anticipation during the weeks before a hearing or trial is particularly upsetting. Witnesses live in fear of confronting the "monster" in person, in the courtroom. Members of the community, feeling as though they are in a war zone with the media playing the part of an occupying army, are reluctant to open their front door for fear that a microphone will be shoved in their face. Strangers accost them on the street. Parents of victims, desperate to cover their medical expenses; to uncover suppressed evidence, real or imagined; or simply to vent their rage, file civil suits. Such lawsuits keep the event alive and fresh in people's minds for years to come.

Following the 1992 shooting by Eric Houston at a high school in Olivehurst, California, Frank Crawford, one of the teachers, gave eloquent expression to his grief: "This is a wound that is so deep, you can't measure it in terms of weeks, months, or even years to heal. It is something I will never be over, and I don't think many who were there will."

HOW THE BOOK CAME TO BE WRITTEN

My interest in SR shootings began in 1998 with the news of the tragic deaths of a teacher and three students in Jonesboro, Arkansas. For many years I had done clinical work with teens and their families in neighborhood agencies, at a school-based health center, and as clinical director of a hospital-based program for children with severe psychological problems. I began teaching at Yeshiva University in 1997 and publishing in academic journals in the areas of aggression, crisis response, and school safety, so the shootings fell within my field of expertise. The day after the Jonesboro, Arkansas shooting, I met informally with some of my colleagues to discuss what preconditions might cause two middle-school boys to shoot and kill classmates and a teacher against whom they had only petty grievances. In the course of arguing about diagnoses and environmental influences, we reached two conclusions that I have returned to often during the writing of this book. First, even if the boys were mentally ill or the product of abusive or neglectful parents, so were many tens of thousands of other teenagers, none of whom had found it necessary to commit such a theatrical, tragic, and pointless crime. In order to show that factor X causes extremely violent behavior, X must be present among those who commit extreme violence, but less common, or milder, or absent altogether among those who are less violent or non-violent. Some researchers call this "variation along the dependent variable," since the degree of violence is a variable that *depends* on the presence, absence, or intensity of X.

Second, we agreed that the SR shooter was motivated by a variety of causes; that factor X had to be a composite of several factors; that any explanation, however simple, had to be multi-dimensional. This is nothing new—Hans Eysenck, a well-known British psychologist, suggested a multi-dimensional theory of criminal behavior over forty years ago—but the fact is often overlooked, particularly by pundits who delight in blaming SR shootings on a single pet peeve such as excessive time spent playing video games, dissolution of the nuclear family, the teaching of evolution, the teaching of values curriculums, ignorance of the Ten Commandments, or even the bleak architecture of the suburbs. Human behavior is a complex thing. People are motivated by many factors: genetic predisposition, pre-natal care, neo-natal health, childhood diseases, psychiatric disorders, familial strengths and dysfunctions, the social life of the school and the community, the influence of the media and the culture, politics, and customs of the land where they live. While the factors are many, they are neither so many nor so subtle that they are beyond our ability to identify and understand.

School rampage shootings present an opportunity to examine a type of predatory mass murder involving "extreme violence," criminologist Lonnie Athens' term for an act of retaliation completely disproportionate to its provocation. Because the SR shooter's criminal career is very much shorter than an adults', the galaxy of variables is constrained by time, and relationships of cause and effect are more apparent and easily established. Many cases are well-documented, and often the information is easily available through newspaper archives, court transcripts, and interviews. Furthermore, SR shootings resemble other kinds of predatory mass murders such as suicide bombings, workplace shootings, and terrorist attacks. The deep understanding of such types of violent behavior may be one of our most important tasks as a global community in the 21st century.

WHAT DO WE ALREADY KNOW ABOUT MASS MURDERERS, VIOLENT ADOLESCENTS, AND SR SHOOTERS?

Most murders are unplanned, spontaneous, and occur when anger and fear produce violent behavior in response to an imminent threat. Such murders are often called "affective," the human equivalent of the fight or flight response seen in animals. Mass murders, "the intentional killing of multiple victims by a single offender within a 24 hour period of time," are rare events, accounting for less than one percent of all violent crimes. This latter style of aggression tends to be "predatory": planned, purposeful, and without emotion. In the 1980s, Park Eliot Dietz, an eminent criminologist, proposed a typology of mass murderers with three categories: "family annihilators," depressed men, highly invested in their families, who kill their wives and children along with themselves because they fear, or wish to believe, that no one else can care for them; "set and run" killers, those who set bombs and disappear, such as Ted Kaczynski, the Unabomber; and "pseudo-commandos," those who are preoccupied with fire-arms and military garb, and plan and deliberate extensively before they act. School rampage shooters, obsessed with weapons and planning, often donning militaristic or terrorist costumes for their shootings and even playing theme music to "pump themselves up," fall into the final category.

A research effort conducted by the *New York Times* following the Columbine High School shooting examined 100 cases of rampage killing committed over a period of 50 years, from 1949 to 1999. It was found that while adult mass murderers operated in isolation, adolescent mass murderers invariably shared their plans with one or more friends. Seung-Hui Cho, who killed 31 victims at Virginia Tech in April of 2007, kept his plans entirely to himself, but he was 23 years old, on the adult side of adolescence. All but one of the school rampage shooters in this study were 18 or younger and all had friends, or collaborators, or those whose status fell somewhere in between, who knew of their plans.

A report prepared by a special investigative team organized by the Secret Service, released a few months after the *New York Times* study, found that SR shooters were often bullied. In over two-thirds of the SR shootings examined,

> . . . attackers felt persecuted, bullied, threatened, attacked, or injured by others prior to the incident. A number of attackers had experienced bullying and harassment that was longstanding and severe. In those cases the experience of bullying appeared to play a major role in motivating the attack at school. . . . (I)n a number of cases, attackers described experiences of being bullied in terms that approached torment. They told of behaviors that, if they occurred in the workplace, would meet the legal definitions of harassment."

Other studies of SR shooters confirmed these findings.

In the most recent and comprehensive study of SR shootings, Katherine Newman, a Princeton sociologist, and her colleagues identified five conditions common to SR shooters. First, the SR shooter perceives himself as "socially marginalized" (whether he is or not). He is the brunt of bullying, teasing, the target of negative rumors, and other exclusionary behaviors. Second, he suffers from psychosocial problems—learning disorders, psychiatric disorders, dysfunctional families, and the like—that "magnify the impact of the marginality." Third, he follows "cultural scripts" for problem-solving, meaning that he buys into the machismo mythology of violence as a problem-solving strategy. *If people are treating you badly, make them respect you through a show of force.* Fourth, he "flies beneath the radar," meaning that his seriously problematic behavior goes unidentified by the traditional gatekeepers: the teachers, guidance counselors, school psychologists, and social workers. His parents collude by being secretive, isolated from the school, or in denial about his problems. The shooter himself may have several strategies for avoiding juvenile court. He may be the class clown, whom no one takes seriously; a practiced and skillful liar; or a boy who keeps to himself. He may be avoided by otherwise helpful adults because he gives off a strange, menacing "vibe." Fifth, he has access to firearms. Without the availability of guns, there are no SR shootings. One used to see a bumper sticker asserting that *Guns don't kill people, people kill people*. The literal truth is that places with more guns have higher rates of adolescent suicide, homicide, and injury than places with fewer guns.

METHODOLOGY

While quantitative research has long been considered, in academic circles, the superior paradigm, qualitative research is more appropriate for an investigation such as this for two reasons. First, SR shootings are sufficiently rare that statistical analysis, upon which quantitative research depends, is meaningless.

Statistical formulas are likely never to be useful for predicting infrequent instances of targeted violence such as school or workplace homicides, because the base rate is so low that, mathematically, high rates of accuracy are nearly impossible.

Seeking to predict acts that occur as rarely as school shootings is almost impossible. This is simple statistical logic: when the incidence of any form of violence is very low and a very large number of people have identifiable risk factors, there is no reliable way to pick out from that large group the very few who will actually commit the violent act.

Second, when little is understood about a phenomenon, qualitative research techniques are more likely to provide the deep and comprehensive understanding necessary for theory building. I chose to conduct this study using a qualitative methodology called "grounded theory" because it is especially conducive to theory-building.

The criteria used to select cases was built upon that suggested by P. E. Deitz and J. Reid Meloy: the shooter or the victims had to be on school grounds during the crime, the assailants had to be adolescents, and the victims had to number two besides the shooter, had he committed suicide too (suicide is nearly always the intended conclusion of the shooter's plan, although more often than not he loses his nerve when the time comes and gives himself up to the police). Thus my criteria excluded cases such as Toby Sincino (Blackville, SC; October 6, 1996), who killed one teacher and himself; Jon William Romano (East Greenbush, New York; February 9, 2004), who threatened students but only wounded one teacher; Dustin Pierce (McKee, Kentucky; September 20, 1989), who brought a shotgun to school, took students hostage, but hurt no one; and perhaps a dozen other cases. The criteria also excluded school disasters perpetrated by post-adolescent males. Two of the worst school disasters in history fall into this category: the Dunblane, Scotland shooting of 1996 where 43-year-old Thomas Hamilton killed 16 kindergarten children before taking his own life; and the Bath, Michigan School Disaster in 1927 involving a disgruntled farmer who detonated a TNT bomb in the local school, killing 39 grade-school children.

The criteria yielded 13 cases. Because the incidents at Columbine High School and in Jonesboro, Arkansas, both involved two boys working in tandem, there are 15 shooters.

SR Shooters Selected for the Study

Name & Age	Date of Shooting	Location
Anthony Barbaro, 17	Dec. 30, 1974	Oleans, NY
Brenda Spencer, 16*	Jan. 16, 1979	San Diego, CA
Eric Houston, 20	May 1, 1992	Olivehurst, CA
Wayne Lo, 19*	Dec. 14, 1992	Great Barrington, MA
Scott Pennington, 17	Jan. 8, 1993	Grayson, KY
Jamie Rouse, 17	Nov. 15, 1995	Lynneville, TN
Barry Loukaitis, 14	Sept. 2, 1996	Moses Lake, WA
Evan Ramsey, 16*	Feb. 19, 1997	Bethel, AL
Luke Woodham, 16*	Oct. 1, 1997	Pearl, MS
Michael Carneal, 14	Dec. 1, 1997	West Paducah, KY
Mitchell Johnson, 13† Andrew Golden, 11†	March 24, 1998	Jonesboro, AK
Kip Kinkel, 15	May 21, 1998	Springfield, OR
Eric Harris, 18*Δ Dylan Klebold, 17*Δ	April 20, 1999	Littleton, CO

* Cases described in depth
†Δ Dyadic shootings

While the cases span a period from 1974 to 1999, SR type shootings occurred prior to this time. On May 19, 1936, a brilliant, eccentric Williams College student named Lewis Jack Somers, Jr. killed one classmate, wounded another, and killed himself with a pair of mail order pistols. While other such cases have occurred, they are difficult to track down and often poorly documented. If far fewer SR shootings were committed prior to the first half of the 20th century, their infrequency may be related to the difficulty in obtaining guns, their cost, and their unreliable mechanisms and limited firepower. For a teenager to commit a rampage killing, he needs a weapon that is easy to obtain, inexpensive, and can fire semi-automatically (i.e. fire rapidly each time the trigger is depressed without having to manually move a new cartridge into the chamber). Such weapons only became widely available in the 1960s when, as a result of violent revolutions abroad, cheap, foreign-made, "assault" rifles such as the Uzi, the Kalishnakov, and the Chinese SKS flooded the American market. I chose to end my study with Columbine because it seemed like a climax to the school shooting story, a worst case that the others presaged. I could not have been more wrong. A school shooting occurred in Alberta, Canada eight days after Columbine. More than 25 school shootings have occurred since then, most of them in the United States but more and more often in other countries such as Germany, Bosnia, Argentina, and even Finland.

On April 16, 2007, Seung-Hui Cho, a 23-year-old South Korean national with a history of mental illness, killed 32 students and wounded another 29 at Virginia Polytechnic Institute where he was a student. Seung-Hui Cho's crime was similar to those described in this book except that he operated without an accomplice or even a single confidante. He shot many of his victims repeatedly to be sure they were dead. The sheer magnitude and viciousness of the killings brought SR shootings back to the front page and the forefront of public discourse. It is unsettling to think that any SR shooter who so desires can become front page news by sufficiently upping the ante. How many young lives will have to be sacrificed to seize the public's attention five or ten years from now?

Each case in the study was reconstructed from documentary evidence, articles from community newspapers, legal documents, and personal accounts. The compilation of the cases, interrupted by the tasks of daily life, teaching and academic committee work, Red Cross volunteering, occasional consulting jobs, and familial obligations, took six years and yielded about 150,000 words of text. A content analysis yielded recurrent themes which were then organized into a theory. Very briefly, "a theory is a systematic and formalized expression of all previous observations, and is predictive, logical, and testable." Readers interested in the details of this process should consult *The Discovery of Grounded Theory*. Although the theory of ceremonial violence can be described in a page or two, creating and then clarifying it—putting it together and then pulling it apart again—was the longest part of the process; at its most intense stage, it occupied my thoughts during nearly all my waking hours.

THE THEORY OF CEREMONIAL VIOLENCE

The thesis of this book is that SR shootings constitute a form of what I have chosen to call "ceremonial violence."

"The candidate," as I will refer to the would-be SR shooter, is a very unhappy child. Circumstances such as childhood abuse, neglect, mental illness, parental separation, and frequent relocations are common. He may have brain damage that makes him behave oddly, be peculiar in appearance, or a have a deformity that makes him the target of ridicule and bullying. A poor fit between a child and his family, be it a very bright child born into a low functioning family, or a socially awkward child in a family of social successes, will exacerbate the situation. Problems of "poorness of fit" may extend to the school and the community. A number of the SR shooters lived in tight-knit, Christian communities where behavioral proscriptions were narrow and rigidly enforced; conditions that encourage the marginalization of the misfit. The candidate's problems reach a boiling point in adolescence. The central crisis of adolescence is forming the foundations of an adult identity. *What kind of person will I be? By which ideals will I navigate the seas of adulthood? What will be my profession? My politics? My faith? In which social milieu will I find comfort and friendship?* As R. F. Baumeister has pointed out, the adolescent who has failed to form an identity often becomes self-destructive and suicidal.

Of all the dimensions of identity formation, that of integration into a social milieu may be central. Most of us are familiar with the strict hierarchical structure of high school "society," a kind of cartoon version of the adult world. Lines of inclusion and exclusion are clearly delineated and fashions in clothes, behavior, and speech must be adhered to rigorously. Talent, charm, good looks, and wealthy or influential parents are the social capitol. Ambition and the ability to endure the stress and discomfort of the competition are also a prerequisite in ascending the social ladder. During the sifting and resifting of freshman year, the candidate drifts to the bottom of the pile: he finds himself in a community of the excluded, the crazies, the rebels, the outcasts, and the delinquents. In order to be *someone*, he and some friends may informally "incorporate" themselves as satanists, skin-heads, Goths, or vampires, anything to suggest a degree of affiliation and power, even if it is only magical or imaginary. Despite this, the rejection continues: girls refuse to date the candidate or break up after a few dates because he is scary, impulsive (in a bad way), lacking in empathy, and barely able to conceal his rage about being disenfranchised. Adults—even his parents—may avoid him for the same reasons. School personnel may pretend not to notice him, secretly hoping that he will graduate before anything awful happens. He may feel betrayed by siblings because of their social and academic success. With every act of exclusion and rejection, he grows more alienated and furious at his peers, school, and family for what he imagines was their contribution to his current dilemma.

Suicide, disturbingly common among American teens, is often the result of alienation due to a changing world, as Emile Durkheim pointed out over a hundred years ago. The candidate might commit suicide at this point were it not for two factors: first, he is a narcissist, or in common parlance, a Drama Queen, a person who craves attention and lacks empathy, two factors which unfortunately operate synergistically in turning a suicide, a private event, into a mass murder, a public event. Second, he has by now found a best friend or soulmate, a member of his disenfranchised group who suffers from a milder form of the candidate's problem and recognizes, in the candidate's rage, a potential proxy, a person through whom he can experience homicide vicariously, and get rid of a few people he hates without sharing the risk. *If you're going to shoot people anyway, get that kid who stole my iPod in middle school.* In some cases this soulmate may take on the role of "violence coach," part of the process of socialization into violence described by Athens and discussed at greater length in Chapter 5 of this book. The coach convinces the candidate to channel his rage into an SR shooting, promising that as a result he will become loved by his similarly oppressed peers, feared by the bullies, or simply renowned throughout the world for being "bad-ass" or cool. This sham ideology is reinforced by books, movies, and rap songs that glorify violence and killing. The coach may keep himself at arm's length from the event, agree to participate in it, or agree and then change his mind when it is too late for the candidate to turn back. He may make a suicide pact with the candidate that they will both die at the end of the shooting, as Dylan Klebold and Eric Harris did before the Columbine High School shooting; or he and the candidate may indulge in a fantasy of denial, involving escape to some magical haven by impossible means. Luke Woodham and Grant Boyette, described in Chapter 5, imagined escaping to Cuba; and Andrew Golden, 11, and Mitchell Johnson, 13, shooters in the

Jonesboro, Arkansas case, convinced themselves that they might be forgiven for their killings after a few weeks of hiding out in the woods.

Once the candidate gets the idea of turning his suicide into a public ceremony, he becomes absorbed in the planning of it, often documenting his thoughts in journals and other media. He may "publicize" the event by telling certain select friends about it, warning them to stay home that day, or suggesting a safe place from which they can view the mayhem. Seung-Hui Cho, mentioned earlier, paused during the Virginia Tech shooting in order to FedEx a press kit with photos, a DVD, and a document explaining his motives, to NBC News. The candidate will purchase special clothing and weapons for the event. He may even choose background music. This kind of ceremony seems to be a throwback to something very ancient and primitive, where the supplicant plays the part of a god, and indulges in a forbidden or privileged activity prior to his own execution or banishment from the tribe.

In the Overview, I present a brief summary of each of the thirteen cases in the study, with a minimum of commentary. *Just the facts, Ma'am*, as Sergeant Friday used to say. The six subsequent chapters are devoted to a more detailed examination of five of the cases, those of Brenda Spencer; Wayne Lo; Evan Ramsey; Luke Woodham; and Eric Harris and Dylan Klebold, who participated together in the Columbine High School shooting, with my commentary interwoven where I believe it illuminates behavior. I have included some details of the trials, how the schools and the communities responded to the shootings, and accounts of the survivors and their tortuous journeys of recovery. The examination of the post-shooting events are valuable to those who have an interest in school safety, crisis response, the recovery of the community from acts of terrorism, and the treatment of trauma. I wanted, for at least a few of the cases, to include the whole story, start to finish. While I was trained late in life as a social scientist, I was raised in a family of storytellers, and I know that to fully understand what has occurred—to get to the heart of it—one must hear the whole story.

SOME THANK-YOUS

Although this book took a long time to write, it would have taken a lot longer (or never have been completed at all) without the encouragement and support of a number of people. I thank the Fink Family Foundation for a generous grant; my agents, Ryan Fischer-Harbage and Kirby Kim at Vigliano Associates; Aaron Schlechter at Overlook, who edited the book; my research assistant, Faith Fisch; Sheldon Gelman, dean of Wurzweiler School of Social Work at Yeshiva University, who enthusiastically supported and guided this project from its inception; my colleagues, including Adrian Ashe and Steve Pimpare, who posed important questions about the work; Lou Levitt, who was my guru throughout doctoral studies and remained a source of guidance and encouragement in subsequent years; Bill Modzeleski, of the U.S. Department of Education's Office of Safe and Drug Free Schools, who graciously let me draw on his knowledge of the topic, and occasionally reined me in; and a host of helpful librarians, courthouse employees, and newspaper archivists in San Diego, Denver, upstate New York, Alaska, Mississippi, and elsewhere around the country, who gave generously of their time and knowledge. Cyn Shepard's Columbine Site (acolumbinesite.com) was a tremendous help in reviewing and organizing the voluminous materials haphazardly released by the Jefferson County Sheriff's Office. Special thanks also to Brooks Brown, for his book, *No Easy Answers: The Truth Behind the Deaths at Columbine* and Jon Bellini, for his book, *Child's Prey*, which were invaluable sources for the chapters on Columbine and Luke Woodham, respectively.

I would also like to thank my family, Barbara, Ben, Dan; Molly Jong-Fast, Matt Greenfield, and of course, Max; Rachel and Avrum Ben-Avi, and my dear friends, Warren and Susan Stern, Debra and Ralph Hafner-Tartaglioni, Frank and Rosella Fanelli, and Jerry and Denny Davidoff, all of whom encouraged me and helped me clarify my ideas by being wonderful listeners and gentle critics.

AN OVERVIEW

THIS OVERVIEW PRESENTS SUMMARIES of the 13 cases analyzed for this study, rather than the case studies themselves which, if reprinted in full, would fill over 600 pages of manuscript, and would involve much tedious, repetitive, and superfluous detail. Thumbnail sketches of the six chapter-length cases are also included here to help the reader keep track of the sequence of shootings over a span of two and a half decades, and to provide a kind of reference section for ideas presented in later chapters.

It is interesting to note that each of the longer summaries in this chapter (1,3,5,6,7,10,11,12) is up to 30 percent longer than the one that precedes it, which is in proportion to the length of the original case study, and reflects the depth and breadth of the documentary evidence that was available to me during the writing of this book. As the public's interest in SR shootings grew, so did the news coverage, the community's willingness to discuss the tragedy openly, the state's eagerness to try the killers as adults and, as a result of the shooter moving out of the juvenile justice system, the public's access to trial proceedings and documents that would have otherwise remained confidential. So while it was difficult to find good documentary evidence about Anthony Barbaro and other early cases, the information about the last three cases—Andrew Golden and Mitchell Johnson, Kip Kinkel, and Eric Harris and Dylan Klebold—was so plentiful that the chore became one of organizing the material, separating fact from hearsay, and choosing between alternate and sometimes contradictory narratives.

The first of these cases, that of Anthony Barbaro, from 1974, defines threads that will weave themselves through the fabric of this book: the smart boy; the infatuation with guns; the social isolation; the journal of self-hatred; the homicidal and suicidal behavior; the apparently normal and affectionate family; the bomb-making supplies hidden in his room; the mass murder during senior year, performed in paramilitary garb; the random choice of victims; and the apparent lack of motive.

What troubled me was that it also seemed to veer the farthest from the theory of ceremonial violence. Where were the events that led to the shooter feeling as though he was damaged goods: the birth defect, the brain damage, the mental illness, the incest, the learning disabilities? Where were the factors that made him an outsider at home and in school? As a social worker, I know about the power of family secrets; I have worked with families whose Leave-it-to-Beaver sheen masked multiple generations of incest and violence. But I have come to believe that an act of public violence will crack the veneer (that may have been an agenda item for several of the shooters). Two messages that came to my attention in January of 2008 may resolve these mysteries. They are included at the end of the case.

1. Anthony Barbaro

Anthony was the eldest of four siblings in an intact, Catholic family that had lived, for three generations, in Oleans, New York, a rural town in the Appalachian foothills. Tony, as he liked to be called, collected firearms, often dressed in camouflage pants and jackets, combat boots and sunglasses year round. He was on the rifle team at school and practiced twice a week at the Oleans armory. He was a loner, an honors student, responsible, helpful, and considerate of others. He enjoyed chess and the novels of Kurt Vonnegut, and wanted to be an engineer. On April 15, 1974, he bought a 30.06 Remington rifle at a local gun store, and at the same time began keeping a diary, chronicling his plans for a rampage killing. He stored bomb-making materials in his room, including black powder, gasoline, and tanks of acetylene. He somehow purchased a self-contained gas mask and boxes of hollow-nosed ammunition, items not available to the general public. During Christmas vacation of the same year, he snuck into his high school and made a sniper's nest in a third floor classroom. To the accompaniment of an Elton John song, *Ticking*, played on a portable tape machine, he began firing out the window, killing three people and wounding eleven others. The night before the trial was to begin, he hanged himself from a bed sheet in his jail cell. A suicide note read, in part:

> I guess I just wanted to kill the person I hate most—myself. I just didn't have the courage. That's one reason why what happened happened I think. I wanted to die, but I couldn't do it; so I had to get someone to do it for me. It didn't work out.

Because the case never went to trial, and people of Oleans were circumspect with reporters, very little information is available about this case.

The widely-reported and unusually tragic Virginia Tech shooting on April 16, 2007, apparently reawakened memories of school shootings for many people who had been directly involved with them, or who had brushed shoulders with them in the past. Because only one website, www.knowgangs.com, described the case of Anthony Barbero and provided a space for visitors to leave comments, former and current Oleans residents, relatives and friends of Anthony Barbero, and others who had heard the story second- or third-hand, began to leave messages there. It became a kind of online bereavement group. Two of these messages were of particular interest, so I reprint them in full:

DAVID
10 SEP 2007, 16:52

I was Tony's best friend in seventh and eighth grade. I found this page on a fluke . . . just thought I would type in his name and see what pops up. Gosh, I remember Ed Connelly in sixth grade . . . saw his comment earlier. Ed, you were one of the best teachers I ever had.

Knowing what we know now about these things I think it is sad that so many people want to believe that everything was normal in his household and in his town and that there were no signs. It really gets old and tired. There were plenty of warning signs all over the place. The simple fact is that nobody was paying any attention. It is the same for all of the shooters.

First off, Tony had been writing notebooks about "invading" Olean and blowing things up since he was ten years old. Nobody thought it was strange. I remember looking at the notebooks and asking him what it was all about.

He had been making bombs since that age out of Estes "rocket engines" that he bought in a hobby shop in town. He would grind out the powder in the rocket engines and compress them in a package and go blow them up in the woods. Lots of people knew about this. I know this because we both were fond of launching Estes toy rockets. However, he liked doing more than that. I just liked flying them. I was always terrified to go near his bomb experiments because I was afraid of losing a hand. He thought it was funny. I know other people who can confirm what I say.

In addition, I don't know how everybody can say everything was perfectly normal in the house. In all the years I knew him I never met the family. He did not want me to meet them because he said they didn't like strangers coming in the house. I always got the impression that things were not cool in that house. I thought this was very odd, even then.

People don't just magically do the things he did for no reason. It is a cop-out on the part of people who want to believe that all families are loving entities. This categorically is not true. There are many, many examples of parents who detest and hate their own children. People do not want to acknowledge awful parenting. It is considered bad form. There are many terrible parents out there.

Especially if they think their child is gay or feminine. This is the great untalked about phenomina. Nobody wants to mention how children like him were mocked and humiliated by their straight peers. Rather, everybody wants to say, "Oh, I just don't know how it happened." Well, I know how it happened and all I can say is that he was mistreated and mocked. As was I.

Tony was gay in a bad time to be gay. Funny how that never comes up in all the stories about him or in any articles. Imagine being gay in a small country town with very religious parents. Do you get the picture of how unpleasant that was? I can tell you that I could never live as I was in that town. Look at how, even now, we have all the crackpots coming out of the woodwork trying to stop two people from loving each other. Think about it, people are obsessed with trying to stop love. Love is a crime, apparently.

And that play that was written about him. I just have to laugh at how ignorant it is. For example, the play says he had a brother who died in Vietnam. That never happened.

Tony was going to the Air Force Academy. He was very obsessed with proving his manliness, I think. However, he went crazy at a very early age, as do all the shooters. The deal was set by the time he was ten or twelve. People are made, they are not accidents. Acting bewildered is a way for communities to avoid collective guilt.

The gay issue needs to be brought out into the open. Tony was gay. I know for a fact. And he had no support for being treated badly, unlike straight kids who have somebody to run to. And many of the modern shooters have been gay. Hmmm . . . but it is hardly mentioned in the press, at least not in the straight press. Could it be that people don't want to see what they have done to others? Or are they just simply so confident that it never even occurs to them? (David, 1997)

ANONYMOUS
30 JAN 2008, 23:03

Tony was my cousin. Some of the things in this article are true, as well as some that are not. For one, Tony wasn't gay. Tony was a very intelligent boy, and he could not handle that. That is what had to drive him to this rage. His family was a tight knit family, but his mother was an alcoholic. His father was the very quiet type, didn't say much unless the kids were annoying him. I last saw Tony's mom (my Aunt Helen) in 1999. We were all mourning the death of her sister (my Aunt Sondra). My Aunt Helen wasn't in a very pleasant state at that time, so we didn't get to talk much. There are questions that I don't have answers to, and I never got to ask Tony's mom. I do feel very sorry for the victims, and their families, but we lost someone too. I wasn't close to Tony, I am closer to his brother's age, but I still love him.

Both these comments are, strictly speaking, anonymous (although they both provide enough detail for an intrepid investigator to track down their authors) but they are written convincingly, and contain accurate details, as far as I can make out. David's account of Tony's homosexuality, of his being bullied, of his alienation from his family because of their religious beliefs, of his long term plans for revenge on the town, are consistent with the other cases described in this book.

I particularly like David's insistence that "People don't just magically do the things he did for no reason." He's a social scientist at heart.

2. BRENDA SPENCER

Brenda Spencer, 16, the youngest of three children, lived alone with her divorced father in a suburb of San Diego. On the morning of January 29, 1979, using a .22 caliber rifle and 500 rounds of ammunition that her father had given her for Christmas, she fired on an elementary school across the street from her home, killing the principal and a janitor, and wounding eight children and a police officer. It was later discovered that Brenda had a seizure disorder and brain damage, possibly from a fall off her bicycle. She was tried and sentenced to 25 years to life. At her second parole hearing in 2005 she stated that she had been sexually and physically abused by her father, a claim he later denied. (This case is described in detail in Chapter 1.)

3. ERIC HOUSTON

Eric Houston grew up in Olivehurst, a small farming community in the Sacramento Valley of California. His father abandoned the family when he was two, and he grew up with his mother, an older sister, and a half brother, Ron Cadell, in a modest house separated by the interstate from Lindhurst High School, which he later attended. Because Ron was 13 years older, became a kind of surrogate father to Eric.

At two months of age, Eric contracted spinal meningitis, and in childhood, pneumonia and other medical problems so severe that his doctor expressed doubts that he would survive to adolescence. As the result of these problems as well as violent physical abuse, Eric suffered from organic brain damage. He was diagnosed learning-disabled in elementary school, and moved into classes for "slow learners." He was a quiet and moody child, with no history of behavioral problems and an IQ slightly below normal.

In high school, academics remained a struggle. Two of his friends self-identified as homosexuals, and Eric's conflicts about his own emerging sexuality may have contributed to two or more suicide attempts involving guns. Following a single homosexual encounter with his best friend, Eric insisted that their relationship be non-sexual. By senior year Eric was described as a quiet, sad figure, who dressed in black and listened to morose rock music, a "nice guy" who didn't take drugs and drank with moderation. Although a gun enthusiast, he never hunted or shot at animals. In senior year he took sophomore U.S. History with a young, handsome teacher who was well-liked in the school. In January, Eric approached the teacher about a paper he had written, and was, according to his testimony, offered a passing grade in return for performing fellatio on him. A second, similar incident occurred about three months later, also in the empty classroom, and perhaps a third. Despite his promises, the teacher treated him disrespectfully and gave him a failing grade. As a result, Eric was not be permitted to graduate, attend the senior prom, or join the army, the only career option that held any appeal for him.

After graduation, Eric found work through a temp agency with Hewlett-Packard, assembling circuit boards. At the same time he began buying guns and ammunition at a rate that alarmed his friends. He spent hours locked in his bedroom, cleaning his guns, watching violent films and reading paramilitary magazines. In February he was laid off from Hewlett-Packard for reasons that were not performance-related, and his girlfriend broke up with him and joined the Coast Guard. One night he jumped the fence surrounding Lindhurst High School and penciled a map of how he planned to attack. On the morning of May 1, 1992, he left the following note under the cover of his waterbed:

> My HATEtrid tord humanity forced me to do what I did. . . . I know parenting had nothing to do with what happen's today. It seems my sanity has slipped away and evil tooken it's place. The mistakes the loneliness and the failures have built up to high. Also I just wanted to say I love my family very much . . .
>
> Also I just wanted to say I also love my friend David Rewert too. And if I die today please bury me somewhere beautiful.

Eric proceeded to the high school, directly to the class of the teacher whom he felt had betrayed him, and killed him. He killed three students, wounded 10 others, and took 60 to 80 students hostage, whom he released gradually over the next seven hours. He gave himself up to the police at 10:35 PM. He was convicted of numerous charges and sentenced to death by poisonous gas.

4. WAYNE LO

Wayne Lo was born in Taiwan, China. His father, a captain in the Taiwan air force, grew disaffected with the local government and immigrated to Billings Montana, where he opened a Chinese restaurant. In middle school Wayne worked long hours at the restaurant, studied intensely at a private Catholic school, and became a prodigy on the violin. In the second semester of his freshman year, he began to show signs of tremendous stress and anxiety. His schoolwork became sloppy and according to one teacher, he took pleasure in his bad grades. Concerned that he would make a suicide attempt, his parents decided he would transfer to Simon's Rock, a boarding school for "exceptional" students in Great Barrington, Massachusetts. Wayne, who considered himself a "jock," did not fit in with the liberal artsy-craftsy culture of the school. He began associating with a small, tough group of conservative students, whose repertoire of "trash talk" included threats to kill other students whom they found annoying. In his sophomore year Wayne stopped practicing violin, explaining to his violin teacher that he had little interest in music and wanted to be a lawyer. At about the same time he began telling friends that he wanted to buy a gun and shoot people in the cafeteria, singling out Jews, African Americans, and homosexuals.

At 10:00 PM on the evening of December 14, 1992, using a semiautomatic assault rifle he had purchased at a local shop and ammunition from a mail-order company, Wayne crossed the campus, killing a student and a staff member, wounding four others, and terrifying everyone. He is currently serving two life sentences (Wayne Lo's story is described in detail in Chapter 2).

5. SCOTT PENNINGTON

Scott Pennington grew up in a rented, ramshackle house in an economically-depressed, rural part of Eliot County, Kentucky. His father was mildly mentally retarded from excessive alcoholism and drug abuse dating back to his own adolescence. His mother's intelligence was also below average, and she was psychotic, hiding behind the barn when people came to visit and ruminating about ghosts. Scott's father physically abused him and his mother; beyond these violent episodes, he had no relationship with his son. The family lived on welfare, and income from odd jobs. When times were particularly hard, they wove and sold grapevine wreaths.

In contrast to his parents, Scott was highly intelligent. By second grade he was exhibiting a passion for science and math, which the school nurtured by providing him with advanced textbooks, and even allowing him to take home an Apple computer over the summer. He was slow to develop physically, and was six years old before he could tie his shoes and 12 before he learned to ride a bicycle.

In the spring of 1992 the house they were renting changed hands and they were evicted by the new landlord. Against Scott's tearful protests, they moved to Grayson, an area with one of the highest unemployment rates in the state, to a house without indoor plumbing, electricity, or a telephone. Scott, now entering his senior year of high school, was enrolled in East Carter High School, a school of 600 students, most of whom had known each other all their lives. Despite joining the academic team, he remained an outsider. His classmates teased him about his appearance, his stutter, his skinny limbs, thick glasses, odd haircut, and "momma's boy" behavior, and called him, "nerd," "geek," and "dork." On one occasion he was savagely beaten for accidentally bumping into another student in the hallway. In December of that year, Scott's closest friend, a girl he had met in 1991, in a summer program for culturally and financially deprived teens, broke up with him.

His English teacher, Mrs. McDavid, a woman with a reputation for her devotion to her students, befriended him, and even gave him her unlisted home phone number. She grew concerned when he handed in an essay on the theme, "The Worst Day of my Life."

The worst day of my life was the day I was born . . . the day I realized that no matter what I did, Dad would never love me . . . the day when I discovered I had no friends, my stuttering became more pronounced . . . I realized what hell life was . . . I have been serving 11 years of hell.

She showed his writing to two administrators, who encouraged her to alert the police and school social workers, but she refrained from further discussions of Scott's case for fear that she would lose his trust or push him into committing suicide or homicide. She also spoke to the director of a local student assistance program, but again decided to hold off from making a referral. In January, she gave him a "C" for a midterm grade. Devastated that it would make him ineligible for a scholarship he had been offered by the State University at Morehouse, he pleaded with her to change it. She refused. Scott told his friends that he was going to shoot her or put a bomb in her mailbox. He wrote in his diary: "Wonder where I'll be this time next year; asylum, grave, jail, home, college? Home and college can be ruled out. Why? Because they don't pat you on the back for what I am planning."

On Monday, January 18th, Martin Luther King Day (a holiday unobserved by the Carter County school district), Scott brought his grandfather's .38 Smith & Wesson to school in his book bag. During English class—seventh period, the last class of the day—Scott entered the classroom as the tardy bell was ringing. He fired twice at Mrs. McDavid, missing the first time, hitting her in the skull the second time and killing her instantly. Other students and teachers crowded the classroom entrance for a look. Some thought it was a play, or an MTV event. The custodian pushed his way through and was rewarded with a bullet in the chest, bleeding to death in a few minutes. Scott then took over the class, reenacting a scene from one of his favorite books, *Rage*, by Stephen King, the story of a boy, a misfit, who shoots his teacher and, while holding the class hostage, becomes a sort of group facilitator/ truth-teller/ heroic figure, encouraging the students to express their authentic selves. Scott was calm throughout this impromptu encounter group; students noticed with surprise that his stutter had vanished.

He released the students in groups of four and, when the room was empty, placed his gun on the desk and gave himself up to the police. The entire incident had lasted only 15 minutes. The jury found him mentally ill and guilty of two counts of murder. He was sentenced to life imprisonment in Kentucky State Reformatory—a prison that provided an array of mental health services—with the possibility of parole after 25 years, when he would be 42. He was also found guilty of 21 counts of kidnapping for which he received a twenty-year sentence that he could serve concurrently.

6. JAMIE ROUSE

Jamie Rouse lived with his father, a truck driver, his mother, and two brothers in Tightbark Hollow, a rural town 75 miles south of Nashville. Many of his neighbors were collateral relatives of the Rouses. Members of Jamie's family, including his grandmother and his father, Elison, had struggled with alcoholism, mental illness, and addiction. Returning from a long haul drunk and ill-tempered, Elison would beat and berate his wife, break things, and punch holes in the walls. He also beat and belt-whipped the children but only as punishment for misbehaving or poor grades, a distinction on which he prided himself. On one occasion, after the family cats had eaten an unattended bucket of Kentucky Fried Chicken, Elison shot them and threw their bodies into the trees.

Jamie was a quiet, well-behaved, but fearful child. He was extremely shy and would walk with his head bent, avoiding the eyes of others. He shared a room with his brother because he could not sleep by himself, but even then he would sometimes run through the house at night in a state of terror. At the age of six he began seeing ghost-like shadows in the hallways and hearing whispering voices. At the age of nine, learning that a previous occupant of his bedroom had committed suicide, he began to believe that a ghost was tapping on his shoulder. In high school, "to be cool," he carved an inverted cross in his forehead and began to sign his name "Satan." He was not a satanist, he told classmates, but rather an atheist or simply someone who rejected Christianity. His parents never noticed the cross because he arranged his long hair to cover it.

When Jamie was 15, his mother decided she could tolerate no more of her husband's drunken behavior, and left him, taking the children with her. To get them back, Elison swore off alcohol and drugs, joined AA, and became a member of the Beechkill Church of Christ, which he attended regularly.

Like his father and grandfather, Jamie suffered from bouts of sudden rage that terminated in blackouts. On one occasion he smashed his CD player because it wouldn't hold a sixth CD in its changer; still unsatisfied, he went outside and battered his car with a lug wrench. He often got into fights with classmates. A fight with his brother, involving a loaded gun, might have ended in a homicide if his mother had not intervened.

In his junior year of high school, Jamie dated a girl for three months, seeing her nearly every weekend. When she broke up with him, he threatened to kill her. As a senior, he was a solitary figure, a poor student, who always dressed in black. He submitted a "last will and testament" to the yearbook, signing it "Satan" and leaving his two younger brothers all the pain and misery that his teachers had inflicted upon him. The editor rejected it. At night he worked at a truck stop, keeping himself awake with over-the-counter stimulants which he "ate like candy," according to his mother. He later told an interviewer:

> I was just going to school and going to work. I just didn't see myself doing anything as far as any goals in life or nothing. . . . But I didn't really know what I wanted to do. I had only two real friends and they were trying to chase girls and go get drunk and I just really didn't care to. People were scared of me. I know girls were scared of me. I couldn't relate to anybody, even my best friends. I really didn't fit in. I didn't see myself reaching out to any adult. I just didn't see anybody I could trust. I didn't see myself being any other way than I was. I didn't see no alternative to it: I thought it would always be like that.

His driver's license was suspended and then restricted as a result of four traffic tickets in nine months. He wrecked a car and bought another, which broke down. When a third car turned out to be in need of constant repair, he began driving his father's pickup. The day before the shooting he experienced something like an extended panic attack, which he dealt with by returning to his truck at various times during the day and listening to his favorite music. In the afternoon he got into a heated argument with a girl, and then asked a friend if he would help him kill people at school, including the girl in question. The friend thought he was kidding. He discussed this plan with at least four other friends that day.

The next morning, November 15, 1995, Jamie dressed in black, selected a gun from the 13 rifles on his father's gun rack, and a partial "brick" of ammunition (a brick is 500 bullets; 443 remained). On his way to school, he picked up his two best friends, who became concerned when they saw the gun in the front seat, but did not intervene.

Jamie brought the gun into school by "boot-legging" it, concealing the barrel in his boot as he walked. On his way to the cafeteria, he shot two teachers, killing one of them. He aimed at a coach, but shot a girl who had gotten in the way, killing her instead. A teacher wrestled him to the floor and teachers and students began piling up on top of him, finally prying the gun out of his grasp.

He was sentenced to two consecutive terms of life imprisonment for the first-degree murders and two consecutive sentences of 25 years for the attempted murders, all to be served consecutively, without possibility of parole. He is currently in the psychiatric unit at Tennessee South Central Correctional Center. Soon after the shooting, Jamie's younger brother was arrested for threatening to finish the work his brother had started. He was convicted of delinquency, and served a two-year sentence in a youth facility.

7. BARRY LOUKAITIS

Barry Loukaitis spent the early years of his life in Iowa and Minnesota. In the fifth grade, just prior to entering middle school, his family settled in Moses Lake, a small town in the Columbia River Basin, about 180 miles east of Seattle. His parents ran a a sandwich and frozen-yogurt shop. Barry's parents were always in conflict about his father's drinking and womanizing, and their arguments often deteriorated into shouting, cursing, and fist fights.

On his mother's side, the family had suffered from generations of mental illness. Barry's grandmother had made at least one suicide attempt, and his mother was often bed-ridden and incapacitated by depression. She had given birth to Barry at 34, and although she had a son from a previous marriage, Barry had been her confidante from kindergarten on, listening and offering solace while she recited the details of her personal life and her unhappy marriage. She relied on him as the only person she could talk to.

Barry was a cheerful and popular child in elementary school. Aside from some school phobia at the age of five, he had no history of behavioral problems. He was a member of the student council, participated in the state chess tournament and entered a project in the science fair. When he entered Frontier Junior High School, however, he began to withdraw from social contact. One of his friends described him during this period:

> In seventh grade he was just a normal guy. But in ninth grade his whole outlook was different . . . [he became] . . . real quiet, clammy, and then cussing at everybody. . . . Some days he was fine, but other days you just couldn't talk to him.

From eighth grade on he occasionally told classmates about how much he hated people—in particular gang members—and how he'd enjoy going on a killing spree. He threatened to kill some students, and asked others if they thought they deserved to die (a reference to the film, *Natural Born Killers*; see Chapter 5). He withdrew socially, spending hours at the library, poring over gun magazines, and immersing himself in violent literature and videos. In ninth grade he wrote poems about killing which he read aloud in class.

> Murder
> It's my first murder
> I'm at my point of no return
> I can't let him live now
> He'd go to the cops for sure
> So I finish
> I look at his body on the floor,
> Killing a bastard that deserves to die,
> Ain't nothing like it in the world,
> But he sure did bleed a lot.

He would take his best friend, Zachary, back to his home, show him his father's gun collection, loading and cocking the weapons, but never firing them. They would discuss where Barry could get ammunition, in particular shotgun shells. Zachary did not take his friend's homicidal threats seriously, or so he stated later.

Barry had a crush on a girl in his fifth period algebra class. When her boyfriend, Manuel Vela, who was also in the class, noticed this, he responded with a campaign of abuse. He called Barry names, spat on him, shoved him in the hallway, and kicked him until his legs were covered with black and blue marks. Vela was a slight, handsome boy, who dressed like a gang member in baggy pants and a bandanna, and hoped to become a professional rap artist one day. Barry's talk about Latinos and gang members "ruining the world" exacerbated the situation.

Two weeks prior to the shootings, Barry's mother told him of her plan to seek revenge on her husband, who was often traveling to Ellensberg, about 70 miles to the west, under the pretext of starting a second sandwich shop, but actually—or so she was convinced—to carry on an affair. She intended to confront him and his suspected lover at gunpoint, lead them to the basement, tie them to chairs, and force them to listen to the ways in which they had hurt her. She would behave as though she had planned to kill them, but then, at the last instant, turn the gun on herself.

> I was going to tell them what they had done to me . . . and I was going to kill myself and make them watch. . . . If he didn't remember my life, he was going to remember my death.

She began carrying her husband's .25 automatic in her coat pocket. Later she took the .22 revolver that her husband kept in the car trunk, and hid both weapons, telling only her son of their location. When asked why she had done this, she replied, "Because I told him everything."

On the morning of February 2, 1996, Barry dressed like a cowboy but all in black. He slid the barrel of his father's rifle into the right pocket of his baggy pants so that the barrel lay along his right leg. He collected his father's handguns from where his mother had hid them, slung three ammunition belts across his chest, put earplugs and speedloaders in his pockets and left for school, but not before watching a few minutes of Clint Eastwood in *A Fistful of Dollars*. He left the video cued to the moment when Eastwood stands over the victim victoriously holding up his rifle.

Barry took a back route to school, walking over a mile in extremely cold weather. Although dressed in this outlandish attire, he attracted little attention. He entered Frontier Junior High School at 2:00 PM. In Room 15 his fifth period algebra class was already in progress. Barry slid the rifle from his pocket and started shooting. He killed his teacher, Manuel Vela and another student, and seriously wounded another. He held the class hostage for 15 minutes, before releasing them and giving himself up to the police.

After nearly two years of postponements, Barry was tried and sentenced to two consecutive life terms plus 205 years of prison. He was delivered to the state's new Youth Offender Program at the Washington Corrections Center in Shelton, Washington, and is currently incarcerated at the same facility's program for adults.

While all school shooters seem to piece together what they consider an appealing negative identity from the popular media, this case is interesting because so much of who he became and what he did was drawn from— although not necessarily catalyzed by—fragments of violent pop culture. The question he posed to his classmates, "Do you deserve to die?" is a quote from the Oliver Stone film *Natural Born Killers*. His carefully assembled "Western" costume seems to have been inspired by the Doc Halliday character (played by Val Kilmer) in the movie *Tombstone*. While holding the class hostage, he quoted a line from Stephen King's short novel *Rage* ("This sure beats algebra, doesn't it?"), and he had watched the video of the Pearl Jam song, "Jeremy," a depiction of a school rampage shooting, so many times that he and his mother both knew all the lyrics (suggesting that they watched the video together and sang along, an image that casts their relationship in an even stranger light). The defense attorney spoke of "emotional incest" occurring between them. Similar relationships can be seen in the cases of Brenda Spencer (Chapter 1, Case 2) and Luke Woodham (Chapter 4, Case 9). When the video was played during the trial in an attempt to prove that Barry was the victim of media persuasion, E!Online cynically labeled it the "Pearl Jam Defense."

8. EVAN RAMSEY

Evan Ramsey, the second of three brothers, was born and lived in Anchorage, Alaska until he was five. His father, Donald, a muscular man of short stature, drove a cab and sometimes referred to himself in the third person, as "Yoda." His mother was part Eskimo, part Athapascan Indian. In 1986, Donald, then 41, became convinced that he was the target of a political plot. Having moved his family to Fairbanks to stay with relatives, he stormed the office of the *Anchorage Times*, setting off smoke bombs and threatening to kill the publisher. He was arrested and sentenced to a ten-year prison term.

Without her husband, Carol began to drink in excess and neglect her children. Her boyfriends were occasionally brutal with her and her sons. The boys were soon referred to family services, and placed in a series of ten foster homes during the next three years. Eventually they found a home with Sue Hare, the district superintendent of schools. She traveled often, leaving the Ramsey boys alone with her other adopted children, one of whom was, in violation of the law, a convicted pedophile.

As a teen, Evan was a goofy kid with acne and an explosive temper. He was rebellious with teachers, and frequently served detention or was absent from school. He was teased by classmates, who enjoyed seeing him go into a rage. Evan attempted suicide when he was 10 and 14. Around February 10, 1997, following a call from his father announcing that he had been released from prison, Evan began to plan another suicide attempt. While smoking marijuana one night, two freshman whom he, a junior, had befriended that year convinced him that if he was committing suicide, he might as well kill some other people and become famous because of the magnitude of his crime. They were all exhilarated by the idea. The next three days were spent planning the event, and inviting friends to watch from the library verandah, where they would be out of harm's way. The FBI later estimated that at least 24 teens had been warned that something very bad was going to happen that day; none had alerted an authority.

On Wednesday morning, February 19, 1997, Evan brought to school, concealed beneath baggy pants and a parka, his foster brother's shotgun, which had been standing, as always, unsecured on the gunrack by the front door. He shot and killed a student whom he disliked, and the principal, and wounded others. Students later described him "laughing, just going crazy." Five policemen arrived while the shooting was in progress, and charged him, forcing him up the stairs to the library, where he found himself trapped against a locked gate. Evan threw down his gun as ordered, and was apprehended.

Evan was sentenced to a 210-year term with a possibility of parole at the age of 70, in 2050.

9. LUKE WOODHAM

Luke Woodham was born in Pearl, Mississippi, a community of 22,000, largely Christian fundamentalists. An older brother, John Jr., tormented and abused him throughout his early childhood. His father, an accountant, fought often with his mother, and after losing his job and experiencing other setbacks, abandoned the family when Luke was in second grade. Luke's mother had difficulty supporting the family on her own. Her parenting was at times neglectful, at other times overly intimate, obsessional, punitive, and occasionally sadistic. She often went on dates, leaving John Jr. to babysit Luke, and did not return until the following morning, behavior Luke found difficult to reconcile with her devout Christianity.

Because he was overweight, socially inept, and wore glasses with thick lenses, he was teased in high school. He wrote violent, inappropriate entries for a journal he kept for freshman English. A girl named Christy Menefee went out with him three times but refused to continue because she found him too controlling. She was made uncomfortable by Luke's mother, who chaperoned them on dates.

Through his interest in role-playing games he met Grant Boyette, a high school senior, who appeared to be a pious Christian in public but, when alone with his clique of role-playing enthusiasts, urged them toward antisocial acts. Realizing Luke's potential as a proxy for his own homicidal urges, he lavished attention on him, and began a campaign of violence coaching. Together, they participated in the vicious and sadistic killing of his pet dog, Sparkle. By the end of September 1997, he had planned to kill his mother so that he might use her car, take his brother's gun to school, and kill Christy Menefee and some other people. He hoped the incident would end with a shootout with the cops during which he would be killed.

On November 30th, he asked his mother if he could borrow the car and she refused. The following morning he killed her in a violent and sadistic manner, left a long and pompous suicide note quoting Neitzsche out of context, and proceeded to school where he killed Christy Menefee and her good friend, and wounded seven others. While trying to escape, his car became mired in the mud. Joel Myrick, an assistant principal, used a pistol he kept in his truck to detain Luke until the police arrived.

In a first trial, Luke was convicted of killing his mother, and in a second, of the killings and assaults that occurred at the school. He received a life sentence for the first crime, and 140 years for the second, sentences to be served consecutively at Parchman Farm Prison, an institution notorious for its cruelty and inadequate conditions. (Luke Woodham's case is described in detail in Chapter 4.)

10. MICHAEL CARNEAL

Michael Carneal was born in Heath, a suburb of Paducah, Kentucky, a close-knit, white, Christian, economically diverse community where his family had lived for generations. Michael was a slight, fragile child who wore over-sized glasses with big frames and his hair cropped in bangs, an under-achiever in a family of over-achievers. His father was a prominent lawyer, who made a point of spending time with his son, playing chess and taking him to sporting events; his mother was an attentive stay-at-home mom with some post-graduate education. Both parents were active in the community, the church, and the high school. His older sister was valedictorian of her high school class and attended an out-of-state college. A devout Christian, she worshipped every morning before school with Agape, a popular Christian youth group.

Michael was a bully and a victim of bullying. In eighth grade he set off a stink bomb and on another occasion, took fish out of an aquarium and stomped on them. For a time he played the class clown, wearing funny hats and childish jewelry, such as a plastic necklace that said,"I Love Smurfs." On another occasion, at a party, he turned the large vinyl "Twister" game board into a cape. In eighth grade the gossip column in the student newspaper reported that he liked another boy in a romantic way. He was widely ridiculed for this, and classmates called him "faggot" and "gay." After this, Michael's grades began to deteriorate and he contemplated suicide. In August of 1997, with high school looming before him, he cut himself on the forearm, a wound he told grownups had resulted from a bicycle accident.

During his 71 days as a freshman at Heath High, he was referred to the principal's office five times for minor offenses, using a library computer to view the *Playboy* website, flecking paint off the wall, scratching another boy with a pen, stealing a can of food from a home-economics class, and bring-ing a pair of plastic nunchuks to school in violation of school rules. Essays and a journal he kept for his English class reflected his sadness, his loneli-ness, and his rage against his classmates. In one assignment he was asked to define himself.

My name is Michael Carneal. Not to offend you but I really hate sports. I have low self esteem and I play guitar. I have a wide variety of friends (1) and I like to run. I have an overachieving sister (Kelly Carneal) whom is a senior. I hate being compared to her . . .

I don't take stuff from teenagers or parents and I am seriously mad at the world . . .

In another essay, he wrote across the top of the page, "Please don't tell anyone very personal (sic)."

They all mocked and slaughtered my self-esteem. After a cruel day at H.M.S. when someone put in the school newspaper that I was gay, I went home and cried yes I admit it I cried.

He described how he had "snorted seven Tylenol 3s," how a friend had persuaded him not to use drugs and how he had ". . . been clean for a year now." Adopting the tone of a hardened addict added a comic twist to the confession, making it hard for teachers to take it seriously. In a story called "Halloween Surprise" he describes a character named Michael killing five "preps," describing their torture with relish, and presenting his mother with the bodies. None of this was reported to his parents or the school staff, perhaps because it was so hard to imagine this fragile little child harboring murderous thoughts.

While Michael was providing glimpses of his alienation and rage in his class writings, he was concealing his most bizarre and paranoid delusions. He believed that a race of miniature people called "Danes" (no connection with people of Danish descent) were living in the crawl spaces and duct work of his home, and he engaged in elaborate rituals to protect himself from their attacks.

He tried to be popular in high school by joining the school band, but he was forced to play the tuba, the enormous size of which only emphasized his own diminutive stature, and made him more comical. After other rejections, he set his sights on a group to which membership seemed most attainable for an outcast like himself, "the Black Group" as they were sometimes called because they dressed in black, or the "the Zoo Crew" because they were odd. They were involved in role-playing games, and intrigued by vampires and witchcraft. While Michael was not interested in RPGs or the occult, he shared their love of computers and bands such as Nirvana and Marilyn Manson. James O'Nan, the de facto leader of the group, claimed to be a vampire himself, and spoke of controlling the weather and having visions. He wore a long black trench coat to school, and a wallet chain, and occasionally affected black lipstick and nail polish. There was talk about midnight meetings beneath a railroad underpass, and remains of animal sacrifices, of crucified cats and dogs later substantiated by the police.

Michael lavished gifts on the Goth group: $100 bills stolen from his father's wallet, CDs paid for with stolen credit card numbers, and a fax machine stolen from a friend's home. When they spoke about taking over the school or the mall, or shooting students they disliked, Michael participated enthusiastically in the discussions and offered to provide weapons. A particular animosity developed between the Goth group and members of a Christian youth group called Agape, of which Michael's sister and a girl named Nicole Hadley, a longtime object of Michael's affection, were members. They formed a prayer circle every morning for 15 minutes before the start of classes. Michael and members of the black group would stand on the outskirts of the circle, mocking the worshipers, mimicking the leader when he or she announced that it was "time to pray" or speaking loudly during prayer.

Shortly before Halloween of 1997 Michael stole his father's .38 special Smith & Wesson pistol out of a locked box in their bedroom and tried to sell it at school. An older boy took the gun but refused to pay for it, threatening to tell the authorities. A few weeks later, Michael and his friend Toby Nace found a handgun in the Nace's garage that Toby's father had neglected to return to his gun safe. He brought it to school and showed it to other students, warning them to be careful about how they treated him.

During lunch period that day, Michael told his Goth friends that he would do something to the prayer group on Monday that would involve "blood and guts." He told at least four other students that Monday would be "the day of reckoning. . . ." He was going to bring a gun to school and start shooting people, and ". . . the hypocrites in the prayer group were going to go down. . . ." He also warned certain members of the prayer group whom he thought of as friends to keep out of the way. No one told an adult.

Thanksgiving day, while the Naces were having dinner, Michael, who had eaten earlier, climbed through an open window in the Nace garage, located the hidden key to the gun locker and took five expensive rifles as well as two pairs of earplugs, four boxes of shotgun shells, and 600 rounds of cartridges, which he transported home on his bicycle and hid under his bed. Later he added two shotguns stolen from his father's closet.

Monday morning, December 1, 1997, Michael loaded his backpack with ammunition and bundled the long guns in a blanket secured with masking tape. When his sister, who was driving him to school, asked about it, he replied that it was "an English project—props for a play."

The prayer circle was already in session when Michael reached the Heath High lobby. He joined his would-be friends in the Goth group, who stood off to one side, observing sardonically. Other students gathered there too, including his sister Kelly. James O'Nan said that he and the others sensed that something unusual was about to happen.

Michael crouched, and raised the gun, his arm outstretched at the shoulder like a police sharpshooter. He fired three shots into the crowd and then five more, in an arc across the room. Although he later stated that he was not aiming at anyone, every bullet struck a student. Less than two minutes later, students were lying the length of the bloodied corridor, while other students huddled over bodies of friends, crying and screaming for help. Eight students had been shot, three of them fatally. He claimed to be surprised and upset to see that he had killed Nicole, whom he counted among his closest friends.

To what extent was Michael the pawn of the Black Group?

". . . at the very least, the older boys manipulated and encouraged Carneal to engage in a variety of illegal activities," said one psychologist who interviewed Michael before the trial. One witness reported one of the group smiling at the crime scene immediately after the shootings. Members of the group were evasive about their role in the crime and the prosecutor never had sufficient information to charge them.

Michael pled guilty but mentally ill. During his incarceration in the Northern Kentucky Youth Development Center, his symptoms of mental illness developed into paranoid schizophrenia. When the Columbine shootings occurred in April of 1999, he felt responsible, and had a psychotic episode and severe depression, which in turn led to two suicide attempts. At 18, he was sentenced as an adult and transferred to the Correctional Psychiatric Treatment Center, a 150-bed facility at the Kentucky State Reformatory in LaGrange, to serve out the rest of his life sentence

11. MITCHELL JOHNSON & ANDREW GOLDEN

Mitchell Johnson was born in 1984 in Spring Valley, Minnesota, a farming community about 100 miles southeast of Minneapolis. His younger brother, Monty, was born two years later. Their father, Scott Johnson, worked in a meat-packing plant and had an explosive temper. During his rages, he punched holes in the walls, and was verbally abusive. While there is no evidence that he physically abused his sons, he was a poor and inconsistent disciplinarian. Mitchell had a sensitive disposition and his father's temper tantrums would leave him trembling and physically ill, a condition from which he found it difficult to recover.

From the beginning, the Johnsons had trouble making ends meet. Mitchell and Monty were sent to live with their grandmother, in a two-bedroom trailer, in a nearby trailer court off Minnesota 16. They slept in the living room, one on the couch and the other on the floor, and kept all their toys and other belongings in cardboard cartons. They attended daycare and when they were older, Kingsland Elementary School, where neighbors described them as successful students. School friends said that Mitchell was teased mercilessly regarding his weight. In photographs he appears as a chubby boy with a sweet smile and short, bristling porcupine hair. Even at this age, he was troubled and emotionally reactive. Andrew, a friend from the trailer park, told how Mitchell decided to commit suicide after breaking up with his girlfriend in elementary school. He got a rope and a gun in order to shoot or hang himself and Andrew had to spend 45 minutes convincing the nearly hysterical boy to abandon the idea.

In 1988 the family's fortunes improved when their mother, Gretchen Woodard, found a job working in the federal prison system. At about the same time, Mitchell and Monty, now six and four, were repeatedly sexually molested, or so Scott Johnson claimed during an interview on the ABC News show *20/20*, after the shootings had occurred. Johnson later recanted the molestation story for fear of a lawsuit.

In 1993, the couple separated and began a contentious divorce. Scott Johnson, while working at the Hill Top Grocery in Spring Valley, was fired for stealing a quantity of meat, but plea-bargained his way out of a prison term. Gretchen complained about inadequate child support, unannounced visits, and abusive behavior.

While working at the prison, Gretchen became friendly with a prisoner named Terry "Buddy" Woodard, who was eight years younger (Scott had been six years younger than she), and serving a five-year sentence for transporting firearms and drugs across state lines with the intention of selling them. Eventually Buddy was paroled, and moved to Bono, Arkansas, a farm town about 130 miles northeast of Little Rock. Gretchen and her boys had set up housekeeping in Bono in preparation for his release. They married and Buddy got a job driving a truck.

Mitchell was upset about the move and wanted to stay with his father and grandmother in Minnesota. Despite his protests, he was enrolled in Westside School, an almost exclusively white Christian school of 250 sixth and seventh graders, where about a third of the students lived below the poverty level. He joined a church youth group, and sang in church and school choirs. He held doors open for girls, charming parents and teachers alike with his good manners and cheerful disposition. But others who knew him well described him as manipulative and sneaky, a conman. Like his father, he had an explosive temper, and was a bully and braggart with the neighborhood kids. On one occasion, while serving detention for refusing to remove his cap, he was asked to write an essay about his behavior. One sentence: "I have a pellet gun and I am not afraid to use it" was construed as a threat and resulted in a meeting with the principal and his parents. Sharon Wright, the English teacher who assigned the essay, became one of the victims of his shooting. On another occasion he was paddled for cursing on the bus. Aside from these incidents, he was not considered a disciplinary problem and was remorseful and lavishly apologetic after every infraction.

Each year Mitchell and Monty returned to Minnesota, to the town of Grand Meadow, where his father, now employed as a truck driver, lived with his girlfriend. Mitchell was conflicted about seeing him. Scott remained easy to anger and often threatened to send him home if he misbehaved. During a visit in the summer of 1996, (6/14) an incident occurred involving Mitchell and a female toddler, a two- or three-year-old, who lived in the trailer park with her mother, and was a relative of Scott Johnson's girlfriend. Mitchell's brother, Monte, who was 11 at the time, walked into the bedroom and saw Mitchell, with his pants down to his ankles, with the toddler. He told their father, who then told the girl's family, who called the police. Mitchell was questioned by members of the Mower County Sheriff's Department, and admitted to touching the girl sexually, but only on that one occasion. Investigators interviewed the mother and the toddler, who demonstrated on anatomically correct dolls exactly how Mitchell had touched her. A doctor at St. Mary's Hospital in Rochester, Minnesota, found no bruising or evidence of penetration during his examination. Cathy O'Rourke, a neighbor and friend from the Minnesota trailer park, said that Mitchell had told her that the whole thing was a "big misunderstanding" and he was simply helping the toddler pull up her pants in the bathroom. The toddler and her mother moved out of the trailer park about two weeks later. Mitchell had appeared in court twice for the offence and a trial was scheduled for June.

When he returned to Jonesboro, Mitchell had changed. He styled himself an inner-city "gangsta," pulled a knife in the school locker room, flashed Blood handsigns, listened to rap music, wore the color red, got into frequent fist fights, and talked about killing. All involved with the case agreed that Mitchell's connection with teenage gangs resided entirely in his imagination. Gretchen took him to see a psychologist who concluded that the molestation was probably an isolated incident, and not a source of concern.

At Christmas Mitchell and his brother went back to Minnesota to visit their father for the last time together. During the bus trip home they were stranded for two days in the Chicago bus terminal because of bad weather before their parents and step-parents realized they were missing.

Around this time, Mitchell began planning an SR shooting with another little boy he had met on the school bus named Andrew Golden. Andrew's parents and Mitchell's parents were unaware that the boys had ever spoken to one another, aside from an incident in 1996, soon after they had first moved to Bono, when Mitchell had bullied Drew on the bus. This made it especially hard to figure out who was the leader and who was the follower. In the April 6th issue of *Time* magazine, Gretchen claimed that Andrew proposed the idea to Mitchell during the bus ride home from school the afternoon before the shooting. "Mitch told me he never meant to hurt anybody," she said. "He just meant to scare them, I guess. But then something went terribly wrong."

Andrew Golden, or "Drew," was a small, frail 11-year-old, whose mother and father worked as postmasters in nearby towns. The result of a reversed tubal ligation, he was considered their "miracle baby" and spoiled accordingly.

Drew's father was the cofounder and an official of a local gun club, the Jonesboro Practical Pistol Shooter's Association. His grandfather, who lived next door, was a state wildlife technician, and boasted of buying Drew guns at an early age. Although he was only 11, Drew owned two rifles, a shotgun, and a crossbow. His parents kept the weapons locked in a vault and the combination secret. While Arkansas law does not permit children to purchase handguns, they are allowed to possess as many long guns as they like.

Drew was considered immature and spoiled. His parents gave him whatever he wanted and rarely disciplined him. A neighbor told how, at the age of four or five, Drew would curse like a sailor, and his father and grandfather would laugh and goad him on, saying it would make a man out of him. His mother would throw her hands up in despair. What could she do when the men encouraged him like that? Andrew was a mediocre student who was placed in remedial math and English classes in elementary school. He was never suspended and rarely required disciplining. Andrew was often mischievous and played the class clown. Teachers cut him a lot of slack because many of them had been in the same class as his father, who was also a class clown. He was just a chip off the old block. Most described him as a boy who always had a grin on his face and largely went unnoticed. Those who knew him well, however, said he cursed and yelled at other children, and threatened to shoot them with his BB gun if they came to his yard. He had shot cats in his backyard and once starved a cat to death in a barrel. Two cousins whom he later shot were told not to play with him by their parents when they learned about his cruelty to animals.

About a month before the shootings, Mitchell began to call sex talk lines and ran up hundreds of dollars of charges on his father's credit card. He was kicked off the basketball team—or was never accepted in the first place—for carving his initials into his own shoulder, and was suspended for refusing to remove his Nike baseball cap. On two occasions he wandered onto the property of a neighbor and fired at his house with a shotgun before the neighbor drove him away.

During this time he wooed and was dumped after three days, by Candace Porter, a pretty little girl with freckles and brown hair. "I thought he was nice but then I found out he was trouble," she said, sounding older than her 11 years. She had heard that he was carrying a list of students he intended to kill. "I thought he was bragging, like always. I didn't think he was going to hurt anybody really." After she broke up with him, Candace's name was added to the list.

In the days before the shootings, Mitchell began to talk about the crime he had planned. He told one friend that he was going to kill all the girls who had broken up with him. He told another, "I've got a lot of killing to do," and another, "Tomorrow you will find out if you live or die," and still another, "Everyone that hates me, everyone that I don't like is going to die." On Monday, March 23, 1998, the day before the shootings, Mitchell brandished a knife at school and threatened to kill Candace Porter and a teacher. He told another student, Jennifer Nightingale, that she would never see him again because he was going to run away. None of the children alerted an adult. When asked why, they explained that nobody had taken the threats seriously.

On the morning of March 24, Mitchell missed the school bus. While his mother was preoccupied, caring for a younger sister and a neighbor's boy, he stole her '91 Dodge Caravan. His mother thought his father had taken it. Mitchell packed the van with camping supplies, and a hammer and a propane torch, intending to cut open the gun safe where Drew's father kept his firearms. When he reached Drew's house—Drew's parents had already left for work—he found that the tools had little effect on the steel safe. They had to be satisfied with the unsecured guns in the house, a two-shot derringer, a .38 snub-nose, and a .357 Magnum. Their luck was better at the home of Andrew's grandfather, where they found, secured only by a cable running through the trigger guards, an arsenal of 48 rifles. The cable was locked to the rack at either end, but Drew knew where his grandfather kept the keys. They took three powerful rifles. Three more handguns were hidden under the mattress and a fourth in another location. A thousand round boxes of ammunition were stacked atop the refrigerator.

When they finished loading the van, it contained—in addition to the long guns and hand guns—sleeping bags, a camouflage jacket, an insulated camouflage vest, a military duty belt with a ten-inch special purpose knife, a crossbow, hunter's camouflage netting, a pair of size seven Doc Marten boots, assorted ammunition, a machete, a survival knife, four other knives, a tent and backpack, a portable radio, a plastic toolbox filled with packaged foods, the propane torch they had used on Andrew's father's gun safe, and Mitchell's hunter-education card (a prerequisite for getting a hunting license in Arkansas and many other states; hunter education courses were instituted in the early 1970s to reduce fire-arm accidents). There was also a Dr. Seuss book, a pink stuffed bunny, a Mountain Dew soda can in a back-seat holder, a single small purple sock, and two bags of Lays potato chips. After the shootings, Mitchell told his mother that they had planned to drive the van to Ravendon, in Lawrence County, where Drew's family owned some land. Drew would hide out, camping, eating the packaged food, which consisted of canned soups and beans, jerky, tuna, crackers, snacks, and candy, while Mitchell returned the van to his father. After a few weeks, they would return home, admit their crime, apologize, and be forgiven.

On their way to the school they discovered that they needed gas. They stopped at a gas station but couldn't figure out how to operate the pump. The attendant, seeing that they were underage, refused to help them but did not alert the police or do anything else to stop them. They visited two more gas stations before finally managing to fill the tank.

Mitchell dropped Andrew off at school, continued up a side road near the woods bordering the middle school, and parked in a cul-de-sac about a half mile from the campus. He carried his armaments to a place in the woods, just beyond the playing field. New construction had left a trench where they could stand and shoot over the lip of the embankment. From here they had a clear view of the school yard, the school, and the exits.

During fifth period social studies, Drew raised his hand and asked to go to the bathroom. It was a few minutes after 12:00. Instead of going to the bathroom, he pulled the fire alarm and ran out the door. The teachers were all surprised since no fire drill had been scheduled for that day, but led their classes outside as required by law. The sun was shining on the rolling lawns around the building. There was an explosion that sounded like a fire-cracker, and 12-year-old Stephanie Johnson fell to the concrete and lay motionless. She had been shot twice in the head and had died almost instantly. A bullet hit Ms. Thetford, Drew's social studies teacher, in the back, piercing her small intestines, and lodged near her spine, just below the hip line. Her leg suddenly numb, she toppled over. She cried out for help. Steve Williams, a fellow teacher, thought she was kidding. "What have you been hit with, a firecracker?" She replied, "I've been shot; get me out of here."

Some students fell, others screamed, and others, believing it was a staged event, began to applaud.

About 25 students, seven boys and 18 girls, were in a music class when the alarm went off. The boys took their time but the girls ran out a side entrance. Whitney Puckett, 12, and Brittany Lambie, 13, were talking excitedly and holding hands as they scampered across the lawn, when Brittany suddenly dropped. "I said, 'Get up, Brittany,' and she said, 'I can't.' When I looked down, there was blood on her legs."

Whitney and a teacher, Debby Spencer, were unable to get Brittany back inside the building because the school doors had locked automatically as they were designed to do during a fire drill. People were banging on the doors with their fists and screaming to be let inside.

Tammy Arms, a sixth grade teacher, said she could tell the location of the snipers by the direction in which the students fell. On the basis of this, teachers told the children to run to the gymnasium, which was on the side of the school away from the snipers. By now people inside the building had become aware of the problem with the exit doors and were holding them open.

As Candace Porter was running toward the gymnasium, a bullet struck her right side. She felt nothing more than a stinging sensation at the time, but when she was safe inside the gym, she saw she was "bleeding a little." A teacher told her to sit up against a wall next to Whitney Irving, who had been shot in the back. All around her children were screaming and crying for their parents. She could still hear the steady sound of gunfire from outside.

Although it seemed to go on forever, the shooting lasted only 15 seconds. At the end of that time, Mitchell had killed a teacher and wounded four students, and Drew had killed three students and wounded a teacher and six students. The boys may have stopped shooting because of a construction worker standing on the roof of the new fifth-grade wing of the middle school, who shouted at them to stop. Mitchell fired a few shots at him and then both boys fled. In terms of casualties, this was the worst school shooting to date.

Deputies John Varner and Jon Moore were driving north on a dead-end gravel road at the edge of the school property when they saw two boys in camouflage clothing, carrying high-powered semiautomatic rifles, come running from behind a line of trees. They got out of their cars and ordered the boys to drop their guns and get down on the ground. "The youngest one, he dropped real quick," Varner said. "The older one hesitated. . . . We had to shout two or three times to get them to raise their hands off the ground." They cuffed the boys and searched them. In addition to the long guns, the deputies found the ten handguns in their clothing, each weapon loaded to capacity and cocked. Varner and Moore asked them why they had fired on their schoolmates. "Both of them just said, 'I don't know. I just don't know.'" However, sheriff's deputy Terry McNatt said that he over-heard one of the officers asking Mitchell why he had done it, and him responding, "Andrew was mad at a teacher. He was tired of their crap." While they were driving to Craighead County Juvenile Detention Center to await the arrival of their parents, Mitchell again told officers that the shoot-ings were Andrew's idea, that he had been motivated by anger, and that he had invited Mitchell to join him.

Mitchell was a picture of calm at the jail. He asked for a bible, spoke to the jail chaplain, and requested a visit with his pastor, the Rev. William Holt, from the Revival Tabernacle Church in Bono. Drew wept and pleaded for his mother. He told the police that he wanted to go home now. The boys asked if they could trade their lunch of corn bread, white beans, and baked chicken for a pizza and were told no. According to Gretchen Woodard, they were treated extremely well during their incarceration. They received 15 to 20 pieces of mail a day, some death threats, but many more expressions of sympathy for them and their families.

Five ambulances arrived within four minutes and the wounded were rushed to St. Bernards Regional Medical Center. The emergency room staff had learned about the shootings at 12:45 PM and invoked the disaster pro-tocol the hospital had practiced in drills, and during tornadoes in 1968 and 1973. Twelve specialists, including neurosurgeons, cardiothoracic surgeons, and urologists, were ready when the patients began to arrive. Some children had head wounds, orthopedic wounds, chest wounds, and stomach wounds, while others had been hurt while falling or fleeing the gunfire. Access to patient rooms and waiting areas was sealed off from the press. One room was set aside as a waiting room for friends and family of the injured. The names of the wounded and their status were listed on two large sheets of paper taped to the wall. Beside the names of each deceased child was a room number and the word "family," and besides those who had died in the ER or at the school was written, "family at home."

President Clinton, visiting Uganda during a 12-day African tour, was awakened in the middle of the night by a phone call. While he had seen an astonishing number of school rampage shootings in his term as president, this latest had occurred in his home state, in his own backyard. "Hillary and

I are deeply shocked and heartbroken by this afternoon's horrifying events at Westside Middle School in Jonesboro, Arkansas," he told the nation. "We don't know now and may never fully understand what could have driven two youths to deliberately shoot into a crowd of their classmates. Our thoughts and prayers are with the victims, their families, and the entire Jonesboro community." He was in constant communication with Arkansas governor Mike Huckabee and other local officials during the days to come. In addition, he asked Janet Reno, the Attorney General, to try to determine the cause of these school rampage shootings and how they might be prevented in the future.

Huckabee promised to create a task force to review the state's juvenile codes with an eye to revising them. The issue was a delicate and disturbing one: the way the laws were now written, Mitchell might only serve four years of jail time, and Drew, seven, sentences that outraged nearly everyone. According to Arkansas law, because they were under 14, they would be tried as minors, and all minors had to be released from incarceration by the age of 21. At 18, delinquents were transferred from the juvenile court system to the Arkansas Department of Human Services Division of Youth Services, which, because of budgetary issues and lack of pressing need, had no incarceration facilities of its own. Lawrence Graves, spokesman for the state attorney general's office, said, ". . . for all practical purposes, at age 18 they walk." Any changes in the law would be enacted too late to affect Mitchell's and Drew's sentences. The Craighead County prosecuting attorney conferred with the U.S. Attorney in Little Rock and Justice Department officials in Washington about strategies to charge the boys with a federal crime, possibly firearms related offenses, to keep them in prison at least until they were 21.

In response to the shootings, Colorado representative Diana DeGette, and California senator Dianne Feinstein, both Democrats, proposed, during the 105th Congress, a budget amendment to ban the importation of high-capacity ammunition clips (clips holding more than ten rounds). Andrew and Mitchell had four large ammunition clips in their possession, and of the 22 shots fired, 15 had come from one 15-round clip. Sales of high-capacity clips were banned by the Violent Crime Control and Law Enforcement Act of 1994, one of our nation's six federal gun control laws, but, in a concession to the gun lobby, existing high-capacity clips were exempted. The stockpile of clips, which had been expected to disappear in a few years, had not dwindled, possibly because of the importation of clips manufactured outside the country. The Republican controlled Senate had little interest in passing the amendment.

Suzanne Wilson, trying to wrest some positive thing from the loss of her daughter, also became an advocate for gun control. "When someone takes away our prize possession, it destroys our lives," she said. "I try to find answers. If I didn't have this [gun control advocacy], I'd probably turn into myself and withdraw and not wake up in the mornings." Ms. Wilson was televised on the Capitol building's east façade alongside Ted Kennedy and Sarah Brady, promoting the Children's Gun Violence Prevention Act (CGVPTA) of 1999, a comprehensive legislation requiring, among other things, child safety locks on handguns and prohibiting the sales of assault weapons to anyone under 18. Among those opposing the amendment, which ultimately failed, was the National Rifle Association, and five of Arkansas' six congressional members. The NRA was concerned that any kind of safety lock might interfere with people accessing their firearms quickly enough to repel violent intruders.

A week later Suzanne Wilson appeared alongside President Clinton in the Old Executive Office Building as he promoted a provision to the CGVPTA that would hold adults liable if a loaded gun or a gun stored with ammunition is taken by a child and used to kill that child or another person. It was an attempt to make federal the kind of "child access prevention" laws that had already been enacted in 15 states. The NRA objected that a single federal gun storage standard could not possibly address all the different conditions under which families keep guns in their homes for protection, and the bill was eventually defeated. Suzanne Wilson's tireless advocacy for gun control legislation, her trips back and forth to Washington, and numerous public appearances arguing for her cause were acknowledged when she was invited to sit beside first lady Hillary Clinton during President Clinton's State of the Union address in January of 1999.

The boys remained jailed, awaiting their trial. Andrew cried and pleaded for his mother. "With dark circled eyes," a jailer told a journalist, "he stares gloomily out into the juvenile cell block. The sleeves of his too-long orange prison shirt extend past his hands when he walks." Neither boy could stomach the prison food and both began to lose weight. Drew was fed Ensure, a dietary supplement. On one occasion they both threw their dinners out of their cells and another time Mitchell threw a shoe at the sprinkler head, causing a downpour in his cell, soaking his belongings. Their shenanigans resulted in the loss of TV and visitor privileges for a month. At the end of that period Judge Wilson ordered the boys to begin attending classes, from 8:45 to lunch, and after lunch until 3:30, in the hope that they could earn their GEDs. Both boys did well, as they had at Westside, and with Mitchell a particularly enthusiastic student, he promptly completed all his assignments. Cheryl Upshaw, an attorney with the state's Public Defender Commission, grew concerned when she heard that jail employees conducting tours of the prison regularly pointed out Mitchell and Andrew as "the Jonesboro killers." Rick Duhon, the prison administrator, denied the allegation. Perhaps they had been pointed out in tours, but they had never been referred to as "killers." Sheriff Haas made light of the complaints regarding food, exercise, and humiliation. "This is not a comfortable environment," he told the press, "but this is not a motel. It's a jail."

Two months after the shooting, just as the Jonesboro community had begun to get their bearings again, news came from Springfield, Oregon of another school shooting, this one involving a 15-year-old boy, Kip Kinkel, who had brought a gun to school, gotten caught, been expelled, returned to school the following day, and opened fire on students in the cafeteria. This was a terrible blow to the community, rekindling their fears. With unfortunate timing, Mike Huckabee's book, *Kids Who Kill*, was shipped to bookstores at about the same time, giving Jonesboro residents a sense that they had been betrayed, that the governor of their state was trying to turn a profit from their personal tragedies.

The adjudication hearing for the boys was scheduled for August 11. The day before the hearing, the families of the deceased, led by Mitchell Wright and Renee Brooks, filed a wrongful death suit alleging that Mitchell Johnson and Drew Golden had shown ample evidence of antisocial behavior and had a "propensity to commit acts which could normally be expected to cause injury." The suit named as defendants Mitchell and Drew and their parents, Drew's grandfather, and the two gun manufacturers whose weapons were responsible for most loss of life, Remington Arms Company and Universal Firearms. Rather than specifying an amount, it asked a jury to set damages above what the defendants might earn from book royalties, movies, or interview fees, and to calculate a number that would deter arms manufacturers from making guns without trigger locks, a number that would compensate the plaintiffs for their loss and expenses, and sufficiently punish the defendants. At the time no guns were made with trigger locks, but the suit alleged that such locks were "technologically feasible and economically practical" and to omit them made the weapons "defective products" that were "unreasonably dangerous."

The complaint against Remington Arms Company, now operating as Sporting Goods Properties, Inc., was dismissed because of "intervening factors," one of which was that the boys had stolen the guns. Universal Firearms, the company that made the .30 caliber carbine used in the killings, had declared bankruptcy and was no longer in existence. Drew's grandfather was dismissed from the lawsuit because he kept his weapons more or less secured. That left the parents and the boys themselves. The company that had issued the Golden's homeowners policy negotiated a settlement, the details of which were not disclosed. Despite this, the families who had brought the suit were pleased that they had alerted the nation to the importance of trigger locks and firearm security. Smith & Wesson had recently announced that they would equip all new weapons with trigger locks, and it was thought that other firearm manufacturers would follow their lead, to guard themselves against litigation if for no other reason. A flood of gun control lawsuits was forcing the smaller gun manufacturers, the "junk gun makers," into bankruptcy.

While juvenile cases are traditionally closed and confidential, Judge Wilson decided that the trial would be open to the public because of "significant public interest in the case." Because juvenile cases are decided by the judge, there was no jury. Mitchell Johnson pleaded guilty and Andrew Golden's lawyers submitted a plea of "not guilty by reason of mental deficit and incompetence" on his behalf. The judge refused to accept the plea; both boys were found delinquent in the face of overwhelming evidence.

Mitchell turned 18 and was released from juvenile incarceration in 2006. Drew turned 18 and was released in 2008. Mitchell was re-arrested on New Year's Day, 2007, while riding in a van with a friend, for possession of marijuana and carrying a loaded 9mm pistol.

12. KIP KINKEL

[People] always wanted to hear that he was some kind of monster, but he was just this little class clown. Nobody had a clue that he was going to do this. . . . Only a handful of people knew that he had any kind of fascination with guns and bombs.

Kip Kinkel's parents and older sister were all smart, competitive, athletic, and socially successful. His father, Bill, an avid tennis player, had a master's in education. Until his retirement in 1991, he was a popular Spanish teacher at Thurston High School and the local community college, and coached the high school tennis team. His wife, Faith, also a Spanish teacher with a master's in education, graduated magna cum laude, served in the Peace Corps, and taught high school in the Springfield school district. Two days before her death, the Alpha Delta Kappa honor society selected her as one of the outstanding teachers of the year. Kip's older sister, Kristin, born in 1976, was a graceful girl with a quick mind and a bubbly personality. She was class valedictorian, earned a cheerleading scholarship for Hawaii Pacific University, and placed fourth in the College Cheerleading National Championship.

Kipland Phillip Kinkel, or Kip, born on August 30, 1982, was physically clumsy, and suffered from learning disorders. While his sister got A's with little effort, he failed tests after hours of poring over his books. In 1986, when Bill took the family to Spain for his sabbatical, Kristin mastered Spanish and made many friends, while Kip, only four, was bullied by a bigger boy, a problem compounded by his inability to learn more than a few words of Spanish.

Kip's parents and teachers decided that he would benefit from a year's delay in starting school because of his immaturity and slow emotional and physical growth. He was placed on a behavioral management plan because of aggressive acts on the playground and his cruel teasing of classmates. When he was six years old he struck an older boy with a steel rod, permanently injuring his arm. In third grade Kip was identified as learning disabled and provided with special classes and teachers. In fourth grade he was placed in a talented and gifted (TAG) program because of his aptitude in math and science. This kind of disparity between cognitive abilities is particularly frustrating to children. While his teachers had an overall impression of him being very intelligent, well-behaved, and a hard worker, they also recall him becoming so frustrated from his struggles with reading and spelling that he occasionally had to be removed from class to calm down.

In middle school, Kip asked his parents for karate lessons so he could protect himself from the boys who continued to bully him. Although all forms of violence were forbidden in their home, his parents agreed, reasoning that it would help his self-esteem. Kip's karate studies eventually led to trophies, certificates, and blue ribbons, which his parents proudly displayed throughout the house. In eighth grade Kip began associating with "skaters," tough kids who smoked, and had spent time in juvenile detention. When Kip was caught stealing CDs with them Bill and Faith responded by giving him Internet access at home, a privilege previously denied to him, because they believed it would keep him in his room and away from his new friends. He visited pornography sites, and sites describing bomb-making, a subject that had come to fascinate him. He ordered bomb-making books on the school computer and had them delivered to the school. When they arrived, school authorities traced the order back to him, and his parents were summoned to a meeting with the principal. Kip told his mother that his interest in explosives stemmed from his desire to become a cop, a member of the bomb squad, an explosives specialist. Among his punishments was loss of Internet privileges.

One night that winter, while attending a snowboarding clinic in Bend, Oregon, Kip and a friend tossed a big rock from an overpass onto the highway, nicking a car passing beneath them. The driver alerted the police, and Kip was taken into custody. His parents were called at 11:40 PM and immediately set out on the 250-mile journey to pick up their son. His case was adjudicated and Kip was required to complete 32 hours of community service, write a letter of apology, and pay for the damages done to the car.

Faith, having exhausted her own resources, including "tough love" and "unconditional love," convinced Bill to send Kip to a psychologist, a practice he considered quackery. Kip met with Dr. Jeffrey Hicks nine times between January and June of 1997. Perhaps wishing to find a common ground upon which to build a relationship, Dr. Hicks told Kip that he too was a gun enthusiast and owned four pistols, two of them Glocks. Kip began campaigning for a Glock pistol of his own. While his parents had forbidden toy guns and soldiers and even Bugs Bunny cartoons, by the time his therapy was terminated, Bill had bought his son a 9mm Glock 19, a semiautomatic weapon whose small size made it easy to conceal.

While this seems like a shocking decision considering Kip's personality, his emotional problems, and his supposedly non-violent upbringing, the fact remains that in prior years Bill had given his son two BB guns and three knives; and, on his 12th birthday, a 336 Marlin, a gun that he had received from his father as a boy. The media made little mention of this. During a pre-trial neuro-psychiatric assessment conducted by Jonathan Pincus, a neurologist whose work is discussed in Chapter 1, the boy "described the gun-drenched culture of his family, the verbal abusiveness of his parents, and his sense of loneliness and being threatened." Bill himself continued to own a Winchester lever-action rifle, another souvenir from childhood, and a .22 caliber Ruger pistol which he occasionally let Kip use for target practice.

Bill's thinking was that if Kip wanted the Glock so badly, he would get hold of it one way or another; better to have him do it under his father's guidance than illicitly. Kip agreed that his father would keep the gun locked in a safe, they would only fire it together, and they would take a gun safety course. When, on one occasion, Kip somehow got a hold of the Glock without his father's knowledge, Bill took the gun away and began keeping it in his locker at the club where he played tennis. After a while he began carrying it back and forth to the club in his gym bag so that he and Kip could occasionally shoot it together. Dr. Hicks was not consulted regarding the purchase. He later stated that he would have never let a parent purchase a handgun for a depressed adolescent. Three months later, following another round of pleading, begging, and tantrums, Bill bought Kip a second weapon, a Ruger .22 caliber semiautomatic rifle, under the same conditions. By the time of the shooting, Kip was keeping the Ruger in his bedroom, possibly with his parents' knowledge.

Kip secretly purchased a sawed-off shotgun from one friend and a .22 caliber pistol from another during the summer before he entered high school, weapons he kept hidden in his room. He accumulated more and more knives until they filled the two storage drawers of his captain's bed. How often he fired the guns and played with the knives and the extent of his parents' awareness of them is difficult to gauge. When police searched the house the day of the shooting, they found leaning against a tree, in plain view of the deck where the family often relaxed together, a four-by-six-foot piece of plywood, a human figure outlined in orange spray paint, with hundreds of chips and gauges in the "kill zone," the area of the vital organs.

Toward the end of April Kip was suspended for two days for kicking a classmate in the head following an argument on the school bus. On another occasion he was suspended for three days for throwing a pencil at a boy.

The following fall he entered Thurston High School. Hoping to make the way easier for his troubled son, Bill, having conferred with his friend and former colleague, Don Stone, the football coach, convinced Kip to try out for the football team. Coach Stone made Kip a linebacker. Because Kip weighed only 120 pounds, he rarely played, and spent most of his time on the bench. Kip became alienated from his teammates and convinced that one of them was picking on him and intentionally injuring him during practices.

In speech class, Kip read a paper he had written on how to make a bomb, complete with detailed diagrams of explosives wired to a clock. Afterwards his teacher contacted one of the school guidance counselors regarding Kip's presentation. The guidance counselor wrote a memo stating that Kip's father knew all about his obsessions with bombs and violence, so nothing more need be done about it. According to Oregon law, a teacher must inform child services if a school paper contains disclosures about a child's physical abuse or neglect, but there are no specific guidelines about how a teacher should respond to writing that is unusually violent or bizarre.

That winter the media lavished attention on the school shootings in Pearl, Mississippi; West Paducah, Kentucky; and Jonesboro, Arkansas. While watching the last of these events on a monitor at school, a friend heard Kip remark, "Hey, that's pretty cool." Another friend recalled Kip analyzing the school shootings the way a coach might review videotapes of a football defeat.

Around this time, the woman who had been the Kinkels' housekeeper for seven years quit because she was uncomfortable with Kip's knife collection, with his wardrobe of black clothing, and his penchant for setting things on fire. When she warned Faith and Bill about their son's activities, they had nothing more to say than, "Thank you for telling us."

At about the same time, a Springfield resident, while shopping at a local hardware store, saw Kip buying PVC pipe and learned that it was intended for making pipe bombs. He was understandably disturbed and warned store employees, who, according to police reports, told him to ". . . mind his own business."

That winter, while studying *Romeo and Juliet,* Kip developed a crush on a girl in the class who was considered very outgoing and "individualistic" by his circle of friends. For their first date, they went to the Thurston Winter Formal which was traditionally held in mid February. To the astonishment of his friends, Kip dressed up for the event. The girl wore ". . . a really weird dress. It was black and white and it was, like, wavy. From one way it looked black, and from one way it looked white. It was weird." In the days that followed she told Kip that she wasn't sure how she felt about him and that maybe she just wanted to be friends. Thrown into a dungeon of despair, he wrote in his journal:

> I gave her all I have and she just threw it away. Why? Why did God just want me to be in complete misery? I need to find more weapons.

In March the Kinkels went on their last holiday together, to a ski resort outside of Seattle. Kristin, who had flown home from Hawaii Pacific College, described her brother as being funny, positive, and self-confident. There was no mention of bombs and guns. Shortly after their return, Bill, growing suspicious about a locked trunk in Kip's bedroom, took a hacksaw to it and found it filled with guns. He confiscated them, locked them away and wore the key on a chain around his neck where both he and Kip could always see it. Kip told his friends that the truce with his father was over; Bill was trying to take away his guns.

In the days that followed he shared his fantasies with his friends about putting a bomb under the bleachers during a pep rally and blocking the doors; about "hitting" the cafeteria with his .22; about joining the army so he would know how it felt to kill people. Classmates jokingly voted him most likely to start World War III. No one ever told an adult about his threats because they did not take him seriously. He was considered a harmless little class clown.

In his journal, Kip wrote:

> I sit here all alone. I am always alone. I don't know who I am. I want to be something I can never be. I try so hard every day. But in the end, I hate myself for what I've become.

On May 19th, Kip got a call from a schoolmate, Corey Ewert, who, knowing of his interest in guns, thought he might want to purchase a .32 Beretta pistol which Corey had stolen from a friend's father, Mr. Scott Keeney. The next day, Kip came to school with $110 in cash. Corey gave him the loaded gun, which Kip hid in a paper bag in his locker. When Mr. Keeney discovered that his gun was missing, he phoned the school, and gave them the names of the boys who had been at his house the day before; he was certain one of them had stolen it. School administrators immediately began calling the boys out of class. Kip became nervous when he was summoned to the principal's office and confessed without prompting. The gun was located in the locker.

Kip and Corey were cuffed and taken to the police station where Kip was charged with two felonies: possessing a firearm in a public building and receiving a stolen weapon. His father was called to school and Kip was released in his custody. Kip described the ride home in his confession. "My dad kept saying how my mom . . . how embarrassed she was going to be and how horrible I was. . . ." When they got home, Kip went to his room, while his father sat downstairs at the kitchen counter, trying to decide how to manage his unmanagable son. Kip's guidance counselor called, as did Scott Keeney, who was a friend of Bill's. He told them that Kip was out of control and he didn't know what to do. According to phone records, he called the Oregon National Guard about their Youth Challenge Program for troubled teens; they would not, it turned out, accept youngsters on parole nor those being prosecuted for carrying a weapon.

Around three o'clock, Kip came out of his room with the .22 caliber rifle and shot his father behind the left ear, killing him. He dragged the body into the bathroom and covered it with a sheet.

Faith Kinkel was late getting home because of a friend's retirement party. Kip waited in the living room so he could see her car when it pulled up. He cried and slipped the .22 pistol into the waistband of his pants and said to himself how sorry he was that he had to do it and that there was no other way.

When his mother arrived, sometime after 6:00 PM, he ran downstairs to the garage to greet her and help with her bags. She knew nothing about the weapon, the expulsion from school, or the death of her husband. As she started up the stairs, Kip told her that he loved her and, drawing the .22, shot her twice in the back of her head. When he started to drag her up the stairs to the basement, he discovered that she was still conscious, and shot her four more times. He covered her body with a sheet and left her on the basement floor.

Kip spent the night alone in the house with the bodies of his parents, listening to the soundtrack from Baz Luhrman's contemporary remake of *Romeo and Juliet*, which he left on continuous replay. In a small, cramped hand, he wrote a note filled with misspellings and cross-outs, and left it on the coffee table in the living room.

> I have just killed my parents! I don't know what is happening. I love my mom and dad so much. I just got two felonies on my record. My parents can't take that! It would destroy them. The embarrassment would be too much for them. They couldn't live with themselves. . . . It's not their fault or the fault of any person, organization, or television show. My head just doesn't work right. God damn these VOICES inside my head. I want to die. I want to be gon.e . . .

His father had brought Kip's Glock home from the club in his tennis bag. During the night Kip loaded the gun and tried to kill himself but could not bring himself to pull the trigger.

Early in the morning of Thursday, May 21, Kip dressed for school, securing two bullets, a .22 caliber and a 9mm, to his chest with masking tape crosses before putting on his shirt. He taped a hunting knife to his leg, filled his dad's tennis bag with ammunition, and donned a cap with the logo of his favorite band, Nine Inch Nails. Finally, he put on a trench coat to hide the Ruger rifle and his two pistols he was carrying. At 7:30 he took the keys to his mother's Explorer and drove to Thurston High. At 7:55 he entered the school building and walked quickly down the breezeway to the cafeteria, overtaking three friends, whom he told to flee.

Ben Walker, 16, approached while Kip was talking to his friends. Kip strode by him, then turned around and, pulling the rifle from under his trench coat, shot at the back of his head. The gun failed to fire. Kip loaded another round and shot and fatally wounded Ben. Seconds later he shot a second student, Ryan Atteberry, in the face, but not fatally. When Kip reached the cafeteria door, he held it open with his foot and began shooting into the cafeteria.

In an instant the atmosphere of bantering conversation, of socializing and flirtation, was transformed into a scene of horror and confusion, of smoke and gunpowder smells, of popping bullets. Bodies crumpled on the linoleum, students screamed and stampeded for the door, literally crushing each other in their rush to escape. Kip discharged what remained of the 50-round clip in the rifle, and one round from the Glock handgun. At the end of the nine-minute killing spree, one student, Mikael Niklausen, 17, was dead, one was fatally wounded (Ben Walker), and 25 more were injured. Nineteen had been hit by gunfire and the remaining four harmed during the stampede to leave the cafeteria.

Jake Ryker, a 17-year-old, six-foot-four wrestler, having witnessed the wounding of his girlfriend, and heard the *click* of the empty ammunition clip, charged Kip, tackling him at the waist. The rifle went flying. Travis Weaver, a senior, grabbed it and ran it to the main office, keeping the barrel pointed at the ceiling as he had been taught by his father, and reassuring those he passed that he was not the shooter.

When Kip drew the Glock from his waistband, Jake seized the pistol barrel. As they wrestled over the weapon, Kip fired it, wounding Jake in the middle joint of his left index finger. "You bastard, you shot me!" Jake shouted. His brother, also a big boy, and three other members of the wrestling team piled on top of Kip, holding him down and punching and kicking him. He pleaded for them to shoot him.

The police arrived within minutes, cuffed Kip and drove him to the station house. The arresting officer locked him in an interview room while he set up the tape recorder in a second room. Kip managed to slip the cuffs around to the front, pried loose the folding pocket knife he had taped to his ankle and, when the officer returned, rose from the chair and lunged at him, crying, "Kill me! Shoot me!" The officer subdued him with pepper spray.

When they learned that Kip had killed his parents, officers were sent to examine the crime scene. They found his parents' bodies, ammunition, firearms, knives, and bomb-making materials. The Eugene bomb squad was summoned. In the crawl space under the house, they found two bombs of sophisticated design with electronic timing devices and two pipe bombs.

Lane County Mental Health division had ten counselors at the high school by 9:30 the day of the shooting, and workers from other organizations arrived throughout the day. That night, Thurston teachers attempted to call every one of the 1,450 students at the high school to touch base, communicate their concern, and inquire about their physical and psychological well-being.

Kristin Kinkel flew back from Honolulu on Friday, May 22, in order to arrange her parents' funerals and oversee the distribution of their estates. When she visited her brother, all he could do was cry. "It took weeks for him to make eye-contact with me," she said, "and even longer to say something. When he finally did, it was 'I am so sorry.'"

President Clinton, in his weekly radio address, acknowledged the nation's grief at another incident of school rampage killings, and urged Congress to pass a juvenile crime bill which would place a lifetime ban on the sale of guns to those who had been declared violent juveniles. He attributed the problem to a culture that desensitized children to violence through constant exposure to murders and brutality in the entertainment media, and the inability of educational and mental health professionals to identify SR shooters before they became a menace to their peers.

Regular classes were suspended on Monday. The school was open for three hours and students and their parents were invited to visit. Free breakfast was served in the cafeteria and also in the courtyard for those who couldn't bring themselves to go back inside the building. By then the area had been professionally cleaned of bullet-casings, blood stains, and tissue. The walls had been patched and painted. It was as though the crime had never taken place.

Three hours after the shooting somebody had slipped two bouquets of white and yellow chrysanthemums into the chain link fence surrounding the school, and by the end of the day, the fence had become a makeshift memorial, like the fence in Oklahoma City, two years before. Despite the rain and overcast skies that Monday, students and their parents seemed drawn to the fence. In addition to the notes, stuffed animals, and flowers, a letter jacket and a graduation robe appeared, in acknowledgement of those who would now never graduate. Black and red ribbons were everywhere, tied to trees and power poles, occasionally imprinted with the words, "Let it end here," the title Springfield firefighters and paramedics had chosen for their campaign to stop youth violence.

Another spontaneous memorial had occurred on the spot, 50 paces down the breezeway, where Ben Walker was shot. Dozens of students had paid their respects by tracing their hands with pens and markers and inscribing messages of faith and fondness. When school recommenced in the fall, the breezeway had been repainted a stark white, and none of the writing remained, even as pentimento. Many students found it unsettling. "You just looked at it and you knew," one student said. "It gave you the most vivid picture of what happened." Another student said of the whiteness, "You don't even want to step on it, like it's forbidden territory." An editor of the school newspaper wrote, "Beneath the fresh layer of white paint glaring off the hallway floor were the blood stains of our fallen friends. A bullet hole was hidden behind a campaign poster on the cafeteria wall; but the scars on our tender hearts could not be so easily concealed . . ."

Many students found it difficult to return to the school, especially the 100 or so who had personally witnessed the shooting. One student said, "The sooner you get started [returning to school] the sooner you get used to it. It's starting to get more normal again, seeing all my friends. The teachers are a good support." Megan Conklin, a classmate of Kip's who had been in the cafeteria during the shooting and had seen a student die a few feet away, found school unbearable. During the days after the shooting she slept only a few hours a night. She tried to explain her fear: "I keep feeling like Kip's in my room and putting a gun to my head." She decided to go on camera and publicly forgive him, but when she saw the glass eye focused on her, she could not speak, and broke down in tears.

Teachers were conflicted about what course of action to take with their students. Some felt that the ". . . only way to get over this is have our grieving period and get back to normal school life as soon as possible." But many students were unable to stay on topic, and teachers who tried to keep to the curriculum found the task like trying to climb a crumbling dune; discussions kept sliding back to the topic of the shooting. To complicate matters, the teachers were struggling with their own guilt, wondering if there was something they could have done to prevent the shooting or reduce the death toll and injuries.

Ben Walker's funeral was held that afternoon at Springfield Faith Center. Five hundred people filled every seat and stood in the back of the room, alongside CNN's live video camera. Rain pounded on the church roof and people tromped through a sea of mud. Ben's girlfriend wore his favorite plaid shirt over her good black dress. A wounded girl hobbled in on crutches. Members of the police and fire department, their badges banded in black, placed wreathes on Ben's coffin. Bill Morrisette, the mayor of Springfield, told the gathering, ". . . if I carried an organ donated by someone who had died, I would be a living memorial for that person. So Ben will live through other people." As they left the church, each attendee was given a carnation to place in the chain-link fence. For years afterwards, Ben's mother, Linda Kluber, visited his grave daily. She chose to home-school Ben's little sister, Kayla, because she no longer felt secure about public education.

On Tuesday school was let out at 10:55 so students could attend the funeral of Mikael Nickolausen at the Eugene Christian Fellowship. Otis

Harden, a retired minister and family friend who had know Mikael most of his life, officiated. "Greater love hath no man," he quoted from First Corinthians, "then that he lays down his life for his friend. If Mikael hadn't been standing where he was, someone else would have died." Relatives, friends, and teachers went up to the microphone to share their favorite stories about Mikael. They recalled him as a tinkerer, a computer nut, a Trekkie, a card shark, and a student who was "easy to teach and eager to please." "Mikael could move his eyebrows in this really weird way," one girl recalled. "He would do it in the middle of class just to see me crack up." Because Mikael had recently enlisted in the Oregon National Guard and, had he lived, would have completed basic training over the summer, he was given a quasi-military funeral with a flag-draped coffin. As the mourners left the chapel, the sun came out for the first time in days.

The school returned to its regular schedule on Wednesday.

Kip's shooting inspired a rash of "copycat" threats. On Wednesday, May 27th, a 14-year-old boy at Fariss Aternative School in Gresham, Oregon threatened to return to school and "shoot everyone" and was arrested and charged with disorderly conduct and harassment. A student at Henley High in Klamath County, Oregon, threatened to kill classmates at the school's graduation. He was admitted to a psychiatric unit at a local hospital for observation. A 15-year-old boy in Astoria, Oregon, made threats after he was suspended for fighting at Astoria Middle School on Friday the 22nd, and a student at North Valley High School in Wolf Creek, Oregon, was taken into custody Saturday after threatening to kill two classmates.

The community continued to protect their children, process their grief, and memorialize their dead in creative and powerful ways. Three Eugene women invited their neighbors throughout the state to submit ten-inch squares of fabric, decorated with embroidery or appliqué, to be assembled into a Thurston Healing Quilt. Hundreds of squares were received. Unlike the AIDS quilt, which was meant to be a single massive exhibit piece, the Healing Quilt was made into many small quilts which were distributed to survivors and their families. Teresa Miltonberger took one of the quilts with her when she visited the White House.

Life in Springfield seemed to be returning to normal. The weather was getting warm, crocuses were poking through the snow, and students were beginning to count the days until summer vacation. Then, on Tuesday, April 20, 1999, at 11:45, the classroom intercoms crackled to life. The principal announced that a shooting was in progress at Columbine High School in Colorado. Immediately a "safe room" was set up for students who needed support or assistance, and the television sets in the library were tuned to

CNN so students could see for themselves what was happening. Some students, outraged by the return of reporters to the school grounds, shouted at them to go away, and made obscene gestures, while others seemed to find comfort in telling them about the thoughts and emotions they were experiencing. Bill Morrisette, now a state representative, spoke for many when he said, "A scab has been ripped off a wound that is now bleeding again."

Trial preparations began in early September: a lottery for courtroom seats; a pool of jury candidates numbering nearly 1200; high security, with metal detectors and personal searches; network news departments litigating to put cameras in the courtroom; and a line-up of expert witnesses, including serial-killer authority, Park Dietz. The Kip Kinkel trial threatened to be a media circus unequalled in local history. At the eleventh hour, a meeting was arranged with David Brewer, an appeals court judge known for his modesty and his ability to broker settlements under adverse conditions. After two days of negotiations, Kip and his attorneys agreed to plead guilty and reserve testimony about his mental state for the sentencing hearing. In return, the prosecution would recommend that Kip be allowed to serve his sentences, the maximum of which would be 25 years, the minimum sentence for a murder conviction in Oregon, concurrently.

"My mind is clear and I am not sick," Kip stated in his written plea. ". . . I offer my plea of 'guilty' freely and voluntarily, of my own accord, with a full understanding of the charges and of the rights that I am giving up by this plea."

The six-day sentencing hearing began on November 2, 1999, and took the form of a small trial with a more relaxed protocol and rules of evidence, as was the practice in Oregon. Expert witnesses for the defense argued that Kip was psychotic; those for the prosecution argued that he was an exceedingly nasty boy who knew exactly what he was doing.

On November 9th, Judge Mattison explained that according to a recent change in the Oregon State Constitution, the protection of society was of greater importance than the reformation of the criminal and, with this in mind, Kip was being sentenced to 1040 months or slightly more than 86 years for the attempted murders and 25 years for the four murders, leaving him with a sentence of almost 112 years in prison. The sentence was immediately appealed by the public defender's office, who called it "cruel and unusual punishment," and "shocking in the moral sense to all fair-minded persons." On October 8, 2002, the state appeals court upheld the sentence, confirming Judge Mattison's interpretation of the new sentencing guidelines. The cost of legal proceedings to the state of Oregon was calculated at $203,815.

Kristin Kinkel married, sold the family home, moved to Portland, and got a job teaching English as a second language in a local elementary school. She continued to visit Kip at least once a month, care for her grandmother in Eugene, and travel the country competing in, and judging, cheerleading competitions, and teaching at cheerleading camps. More than a year after the shooting she stated:

> The shock that my parents were dead and that my brother had done it and he hadn't stopped at that. . . I don't know how to describe it. It's still just too much. Now, more than a year later, I'm just barely starting to grieve my parents' death. I haven't come anywhere near to learning how to deal with the fact that my brother did it. . . .
>
> Overwhelming isn't the word. If there's a word bigger than overwhelming, that would be it. . . . It's going to be years before I'll even be able to feel it, to feel what happened.

CASE 13. ERIC HARRIS & DYLAN KLEBOLD

Dylan Klebold, a pathologically shy child, was teased relentlessly from a very early age. His parents were intelligent and loving, if perhaps guilty of a high degree of denial regarding their son's later activities. While Dylan was initially very close to an older brother, Byron, by the time he reached high school Byron had joined the ranks of the bullies who were victimizing him. In high school Dylan came under the sway of Eric Harris. Eric had been born with a caved-in chest, or *pectus excavetum*, which made him the brunt of bullying. This, along with frequent family relocations, and the need to continuously reestablish his identity among new communities of children, led to homicidal and suicidal inclinations, which he expressed in a website filled with racist and terrorist rants, in midnight raids on the homes of his "enemies" (schoolmates by who he had felt disrespected), and in a fascination with bombs, firearms, and violent entertainment.

Dylan knew Eric from middle school, but the boys became close friends in high school, when they began working together at Blackjack Pizza. In January of their junior year they broke into a parked van and stole $400 worth of electrical equipment. They were apprehended by the police and sentenced to a juvenile alternative incarceration program. Soon afterwards they began plotting an assault on the high school involving explosives and shootings. This act, they believed, would result in them becoming mythologized, like Charles Manson, and creating a "revolution of the dispossessed," a term coined by Karl Marx.

On April 20, 1999, they planted bombs around Columbine High School, many of which failed to detonate. They strode through the school, seemingly choosing their victims at random, shooting and killing 12 students and a teacher, and wounding many others, some very seriously. Soon after noon they both committed suicide in the school library. (The Columbine High School shooting is described in detail in Chapters 5 and 6.)

CHAPTER 1

CASE 2: BRENDA SPENCER

Conduct Disorder / Malignant Narcissism / Brain Damage and Disinhibition

IN 1979, A PETIT, TOUGH, mercurial teenager named Brenda Spencer killed two adults and wounded eight little children in a school shooting in San Diego, California. In newspaper photographs, with her small, sharp nose, aviator glasses, and defiant air, she resembles Patty Hearst during her stint as a radical; but instead of a black beret, she wears a cowboy hat. Her skin is freckled and her bright red hair lies limp to her shoulders. She is five-foot-one and weighs 90 pounds.

Sixteen-year-old Dawn White, who claimed to be among Brenda's close friends, described her as "pretty happy" and said that she "wouldn't hurt anybody." She knew of no reason why Brenda might be upset enough to shoot at children she'd never met. Raelynn MacDonald, a senior, said "She had the brains to do whatever she wanted. She just didn't put them to use. I was talking to her Friday and nothing seemed to be wrong with her." Another student saw another side of her: "She was nice but she was really crazy. We were nice to her because we were afraid of her . . . I didn't like her because she always talked about killing things." A student from her history class recalls Brenda wondering aloud how it would feel to shoot people. Adults were also confused about her character. Mary Lipe, a neighbor of Brenda's, described her as a quiet girl from a nice family who was looking for attention, a bright girl who did not like school. Mrs. Lipe's five-year-old son, David, often visited the Spencer home to play in Brenda's father's pickup truck or help care for Brenda's pets. Neighborhood children agreed that Brenda loved animals and talked about little else, but they also recall her chasing neighborhood strays with a can of lighter fluid, with the intention of soaking their tails and setting them afire. According to a story Brenda had told a classmate, when she was younger her grandmother had forbidden her visiting unless accompanied by her older sister, who was expected to keep an eye on her.

These Jekyll-and-Hyde descriptions of SR shooters are not uncommon; they are the result of the shooter's skill at concealing his violent and anti-social urges from all but a perceptive few. This is the "flying below the radar," behavior noted by Newman and his colleagues. The SR shooter's family is equally adept at keeping his secret, or remains in denial about it. Because he keeps a low profile at school, he may be unknown to the counseling staff. Thus, in the first wave of media reports, the SR shooting seems to come out of nowhere, astonishing the community and contributing to the apparent mystery and mystique of these events. Had the shooter lacked this ability to hide in plain sight, he would have been identified early on and diverted to a therapeutic placement, a boarding school, or children's psychiatric inpatient unit.

Brenda loved guns and knives, and was an excellent marksman. "I went into the desert with her last year to go target shooting," Dawn White recalled, "and she killed a lot of lizards and squirrels. She almost never missed." When she was 11, Mary Lipe had scolded her for shooting at birds with her BB gun. Another friend said that Brenda dreamed of making her living as a sniper. She always carried a small knife. "She always had a lot of knives," Dawn said. "She loved knives."

Her favorite course at school was photography. Her teacher described her as introverted and undistinguished except for her better-than-average ability to compose an image and her bright red hair. She won a color TV, first prize in a Humane Society photo contest in October, four months before the shootings. The winning photograph, reprinted in a local paper, showed a man leading his dog through an obedience trial at a neighborhood dog show. Well-composed and full of vitality, it might easily be the work of a professional photojournalist.

Brenda had bought into the decaying revolutionary counterculture of the 1970s, now a dumping ground where students who belonged nowhere could pretend to have some kind of social affiliation. According to the neighborhood kids, she was, by her own account, often "stoned on LSD, pot, or pills." While watching TV, she would exclaim "All right!" whenever a cop was shot. She often talked about how she wanted to kill cops, to "blow one away." It should be recalled that "Off the pig!"—an admonition to kill police—was a popular catch phrase of the revolutionary counterculture in the late '60s and early '70s. For example, a 1968 film about the Black Panthers was called, *Off the Pig*. An article from an educational journal of that era, suggesting a revision of elementary school social studies curriculums, is called "Law and Order: The Policeman is Our Friend—Off the 'Pig.'" Brenda's disdain for the police, a friend suggested, had been exacerbated by encounters with the law. She had been arrested at least twice prior to her crime, once for shooting out windows at Cleveland Elementary School the summer before her SR shootings, and again for shoplifting ammunition from a local drugstore. As a result, she was receiving counseling from a probation officer at the county's Youth Services Bureau. Another classmate, Tracy Mills, said that Brenda often boasted about her skill as a shoplifter. Tracy described her as "a radical," and added that she cut school often. In fact, she had been suspended for excessive truancy the previous year. While in the 1970s theft was considered a politically radical act—as evidenced by Abbie Hoffman's book, *Steal This Book*—post-millennial Americans, in particular child therapists, will recognize in this and Brenda's other antisocial acts the symptoms of conduct disorder, the diagnostic label applied to children embarking on the path to adult criminality.

The *Diagnostic and Statistical Manual of Mental Disorders, Fourth Edition, Text Revision* or DSM IV-TR for short, is a book with the heft of a dictionary, published by the American Psychiatric Association and periodically updated, which lists every currently recognized psychiatric disorder (as well as their Medicaid reimbursement code, which must be entered on insurance forms if mental health workers are to be paid). Since its first edition in 1955, the DSM has become the arbiter of what constitutes a psychiatric disorder, how these disorders should be understood, and how people who suffer from them should be labeled. In order to assign the diagnosis of conduct disorder, the DSM uses its convention of identifying a subset of symptoms from a larger set; in the case of conduct disorder, at least three symptoms from a list of fifteen. Although we know little of Brenda, we can say with some certainty that she:

1. stole "items of nontrivial value without confronting the victim (e.g., shoplifting . . .)"

2. was ". . . physically cruel to animals," and

3. ". . . deliberately destroyed others' property."

She might qualify for more symptoms if we had more information. We know that she was frequently truant from school. Frequent truancy is listed as a symptom of conduct disorder, but it must occur *before* age 13 (sad to say that beyond that age truancy is sufficiently common to be a norm). Carrying and using weapons is another listed symptom. Brenda loved knives and may have carried a knife around with her, but, according to police reports, she never used a knife to harm a person so it doesn't quite fit. However, three out of 15 is sufficient to make the diagnosis. People often question the value of this particular diagnoses, arguing that poor conduct is a moral issue rather than a psychiatric one, that it is recursive (because conduct disorder is a list of childish crimes such as shoplifting, the diagnosis tells us little more than that the child commits childish crimes); and "sticky" (the diagnosis follows a child into adulthood, making it difficult for them to get certain kinds of jobs or serve in the military); and that such labels encourage people to think of themselves as criminals or mental patients. These criticisms are well-founded, but the DSM IV-TR also has real value in that it represents the current "paradigm" of psychiatric science in the Kuhnian sense, arrived at through empirical studies, laborious statistics, and an effort to be atheoretical. In a study such as this, the DSM provides valuable grounding and clarity.

Brenda's parents, Dorothy Nadine Spencer and Wallace Edward Spencer, were married on December 12, 1954 in Chula Vista, California. He was 25 and she was 19. They lived at 6143 Boulder Lake Avenue in a house worth about $18,000 ($140,638.88 in 2007 dollars according to the Consumer Price Index) at the time of their divorce. Dorothy had a bachelor's degree in business from the Woodbury School, a local college, and had taken another three years of college courses in accounting. For six months of the year, she was the head bookkeeper at the Andy Williams Open Golf Tournament. She had an office in her home and her other clients included a local church, the Del Mar Fair, and the Community Bookstore at the University of San Diego. She was well-known and well-liked in the community.

In 1956 Dorothy gave birth to a son, Scott Mathew Spencer, and two years later, a daughter, Theresa Lynn. Brenda Ann was born on September 3, 1962. In January of 1972, when Brenda was nine, Dorothy petitioned Wallace for divorce. She asked for custody of the children and modest child support and alimony. After a private meeting with the Spencer children in chambers, the judge awarded custody to Wallace, a decision nearly unheard of in San Diego in 1972. Dorothy got the usual visitation rights, although it is not known whether, or for how long, she maintained contact with her three children. Wallace agreed to pay her $200 ($1,562.65 in 2007 dollars) a month for two years, then $1 a year for three years, an amount that must have been symbolic and may have been punitive by being humiliating. Wallace, who was 43 at the time, had take-home pay of about $9,500 ($74,226.08 in 2007 dollars) a year, and Dorothy, who was 37, made about $3,700 ($28,909.10 in 2007 dollars). She drove a seven-year-old Rambler station wagon, and he a 12-year-old Ford pickup truck. The house had a substantial mortgage.

Wallace and the children moved into a little yellow house at 6356 Lake Atlin Avenue, in San Carlos, a blue-collar suburb of San Diego. It was convenient in that it was located directly across the street from Cleveland Elementary School, which Brenda attended through 1974. The proximity was such that you could see the entrance of the school through the small rhomboid windows in her front door.

As an equipment technician at San Diego State University, Wallace found it difficult to make ends meet. In June of 1973, he fell into arrears on his alimony and, in May of 1974, he asked the court if he could discontinue payment. Now he requested that Dorothy pay him child support of $150 for the three children.

By 1976 both Scott, then 20, and Theresa, 18, had moved out of the house, leaving 14-year-old Brenda living alone with her father. A colleague at the office described him at that time as a quiet, shy, and soft-spoken man who sometimes seemed overwhelmed by his role as a single father. He appeared to be very depressed. People considered him a good father because he encouraged his daughters to pursue their interests; for example, he gave Brenda a camera for her birthday.

However, for Christmas of 1979, Wallace gave Brenda a .22 caliber semiautomatic rifle with a telescopic sight and 500 rounds of ammunition, a questionable gift for a child with a history of arrests and serious psychiatric problems. About a month later, Brenda told her "boyfriend" that she was planning something "big" that "will be on television and everything." She told friends that her "battle plans" included turning the garage into a fortress and digging a hideout tunnel in the backyard. This kind of planning and publicizing of the event are characteristic of all school shootings. Details are worked out in advance (although not necessarily realistically); friends are forewarned, and sometimes invited to watch from a safe shelter.

Four years earlier, Patty Hearst, granddaughter of newspaper magnate William Randolph Hearst, had been kidnapped and brainwashed by a ragtag band of revolutionaries who called themselves the Symbionese Liberation Army. The TV and newspaper coverage, particularly copious in California, continued through March of 1976, when Hearst was sentenced to prison (the sentence was later commuted by Jimmy Carter). A poster depicting the scowling, politicized Patty in combat fatigues and black beret, cradling a submachine gun, with a seven-headed cobra painted on the wall behind her, became a symbol for rebellious, badass behavior, qualities often admired by teens. When Brenda spoke boldly about "shooting pigs" and told her friends that she was a "revolutionary," she was echoing their rhetoric and ideology. Patty Hearst had turned violent, committed a crime (participating in the robbing of the Hibernia National Bank in San Francisco), and became a celebrity, a symbol of rebellion. Brenda may have thought she would do the same. Newman and her colleagues refer to this as "following a cultural script," but I think it is more useful to see it as an attempt to create significance in one's life through a ceremonial, public act rationalized by a sham ideology. Because she was proficient as a sniper, and had achieved notoriety for this in the past (shooting out the windows of Cleveland Elementary School), it became her preferred mode of violence.

On the morning of January 29, children who had arrived early at Cleveland Elementary School were chasing one another around the playground, while a line of cars moved slowly past the entrance, dropping off children with backpacks. Cleveland was a small school with 319 students, 13 teachers, and six support staff. The first bell rang at 8:50 AM. Across the street, Brenda broke two of the diamond-shaped panels in the front door, stuck her rifle barrel through the hole, and began to fire. Over the next 15 minutes she discharged 40 rounds. The school driveway, bordered by an ivy-covered fence on the left, and the "el" of the school building on the right, created a corridor, giving her a clear shot from her own front door to the entrance of the school. The distance from her home was less than 50 feet.

Burton Wragg was 53 and had just been appointed principal of Cleveland Elementary School. This was his first day on the job. He and Daryl Barnes, who taught sixth grade and was the school's senior teacher, were standing in the vestibule, welcoming the children and maintaining order, when they heard two shots. Wragg rushed outside and was immediately hit in the shoulder by a bullet and then again in the chest. The impact spun him around and knocked him into a small ivy garden at the south end of the school parking lot. Daryl Barnes ran outside moments later and found him lying on the ground, on his back. "There were children running everywhere," Barnes remembers. "He was badly wounded in the chest. I opened his shirt. He appeared dead." When Barnes stood up, a bullet missed him by a breath. "I guess God's hand was on my shoulder," he said later. He scooped up two children, one under each arm, and ran inside.

Michael Suchar, the school custodian, unaware of or indifferent to the deadliness of the sniper fire, came outside with a blanket to cover Wragg, to keep him from going into shock. Barnes, who was watching from the window of the nurse's office, described what happened next. "I saw him lean down over Wragg and almost immediately two bullets hit him, spinning him around and to the ground."

Wanda Carberry, a fourth grade teacher with 23 years in the school system, went outside, blew her whistle, and shouted for children to come in.

"The sniper seemed to pick them off easily as they ran towards the school," she told the press. She could hear bullets ricocheting off the steel posts above her head. Other teachers followed her lead, saving the children without consideration for their own safety.

The first police ambulance arrived minutes later. Hunkered down and shielded from view by masses of ivy, patrolman Dennis P. Doremus and his partner, Robert Robb, herded the children along the chain link fence, to safety. While Robb was examining Wragg's and Suchar's bodies, he was struck by a bullet that found its way through the armhole of his bullet-proof vest and lodged under his right shoulder blade. He fell, but in the chaos of the moment, stimulated into overdrive by his own adrenaline, he remained unsure that he had been hit. He was 28, a recent graduate of the police academy.

Seventeen minutes after the first shot was fired, Alvarado Hospital, an acute-care facility about three and a half miles from the school, was placed on "general blue alert." The first victims arrived at 9:15 by police car and van, and Principal Wragg was among them. He was rushed to surgery and died on the operating table 35 minutes later. Custodian Suchar was pronounced dead on arrival. The less seriously injured were taken to Grossmont Hospital in La Mesa, an older facility.

When editors at the *San Diego Evening Tribune* heard about sniper fire at Cleveland Elementary, they assigned reporter Gus Stevens to investigate. He consulted a reverse directory (a listing of phone numbers by address rather than name) and began calling the homes nearest the school to see if anybody had an idea whence the shooting originated. He placed his first call to the house opposite the school.

The girl who answered the phone gave her name as Brenda.

Did she know anything about the shootings?

"Yes," she replied. "I saw the whole thing."

Did she know who did it?

A 16-year-old kid who lived at 6356 Atlin Avenue, she replied.

"Isn't that your address?" Stevens asked, puzzled.

"Sure," she said, giggling. "Who do you think did it?" And she hung up. Stevens called back and asked if Brenda would mind being interviewed.

Brenda explained that she had told her father that she was sick so she could stay home from school. After that "I just started shooting. That's it. I just did it for the fun of it." She went on: "I just don't like Mondays. Do *you* like Mondays? I did this because it's a way to cheer up the day. Nobody likes Mondays." Later she said, "It just popped into my head. About last Wednesday, I think."

Was she alone in the house?

"You think I'd be doing it if someone was home?"

Stevens described her attitude as calm and matter-of-fact. She claimed that she found nothing odd about shooting at people she did not know, but she did admit to being worried about what her father would say.

"My dad's gonna kill me when he gets home and finds out about this," she told Stevens on the phone. "He's going to flip. This will really blow him away."

Stevens pointed out that she may have killed three or four innocent people.

"Is that all?" Brenda responded. "I saw lots of feathers fly."

She went on about splitting open people's "skulls with a cleaver," something she probably never did, and admitted to her prior arrests for burglary and shoplifting. Before hanging up on the second call, she said, "I have to go now. I shot a pig, I think, and I want to shoot some more."

While Stevens was on the phone, other staff at the *San Diego Evening Tribune*, alerted to his strange interview, contacted the police. They, in turn, fed questions to Stevens that he relayed to Brenda, yielding information that would later result in her being arrested without additional injuries.

MALIGNANT NARCISSISM

What induced Brenda Spencer to grant a phone interview in the middle of a killing spree, and why did she say the things she did? This extraordinarily callous behavior foreshadows that of Seung-Hui Cho, who paused during his killing spree to mail his own "press kit" to NBC News.

When one has a grandiose sense of self-importance and is indifferent toward the feelings of others, he is called "narcissistic." In the psychiatric literature, this kind of behavior is referred to as narcissistic personality disorder, or NPD. In his seminal work, *On Narcissism* (1914), Freud wrote that, prior to age three, every child experiences "primary narcissism," the belief that he is the center of the universe, as indeed most infants are. This is healthy and normal. The infant's every need is attended to, more or less immediately, and he has no need to concern himself with the welfare of others. John Bowlby (1982) writes of a bonding process that takes place early on, the forging of the initial, enduring emotional tie between the infant and the caregiver. By bonding with the caregiver, the infant discovers that the caregiver is a sentient person like herself, who feels pain and sadness, and joy and love, not simply a device to provide food and care in response to howls for attention. His relationship with the caregiver lays the groundwork for subsequent relationships with siblings, playmates, boyfriends, spouses, and others. Current research suggests that the bonding must take place within a certain period of a child's development; if it does not, then establishing it later in life becomes a task of great effort. Without bonding, the infant never learns to experience empathy. As he grows older, he continues to employ infantile strategies for gaining while treating others like unfeeling devices. In the worst cases, sometimes referred to as "malignant narcissism," other people are dehumanized to the extent that they can be killed without remorse.

In order to overcome his low opinion of himself, he focuses on the aspect of himself of which the parents most approve—physical attractiveness, intellectual acuity, a talent for drawing or singing—and tries to bury the part which they reject. If the Self were a house, the supposed competence would be a trophy displayed on the mantle. *Handsome,* the engraving on the base might say, or *Brilliant,* or even *Superior Sniper* or *Infamous Radical.* The split-off part, which might be labeled *Unlovable,* or *Friendless,* or *Broken-brained,* is disowned, hidden in the cellar, where it can be forgotten, at least until someone has the nerve or foolishness to confront him with it. Those who offer praise or publicity—they are sometimes referred to as "narcissistic sources"—are prized by the narcissist because they keep the split Self's fragile fiction of superiority intact. Gus Stevens was a narcissistic source, as are all reporters. Brenda kept talking to him even though (or because) it was outrageous behavior, because she believed that he would spread her story, and build her reputation as a radical and a dangerous cop-killer. To help the story along, she made up details about splitting heads with cleavers, and killing on a whim, because it was Monday and she didn't like Mondays. How badass can you get?

Across the street at Cleveland Elementary School, children and teachers sought shelter in the bathrooms and in the classrooms, sitting on the floor in order to be out of the range of bullets fired through the windows. About half the students had been herded into the auditorium, because the walls in that part of the building were brick, and afforded better protection. When the police finally located the source of the bullets, they set about evacuating the children from the opposite side of the building. The only path to the exit, however, crossed a corridor exposed to sniper fire. Police blocked the corridor with a truck and made a barricade of tables and chairs. Around 11:30 the children marched out the rear of the school in a single file and boarded buses waiting on Lake Angela Drive. Parents, some nearly hysterical with anxiety, watched from behind police lines, pleading for information about their sons and daughters. Some of them had binoculars. Onlookers were astonished by the total silence and orderliness displayed by the children, who were at other times so boisterous and rowdy. When they spotted their own children alive and well, they wept and shrieked with joy. The children were taken to the auditorium of Pershing High School, three blocks away, where their parents could retrieve them in a safe and orderly way.

Detective Paul E. Olson, a member of the specially trained hostage negotiation team, contacted Brenda by telephone at 12:06 PM. Why had they taken so long to reach her? Brenda asked. The reporter had found her hours ago. The negotiations were difficult because, unlike other hostage situations, Brenda had everything she needed. There could be no bargaining for food, drink, an escape vehicle, or amnesty. She was, after all, in her own home. Olson kept her engaged for the next three hours, trying to establish a relationship of trust.

More crowds had gathered beyond the barricades that surrounded the little yellow house on Lake Atlin Avenue. Onlookers shouted, "Shoot her!" and urged the police to storm the house. "As long as she talks," SWAT team members countered, "we wait."

Brenda's classmates at the high school, many of whom had little brothers and sisters at Cleveland Elementary, were appalled, not by the fact that she had "gone postal" and murdered the principal and the custodian, but that she had shot at and wounded little children. As one of them commented, ". . . you don't hurt kids. That's like setting fire to the church. Kids are sacred."

A little after three o'clock, Detective Olson convinced Brenda to surrender her weapons. She emerged from the house, placed the .22 rifle and a pellet gun on the driveway, and went back inside. Next Olson convinced her to give up her ammunition. After she had placed several hundred rounds of ammunition on the driveway, she was cuffed and led to a police van parked nearby. She was driven to police headquarters and from there to Juvenile Hall, where she was confined.

Members of the school board spent most of the night in the hospital, comforting Suchar's and Wragg's distraught widows and supporting the parents of the wounded children.

At 8:30 the next morning, Carl M. Cannon, a *San Diego Union* reporter, knocked on the door of Brenda's home, hoping to interview her father. Peering through the window, he could see Wallace Spencer sitting in a straight-back chair in the living room, staring into space, but the man didn't budge. By noon a family friend had taped a sign to the door: Wallace was "in shock and agony over the events of yesterday—the deaths of the principal and custodian, the wounding of the children and policeman, his daughter Brenda . . ."

Later that day the district attorney's office made a statement that they would seek to have Brenda tried as an adult in Superior Court so that she would be eligible for a life sentence. In juvenile court, regardless of the severity of the crime, she would be freed upon her 23rd birthday.

Daryl Barnes, having taken over as principal, decided, with the support of his staff, that the children should return to class that day. "Each teacher then spent time in their own way trying to explain what had happened and how the healthy students could help those who had been hurt. Mostly we just talked it out—in class, in assemblies, in one-to-one counseling for those kids, teachers, and parents who needed it. People were told to not be afraid to talk about it, to show emotion. We said time would heal." Despite his decision, 69 children, 20 percent of the school, were absent as opposed to six percent on a normal day. Some children seemed relatively undisturbed by the event while others were afraid to go back. A third group made a point of going back and confronting their fears and perhaps making a public show of their courage. Sometimes these diverse feelings appeared within the same family. Veronna Rodgers said that her six-year-old daughter, Tanisha, was too frightened to go to school the morning after the shootings, while her eight-year-old, Trina, insisted on walking to school by herself. Representatives of the city school district's counseling office, and from the San Diego County Mental Health Services Department, helped teachers and students deal with their grief. Student council representatives and teachers planned a memorial service for Principal Wragg while children made cards and sent flowers to the widow of "Mr. Mike," as the kids called him.

On March 19, two months after her arrest, Brenda underwent a series of neurological tests at Scripps Memorial Hospital, including X-rays and EEGs. On March 28, her attorney, Michael McGlinn, filed a writ of habeas corpus, an emergency appeal stating that Brenda had a mental illness that may have been caused by a fall on her head from a bicycle when she was 14. She was found to have "grossly abnormal" brain waves indicating, in all likelihood, temporal lobe epilepsy.

If the brain is pictured as a boxing glove, the temporal lobes are where the thumb might be. The magnitude of the seizure depends on the areas of the lobes and the neighboring brain affected. The International League Against Epilepsy recognizes three types of seizures. The third type, where the seizure spreads from the temporal lobes to the rest of the brain, results in the behaviors commonly associated with epilepsy: the stiffening of the arms and legs followed by a period of uncontrollable jerking of the limbs. Had Brenda suffered from this, it would have been known to all because such behaviors are nearly impossible to hide. This leaves the first two types of seizures, the simple partial seizure (SPS), and the complex partial seizure (CPS). The symptoms of SPS are mainly odd sensations such as déjà-vu, or minor hallucinations involving taste, touch, sound, or sight, sometimes accompanied by un-elicited and incongruous feelings of fear, anger, depression, or exultation. During CPS, a somewhat more severe affliction, the seizure spreads to a larger portion of the temporal lobes, causing disruptions in consciousness. The sufferer might appear to "zone out" in an obvious way, staring into space for minutes at a time and failing to respond to others, or exhibiting repetitious behaviors or bizarre speech. Impaired judgment is another symptom. It is easy to imagine the teasing that undiagnosed SPS or CPS might have elicited from Brenda's classmates (*Look, Brenda's zoning out again! Brenda's such a space cadet!* etc.) and the scoldings from teachers (*Brenda! Why are you always daydreaming in class?*).

Most of us who took an introductory psychology course in high school or college learned about Phineas Gage, a hardworking foreman of a railroad crew who, in 1848, during an accidental explosion, had a six-foot-long iron tamping rod driven like a projectile through his skull, entering under his left cheek bone and exiting out the top of his skull. Miraculously, he survived with all his faculties intact; however his personality was permanently altered. Where before he had been pious, honest, and hard-working, he now cursed, lied, and behaved abominably to others (but did not, to our knowledge, murder anybody). No autopsy was performed when he died in 1861, but his skull was later recovered and examined to determine where the brain had been damaged. In the early 1990s, Hannah Damasio and her colleagues from the University of Iowa Medical School borrowed Phineas Gage's skull and, using three-dimensional computer imaging techniques, located the precise location of the lesions. They found that the damage involved the left and right prefrontal cortices in a pattern that, as confirmed by the most current research, "causes a defect in rational decision making and the processing of emotion." Several well-conducted studies by Adrian Raine, a researcher at UCLA, and his colleagues, using modern imaging techniques such as the PET (Positron Emission Tomography) scan, have confirmed the association between antisocial, violent, and predatory behaviors and frontal lobe damage and deficits. A theory developed by Jonathan Pincus and Dorothy Otnow Lewis suggests that some disinhibiting form of brain damage is one of three precursors to most homicidal behavior, the other two being childhood abuse and paranoia. Pincus is a professor of neurology at John Hopkins Medical School, and the author of a popular neurology textbook, and Lewis is on the faculty of the Yale Child Study Center. They base their theory on 25 years of experience interviewing over 100 convicted murderers, including serial killers, those who had killed impulsively during the commission of a robbery or other crime (affective homicide), those who planned their killing (predatory homicide), and at least one SR shooter (Kip Kinkel). All that we are told is that Brenda Spencer's brainwaves, her EEGs, suggested some kind of epilepsy, possibly the result of a impact to her skull during a bicycle accident. The unusual frequency of epileptic behavior among violent prisoners has been the subject of study for over a hundred years, and has attracted controversy because of its disingenuous use as a legal defense. Although surveys have confirmed that epilepsy is two to four times more common among violent offenders, Pincus has this to say on the subject:

> My view . . . [is that] brain damage, not epilepsy, increases the chances of violent behavior. Brain damage, especially in limbic areas, can cause paranoia, and frontal damage can cause disinhibition. Paranoia and disinhibition are significant precipitators of violence, especially when combined with a history of childhood abuse. Limbic and/or frontal damage can also cause seizures, but seizures themselves rarely cause violence. Though the presence of seizures can be indicative of brain damage, it is the brain damage, not the seizures, that disinhibits.

Because of the discovery of Brenda's brain damage, and its possible affect on her behavior, McGlinn urged that the case be sent back to juvenile court and reconsidered. Two consulting psychiatrists, Dr. Thomas A. Rodgers and Dr. Haig A. Koshkarian, wrote letters stating that Brenda would receive better treatment, including medication trials and psychotherapy, in the custody of the California Youth Authority.

The appeal was denied.

Brenda was scheduled to be tried as an adult on two counts of murder and nine counts of assault. On October 1, for reasons that were never explained, she changed her plea to guilty and the trial never took place.

On November 31, Orange County Superior Court Judge, Byron K. McMillan, sent Brenda to the Ventura School, a California Youth Authority facility, for a 90-day psychiatric evaluation. At that time, McGlinn stated that Brenda had no recollection of the shootings. "She doesn't recall the actual incident itself," he told reporters. "She's blacked that out of her mind." He added that she had "a lot of very serious psychological problems."

Criminals who were sexually or physically abused as children some-times claim amnesia for the crimes they themselves commit as adults. It has been suggested that childhood abuse sufferers become adept at disso-ciation, at separating their consciousness from the body, so that the repel-lant experience becomes dream-like or forgotten altogether. Freud consid-ered this a "defense mechanism," a way of surviving intolerable ordeals, even if the ordeals were of one's own making. Sometimes dissociation occurs in the manifesting of multiple personalities, only the most antiso-cial of whom may recall committing the crime. The other "selves" are amnesiac about the event and may even believe that they were somewhere else when it occurred (and in a sense they were!). To skeptics, such claims seem, like the epilepsy-violence connection, a disingenuous ploy for an otherwise hopeless legal defense. Research by Lewis and her colleagues, by James Chu of Harvard Medical School, and by other respected scien-tists support a strong correlation between childhood abuse and dissocia-tive disorders. Lewis's research suggests that most claims of dissociative disorders among murderers are often legitimate. The DSM IV-TR which, as I have mentioned, is the arbiter of such matters, and is by its very nature scientifically conservative, recognizes the existence of multiple per-sonality disorder, although it refers to it as "dissociative identity disorder" to emphasize its place in the categorical scheme which it employs. Kenneth Bianchi, nicknamed by the Los Angeles press "the Hillside Strangler," claimed to have no recollection of the twelve women he had raped and murdered, but a tough-talking alternate identity named "Steve" bragged about the killings. Some of the psychologists who assessed Bianchi believed him to have multiple personalities but others thought it was an act. Many years ago I met one of the believers, psychol-ogist John G. Watkins, at a conference, and he told me that the prisoners in the adjacent cells were kept awake by several different voices from Bianchi's cell (he was the only occupant) arguing fiercely with one anoth-er. Watkins took this as conclusive evidence of the legitimacy of his disor-der. What would a prisoner stand to gain from faking the behavior under those circumstances? Lee Boyd Malvo, John Muhammad's young partner in the more recent "Beltway Snipers" killing of ten men and women, was diagnosed as having a dissociative disorder as a result of being "brain-washed" by his elder partner. This diagnosis was one of the factors that got him a life sentence rather than an execution. Brenda Spencer had noth-ing to gain by fabricating a dissociative episode because she had already pleaded guilty to her crimes (in fact in 1979 the link between child abuse, dissociation, and violent acts was still tentative).

Why did Brenda Spencer change her plea? The public was never told. However, this much we know: had the case gone to trial, much personal information about her and her relationship to her family would have been made public. Brenda may have had "a lot of very serious psychological problems," as her attorneys told the press, employing the vaguest language at their disposal, but the nature of these problems remains unknown. It is interesting to note that of the 15 SR shooters investigated during the writing of this book, the only cases that did not report childhood abuse were those where a trial had been averted by a guilty plea or the suicide of the shooter.

Brenda Spencer was sentenced to 25 years to life at the California Institute for Women at Frontera, an adult facility. CIWF is located in Chowchilla, seven hours north of San Diego, requiring a commitment of at least two days of travel for anyone who chose to visit her. Many aspects of life at CIWF seemed cruel or exploitive. Prisoners wishing to call friends and family were charged three dollars or more by the telephone companies (MCI was among the offenders; they claimed that telephone connections from prisons were more expensive because of "security measures") in addition to the usual per-minute toll to place a collect call. Guards regularly observed the prisoners while they were showering, dressing, and using the bathroom. They were searched continuously, patted down after meals, and subjected to strip searches and body cavity searches after all personal visits. In the 1990s—Brenda was in her late twenties by then—following the passage of mandatory sentencing laws for drug possession, the CIWF prisoner population began to increase rapidly, and by the end of the decade the institution was operating at twice its capacity. In 1995 a class action lawsuit was filed against CIWF, accusing the prison's administrative and medical staff of:

> . . . cruel and unusual punishment and . . . "deliberate indifference" to the health needs of inmates. Among the cases . . . were instances of untreated or poorly treated pulmonary and cardiac problems, hypertension, sickle-cell anemia, and cancer. Attorneys also attributed at least two prison deaths to the poor quality of health care, including the case of a mentally ill woman with gastrointestinal problems. Confined naked to a prison cell, the woman ingested her own body waste and eventually died of untreated pancreatitis and starvation.

Twenty-three years later Kathe Wragg, Principal Wragg's widow, still had not remarried. She was overwhelmed with grief but forced herself to put her husband's death behind her for the sake of her three teenage sons.

She took it as an affirmation of her behavior when her husband appeared to her in a dream and told her, "You're doing so well." Years later she told a local journalist, "This is always on my mind. You never forget. It did a lot to our family."

Christy Buell, one of the eight children wounded that day, remembered standing in front of the school and hearing a sound like a popgun. A voice told her to run but before she could, she was shot in the abdomen. She crawled across the sidewalk and lawn and into the school building, where a teacher pulled her into a room. Two more shots grazed her head before she was out of the line of fire. Christy was hospitalized for 42 days and had two operations. Years later, possibly inspired by the heroism she saw that day, or by a need to face the moment of her fear over and over again to come to terms with it, she became a preschool teacher and continues to live in the same neighborhood with her father. The sight of the school no longer upsets her, but of the shooting itself, she says, "It will just never leave my mind."

Patti Satin-Jacob's son Scott was in the fourth grade when the shooting took place. "When he was walking into school he saw a child shot, and then he hit the ground. Then he saw the principal on the ground and heard popping sounds and teachers screaming." Although her son was not wounded, he was "a very upset child for a very long time." In time, with the help of a crisis management team organized by the school, he was able to attend classes and concentrate on his lessons.

Monika Selvig, who was eight at the time of the shooting, still bears the scars where the bullet entered her stomach and came out her back. Praised by grown-ups for being so brave and cheerful afterwards, she took pride in refusing help. At the age of 14 she began drinking alcohol and smoking pot, habits that worsened during the following 15 years, the alcohol becoming habitual and the pot giving way to hard drugs. In 2001 she was arrested for dealing drugs and sentenced to 180 days in a clinic. She believes that her dependence on alcohol and drugs was a result of her unwillingness to talk about the traumatic events of that morning.

Mathew Hardy, then five years old, had been walking to school with his big sister, Crystal, when she was suddenly shot in the hand. "We didn't really know what was going on. We thought it was fireworks." Mathew believed that the incident influenced the course of his life for years to come. At first he was angry and abandoned religion, but later his faith returned and he became a pastor at Horizon Fellowship. For years afterwards, his sister would crouch down or take cover at any shot-like sound.

The contrast between the cavalier attitude Brenda had displayed during her interview with Gus Stevens, and the enormity of her crime had considerable shock value. She became a minor celebrity, and even had a song written about her by the Boomtown Rats, an Irish new wave band of the 1970s. "I Don't Like Mondays" became the number one song in the UK for a month in 1979 and was "covered" by the likes of Bon Jovi and Tori Amos.

I Don't Like Mondays

The silicon chip inside her head
Gets switched to overload.
Nobody's gonna go to school today,
She's gonna make them stay at home.
Daddy doesn't understand it,
He always said she was good as gold.
He can see no reason,
'Cause there are no reasons,
What reasons do you need to be shown?
Chorus:
Tell me why
I don't like Mondays
I want to shoot
The whole day down

Lyrics by Bob Geldof, from the album
The Fine Art of Surfacing

In 1993, during her first parole hearing, Brenda, now 30, told the three Board of Prison Terms members that she had been under the influence of PCP and alcohol during the shootings, and that the mixture of the drug and the alcohol had caused her to experience hallucinations of "commando types" in paramilitary gear closing in on her house. Believing that she was under attack, she had barricaded herself inside the house and started shooting. The consciousness-altering substances had not shown up in the blood test taken upon her arrest because the police, the prosecutor, and her defense attorney had conspired to falsify the results. Wragg, Suchar, and the wounded children had actually been shot by the police, who had lied about the number of rounds they had fired. She believed that during the first two years of her incarceration she had been receiving mind-altering drugs, and did not realize until a few months before the parole hearing that she had signed an agreement acknowledging her guilt. Her parole was denied and she was criticized for refusing to accept responsibility for her action.

During her 2001 probation hearing, an aging, graying Brenda Spencer announced that she was an incest survivor, that she had shared her father's bed until she was 14. She described frequent beatings at his hand, and sexual abuse. Brett Granlund, the chairman of the parole board, was unconvinced, the revelation coming 22 years after the crime. In fact it is not unusual for an incest victim to go to great lengths to protect her family.

> The pressure for secrecy is an inevitable component of the incestuous relationship. . . . The intense dependency and insecurity operant in the incestuous family function to increase the child's investment in maintaining her family unit. The child may adopt a protective stance toward one or both parents, maintaining her silence in an attempt to shelter them . . .

> Victims [of incest] report a fear of abandonment, fear of not being believed, fear of punishment, and fear of being blamed for allowing the incestuous activity to occur and continue . . .

Delinquent "acting-out" behavior is also consistent with incest.

> While the child may not be able to take direct action in response to the incest, she may express her anxiety indirectly through [acting out behaviors]. The older child may act out by engaging in delinquent behavior or running away.

Brenda also stated during the hearing that she would have preferred a radio to the rifle and felt as though her father had given it to her so she would kill herself. She, obligingly, had shot at the school in the hope that the police would kill her. "I had failed in every other suicide attempt. I thought if I shot at the cops, they would shoot me." Other SR shooters have expressed similar sentiments.

Despite these revelations, parole was denied. At the time of writing, Brenda Spencer remains incarcerated at Frontera.

Cleveland Elementary School was closed down in 1984 because of declining enrollment. For a time it housed a private Lutheran school, and it is currently the home of the San Diego Hebrew Day School.

Wallace Spencer, now in his sixties, married a second time to a woman some 30 years younger than he who had shared a cell with Brenda at Juvenile Hall in 1979. The couple lives in the same yellow house and they now have a child. To bring the story full circle, the child attends daycare, and one of the teachers at the daycare center is Christy Buell, whom Brenda wounded in her attack.

CHAPTER 2

CASE 4: WAYNE LO

Identity Confusion / Cycle of Violence

WAYNE LO WAS A DUTIFUL CHILD, an A student, so proficient on the violin that he twice won the Montana Young Artists' Concerto competition. After school, he cleaned the house or worked at the restaurant started by his enterprising immigrant parents, and studied late into the night. People spoke of his respectfulness to others and his excellent manners. He might have been the protagonist of a modern-day Horatio Alger story, an exemplar of the Asian-American "model minority," had he not gone on to commit a mass murder.

Wayne was born in Tainan City, the fourth largest city in Taiwan. Although Tainan's population numbers less than a million, it has a rich cultural tradition, many ancient temples, buildings of striking classical architecture, and three universities. Wayne's father, Chia-Wei (or Jawei), also known as C.W., was a career officer in the Nationalist China Air Force. For many years he flew combat jets; however in 1981 he was assigned to the Taiwanese embassy in Washington and the experience disillusioned him about the politics of his homeland. Until 1949, all of China had been ruled by the Kuomintang, the Chinese Nationalist Party, a remnant of the authoritarian, cruel, and often corrupt dynastic system that had held China in its sway for 5,000 years. In December of 1949, the Communist Party gained control of the mainland, and Kuomintang was left with the isle of Taiwan and the surrounding smaller islands. In 1986, when C.W. and his wife, Lin-Lin, a piano teacher, immigrated to the U.S., the political and economic climate of Taiwan had begun to improve. Later, in the 1990s, it would undergo a peaceful transition to democracy and, in 1996, would elect its first president—but that was still far in the future. At the time of their immigration, C.W. and Lin-Lin felt as though life in the U.S. offered the best opportunities for their children's future.

C.W. resigned from the air force, signed over his pension to his mother, liquidated his assets, left his sons in the care of relatives, and relocated with his wife to the U.S. They settled temporarily in South Dakota, where a Taiwanese friend who owned a successful Chinese restaurant had agreed to teach them the business. When they felt competent, they moved on to Billings, Montana and started a Chinese restaurant of their own, The Great Wall. Wayne, 12, and his younger brother Ryan, 7, joined them, flying the long journey from Taipei to Montana by themselves.

Adapting to the new culture was a challenge. Even simple tasks such as mailing a letter were initially confusing for Lin-Lin. Wayne attended Lewis and Clarke Middle School and started Billings Central Catholic High School in the fall of 1989, where he was the only Asian among 340 students. While the Los were not Catholic themselves, their thinking ran thus: America is a Christian country, and nothing could be more Christian than Catholicism. Wayne maintained a 3.6 grade point average, and was liked and respected by students and faculty. While he had no history of misbehavior, he was sometimes stubborn and arrogant, disagreeing with teachers whom he took to be intellectual inferiors, and refusing to complete assignments which he considered pointless. Despite this, he maintained a peculiar affection for many of his Catholic school teachers, visiting them during vacation, and sending sentimental Christmas cards, even after he had transferred to a New England boarding school.

On weekdays Wayne took care of the house while his parents worked day and night at the restaurant. He would clean (he asked for, and received, a vacuum cleaner for his 14th birthday), make dinner for himself and his brother, put Ryan to bed, and then spend the rest of the evening doing homework and practicing the violin. On the weekends he bussed tables at the restaurant. April Coolidge, who managed The Great Wall, said that Wayne was "fun to be around, nice, polite. He never seemed depressed. He seemed to like his school, he really did... [the shooting] comes as a shock to us, if that helps explain his character at all." But Brian Skinner, the assistant manager, said that Wayne would often bristle at his father's strict instructions, and talked about how much he hated him. In fact C.W., for all his charm and intelligence, displayed the rigid and authoritarian parenting style one might associate with a military commander who had served under a totalitarian regime. A strict disciplinarian, he would beat Wayne with a riding crop when he disobeyed an order.

Authorities have long questioned whether there is a "cycle of violence," whether those who are abused as children become violent adults, and whether violent adults were abused as children. Jonathan Pincus, whose work is discussed in Chapter 1, has this to say:

> The frequent and prolonged history of physical and sexual abuse committed by a parent or parent substitute has been pervasive and extreme among the 150 or so murderers I have seen. It has been the life experience of 94 percent of all the murderers I examined in a consecutive five-year period and reported in 1995. Extreme abuse was also present in the histories of thirteen of the fourteen individuals Dr. Lewis and I examined who were on death row for homicides committed before they were eighteen years old and in fifteen condemned murderers we had examined just before scheduled executions.

Similarly, in Athens' 1992 qualitative study of 110 convicts who had committed extreme violence (which may or may not have involved murder), 100 percent had been victims of childhood abuse. Quantitative researchers using larger samples and statistical methods found that children who had suffered from parental abuse were more likely to become violent criminals than non-abused children, but in much smaller percentages than the qualitative studies. In C. S. Widom's study only 21.1 percent of the physically abused children went on to be arrested for a violent offense, as opposed to 13.9 percent of those who had not been abused. Two issues are worth noting: first, that none of these studies distinguished between predatory and affective violence; and second, none distinguished between the types of physical abuse that children received, its duration or intensity. I suspect that the psychological effects of a parent who delivers a beating because he is suffering from enormous stress and has lost his temper, and a parent who beats a child methodically and deliberately as a punishment or to satisfy sadistic impulses, are fundamentally different but no research, to my knowledge, has examined this distinction.

C.W.'s motives may have been altruistic. He may have believed that a beating was the only way to teach Wayne how to behave, or that a child should be treated like small a soldier to bring out the best in him. Perhaps he himself had been beaten as a child, and his father before him, and it seemed like the normal thing to do. Parenting practices tend to be inherited from one generation to the next. I suspect C.W. administered his punishments in a methodical way, dispassionately, as a ship's captain might sentence a sailor to a flogging, making sure that the number of lashes was commensurate to the crime. In my clinical practice I have heard parents argue that certain children require corporal punishment because they are "thick-skinned" or dull in some way, or because they live in violent communities where society functions according to different, more primitive rules. While I cannot definitively dismiss either of these contentions, my belief is that no person, child or adult, benefits from violent treatment.

As a child, C.W. had dreamed of becoming a concert violinist, but a broken finger, a baseball mishap, put an end to his plans. Determined that Wayne would succeed where he had failed, C.W. started him on the violin at the age of four. When Wayne begged to play baseball with the local American Legion team, his father forbade it, lest Wayne's career be cut short by a hand injury. A friend reported Wayne crying afterwards, when he spoke of his frustration.

When Wayne was 12 and 13, he was a regular member of the Billings Symphony Orchestra. Uri Barnea, its conductor, said that Wayne ". . . has a tremendous talent, no question about it. We were very sorry to see that he left because we lost a very valuable member of the symphony." He won the Montana Association of Symphony Orchestra's Young Artist Competition in 1990 and again in 1998. That summer—the summer after his freshman year of high school—he attended the Aspen Music Festival where he studied with the famed violin pedagogue, Dorothy Delay.

According to Gary Gaudreau, one of Wayne's teachers at Billings Central Catholic High School, he did very well during the first semester of his freshman year, but in the second semester there was a "buildup . . . of tremendous stress, tremendous anxiety." This is no surprise, considering that he was expected to be a housekeeper, a busboy, a concert violinist, and a straight-A student, all while navigating the social maze of hight school and the cataclysmic changes of puberty. Given that he was the only Chinese student in his school, he may have also encountered bullying and social isolation.

Additional stress came in the form of his parents' high expectations for him. "Our whole hope is our two boys," C.W. once told a reporter. Asian Americans of this era were considered "the model minority," a term defined by legal scholar Rhoda Yen as "a non-white group that has achieved economic success and social acceptance through hard work and conservative values." The Immigration Act of 1965 insured that the Asian immigrants accepted into the U.S. were drawn from the wealthiest and most educated pools in their native countries. The selectivity of this policy created a lasting impression among Americans that Asian immigrants were innately culturally or racially superior to other immigrant groups. President Reagan expressed the sentiments of most Americans when, addressing a group of Asian and Pacific-American leaders in the old executive office building in 1984, he said:

> Asian and Pacific Americans have helped preserve that dream by living up to the bedrock values that make us a good and a worthy people. I'm talking about principles that begin with the sacred worth of human life, religious faith, community spirit . . . tolerance, hard work, fiscal responsibility, cooperation, and love.
>
> It's no wonder that the median income of Asian and Pacific-American families is much higher than the total American average . . .

In 1985 the *New Republic* ran a story called, "The Triumph of Asian-Americans: America's Greatest Success Story." In 1987, the year C.W. and Lin-Lin arrived in Montana, *Fortune* magazine ran a headline describing Asian Americans as "America's Super Minority." Yen points out that the model minority stereotype stops Asian Americans from defining themselves as individuals, resulting in a variety of psychosocial concerns.

> [T]hreats to cultural identity, powerlessness, feelings of marginality, loneliness, hostility and perceived alienation and discrimination remain unredressed and hidden under the veneer of the model minority myth. Both social and psychological forces to conform to the model minority stereotype place an inordinate amount of pressure on Asian Americans.

Mr. Gaudreau, fearful that Wayne's anxiety would translate into a suicide attempt, discussed the student with Sister Barbara, the school counselor. While she acknowledged the problem, the culture of the school discouraged her from contacting Wayne's parents. His English teacher, Michelle Mattix, was also concerned about Wayne's emotional health. His schoolwork had become sloppy, and he seemed to take pleasure in his bad grades, boasting about them in class. Right before Easter vacation he told Mrs. Mattix that, since this would be his last class, she need not return his papers. He behaved oddly and displayed a "bizarre euphoria." But instead of a suicide attempt, he stole his mother's car, drove to Oregon, and spent five days with a girlfriend who lived there. There are many possible explanations for a behavioral change such as this. Some psychiatric disorders, such as bipolar disorder and schizophrenia, often begin during adolescence with a peculiar incident such as this, but the behavior also falls well within the limits of normal teenage acting-out. William Glaberson, a *New York Times* reporter who interviewed Wayne in prison in April of 2000, was struck by his controlling and manipulative character. As we shall see later, Wayne was capable of pretending to be crazy when he thought it would serve a purpose. It is not far fetched to believe that he dropped hints about his suicidal ideas to his teachers and staged his disappearance to frighten his parents into letting him transfer to a school in another part of the country where he would be out from under his father's thumb. He had used an insincere suicide threat during his summer at the Aspen Music Festival, to manipulate circumstances in his favor.

> I was really into this Mormon chick but she won't give me the time of day so being pathetic I said I would kill myself and she called the cops on me! So the Aspen police shows up and asks me if everything is ok. So that's that. Wayne Lo, 2007

Simon's Rock College must have seemed like a perfect destination to Wayne and for his parents to whom he had suddenly become a different person, uncontrollable and unpredictable. Simon's Rock was located far away in Massachusetts and was described as a haven for bright 10th and 11th graders who found high school tedious. Students could stay for two years and go on to a four-year college or remain for four years and graduate with an associate's degree. Simon's Rock was ranked by *U.S. News and World Report* as one of the two or three best schools of its kind, with a small enrollment (about 320 students at the time) and a rigorous but informal course of study. What no one had taken into account was cultural shock. Billings, Montana was a historically conservative state steeped in the tradition of guns and game hunting, while Great Barrington, Massachusetts, was a summer haven for liberal academics and intellectuals from the Boston area. In the Glaberson interview Wayne complains of feeling "Taiwanese in Montana, Montanan in Massachusetts." Simon's Rock was administered by Bard College, which was ranked by the *Princeton Review* in 2005 as the second most liberal college in the United States. Anne Coulter, a critic of liberalism sometimes given to hyperbole, described Bard as a "Safe Streets program for traitors and lunatics." While the Billings Central Catholic High School prohibited sexual behavior and drug use, a member of the Simon's Rock counseling staff said nonchalantly of the incoming students that ". . . when they come here there's a lot of acting out—sex, drugs. They're trying things on for size." The tuition was more than the Los could afford, the equivalent of an Ivy League college—$20,000 in 1992 when Wayne applied for admission,

$44,644 in 2008—but Wayne was awarded a scholarship reserved for minority students with exceptional academic ability. The director of admissions was impressed by the thoughtfulness of his application, in which he expressed his desire to explore areas outside music, in particular the social and natural sciences.

Wayne started at Simon's Rock when he was 16, in September of 1991. An excellent violin teacher in the Great Barrington area agreed to take him on as a student, but now that Wayne was out from under his father's shadow, he stopped practicing and frequently missed lessons. He told his new violin teacher that he wanted to be a lawyer and was no longer terribly interested in music.

During the summer between 10th and 11th grades—the summer before the shooting—he explored other interests, taking six-week courses in astronomy and international relations at Cornell University, and earning B's in both. Free to engage in sports, he joined the Simon's Rock basketball team, where despite his stature—he was five-foot-five—he was considered an asset. But his athleticism, which might been a social advantage at other schools, worked against him here, or so he believed, because of the school's offbeat culture.

> Simon's Rock is a high school for outcasts. Although they may not officially acknowledge it, everyone knows it. I attended SRC to get away from home, not H.S. I became an outcast at SRC because all the outcasts became the majority. So there weren't any jocks or preppies at SRC. I guess I was the jock, so it was a reverse Columbine. *From an interview on the Wayne Lo website "Zach"*

In the spring of 10th grade, Wayne asked a young man named Robert Schork, an upper-classman who was tutoring him in economics, if he could borrow his car and drive to Pittsfield to buy a gun. "No way in hell," Robert responded. When he came home on break, his former classmates from Central Catholic High noticed Wayne's heightened interest in guns and violence. He showed his best friend, Casey Stessman, a set of brass knuckles he had obtained in the Berkshires. He told Debra Junnila, another former friend and classmate, that he needed a pistol to protect himself and was dismayed to learn that a local firearms course was fully-enrolled.

After so many cultural dislocations, Wayne found little in common with the majority of the students, but there was a small clique of tough kids who shared his rage and accepted him. The group included Kevin Wolak, Jeremy Robinson, and Eddie Caruso, young men who occupied the bottom rung of the social ladder at Simon's Rock, relating to other students through intimidation, and defining themselves by becoming their ideological opposites. Erik Erikson called this poor solution to the crises of identity formation, a "negative identity." While other students embraced liberalism and diversity, Wayne and his clique practiced a conservatism of exclusion, listening to Rush Limbaugh together and peppering their talk with angry racist and sexist remarks. The fact that Wayne himself was a member of a racial minority did not interefere with this practice or seem inconsistent to him at the time, although he later remarked on it in his blog. This conservative posturing also gave Wayne an opportunity to master his own real or perceived marginalization by marginalizing others. This, a common psychological defense mechanism among the abused, is called "identification with the aggressor." Other students gave Wayne and his clique a wide berth. "It's not like we haven't been afraid of Wayne and his friends," said a senior named Ziadee Taekheir, 20, from Portland, Maine. "My friends and I had been talking daily about how scary he is."

Wayne, Kevin, Jeremy, and Eddie were described as "perennially angry." They would sit in their own corner of the dining room scowling at others and joking about killing people they didn't like. "Wayne often spoke about getting an automatic weapon," Kevin Wolak later told the public, "and going into the cafeteria and shooting people at random. He would target African Americans one time and then Jews or homosexuals another time. . . ." A favorite bit of banter was, *Stay away from the dining hall, I'm in a bad mood today*. After the shootings, Wayne's friends claimed this was all in jest and they had assumed that Wayne was joking too. The group grew smaller when Eddie Caruso was expelled for threatening a female student, an act which martyred him in the eyes of his friends. Like Eric Harris and Seung-Hui Cho, Wayne was involved in an incident of intimidating a girl, which he describes on his blog. Notice how he impugnes the girl's reputation by off-handedly mentioning her hanging out in the boy's dorm and contracting mono.

> I met this girl Alison and we hit it off, but then I guess she got tired of me, but I still pursued her. She then told my faculty adviser I was annoying her. When my adviser informed me of this, I got scared as well cause I didn't want to get in trouble so I totally backed off. Pretty much ran the opposite way when I saw her coming. But SRC is so damn small! Only one library and one dining hall, not to mention the fact she hung out in the boys' dorm a lot. So no way I could

actually avoid her. Anyway, she left like the second semester of freshman year because she contracted mono. Obviously not from me! Let your own imagination explain it. But then years later when she appeared on the A&E [Arts & Entertainment Channel] documentary "Rampage Shooters," she claimed she left SRC because of me!   Wayne Lo, 2007

During his second year at Simon's Rock, Wayne continued along the same course. In the fall, he and an unidentified friend visited Bob's Corner Store in Lee, Massachusetts, about 12 miles from the school, and asked if they sold assault weapons, or if they could steer them to someone who did. That night the shop owner told his wife about the incident, observing that the boy appeared to be crazy and dangerous, and that something bad was going to happen. On two occasions before Thanksgiving, Wayne asked a basketball teammate, a boy from Brooklyn, if he could get him a gun, not because he was a particularly close friend or a reputed weapons dealer, but because he was from Brooklyn, where, Wayne had heard, guns were plentiful and inexpensive. When asked to write a paper for his Sophomore Seminar class suggesting a model for social change, Wayne proposed that people with AIDS be quarantined in Canada, or perhaps killed. While the professor found the moral and ethical content "distressing," he gave the paper a B because the argument was well-structured.

Wayne had been focused, since the age of four, on developing his father-pleasing, inauthentic Self, the "trophy on the mantle." What remained of his Self, once he had distanced himself from his father and abandoned his career as a violinist, was fragmented and ill-equipped for dealing with adolescent society. The students at Simon's Rock disliked and feared him. Girls felt stalked and harassed by him. The more he explored alternative careers, the more obvious it became that the law, the natural sciences, and the social sciences would never offer the narcissistic thrills he had experienced playing violin concertos: the rapt audiences, adoring gazes, and thunderous applause. Yet the career of the concert violinist was his father's dream, not Wayne's.

The week before Thanksgiving vacation, Wayne came down with chicken pox. The airlines refused to let him fly and he was forced to remain at Simon's Rock during the break. The few students who remained on campus were obliged to stay in one dorm area so that the residence directors could keep track of them. Wayne acquiesced but then moved back to his room in Kendrick House prematurely, without anyone's knowledge or permission. Wayne's bigotry had led to an antagonistic relationship with the Kendrick House residence director, Floyd Robinson. Floyd, an African American, was married to Trinka, a white woman, who was also a residence director. They lived together in Kendrick House with their two young children. When Floyd discovered that Wayne had moved back to Kendrick against regulations, he punished him, and Wayne was outraged. He told Floyd, "If I'd known you were going to throw the whole book at me, I would have gotten my money's worth. I have the power to bring the whole school down to its knees." In the weeks before the shootings, Floyd and his wife had received an anonymous death threat. Although other students had no proof, they assumed that Wayne was the author, such was his reputation at the time.

Wayne's mother, his brother Ryan, and a family friend came to Simon's Rock for a visit in the beginning of December, ten days before the shooting. They found their son in an optimistic mood, studying for exams, and writing transfer applications for four-year colleges. He showed them his dorm room and talked about coming home during spring break. The following week Wayne phoned Sherry Keziah, the co-owner of Classic Arms, a mail-order gun dealer in North Carolina, and ordered from their catalogue using his mother's credit card. He bought several 30-bullet clips, a folding plastic stock, and 200 rounds of copper-jacketed, steel-core bullets packed in a sealed metal tin. He paid extra to ensure a Saturday delivery, but a weekend snowstorm was so severe that delivery was postponed until Monday.

On Sunday evening, December 13, Jeremy Robinson ran into Wayne in the library. Wayne told him he was planning to bring a gun on campus and shoot people. Later that evening, Jeremy called Wayne in his room. During the course of the conversation, he asked if he was studying for finals. Wayne replied that he was copying the Book of Revelations into his notebook so that people would think he was crazy. Jeremy thought Wayne was kidding.

Wayne's package arrived a little before 10 AM on Monday, December 14. The college receptionist, noticing the "Classic Arms" label, called the Office for Student Life, who in turn contacted the Robinsons. Floyd and Trinka brought the package to their regularly scheduled 10 AM meeting with Bernard Rodgers, the college dean, to discuss how they should proceed. If the package contained a weapon, that would constitute a violation of school policy, but opening the package without Wayne's permission would be a federal offense. Furthermore, they would be violating a student's privacy, an important issue at a college that made a point of valuing human rights. They decided to return the package to the mail room unopened.

There are different accounts of what occurred next. According to a ten-page press release prepared by Simon's Rock and circulated on December 25, 1992, attendees of the meeting agreed that when Wayne picked up the package, Trinka would follow him back to his room and question him about it. Wayne had previously scheduled a meeting with the dean for 11:30 to discuss his transfer, a regular practice for college-bound students. The dean would have an opportunity to question him at that time. According to Trinka Robinson's deposition, however, she left the meeting thinking that the dean would arrange for the package to be opened in his presence, perhaps by keeping it with him until his meeting with Wayne. Trinka was surprised when, a little later that morning, a staff member told her that Wayne had picked up the package and was on his way back to the dorm. She called the dean, who told her to examine the contents of the package but forbade her to search Wayne's room. She hurried to his room and knocked. He took a long time to respond. Here again the accounts differ. According to Trinka, when Wayne finally opened the door, the contents of the package were spread out on the bed—everything except the ammunition.

According to the Simon's Rock statement, the unopened package was in plain sight. She asked Wayne to open the package in her presence and he argued that according to the student handbook, two college officials had to be present during a room search. Stymied, Trinka left Wayne alone in the room and phoned the dean. When she returned, the package was open and the contents spread across the bed, all but the ammunition. Trinka asked about the individual items and Wayne replied that he would be taking them home to Billings over spring break to modify the semi-automatic rifle he kept there, all except the ammunition box, which was a present for his father's birthday. Ammunition boxes are heavy duty, waterproof, and fireproof containers about the size of a car battery, with a carrying handle and a clasp which you can operate with one hand, making them excellent storage containers. She did not search his room, nor ask to see the packing slip, which was understandable considering how upset she must have been. When Trinka returned to her apartment and called the dean, he asked that Wayne be sent to his office immediately.

Wayne met with the dean from 12:00 to 12:30 (he had failed to show for his 11:30 appointment) and repeated his story about the ammo box for his father, the gun parts for a spring vacation project. He was respectful and pleasant; not at all agitated or angry.

Earlier that morning Wayne had called Dave's Sporting Goods in Pittsfield twice, asking how he would go about buying a gun, being from out of state. Before a Massachusetts resident can buy a gun, he must obtain a Firearms Identification Card (FID), a month-long process involving a screening for felony convictions, mental illness, drug addiction, or other disqualifying circumstances. The time provides a "cooling off period" for those who might be acting on a violent impulse. Workers at Dave's Sporting Goods, consulting the gun laws, learned that because Wayne was 18 and a resident of Montana—a fact established by his driver's license—he could follow the gun laws of that state, which had no regulations whatsoever regarding the purchase, possession, or use of firearms. This queer loophole in the Massachusetts' gun laws, which makes a weapon purchase easier for a transient than a member of the community, was passed in 1991 as an accommodation for Kevin McHale, a player for the Boston Celtics. One day McHale felt a need to go bird hunting and couldn't understand why he had to wait a month to buy a firearm. Where he came from—Minnesota—a man could walk into a gun store, lay down his money, and walk out with a shotgun. Like a court toadying to a king, the Massachusetts legislature retooled the law for McHale's pleasure—and to the detriment of the Simon's Rock community.

Following his meeting with the dean, Wayne took a cab to Dave's Sporting Goods and purchased a semiautomatic SKS, a cheap Chinese-made copy of the Soviet AK47 assault weapon, for $129. Before the sale was completed, Dave himself, the store's owner, took a few minutes to chat with Wayne to ascertain that he was truly from Montana. The test included pronouncing the name of the state capitol. Wayne snuck the weapon onto campus in a guitar case.

Because the purchasing of the gun took longer than anticipated, he arrived 45 minutes late for the Sophomore Seminar final. He dashed off two essays, one on the meaning of "power" and the other of "civilization," and was done after only an hour. It was 3:00 PM. At the end of his exam book he wrote, "Anyone adding to this book, God will add to him the plagues mentioned here. Anyone taking away from this book, God will take away his tree of life. Amen. God be with you." His use of the cadence and the oblique style of the Book of Revelations suggest a further attempt to convey insanity.

Hurrying back to his dorm room, he replaced the SKS's wooden stock with the folding plastic one. When Wayne ran into Kevin later that day, he told him excitedly that he had gotten the "gun stuff" and that it was for his father. "That stuff is for my dad's gun at home . . ." he said, equivocating, "but maybe it's not." Rumors that Kevin had helped Wayne order and modify his weapon were never substantiated.

Before dinner Wayne visited the weight room to "pump up."

When his friends dropped by his dorm room to pick him up for dinner, they saw the empty ammunition box lying on his bed. At the dining hall that evening, Wayne repeated his statement about getting a gun and bringing it on campus to shoot people. One member of the clique responded that if this were so, it would be Wayne's "Last Supper," and in commemoration of that idea, Wayne performed a mock communion, drinking cranberry juice as though it were wine and receiving white bread as though it were wafer. Later, when the others had left, Jeremy asked Wayne why he would ever consider killing people. According to Jeremy, "He changed his mood. He got very serious. I had never seen him that serious. He said, 'Because I don't care anymore. I don't want to live.'" This sincere admission of suicidal ideation sheds some doubt on Wayne's disavowal of previous incidents. Just as pretending to be crazy would not necessarily be evidence of sanity, pretending to be suicidal would not preclude the possibility of being suicidal. Jeremy, who knew Wayne very well, took his suicidal and homicidal threats seriously and notified the residence directors.

In an alternate account, it was another friend, someone on the periphery of the click named Jeremy Robinson, in whom Wayne confided. Jeremy also sensed that Wayne was no longer joking, that he might have a gun and be serious about using it. After dinner, Jeremy made several attempts to reach campus security, but his calls were intercepted by an answering machine. Then he tried calling the Robinsons. Trinika was alone in the apartment with the children, and Floyd was elsewhere in the building, conducting a dorm meeting at which Wayne was an attendee. When she picked up the receiver, Jeremy refused to give his name but warned that Wayne was planning to kill her and her family. He was under the impression that it might happen the following night.

Trinka called the dean, and then the provost, who immediately drove over to the dorm and waited with them for her husband's return. When Floyd came back from the meeting, about half an hour later, he was astonished to hear about the threat. Of course he and Wayne had argued during the meeting—that was business as usual—but nothing had suggested that the boy was contemplating anything as drastic as homicide.

Wayne returned to his room following the meeting and called Jeremy to say goodbye.

Floyd, Trinka, and her children were taken to the provost's home to assure their safety, arriving around 10:00 PM. After some discussion, they decided that the provost and another residence director would return to the dorm, find Wayne and search his room for a weapon. If they met any resistance, they would call the police. The provost called the dean to tell him of their plans. While they were talking on the phone, they heard gunshots.

It was 10:15. Teresa Beavers was on duty at the guard shack at the entrance to the college. Embankments of snow rose several feet on either side of the road, the result of the weekend storm and multiple plowings. The night was frosty and clear, the stars glittering like icicles. Teresa was on the phone, making Christmas plans with her husband, Bruce. He was on disability leave from his job because of a back injury, and Theresa had gone back to work after 15 years of homemaking to support him as well as her four teenage daughters, who were still living at home. She had been delighted to find this job as a campus guard near home, 40 hours a week, four nights and one day shift.

Now Teresa saw a figure walking toward her, a small, wiry boy, wearing a jacket and a black knit cap with the words "over the edge" embroidered along the front. He wore a backpack and carried an assault rifle. At certain times during the evening he also wore a black knit hat with the words "Over the edge" embroidered along the front.

"Hang on," she told Bruce, calmly, "there's a kid out here with a gun." She put the phone down on the counter. He heard her say, "Oh my God, no!" then gunshots and her screaming. Bruce hung up, called the police, and drove as fast as he could to the college.

Later Teresa described it from her point of view:

> I opened the door to talk to him and he stuck the barrel of the gun through the door. . . . I tried to push the door shut. He shot twice. I finally got the door closed . . . he pushed the gun barrel through one of the windows and shot two more times . . .

Her initial tones had reflected Wayne's calm and composed presentation. It was difficult to imagine that he was about to commit an act of violence. Wayne describes his own state of mind during an interview some years later:

> I was calm when I went on the shooting. I thought I was on a mission from God. I know, it sounds ridiculous now, but I actually believed it then. I wasn't nervous or disorganized. I was calm but with a lot of anger. I just shot at anything that moved in front of me. The plan was to attack Simon's Rock College so I guess I succeeded. I didn't really have a step-by-step plan as to who or where I was going to shoot at.

Nacunan Saez, who taught language and literature, was returning to the college to pick up a stack of papers that he had neglected to grade. He steered his car, a little blue Ford Festiva, up the serpentine drive, then slowed by the guard shack, perhaps puzzled by the sight of Wayne standing by the shack with his rifle. As he passed, Wayne fired two shots; the first cracked the driver's side window, entered Saez's left temple and exited the right side of his jaw; the second penetrated the door just below the side view mirror, tore a piece off the steering column, passed through his thigh and out the passenger-side door. The Ford continued to roll, coming to a stop in a snow bank, the driver's side door hanging open at an odd angle. Saez slumped across the seat, a tinny patter of voices drifting from the dashboard radio. Saez was a charismatic teacher, and frequently the object of student infatuations. An accomplished linguist with a doctorate from the University of Connecticut, he was fluent in French, Italian, Spanish, and English. He had been planning to return to his homeland, Argentina, for Christmas, to celebrate his 38th birthday with his mother, who had been recently widowed. Wayne had never been in any of his Dr. Saez's classes and hardly knew him.

Tom McElderry, 19, a recent transfer from Kotzebue, Alaska, and two other students were driving onto campus when they saw the nose of Saez's car stuck in the snowbank, the open door, the motionless body. On their way to the library to get help, they stopped to gawk at Wayne who was standing in the shelter of the pines, struggling to eject a shell.

"Get the fuck out of here!" Wayne shouted at them.

The trail of unfired shells that marked Wayne's passage through campus was evidence of the gun jamming repeatedly, forcing him to insert and eject cartridges by hand. Later, Sergeant Phillip Langton, a ballistics expert with the state police, traced the problem to the poor fit of the magazine. A newly purchased gun often comes coated in grease to protect it from moisture and grit, and Wayne, out of ignorance or a lack of time, had neglected to remove the coating, which contributed to the problem. If not for this, the list of dead and wounded would have been longer.

Galen Gibson would have been at the college theater, doing tech for the Christmas concert, had the event not been ended early due to a snow storm warning. He had gone to the library with his friend, Rob Horowitz, to cram for finals. The young men paid little attention to the muffled explosions as they were accustomed to the sounds of hunters, fireworks, and backfiring cars. Then the doors flew open and Tom McElderry rushed in, explaining that there had been an accident. The student at the circulation desk called for help on the library phone.

Galen was crossing the atrium, putting on his coat, on his way to help Dr. Saez if helping him was possible, when Wayne shot him through the glass door twice, once in the chest and once in the side. The first shot was fatal, shattering his sternum, severing blood vessels in the chest cavity, tearing through lung and trachea, cracking a rib, and exiting from his back. Galen hobbled back to the table where he had been studying, holding both hands over his chest.

"I've been shot," he said. "Get help."

Rob thought he might have been kidding, but when Galen took his hands away, they were covered with blood. A bloody cavity had been punched in his chest. Seconds later . . .

> . . . the room exploded with gunfire. Everyone . . . went down. Glass was flying, the gun banging, bullets zinging around. Tom McElderry was shot in the leg. Rose was on the floor with the phone, still trying to call for help. Kids were screaming. Rob ran out the back door and through the woods to get help at the guard shack.

Wayne left the library and walked through the frigid night toward the dorms, Kendrick House, Dolliver House, and Crosby House. When a student emerged from of the entrances, Wayne fired a volley of shots, not to kill him but to scare him back inside, or so he later told the jury.

Mathew David, 18, a sophomore from Montclair, New Jersey, a slight young man with glasses and a beard, and his roommate, Josh Faber, 15, a freshman from Pittsfield, New York, were watching *Monday Night Football* in the basement of Dolliver House. During halftime—a little after 10:00 PM—they headed for their room, stopping to talk to friends in the first floor entranceway. The sound of shattering glass from the library drew their attention. The moved to the door for a better look and within seconds they had both been shot through the glass panels. Mathew described it:

> . . . [I] felt a pressure in my side. I curled up and rolled into a nearby hallway. I lay there and I wasn't sure what had happened . . . [Friends] were telling me I was shot. I took a look and said 'It looks like it just grazed me,' but I was told, 'Nope there's a hole in the other side.'

Joshua was similarly confused by what had happened:

> I heard an explosion and noticed that I was suddenly sitting on the ground. I first thought a firecracker had gone off. I looked down at

my legs and noticed that I was bleeding from two holes in each of my thighs . . . I could tell my heart [was] beat[ing] because with each heart beat, more blood came out.

His left leg hanging limp from his hip, he hopped up the stairs on the right, steadying himself with a hand on the banister. On the second floor a girl was screaming. A friend helped him to the door of the residence director, where he asked, with the politeness that comes of habit, if he could come in for a moment. He was made comfortable on the floor, a tourniquet tied around one leg, pressure placed on the other to reduce blood loss. Josh recalled thinking that if he passed out he would die, and sang to himself to stay awake. Forty minutes passed before the EMTs arrived. An ambulance took the boys to Fairview Hospital where Joshua was rushed into emergency surgery. Mathew was released after his wounds had been cleaned and dressed.

At 10:23, two officers were driving north on Main Street, six and a half hours into an unremarkable shift. Through the crackle of the police radio came the kind of message they dreaded: "People down at Simon's Rock guard booth." They made a U-turn, started the sirens, and raced to the college, the tires sliding on the icy road. The first thing they saw as they came through the gate was Saez's car in the snow bank. One officer left the patrol car and proceeded on foot. Reaching the Ford, he bent over the body, searching for a pulse. Meanwhile the second officer approached the guard shack. Teresa Beavers was propped against the wall, crying hysterically. Her liver and intestines had been torn by the bullet and her pelvis shattered. In her distress, she mistook the officer for the killer and began screaming, "Please stop, please don't shoot me again, please, please. . . ." More shots echoed from the direction of the library. After radioing for backup and an ambulance, he asked Teresa if she could identify her assailant.

"One of the students," she said. "Wayne Lo."

A student named Simon Bromberg was returning from singing in the chorus at the abbreviated Christmas concert when he heard gunshots. He entered the now deserted student union and, through a plate glass window in the large room known as the "dance hall," saw Wayne coming from the dorms. Wayne entered the building and said to Simon, "Don't move or I'll fucking kill you." He sat down on a couch, took off his backpack, and removed the ammunition clips from the gun.

"What are you doing?" Simon asked.

"I'm killing people. I'm fucking shooting people."

Wayne told Simon to call the police. Under the pressure of the moment, Simon couldn't recall how to place an off-campus call. Embarrassed, he said the phone was broken. Could he leave?

Wayne agreed.

Simon got as far as the door before remembering that he had left his jacket and choral music on the couch. He went back for them and left the building unharmed.

Wayne called the police himself, but had difficulty getting through because so many students were calling 911. Eventually reaching the officer at the dispatch desk, he turned himself in. "I'm the person who shot the people at Simon's Rock . . ." he said, and added, "the people at Simon's Rock needed to be taught a lesson." It was 10:33 PM, 18 minutes after the first shot had been fired. No record exists of Wayne's call because the two tape recorders were occupied by the stream of incoming 911 calls on the other two lines.

The dispatcher kept Wayne on the phone while two more patrol cars headed for the college. They cruised silently along the campus drive with their headlights off. They could see Wayne's face through the window of the Student Union, illuminated by the shifting light of the TV. He was watching *Monday Night Football* while talking on the phone, describing his killings to the dispatcher. He admitted that he was worried about getting hurt if he didn't get killed. He didn't want to be maimed or paralyzed by a sharp-shooter's bullet.

The patrol cars parked and the officers surrounded the building, taking care to tread lightly across the skin of ice. When they were in place, they called the dispatcher and told him to order Wayne to put down his weapon, come out with his hands up, and lie on the ground. Wayne obeyed. They pulled off his knit cap "to see what he looked like" and saw that his head was shaved like a Buddhist monk. Under his jacket he wore a black t-shirt that said in red letters, "sick of it all," the name of a hardcore punk band and probably and accurate description of Wayne's mood. They read him his rights, pulled him to his feet and cuffed him.

"Wayne, are you on any kind of drug?"

"No sir."

"Is there anyone else with you?"

"No sir."

"Do you have any more weapons on you?"

"Yes sir, a can of mace in my back pocket."

They confiscated the mace.

The officers were surprised by Wayne's calm manner and polite attitude.

He wasn't sweating, shaking, or hyperventilating. He took them inside and showed them the assault rifle, which he regarded with disdain. He had only fired 13 of the 200 rounds. "I think one of the reasons he stopped shooting was because he got disgusted with the gun," an officer suggested several days later. When they arrived at the stationhouse, Wayne asked an officer, "What did I do tonight?" He appeared puzzled about his own actions.

An officer went to Wayne's dorm room in search of accomplices, wounded students, or more weapons. Legally this kind of exploration is allowed in the aftermath of a crime, although they had not yet obtained a search warrant. He found papers on the desk covered with doodles, including a picture of a little man aiming an assault rifle at a tower, and the word "redrum" written over and over again. This nonsense word appears in the Stephen King novel, *The Shining* as well as the film adaptation, the story of an alcoholic writer who, with his wife and seven-year-old son, travels to the mountain fastness of Colorado as winter caretaker of a resort while completing his novel. The evil spirits of the hotel urge him to murder his family. The son sees the word "REdrUM" on the bathroom door, written in red letters. Later he views it reversed in the mirror of the vanity cabinet: "MUrdER," an omen of the violence to come. The officer also found a handwritten copy of biblical scriptures, and a notebook of miscellaneous writings. Because a search warrant was not obtained until the following day, when a second search was conducted, none of this first group of items could be entered into evidence.

During a "legal" search the following day, a private investigator found transfer applications to Harvard, Yale, and other first rank colleges; two boxes of traditional Christmas cards, sealed, stamped and addressed to old teachers, friends, and family members back in Billings; and a well-worn bible with many annotations in Wayne's hand. Revelations 20, the chapter which speaks of divine retribution and "the mark of the beast," a popular signifier of evil, was paper-clipped for easy reference.

> . . . And *I saw* the souls of them that were beheaded for the witness of Jesus, and for the word of God, and which had not worshipped the beast, neither his image, neither had received *his* mark upon their foreheads, or in their hands; and they lived and reigned with Christ a thousand years.
>
> But the rest of the dead lived not again until the thousand years were finished. This is the first resurrection.
>
> Revelations 20:4 - 20:5, King James ver.

A sheet of paper was inserted at Mark 15, also a well-known passage describing how Jesus gathered his apostles.

And saying, The time is fulfilled and the kingdom of God is at hand: repent ye and believe the gospel.

Now as he walked by the Sea of Galilee, he saw Simon and Andrew his brother casting a net into the sea, for they were fishers.

And Jesus said unto them, Come ye after me, and I will make you to become fishers of men . . .

Mark 15:1 - 15:17, King James ver.

Wayne had drawn Jesus on the cross on the contents page, and on another page, Satan with an angel on a cloud over his head. Later, when he was awaiting trial, Wayne's artwork was sought after by other prisoners, because of his celebrity status, but also because he was a talented artist.

Throughout the night students wept and comforted one another. The sounds of their wailing and keening could be heard across the still, ice-glazed campus.

At Fairview Hospital, surgeons spent the night operating on Teresa Beavers, reconstructing her hip, removing a quarter of her liver. By the end of the week her condition had been upgraded to "serious but stable." She remained in the hospital for a month, then spent six months at home with professional nursing care, then returned for further surgery.

The morning after the shooting, the Berkshire Mental Health Agency and Austen Riggs psychiatric hospital dispatched a crisis intervention team of 15 psychiatrists, psychologists, and social workers to the college. Because members of both institutions regularly provided counseling to Simon's Rock's more troubled students, they understood the culture of the school and could engage easily with those who needed help. Nearly 200 of the school's 318 students and 35 faculty members received counseling within the first 48 hours. Many of the students expressed anger at Wayne; at the electronic news media, for sweeping down on their school like jackals; and at the Simon's Rock administration, which, it was generally believed, could have stopped the shooting had it been more proactive in examining the Classic Arms package. Members of Wayne's clique also visited counselors, expressing concern that the community would alienate and persecute them for Wayne's crime.

The day after the shooting some 350 students, faculty, administrators, friends, and relatives of the deceased gathered in the dining hall for a private memorial service. Students had covered the walls with posters and pictures created in tribute to the deceased. Mourners read poems by Galen Gibson and shared memories of Galen and Nacunan Saez. The memorializing continued for so long that it had to be interrupted so that the students could go to dinner. A more traditional memorial service was held at St.

James Church on Main Street, on Thursday morning, December 17.

Despite occasional friction between the town and the school, Great Barrington rallied in support of the grieving students: a local bakery donated baked goods, the town's three florists sent floral arrangements, and local inns and bed-and-breakfasts offered rooms free of charge to parents and other visitors.

Simon's Rock cancelled final exams and students were dismissed early for Christmas break. Because they would be dispersing to homes all around the country, the college set up an 800 number that they could call for information and support during the break. About a third of the school's students remained on campus, most to be near one another and mourn together.

Although Rob Horowitz, Galen Gibson's best friend, was supposed to graduate in the spring, he stayed on at Simon's Rock an extra semester to care for Danica, Galen's distraught girlfriend. He rented an apartment off campus and she stayed there with him. Often they woke during the night and spent hours talking before they could fall back to sleep. According to Galen's friends, their relationship never became romantic or sexual; it was nothing more or less than a grieving project of unusual but effective design.

Wayne was arraigned in Southern Berkshire District Court on 17 counts, including two counts of murder, four counts of assault with intent to commit murder, and four counts of assault and battery by means of a dangerous weapon. It was the first murder in the county in eight years. Police held morning and afternoon information sessions to keep students and faculty abreast of the news.

When the school called Wayne's parents to tell them of their son's crime, Lin-Lin didn't understand what she was being told, and then thought that Wayne had been one of the victims. When she finally realized what had happened, she immersed herself in cleaning the house. C.W. and Lin-Lin waited until the next morning, at breakfast, to tell Ryan. Then both parents wept and Ryan ran up to his room.

Two days after the shootings, on Wednesday, December 16, Wayne's father flew to Boston and took a car to the jail in Pittsfield where his son was being held. Wayne told him that he had been told by God to study the Book of Revelations and to cleanse Simon's Rock of sinners, the sins in question being homosexuality, drug use, and lying. Using the gun had been his own decision. He had shot at anything that moved. Had C.W. been there, he would have shot at him too.

"I couldn't believe it," his father later told the court. "It was a shock to me . . . I looked at him. He was different. It seemed to me to be a different soul inside. It was not Wayne."

When Lin-Lin visited him in the jail the following week, she concurred. "The Wayne I saw there was not the son I have. I look at him and he looks empty." She asked him, in Mandarin, "How do you feel now?" He replied, also in Mandarin, "My mind is peaceful."

To protect their modest estate from litigation, Wayne's parents had him declared indigent and an attorney was appointed by the court to represent him. Unlike many other states, where public defenders may be the least competent or qualified attorneys, Massachusetts maintains a Committee for Public Counsel Services that keeps lists of attorneys experienced in different types of crimes; they agree to serve as defenders for a low wage in order to fulfill their professional pro-bono obligations.

Wayne's court appointed public defender was Janet Kenton-Walker, a past president of the Hampshire County Bar Association and vice president of the Massachusetts Bar. Stuart "Buzz" Eisenberg, a practitioner and law professor, second-seated her. Money to pay for expert witnesses, psychiatric assessments, and the like, had to be granted by the court, but this proved no impediment to the attorneys presenting the strongest possible case for Wayne.

The trial began on January 11, 1994 with Wayne's lawyers entering a plea of not guilty because of insanity. Just ten years earlier, the lawyers representing John Hinckley, Jr., who had tried to assassinate President Reagan, had successfully used the insanity defense to keep their client out of prison. As a result of the public outrage, several states, including Wayne's home state of Montana, disallowed the insanity defense altogether. Congress toughened the law, specifying that it would apply only to a defendant who, "as a result of a severe mental disease or defect, was unable to appreciate the nature and quality or the wrongfulness of his acts. Mental disease or defect does not otherwise constitute a defense." In fact it was probably not necessary as the insanity defense is used in less than two percent of all felony cases, and fails in 75 percent of those cases. While narcissistic personality disorder is arguably a mental illness—it is listed in the DSM IV-TR—it is not the kind of disorder that interferes with one appreciating the wrongfulness of his acts. A person with NPD might say to himself, *I know it's wrong to kill people but I'm going to do it anyway. I am so smart that I can get away with anything. I'll pretend to be crazy and they'll forgive me and let me go on to college.* A person who has had a psychotic break, on the other hand, as often happens during schizophrenia or severe mood disorders, might sincerely believe that he hears God's voice telling him to kill and that God's word takes precedence over Man's law. Both people are very dangerous, but only the latter fits the legal criteria for an insanity defense. Because of public opinion—the injustice of the Hinckley case was still hanging in the air like an offensive odor—and the nature of Wayne's mental illness, the insanity defense may not have been an appealing alternative; but it was the only alternative. Wayne had admitted his guilt and left irrefutable evidence of his intent. Furthermore, there were many witnesses.

The defense argued their case first. David Smith, a psychologist from the Berkshire County House of Correction, had interviewed Wayne the day after the shooting to determine if he was a danger to himself or the other prisoners. He described Wayne's peaceful state of mind following the killings. When Smith asked Wayne about it, the young man replied that he had done what he had been meant to do; he had carried out God's commands.

David Andregg, another psychologist for the defense, gave Wayne a battery of psychiatric tests after the shooting and again in April, and concluded that he was schizophrenic. Responses to a Rohrshach test were "characterized by a lot of aggression . . . and grandiosity of a religious type."

Erik Plakun, a psychiatrist and director of admissions at the prestigious New England psychiatric hospital, Austen Riggs, assessed Wayne in four two-hour sessions, twice in December of 1992 and once in January and March of 1993. He testified that Wayne was suffering from a "psychotic disorder with command hallucinations and paranoid delusions of grandiosity" and "paranoid schizophrenia" that "interfered with his ability to appreciate the criminality of his acts." Using punishment to bring about purification was a tenet of Wayne's upbringing, Plakun told the court, referring to C.W.'s method of punishing his son. Wayne ". . . felt he was a fundamentally bad person who would be made good by the beatings. He felt that after the beatings, he was a good person until he became bad again."

The next expert for the defense, Dr. Albert Gaw, a psychiatrist fluent in Mandarin who served as an advisor on cross-cultural issues for the DSM III-R, diagnosed Wayne as having a delusional disorder. A delusion is a "fixed, false belief that is resistant to reason or confrontation with fact" and *delusional disorder* is the diagnostic term for a person whose life has been impaired by a delusion. Delusions, along with hallucinations, and other impairments of the sensorium may be features of psychotic disorders such as schizophrenia and severe mood disorders.

Because he was fluent in Mandarin, Dr. Gaw could interview Wayne in both languages, and perhaps perceive finer nuances of expression than his colleagues who did not speak Chinese. Wayne's command hallucinations, he learned, were received somatically, as though they were electrical currents running through his body. Dr. Gaw suggested that Wayne had told no one about his delusions because the Chinese culture, in which he had been raised, values the privacy of feelings, and because God had instructed him to protect the secrecy of his mission. Dr. Gaw told the court that Wayne was "misjudging reality at this point, engaging in illogical thinking that only makes sense to him. For example, Revelations was written to the churches in Asia. Wayne said, 'I am Asian, therefore Revelations is being written to me.'" He told the court that Wayne interpreted the failure of the school to intercept the Classic Arms package, and to successfully search his room, as further evidence of God's sanction. Regarding another witness's statement that Wayne had been boasting about his shooting to other prisoners, Dr. Gaw suggested that such posturing was a normative part of prison life, and revealed little about Wayne's mental state. As for Wayne's statement that he had copied out Revelations in order to appear crazy, Dr. Gaw admitted that it was "a very significant statement and that it bothered me... I felt it was inconsistent." However, he expressed no doubt that Wayne's psychotic (or delusional) behavior was in earnest.

The fifth expert witness for the defense, Dr. Ronald Schouten, a psychiatrist at Massachusetts General Hospital, testified that Wayne was suffering from a "psychotic disorder not otherwise specified," meaning that it involved psychoses but did not fit neatly into any of the DSM III-R's diagnostic categories. Schouten said that Wayne viewed his 13-month incarceration as an extended winter vacation and believed that he would return to school at the end of the trial. He likened himself to the biblical Abraham, whom God had told to sacrifice his only son, and wondered if God might intervene at the final instant, as He had with the sacrificial slaughter of Isaac. He told Schouten that as he walked around the campus, shooting people, he felt nothing.

Prior to the time of the shootings, Wayne had been an "outspoken atheist," a fact confirmed by one of Wayne's high school religion teachers, who was called as a witness. How could he have been an atheist and received messages from God?

Wayne's father testified about a conversation with his son that had taken place during a prison visit:

> No one believed in UFOs, Wayne said, but if you had been abducted by one, you couldn't help but believe in them after that. The experience of being commanded by God was the same. He had never even believed in God, but when God had come to him he had been powerless to resist, powerless to conceive any other reality than that which had issued the command.

The two psychiatrists for the prosecution, Wesley Profit and Michael Annunziato, testified that Wayne was suffering from a narcissistic personality disorder rather than a psychotic or delusional disorder, which gave him an inflated sense of his own importance. His planning and evasive activities demonstrated that he was in control of himself, and that his ability to perceive right from wrong was unimpaired. Dr. Profit was particularly struck by Wayne's need to take control of the conversation during their 20 hours of pretrial interviews, a behavior also noted by Glaberson in an interview conducted eight years later.

The jury began deliberations on Tuesday, February 1. They returned to open court the following afternoon to ask the judge to repeat his definition of legal insanity. On Thursday, they filed into the courtroom and delivered their verdict: Wayne was guilty on all 17 counts. He was given a mandatory sentence of life imprisonment without the possibility of parole.

During the trial, C.W. had apologized personally to the families of each of the boys killed or maimed by his son. Evelyn David, Mathew David's mother, probably echoed the pity felt by many of those in the courtroom when she said, "I feel badly for the Los. It's a dreadful experience. They lost their son. I still have my son."

After the trial, Wayne told friends that he was angry at his attorneys. He believed that he was perfectly sane, a contention he has repeated frequently in interviews and his own writings, and rather than wasting their time trying to prove otherwise, they should have investigated the victims. He was sure that had they learned more about the victims, they would have understood why God had chosen them to die, and Wayne would have been exonerated.

Wayne spent nine months at MCI (Massachusetts Correctional Institution) Cedar Junction prison in Walpole, Massachusetts, a maximum security prison as is standard procedure for anyone convicted of murdere in that state. His parents reported that when they came to visit, he seemed "vacant," saying little and rocking back and forth, mute, when the conversation turned to the subject of his shooting. After nine months, he was transferred to MCI Norfolk, a medium security prison where he remains today.

The parents of Galen Gibson and Mathew David filed civil suits against Simon's Rock College for failing to avert the killings. A third lawsuit was filed by the estate of Nacunan Saez, and a fourth by Teresa Beavers, who was permanently disabled by her wounds. Simon's Rock College refused to admit negligence but eventually settled the lawsuits for undisclosed amounts.

On May 4, 1998, Wayne's lawyers argued for a mistrial on the basis that Dr. Wesley Profit was openly gay, and that may have biased him against

Wayne, who made no secret of his homophobia. Unimpressed by the argument, the State Supreme Court denied the motion.

Three days after the shooting, William Weld, the Republican governor of Massachusetts and an avid hunter, publicly stated that the shootings would have occurred even if tougher anti-gun laws had been in effect. "I'm not sure there is anything a society can do to guarantee you are going to keep weapons out of the hands of people who are crackers and determined to act out their fantasies," he said. He also suggested reinstating the death penalty. "Who's to say if this guy might have thought twice if we'd had a death penalty." Later, however, Weld introduced new gun control laws as part of an anticrime package, which included mandatory penalties for gun traffickers, and seizure of weapons and revocation of gun licenses for those convicted of domestic violence. A law banning assault weapons and raising the legal age for gun ownership from 18 to 21 was tabled. During a hearing, Josh Faber, 15, still partially crippled by the shooting, invoked Galen Gibson's memory while arguing against the loophole that permitted Wayne to buy an assault weapon with such ease. Eventually a law was passed assuring that an out-of-state buyer wishing to take possession of a gun purchased in Massachusetts would have to do so through a dealer in his home state.

Students at Simon's Rock proposed two laws to the town of Great Barrington, one that automatic and semiautomatic weapons be banned in town, another calling for a state-wide gun buy-back program, or at least a referendum on the matter. Both suggestions were tabled. In May of 1994, President Clinton renewed "most favored nation" trading status for China, but banned the importation of Chinese firearms such as the SKS. It is interesting to note that firearms are illegal within China, and are produced entirely for foreign markets. More than a million Chinese firearms, mostly assault weapons, were imported into the U.S. in 1993, the year prior to the ban.

In an attempt to work through his grief, Galen Gibson's father, Gregory, spent seven years investigating the details of his son's murder, a journey of discovery that he later made into a book called *Gone Boy, a Walkabout*. In it he speaks about the "country of grief," how the loss of his son led him there and his struggle to find a way back. When he began the book, he was motivated by the desire for revenge.

> Anger was the fuel for what I did. I wanted to teach those people [Simon's Rock administration] a lesson and I think I did my job. Anger can be empowering, but if you maintain it past its usefulness, it becomes sick. [Writing the book and the lawsuit] . . . transformed me from being just some poor schlub. I could do something. I could

write it down. I could record and analyze it. It made me realize I'm not just a victim, I'm an agent.

After the book was published, a former employee of Simon's Rock contacted him, explaining that she had a message from Wayne, with whom she had remained in touch since his incarceration. He had read *Gone Boy* and wanted to write to its author. Gregory Gibson agreed to correspond on the condition that Wayne acknowledged "the terrible cost of his actions to our family, the other victims, and his own family." Wayne wrote back that "he accepted full responsibility for his crimes. He regretted them more than words could say. . . . he was sorry for what he had done." Gregory, suspicious at this sudden conversion, called C.W., who confirmed his son's sincerity. C.W. said that during the prior year, Wayne had still been in denial, but this year, he had begun to accept responsibility for his actions. C.W. credited *Gone Boy* as the catalyst of his change.

A journalist from the *New York Times*, interviewing Wayne in prison in 1999, described him thus:

Amiable, with smooth, slightly dimpled cheeks and a sparkling intelligence, Wayne Lo often spoke with disarming frankness. He was also manipulative, controlling, and so eager to portray himself in a positive light that it was sometimes impossible to believe he thought he was telling the truth.

During the interview, Wayne spoke of a personal conversion experience, likening it to the lifting of a cloud. For the first few years after the shooting he remained certain that he had been doing God's work, but in the summer of 1999 he had begun to consider the possibility that the messages had come from elsewhere, perhaps from Satan or another supernatural force. With this revelation came the possibility that he had done wrong. By October he was experiencing intense remorse and wishing he could go back and undo what he had done. He further insisted that, despite reports to the contrary, he had been a happy child prior to receiving his commands from God. He insisted that he had never been mentally ill. "Personally I am, I guess you could say, a proud person. I would like to think that I have control of myself, that I am not impaired in any way."

Gregory Gibson and Wayne Lo began to correspond and in his last public interview, Gregory spoke of the possibility of visiting him in person. This is all the more striking since it is one of the few examples a parent of a school shooting victim exploring the possibility of forgiveness.

Wayne Lo currently has a website resembling that of a pop singer or movie star, which contains an interview, pictures (including some of his happy childhood, as if to prove a point), a link to his Wikipedia entry, to his MySpace blog, and finally to his online store, which sells his prison artwork; books that he has read, autographed in English and Chinese; and violin pieces that he played when he was a child, annotated by devoted teachers. Profits go t a scholarship fund established in Grey Gibson's name. The site includes a testimonial from James Gilks, an Internet-based dealer in "murderabilia" and one of the creators of the "serial killer calendar":

> Zach and Wayne are very easy to deal with. Honest, friendly, and very eager to get your items out as fast as possible. It's just not possible to find murderabilia at a lower price anywhere else on the internet.

CHAPTER 3

CASE 8: EVAN RAMSEY

*Childhood Abuse / Environmental Stressors
(the School System from Hell) / Parental Alcoholism &
Foster Care / Impulsive Anger*

Although Evan Ramsey was only five at the time, his life took a downturn from which it never recovered. The year was 1986 and he and his family were living in a small apartment in Anchorage, Alaska. Donald, his father, was four-and-a-half feet tall and well-muscled. He sometimes referred to himself as "Yoda," evoking the wise Muppet guru from *Star Wars*. Driving a cab in Anchorage, Alaska was his vocation but his passion was uncovering a complex conspiracy that he believed was being played out in local politics. For the previous year he had been circulating petitions to recall Tom Knowles, the mayor of Anchorage, because of corruption, but their frequent disappearance suggested, in his mind, conspiracy. When his car stopped working, it seemed to validate his suspicions. Donald ran a full-page ad in the *Anchorage Times*, a sizable investment for a man of his income, deriding the previous mayor, Tom Fink, as well as U.S. senator Frank Murkowski, and Alaska Governor Bill Sheffield. It appeared in one edition on August 19, 1986, before it was discovered and pulled by the newspaper's management. On August 21, Donald's apartment caught fire. Years later he tearfully recalled looking into the apartment window and seeing his sons' new bicycles being destroyed by the flames. It "proved," he wrote in his diary, "that a conspiracy factor exists." He accused Murkowski and his colleagues of torching his apartment, wrote threatening letters to the senator, and vowed to "go to war." His wife, Carol, who was half Eskimo, half Athabaska Indian, and his sons, John, 8, Evan, 5, and William, 3, were dispatched to the home of relatives in Fairbanks while he worked out a plan for revenge.

He chose as his initial target, Robert Atwood, the editor and chief of the newspaper that had refused to carry his ad. Atwood was a wealthy and powerful figure in Alaskan politics. With the help of his father-in-law, he had purchased the struggling newspaper in 1935 and turned it into the largest paper in the state. Using it as a platform, he had lobbied for Alaskan statehood. His influence was acknowledged in 1959 when President Eisenhower invited him to the White House to be present at the signing of the proclamation of statehood.

At 9:30 AM on the morning of October 21, 1986, Donald entered the *Anchorage Times* office building armed with a rifle, a .44 caliber Magnum pistol, a knife, a rope, a club, and fireworks. Having chained the front door closed, he set off smoke bombs and a string of firecrackers, starting a small fire in the lobby. He climbed the stairs, and strode down the hallway, looking for Atwood's office, finding, instead that of Atwood's daughter, Elaine, the assistant publisher. She was working at her desk. He fired at the ceiling, terrifying her, shooting out the lights and creating showers of broken glass. The noise alerted Robert, who came to her defense from an adjacent office. Ramsey tried to back them both into the elder Atwood's office at rifle point, but they attacked him. While father pinned him to the desk, daughter struggled to aim the barrel away from human targets. Ramsey drew his pistol with his free hand but before he could fire, Jim Rose, the paper's comptroller, had appeared and was wresting the pistol from his fingers. Dan Burns, a pressman, had arrived by then, wielding a type of knife commonly used by newspaper production workers. He cut the strap holding the rifle to Ramsey's body, and yanked the weapon away from him. By then the police had arrived. Donald was convicted of attempted kidnapping, three counts of felony assault, and two counts of reckless endangerment, and sentenced to ten years in prison. He would be released in January of 1997, ten days before his son would commit an SR shooting.

Carol Ramsey claimed that, prior to the rampage, Donald had been a caring, loving spouse. After he left for prison, she began to unravel. "That's when I started drinking," she said. "I didn't know what else to do." On December 14, 1987, the Department of Families and Youth Services (DFYS), acting on a tip from her sister, Ida, came to the house and found Carol too drunk to speak. The boys were huddled together for warmth in a room where the temperature had fallen to 22 degrees below zero, Fahrenheit. Three months after DFYS took charge of the Ramsey boys, a state psychologist wrote of Evan that he was "beginning to develop a real depression. He has no nice dreams. The only beautiful thing he can think of is his cat, which died: and it hurts when he cries."

Over the next three years Carol Ramsey lived a life of "welfare and drinking," according to John, her eldest son. "My mom was always messing things up," he said of her. Eventually Carol and her sons found themselves in Napakiak, a village of about 350 on the Kuskokwim River, where half of the adult population was unemployed. Most of the inhabitants were Yup'ik, the indigenous people of the area, who survived by fishing for salmon; hunting waterfowl, moose, bear and seals; and selling their crafts. Because of Carol's drinking and promiscuity, and the family's ignorance of the Yup'ik language, they were shunned by the community, which made survival all the more difficult. The adage *It takes a village to raise a child* is particularly true in the face of poverty, alcoholism, a fractured family, and weather so cold it could quickly be lethal. It is hard to know the extent to which tales of Donald's attack on the *Anchorage Times* pursued the family as they moved from one home to the next. Such dramatic stories take on a life of their own. Carol, being vulnerable in so many ways, would be the target of gossip wherever she went, and the narrative of her fall would include details of her husband's quixotic exploits. I suspect the gossip also contributed to Evan being teased and bullied by other children.

John Ramsey had promised his father that he would care for his brothers, a promise that was repeatedly put to the test in the years to come. One night a fistfight broke out between Carol and her current boyfriend. When nine-year-old John tried to intervene, he was punched in the chest. After his mother and her boyfriend had passed out, John wrapped his brothers in sweaters and coats, and snuck them out of the house. Tired and cold, with nothing to eat but some bubble gum, they wandered through the streets of Napakiak, begging for a place to stay, and getting turned away at every door. Exhausted, they eventually took refuge in the enclosed porch of the principal of the local school. The principal's wife was awakened by a clatter at 3:00 AM. "I heard a noise and thought it was a dog, but I went to take a look and it was the three boys. They had their jackets but no hats or gloves. So we gave them breakfast and in the morning washed them and called DFYS [Department of Family and Youth Services]."

Over the next three years the Ramsey boys lived with ten foster families. In one placement a foster brother bruised Evan's face and neck and, according to Evan, forcibly urinated in his mouth. Evan often found himself unable to sleep at night, and prowled the streets, throwing rocks at stray dogs. He began to smoke pot regularly and made his first suicide attempt. During the summer, he always tried to visit his mother. "When she's sober she's the type of person you wouldn't mind hanging around with," he said of her.

The Ramsey brothers finally found a stable home with Sue Hare, the superintendent of the Lower Kuskokwim School District. Mrs. Hare had moved to Alaska from Georgia, and had married a Yup'ik Eskimo named

David. Early on he had taken his nephew and some other boys fishing on the Kuskowim River. His nephew fell in the water and David drowned while trying to rescue him. Remembering the incident, Sue Hare said, "You always think the thing that's bad is the worst thing that'll ever happen . . . and then you live a little longer." Prior to taking in the Ramsey boys, she had cared for 21 foster children, including a child with leukemia who had died in her arms. She had two adopted children but she could not turn away the homeless Ramsey boys. It was well below freezing outside and the DFYS social worker told her that they had no place else to go.

Sue lived in Bethel, a town of five thousand, which served as the hub for the fishing villages up and down the Kuskokwim River. Although the river delta is vast—the size of Oregon—it has only 16 miles of roads. Most transportation is by small plane and, during the months when the river is not frozen, by boat. Instead of drag racing at stoplights, the teenagers race snow mobiles across the tundra. The high school basketball team, the Warriors, flies to away games in a small plane. The post office uses a hovercraft to deliver the mail. During the days between the end of the short summer and the start of the long winter, much of Bethel is mud, and the mud is deep. Instead of sidewalks, the ground is crisscrossed by fragile wooden boardwalks on stilts. Because the ground turns to permafrost about a foot and a half down, pipes and wire remain unburied, giving the landscape a half-finished look. Internet and telephone lines link to the outside world via big dish antennas set at street level.

Soon after they moved in with the Hare family, John was placed in a nine-month residential program at Charter North Psychiatric Hospital in Anchorage for anger management problems. Evan must have felt as though his family was being whittled away before his eyes. After John was discharged from the hospital, he stayed with relatives in Anchorage. His problems with anger had not been solved. By the age of 12, his criminal record included charges for theft, gun possession, and assault. At the time of Evan's rampage shooting, he was in prison, serving time for the armed robbery of an Anchorage porn store.

Despite her experience as an educator, Sue Hare's home was not an ideal placement. She traveled frequently—her school district was about the size of Ohio—and left the children with friends. When they were little the children got along, but as they grew older Evan fought with his adopted sister and brother, and sometimes became violent. In 1996 the police were called when Evan threatened Sue's adopted daughter, Pam, and kicked a hole in the wall. Sue's adopted son, Sam, had been convicted of sexually abusing a minor in 1992, when he was 27 years old, and continued to live in her home with the Ramsey boys and the other children, in violation of a state law that prohibits children being placed in homes with convicted sex abusers. The shotgun used in Evan's SR shooting belonged to Sam, in violation of his probation and of federal gun laws. Sue had bought it for him to hunt geese, ducks, and ptarmigan. In this part of Alaska, hunting was a way of life and sometimes a means of survival. The gun sat in the rack by the door for years, unlocked and available to anyone who wanted to use it. "It's so normal here to have access to guns . . ." Sue explained. "It was a bird gun. I don't think I even connected the fact that you can kill a person with a gun that you use to shoot birds."

Evan had made his first suicide attempt at ten, about the same time he had begun smoking marijuana. "He went to a cliff, got in the water, and was planning to wade out to sea and drown himself." A second instance occurred when he was 14. Depressed about his home life and harassed at school, he threatened to kill himself with his shotgun. He called up a close friend, Wilson Naneng, and said, "You've got five minutes to get over here or I'm going to shoot myself." Wilson arrived in time to take away the gun and comfort Evan. He never mentioned the incident to Sue Hare, who only learned about Evan's suicide attempts when she read about them in the paper, after his rampage shooting. "I didn't really tell anybody about that," Wilson explained, "because of how friends are."

As a teen Evan was a slight, goofy kid with acne, who wore black t-shirts and jeans, and winter hats in the summer. Sometimes he kept his head shaved and at other times sported a head of curly brown hair. As a student, he was considered an underachiever and was often absent from school. His rebellious attitude with teachers and with the principal led to frequent punishments and after-school detentions. He had been suspended at least three times for fighting. There were also areas where he excelled. He was an excellent chess player and counted among his few friends some of the smartest kids in the school; however they were the clique of students who, according to Evan's ex-girlfriend, "were not really wanted by anyone else." Wilson Naneng was an example of this, a smart, college-bound student who was shunned by the social mainstream.

According to his fellow students, Evan was "more an object of ridicule than a source of fear." Students would often provoke him just to see him explode. "Kids made fun of him," Sharin Mojin, 14, said. "He would do one of his things and kids would call him a 'spaz'." They also called him "brain-dead" and "retarded." For years Evan had struggled to control his explosive temper. "He's like me in one respect," Donald Ramsey said of his son. "He's slow to anger, but when he angers he blows up." Jon Simmons, a friend of

Evans who had moved to Anchorage the year before the shootings, agreed. "He'd blow his top and just go off. His mind would shut off. He wouldn't listen to anybody." But Jon added that he had never seen Evan go after anybody with a gun. When Evan lost his temper, he would throw trash cans or books, toss a chair, or push aside a teacher who tried to restrain him. Once he threw around the chairs in the library, "actually picked them up and winged them around the room." Sometimes the episode would climax with him running, crying, to his foster mother's office across the street from the school. These episodes occurred so often that Wilson Naneng's older sister good-naturedly nicknamed him "Screech" after the geeky, odd-looking, socially unsuccessful, and accident-prone character on the TV series *Saved by the Bell*. The name, to Evan's displeasure, stuck.

Evan got into fights with other students, notably Josh Palacios, the boy he later killed. Josh, a popular sophomore and an outstanding basketball player, had a reputation for making cutting remarks, and Evan had been the victim of his teasing on more than one occasion. Different accounts of the fight circulated around school, but everyone agreed that Evan, or a friend of his, had made a racial slur against Josh, whose father was black and whose mother was Mexican American, and, after school one day, in a vacant lot, in front of a crowd of high school students eager for a distraction, Josh had beat up Evan, or one of Evan's friends, to get even. Evan fled, and returned brandishing a steel pipe, at which point the crowd disbursed. Brock Rapoza, one of Josh's best friends, who also played on the basketball team, witnessed the event. He described Evan as ". . . freaking out. It was like he snapped or something."

Donald Ramsey, John Ramsey, and Evan Ramsey all suffered from fits of uncontrollable rage. This kind of impulsivity is the most common underlying factor of the narcissistic, antisocial, and borderline personality disorders. These are also referred to as the B cluster, or "dramatic" cluster, because patients with these diagnoses frequently indulge in *sturm und drang*. Impulsive anger contributes to a teen committing an SR shooting but not in the way one might anticipate. The teens in question do not "snap" under pressure, fly into an uncontrollable rage, grab a gun, and shoot other students. SR shootings are acts of predatory, not affective, violence, planned out with a cool head well in advance, as we have seen in previous cases. Fits of rage constitute a stigma, a kind of behavior that separates the candidate from his better-behaved peers. The knowledge that he can be made to explode through teasing and provocation is a source of amusement to others, in particular malicious bullies. Being bullied adds to the candidate's anger and his sense of being marginalized, while increasing the likelihood of him becoming aggressive and a bully himself, in an attempt to master his humiliation.

During the months before the shooting, a series of events further contributed to his misery. A girl he had been dating for months, whom he hoped could relate to him because of a mutual history of foster care, broke up with him without warning. Ten days before the shooting, he received a call from his father, who had recently completed his prison sentence. Donald Ramsey was now 51 years old, wheelchair bound and living in a residential program for homeless veterans in Anchorage. He passed his time going to counseling and trying to strengthen his legs with Nautilus equipment. "I got no real vibes that he was having problems or anything," Donald Ramsey said of their phone conversation. "We were just talking. He had just woke up; I could hear him crunching on a bowl of cereal . . . I just called to let him know I got out of prison." They spoke for 20 minutes or a half an hour. "It was just, 'You know I love you, don't you, son?' And he told me, 'I love you too, Dad.'"

Evan began to plan his suicide at about this time but we can only speculate as to whether his father's release from prison was the primary cause, a contributing factor, or a coincidence. My guess is that news of his father's freedom spiked his anxiety and he dealt with this through a coping strategy he had used successfully in the past: a parasuicidal performance. Parasuicide, a term more often used in Europe and Scandinavia than in the U.S., describes a suicide attempt, the goal of which is not primarily to kill oneself but rather to attract attention. SR shootings are a form of parasuicide because they involve a public display of violence—an act of *ceremonial violence*—which the candidate describes to his friends as a prelude to suicide, but which often culminates in a docile surrender to the police. While all unsuccessful suicides resemble parasuicides, they are differently motivated and are associated with different psychological conditions, the former with mood disorders and alienation, the latter with narcissism and a taste for excessive dramatics. The sympathetic attention of friends elicited by parasuicide is the kind of attention the narcissist needs to reinforce the fragile construct of his identity after it has been threatened by events such as rejection by a girlfriend, a failure at school, the disappointment of a parent, or, in Evan's case, the return of a family member with a history of violent and destructive behavior.

How did Evan's suicide plan turn into an SR shooting?

Evan had made two new friends that year, James Randall and Matthew Charles. They were freshmen and he was a junior. James, a distant cousin whom he had known for years but had never been close to, had an intact family, a mother who brought snacks to his room and a father who took him hunting for bear and moose. He had his own Playstation, VCR, TV, stereo, and dozens of speakers he had bought at garage sales. Matthew Charles was socially awkward (after the shooting it was suggested that he suffered from Asperger's Disorder, a form of autism) but had an appealing younger sister, Theresa, who James was dating. The three boys spent hours walking the boardwalks, smoking unfiltered Camels with marijuana mixed in, and playing *Doom*.

Doom was among the earliest "first person shooter" computer games to offer an "immersive 3-D graphic" environment, where the player could move about, as though he were in a realistically animated film, navigating labyrinthine corridors, shooting monsters and zombies, and fulfilling quests. The player takes on the persona of a space marine, an idealized character of great combat skills, who has an armory at his disposal containing everything from rifles to chainsaws. Having disobeyed a commanding officer's order to kill his comrades, the space marine is exiled to Mars, where he must labor for a corrupt military contractor. When one of the projects goes awry, human beings begin changing into zombies, and it falls on the hero to rid Mars of the dangerous creatures.

Violent video games are often scapegoated for violent adolescent acts. Let me be perfectly clear: I am not suggesting that playing *Doom* causes teenagers to commit SR shootings. An overwhelming body of research suggests it does not. What I am saying is this: The same factors that contributed to him becoming an SR shooter contributed to him enjoying the game—not simply the blowing away of zombies but also the role-playing opportunities it offered. Evan's prospects of ever becoming a respected, powerful adult were so slight that the opportunity to pretend to be one, however briefly, was welcome. In addition, *Doom* let him act out his present dilemma symbolically, as if in a dream—or a nightmare. During game-play he became a big, tough space marine (but rebellious and misunderstood), with limitless weaponry, betrayed by authority figures (parents, teachers, and principals), exiled to a strange planet (high school), and put up against an endless army of zombies (his teachers and classmates). Zombies resemble human beings but have no feelings, thoughts, or inner life, and therefore may be killed with impunity. This is how a narcissist perceives other people: as though they are hollow shells.

The Saturday before the shooting, James and Matthew slept over at Evan's house. Theresa joined them and, huddled in the crawl space beneath the house, smoking marijuana, Evan told them about his suicide plan. He intended to "go out with a bang" by shooting himself in the school lobby. "I figured I'd . . . scare the holy crap out of them, and kill myself. But James had some disagreements on that." Evan accused James of suggesting an SR shooting. "He said that my face and name would go across the world. He said I'll become famous. . . . He said I should live the fame." The idea of killing a few of his most irritating classmates before turning the gun on himself was not without appeal to Evan. When James and Matthew realized their friend was seriously considering the suggestion, they egged him on, proposing more names for the list, including the principal. Exhilarated by their plan, Evan retrieved his foster brother's shotgun from the rack by the front door. Matthew, who was interested in photography, borrowed a camera belonging to Evan's younger brother, and they photographed him holding the gun.

Even before the idea of an SR shooting is suggested to Evan, he has planned to commit suicide publicly, in the center of his community, the school lobby, where he could "scare the holy crap out of them." When James Randall suggests that he kill others, Evan embraces the idea because it increases the terror and consequently the significance of the act. Real life becomes more like *Doom*, and perhaps he will re-experience the elation he felt playing the character of the space marine. Unlike a covert murderer, who plans how he will dispose of the gun, the ceremonial murderer begins by having himself photographed *with* the gun, creating evidence of an irrefutable sort. This kind of public relations campaign reaches absurd proportions in Columbine, with its six hours of video tape documentation conceived in the style of a "making of" bonus feature on a DVD, and the press kit Seung-Hui Cho mailed during the Virginia Tech shooting.

On Sunday night Evan called Carol Rodgers, 18, apparently someone he liked very much and possibly hoped would talk him out of his lunatic plan, and told her not to go to school on Wednesday. When she pressed him about it, he described what he intended to do. She refused to hang up until he had promised her not to go ahead with it. Out of respect for him—the unwritten code that forbids "tattling"—she mentioned it to no one.

Evan's last class on Monday was Yearbook, which was taught by Reyne Athanas. Despite her age—she was approaching 50—Reyne was youthful, taught informally, and came to work in jeans. She had a strong connection with her students, encouraging them to call her by her first name. Evan had not completed his assignment, which was to create a yearbook pictorial on special needs students, and she asked him what he was planning to do about it. "I don't know," he replied. She turned her attention to another student, and the next thing she knew, he had put on his backpack and left the class. This was so out of character for him that she grew concerned. She sought out the guidance counselor, who was busy, and the dean, who looked for him in all the boys' bathrooms. Finally she went to the school social worker, Jacqueline Volkman, who had just been hired that year. "The problem was," Volkman said later, "I wasn't even sure who he was; I had to have someone point him out to me."

The fact that she didn't know Evan in a school of only 450 students did not reflect on her lack of competence or industry, but rather on Evan's ability to "fly beneath the radar," and the severely dysfunctional behavior of many of the other students. In the words of Cynthia, a classmate of Evan's whom he had once dated, "My friends carve themselves up with razors, burn themselves, pierce themselves. One of my friends has slit her wrists several times unsuccessfully. There's probably something with every single one of my friends." Three students had died during the previous year, two of them involving suicide with guns. In the fall of 1996, a 13-year-old boy, threatened with a beating if he came to school the next day, went home and killed himself with a rifle that his parents kept in the closet. Later in the year, within the course of a week, one student, a gifted athlete, was accidentally crushed to death while he and his father were lowering the shell of their house onto its foundation, and another involving a disturbed 16-year-old who got drunk and shot himself in the head. While adolescence can be a difficult time for some children, the extent and severity of suffering and self-destructive acts at this school and in this community far surpassed the norm. To better understand this, we must take a brief look at the sociology of the town of Bethel and the educational history of the region.

In the 1890s, when whites first came to the Yukon to pan for gold, or provide support services for the prospectors, they lobbied for schools for their own children—white children. By 1903, nine all-white public schools had been established in southwest Alaska, and by 1930 at least 19 towns and villages had a two-tiered system: a white school that went through grade twelve, and a native children's school that ended at grade eight, institutionalizing the idea that native children had less intelligence and potential than whites and therefore required less education. Native children with exceptional aptitude were sent to boarding schools on Indian Reservations in the Lower 48 for vocational training and "acculturation." Most of them returned home after a few months with tales of their mistreatment while others simply disappeared—victims of who-knew-what terrible kinds of exploitation. In response to this disastrous experiment, the Alaskan government built four of its own vocational boarding schools which were consolidated, after World War II, into one school, Mt. Edgecumbe, constructed on an abandoned naval air base at Sitka and administered by the Bureau of Indian Affairs. For almost 20 years this remained the only tax-supported high school for the region's native children. In 1966, overwhelmed by the number of native children seeking high school educations, Alaska began construction of six regional high schools, each with its own dormitory, in an explicit attempt to destroy the culture of the small villages, which were believed to "retard the development of rural folk into a disciplined and reliable workforce." Bethel Regional High School, attended by Evan, had originally been constructed as was one of these regional boarding schools.

Because the building of the dormitories was progressing so slowly, the government passed a Boarding Home Program which paid local families to take in native children during the school year. The program was meant to be temporary but because the number of applicants always exceeded the number of beds, it was indefinitely extended and became part of the town's culture. Some villages sent a native woman to accompany the child during his nine-month stay and these children faired better than others, but in most regards both programs caused far more harm than good. Boarding Home Program children suffered the same problems as children placed with bad foster families: they were treated like servants, scapegoated and abused.

A University of Alaska study conducted in the early 1970s concluded that the locus of the problem lay in the towns where the six regional schools had been located rather than in the quality of the teachers or the curriculum. In 1972 Bethel's population had been 2,416; in 2005, it was 6,262, having more than doubled, creating confusion and social disorganization. The society had three tiers: the old Eskimo families who were leaders of the community, involved in government and civic projects and often traveling around the state; the whites, who were often government employees, teachers, doctors, and health care workers, many of whom were there temporarily; and the villagers who had relocated there, some for better jobs, but others because they had been exiled from their communities for fighting or drinking. In addition, there were groups of unemployed young men who traveled from town to town looking for work, were often involved in drugs and drinking, and tended to prey on the female boarding students who were away from home for the first time. The University of Alaska study questioned the basic premise of placing the schools in the towns:

> These towns are very poor places to locate high schools for [native] village children. . . . boarding schools for middle class children both in the other states of the U.S. and in England have traditionally been placed in rural areas . . . Yet, in Alaska, the absurdity is that children are taken from small villages and placed in regional towns which usually have much higher rates of social problems than the surrounding villages.

A series of class action lawsuits filed by teens from 126 native villages between 1972 and 1975, demanding educational equality with whites, convinced the Alaskan government to issue a consent decree providing for the establishment of a high school in every one of the 126 villages except those that chose to exempt themselves (none did). "Almost every village with an unused building larger than a broom closet pushed ahead with a high school program." But by that time a negative culture had been established in Bethel and other regional high schools. Townspeople had become cavalier about taking in native children and providing them with the meagerest supervision. Native students were literally a third-class population, vulnerable to drugs, alcohol, and predatory young men. Isolation, long winters, and a highly stratified class structure made matters worse.

Tuesday, the day before the shootings, Evan, James, and Matthew skipped school and wandered through Bethel, visiting friends, and smoking pot in one of their hideouts. When school was over, they returned to Sue Hare's house. Evan took the shotgun to his bedroom where James, who had experience with guns, showed him how to load it, and prepare it for firing—everything except how to fire it. "He told me I'd have to be a fucking moron if I didn't know how to fire a gun," Evan said. Matthew offered to back up James with a .22 caliber revolver he had at home but decided against it "because I'm only 14." Instead he borrowed William's camera. He planned to photograph the shooting, and enlarge the pictures and hang them on the wall. Such "clueless" behavior probably contributed to his diagnosis of Asperger's.

That night Sue Hare came home, tired, ill, and upset that Evan had cut school. She had dinner and went straight to bed. Evan stayed in his room with Matthew—James had gone home earlier—playing music and drawing cartoons. Later, Evan began calling his friends. He called James, crying, and talking about killing himself. "It's either them or me," he said. James tried to talk him out of it. He also called Wilson Naneng, who seems to have been his moral compass, and spent an hour with him on the phone, dropping hints about what he had planned for tomorrow.

He said, "Go up to the library. Something really bad is going to happen tomorrow." I asked him, "What do you mean something bad's going to happen?" He said he would let people know on the bus and let them know out loud in the lobby. I said, "Is it going to be like a fight?" And he said, "Yes." . . . somebody was going to get hurt. He said, "I'd like to tell you more, but I just can't." Then Sue told him he had to go to bed.

Evan called other friends, inviting them to gather the following morning in the library, located on the mezzanine overlooking the lobby, where they could observe Evan's activities without exposing themselves to harm. He spoke of planning "an evil day" and wanting to see his victims "suffer," a comment which came back to haunt him time and again during his trial.

Later that night he wrote two letters in his notebook. The following, an excerpt from the first, was crumpled up and discarded.

> I have thought to myself, what kind of damage can a 12 gauge slug do to a human's internal organs or their head? Well, today I found out and so did everyone else that is in school . . . No, I am not on drugs . . . ciggerettes (sic) that's all. I am not really depressed just that the fact that I want people, the world, or maybe just Bethel, to know how mean and cruel the world is or can be. This school has got to get its shit together 'cause there are too many deaths this past 2-3 years . . .

Evan may have discarded this note when he realized that his admonitions about improving mortality rates were nonsensical if followed by a killing spree. Like Wayne Lo, Eric Harris, and other SR shooters, he emphasized that he was not crazy, or at least not depressed or confused by drugs. He wanted to take full responsibility for his actions, just as he wanted a photograph of himself holding the murder weapon.

The second note, left folded on his desktop, with a request that Sue Hare read it to everyone after Evan had killed himself, shied away from public moralizing.

> Hi, every body!
>
> I feel rejected. Not so much alone but rejected... I figure by the time you guys are reading this I'll probably have done what I told EVERYONE I was going to do. Just hope 12 gauges don't kick too hard, but I do hope the shells hit more than 1 person because I am angry at more than 1 person. One of the Big [expletive] is Mr. Ron Edwards . . . I was told this would be his Last year, but I know it WILL BE HIS LAST YEAR . . . The main reason why I did this is because I'm sick and tired of being treated this way everyday . . .
>
> So I killed a little and killed myself. Jail isn't & wasn't for me, ever.

While Evan was writing his notes, Ron Edwards was attending a school board meeting to discuss the deteriorating social climate of Bethel Regional High School. Students were coming to class wearing gang colors, pretending to be gang members. Others had been busted for drugs in the school parking lot, and the boys' bathroom often smelled of marijuana. Edwards had just returned from the state basketball championship at Anchorage, where he had heard chilling stories of school violence from other administrators. In Anchorage they were talking about metal detectors to reduce gunplay. Edwards pounded his fist on the table, and stated with exasperation, "I do not want my school to be like that."

He was 50 at the time, a former marine and National Guardsman who had served in Vietnam; a seasoned educator who had risen through the ranks of the Kuskokwim Valley School District; a fanatic basketball fan who flew to away games with the team when he could manage the time; an amateur hunter of moose and prospector of gold; and a devoted father of four children. As a teen, in his home town of Kalispell, Montana, he had been an athlete and champion bodybuilder, and his weight was an ongoing concern for him. After his death, they found rice cakes and tuna in one desk drawer and a mountain of candy in the other. When he came home he would sprawl in his favorite chair, announce that "The captain is in the command module," and turn on *Monday Night Football*.

On Wednesday morning, February 19, Evan woke to find himself alone. Sue Hare, still sick, had stayed in bed, and William had taken a cab so he could get to school early, before the excitement began. Evan dressed in baggy black pants he had bought from William for five dollars, his lunch money. After loading the shotgun, he poured some shells into his pocket and took more in a brown paper bag. By sliding the shotgun down his pants leg, and zipping his black parka to the knees, he could hide the weapon completely, although the flexing of his right knee was inhibited, giving him the appearance of a limp. When he set off for school, the temperature was around zero, the ground covered with snow, the sky still dark. At that time of year the sun rose at 10:30 and set at 4:00, so students rarely saw daylight. He stood at the bus stop, talking with his friends, and bumming smokes. When he climbed on the school bus some students noticed his odd gait but nobody made anything of it.

Bethel Regional High School was a hulking, dark wooden box, its lobby decorated with the heads of moose, musk ox, brown bear, and caribou. Friends of Evan's were arriving early, excited and curious about what he had planned. One girl had heard rumors of a disaster that would make people want to leave town, another that something really big lay in store. James and Matthew and others who were in on the plan directed them to the library, or to their lockers. Don't try to play the hero, they warned, and keep out of they way. Some students thought Evan was simply going to kill himself.

Although by now at least twenty students anticipated some kind of violence, no one alerted an adult.

While Evan's friends gathered on the mezzanine, those less favored, the 60 or so most popular and athletic students, were socializing down below, in the lobby, waiting for the bell. Josh Palacio, Brock Rapoza, Raul Sanchez, and Ryan Curda, still sweaty from their early morning game of hoops, had taken their usual seats around a table in the part of the room that doubled as a cafeteria. Brock was breathing hard from their workout and Josh joked about him dying of heat stroke. Brock replied that Josh would die first because he was a black man and their mortality statistics were infamous. They wagered a hundred dollars on who would live longest, a bet that tempted providence too far. Evan appeared at the entrance, holding the shotgun in one hand, the bag of shells in the other. The boys rose, apprehensive, and moved away, then decided that Evan was harmless and returned to their seats. A student named Andy Angstman gave a firsthand account of Josh's murder within days of its occurrence.

> The kid came in with the shotgun and everyone was "Whoa." But we have an ROTC program here, and a lot of kids thought it was probably from that, so there was a delayed reaction. Then Josh said, "Hey, that's a shotgun." He stood up and said, "Hey, why do you have the gun here?" He had the gun at his hip and basically aimed at Josh . . . [Josh] just said, "I'm going to get out of here." When he got up, he got shot.

Evan was standing 12 to 15 feet away from Josh when he fired. Josh grabbed his stomach and tumbled backwards. As he lay on the floor, at the center of an expanding pool of blood, he asked, "Why did you shoot me?" Evan didn't reply. Raul knelt beside his friend and, at his request, pressed Josh's gold crucifix into his hand. Then he crawled under the lunch table and sat with him, holding his hand as his pulse grew weaker.

"You guys better run!" Evan shouted, firing a shot at the ceiling so it rained plaster on their heads.

Jeffrey Chon, 14, described what happened next. "A lot of kids were like, 'Run, run.' I just started running. The whole school was in tears." Eric Hodgins, 18, trapped behind a planter in the corner of the room, recalled Evan's pleasure in firing the shotgun. "He was laughing, just going crazy." A secretary who saw the mayhem, described Evan's expression as "gleefully evil." Students hid under tables and behind planters, and jumped out the windows. When anyone came close to him, Evan swung the shot gun in their direction. He shot again into the crowd, spraying two students, Shane

McIntyre and Russell Lamont, with buckshot. Russell remembered dropping to the floor and crawling away before losing consciousness. Shane didn't realize that he had been hit. It was only after he had had run to the diesel shop to get help that he noticed the bleeding from his shoulder.

Evan strode down the hallway, shooting into the ceiling while teachers pleaded with him to put down the gun. He passed a room where Lynne Lavendar, a substitute and another teacher, Ms. Polli Pete, had been conducting their class. They turned out the lights, hid behind the desk, and prayed together that Evan wouldn't find them.

Reyne Athanas rushed from the teachers' lounge, concerned by the commotion. There was Evan in the middle of the room, waving his shotgun. She approached him cautiously, asking him to put down his gun. "He just couldn't stop," she said later. "I don't know how to describe it. He looked like he wasn't even there."

She held out her hands and asked for the gun.

"Do you. Want. This. Gun?" Evan asked, pausing oddly between every word.

"If you'll give it to me." She stepped forward, hands outstretched.

He swung the barrel toward her as if he was going to shoot her but then thought better of it.

A phys ed teacher, Gale Power, set off a fire alarm. Kids began to scream and run in every direction. One of the boys in the library began laughing and counting off the bodies.

Ron Edwards emerged from his office. He started toward Evan as if to disarm him but then, seeing the gun barrel aimed at him and the look in Evan's eyes, he turned and ran. Evan shot him in the back, behind the left shoulder, the birdshot perforating his lung, heart, and aorta. The blast blew him up against the door and he fell. Nancy Elliot, a special education teacher who had been waiting in his office, dragged him inside. The small entry wound didn't look serious and when Edwards told her twice that he was going to die, she disagreed. Edwards' wife, Cindy, was in school that day, substitute teaching. Trapped on the other side of a folding room divider that was either locked or stuck, she could hear her husband suffering but could not reach him.

Again, Reyne pleaded for Evan to give her the gun.

"They're not going to take me alive," he told her, pulling a single shotgun shell from his shirt pocket. "This one's for me." He put the gun up to his chin. Reyne pleaded with him to stop. She said later that she felt that Evan had little control over what he was doing. Stopping him would have been like stopping an avalanche.

By now a senior named Hans Halverson had phoned 911. Within minutes four officers and Police Chief Gary Eilers—half of the Bethel police force—had converged on the school. Peering past the door, they saw a battlefield tableau, wounded bodies on the carpet, others applying tourniquets and trying to staunch the blood with bandages made from a torn shirt; they heard gunshots, and praying and wailing, and smelled burning powder in the air. After conferring, they decided to take aggressive action, diverting the boy's attention from the students and school personnel. They strode into the building shouting for Evan to put down his gun. When Evan saw them, he ran across the lounge and up the stairs to the mezzanine, where his friends were gathered, but the gate at the top of the staircase had been locked. Trapped there, he turned and aimed the gun at the wounded and terrified victims below. At first the officers stood behind a wall. One stepped into view, attracting Evan's fire. Now a second officer did the same and fired two rounds at Evan. The terrified boy threw the shotgun off the balcony, crying something like, "I'm done, I don't want to die." When the gun hit the floor a part broke off. An officer named Walker kept ordering Evan to "Get down!" as he sprinted across the room, leaping over the dozen or more cowering students. He rushed up the stairs, grabbed Evan, who had started to descend, struggled with him and eventually subdued him.

Evan was cuffed and led from the building. Only three minutes had passed since the police arrived, although the subjective time seemed far longer. Medics who had arrived outside some minutes before hurried in to care for the casualties, while police searched the building for collaborators. "I found students hiding under the toilets," Officer Walked told a reporter. "Every nook and cranny had a student in it, just petrified."

Sue Unin, a teacher in the elementary school, had heard about the shootings and rushed to the cafeteria to help settle the kids. Matthew Charles sat down beside her and began babbling about Evan's rampage. He couldn't believe his friend had actually done it! he said over and over again with excitement. He pulled out a camera and told Ms. Unin that he was supposed to have taken pictures but he got so excited that he had forgotten, and by the time he had charged the flash, it was too late.

Now that the danger had passed, Cindy Edwards ran to her husband and knelt on the carpet, holding him in her arms and trying to comfort him until the paramedics arrived. He was taken to the Yukon-Kuskokwim Delta Regional Hospital and was pronounced dead shortly after arrival.

Joshua Palacios was taken by small plane to Anchorage, and then, by a waiting ambulance, to Providence Alaska Medical Center. Despite everyone's best efforts, the trip took six hours, and he did not arrive until 3:00 PM.

He was in the operating room for three hours and he died on the way to the intensive care unit, some nine hours after being shot. For lack of something better to do, his friends and classmates spent the afternoon making a get well card for him, which he did not live to see. Josh's grandmother had moved to Bethel from Dallas to get away from inner-city violence. Josh, his mother, and his brother, also Dallas residents, had followed in 1988, after her marriage broke up. Although only a sophomore, and five-foot-four, he had made the school's eight-man traveling varsity squad. All Joshua wanted to do was play basketball. On one occasion after his grandmother had passed a rule prohibiting hoops when the wind chill was ten below or worse, Josh and Corey called her at work, arguing that it was only nine below and couldn't they go out and play? With his exotic looks, he was popular with the girls, and always the center of a crowd. When, one summer, the family couldn't find the money to send him to basketball camp, his wide circle of friends got together the needed tuition.

Back in Bethel, parents were in a panic about their children. Velda Miller, who worked at the Tundra Women's Coalition, recalled how it felt to be a parent that morning.

> I became aware of the shooting as Cheryl, my coworker, yelled for me to come listen to the radio in another office . . . As the voice on the radio told parents to get to the high school to pick up their children, we saw students jumping out of the windows and running across the tundra. [The high school was across the street.] I left TWC immediately and passed many parents driving distraught to the high school . . . I could only get so far in the traffic so I parked off the road and ran searching for my daughter. I asked anybody (sic.) if they had seen her. Finally one person told me she was fine and in the dormitory with the other students. I ran to her, held her and cried with her. I was at a loss for words and all I could do was hold her.

Carmen Lowery, director of the Tundra Women's Coalition, immediately began making arrangements to bring school guidance counselors, social workers, and other mental health workers to the Yup'ik Cultural Center. Within a few hours, students and teachers were streaming into the center, hoping to make sense of what had occurred. Around dusk, 60 of the visitors gathered in a large meeting room and took turns recounting their experiences of the morning. At the end of the meeting, they formed a huge circle while one woman sang a mournful Yup'ik purification song, and some of the students sang along. Afterwards, everybody joined in the Lord's Prayer.

Evan's father, contacted in Anchorage by curious reporters, was astonished by the news. "I can't believe that. He's the mellowest kid. My Evan shot somebody? He's not but 16 years old." When asked if he thought his own assault on the *Anchorage Times* had inspired his son's behavior, he replied, "I doubt seriously if it had any impact on him, but who can say? I don't think he's trying to emulate the old man, impress the old man, but who can say . . . ?" Growing tearful, he added, "This comes as a total shock to me. This ain't no family tradition."

Thursday morning the local radio station, KYUK, a PBS affiliate, held a two-hour, open-phone session hosted by Evelyn Day and Liz Sunnyboy, representatives from the Yukon-Kuskokwim Health Corporation who were active in the mental health and recovery community. Sunnyboy, a native Alaskan, was a Yup'ik speaker. Listeners from the length and breadth of the Delta spoke of their feelings of grief and distress, in Yup'ik as frequently as in English, as though they were sitting together in a friend's living room. People listened on their car radios, and in their shops, and cafes. They crowded around the radio at the Yup'ik Cultural Center, nodding their heads to some comments, disagreeing with others. Sentiments commonly expressed were that the community had to learn to listen to their children and instill in them better values. "That young man is hollering for help," Evelyn Day told her audience, and this was "his way of getting our attention right now."

Cathy Sampson Kruse, a Native American, offered to organize a purification ritual. She told the board, ". . . when a tragedy happens there's sadness that stays in the building. I offer to the group that some spiritual leaders should quietly come together and start cleansing this building." The board agreed and the following night, at 9:00 PM, Cathy Sampson Kruse, Myron Naneng (Wilson's dad), and Tom Taylorf led a small number of men, women, and children through the halls, the classrooms, and the cavernous gymnasium of Bethel Regional High School, praying silently. Some carried abalone shells filled with burning sage, sweetgrass, and tobacco, while others fanned the smoke with feathers. This process, called "smudging," is an ancient ritual practice of the Lakotas. A tribal elder had instructed them to use the smoke "to lift you, strengthen you, and protect you." Over 100 students and parents who came to observe stood by the doors, praying in Yup'ik, English, and Hebrew. Afterwards they were invited to enter the lobby area. Although the room had been scrubbed clean, the walls were still riddled with holes, and pellets remained caught in the weave of the carpeting. Friends formed "crying huddles" and others occupied themselves by picking the pellets out of the carpet. Leaders of the service spoke informally about the necessity of sticking together, of treating each other with honor and respect. There were warnings about vigilantism. "Whatever your religion," one speaker said, "they all say vengeance isn't ours." At the end of the evening everyone was asked to face east and recite the Lord's Prayer, to drive the evil spirits out the east entrance of the school, the doors of which had been left open to the cold. In its grieving, the school achieved an understanding across cultural barriers that had previously eluded it.

A Lower Kuskokwim School District Board of Ed meeting had been called for the next day. It was scheduled to be held at the district's board room, but when more than 100 teachers, students, parents, and community leaders showed up, it was moved to the Yup'ik Cultural Center and became, in effect, a town meeting on the subject of school safety. Bob Herron, the board president, announced that starting on Monday, state troopers and Bethel police would be continuously patrolling the local schools, that there was a short-term plan for intensive coverage and a long-term plan for later, when emotions had cooled. Other priorities included a communications system for every classroom, and stricter rules and regulations. "Staff security and student security should be at the top of this school board's agenda," one speaker declared. "Education will have to come second." One student, Eric Hoffman, spoke on behalf of Josh Palacios's friends: they wanted to be heard, and to be involved in the "decision process," and acknowledged by the board. Sue Unin's daughter, Shiela, spoke on behalf of Evan, how he was always picked on, how he had gone to counseling to no avail, how he would have to live with the memories of the people he had killed. Erick Hodgins, a friend of Josh Palacios's, expressed anger at hearing Evan called a victim. He had personally witnessed Evan's pleasure during the shootings. "I saw his eyes and he was enjoying it." Finally they discussed the importance of James Randall and Matthew Charles experiencing consequences for their part in the killings. "It will be a war zone if this isn't taken care of," said Myron Angstman, a local attorney.

On Friday, 2,000 people, nearly half the population of Bethel, gathered in the school gymnasium to "reclaim the school." Alaska state troopers and Bethel police department officers guarded the entrances. Bob Herron opened the ceremony by welcoming back to school ". . . our brave faculty and students." The crowd provided a standing ovation. A Russian Orthodox pastor who had graduated from the high school in 1979 began the assembly with a prayer and sprinkled the bleachers with holy water. Friends sobbed and embraced one another. Les Daenzer, the newly appointed acting principal of the high school told the assembly, "I shudder to think that this is only the tip of the iceberg. There's more out there—I've seen it." He was referring to the troubled children and teens living in the outlying villages of the Delta.

Four case investigators from the Criminal Investigations Bureau and the crime lab arrived by plane that weekend and interviewed more than fifty witnesses. Among the issues under investigation was the extent to which James Randall and Matthew Charles knew about and were involved in the killings. On Sunday morning, February 23, both boys were arrested, charged with first-degree murder by complicity, and held at the Bethel Youth Facility. They were both 14.

School reopened for classes on Monday. Students trudged up Ridgecrest Avenue, leaving footprints in the previous night's light snowfall. Buses arrived and lines of cars discharged students in the twilight. Attendance was high. Parents were invited to accompany their children to school and to spend the day with them, and many accepted the offer, sitting in class with them or congregating in the halls. A counselor was assigned to every classroom and every student was given an opportunity to talk about the events of last Wednesday. Students, wary of more violence, appreciated the police presence.

School ended at 1:00 PM so that students and faculty could attend a memorial service for Ron Edwards. A memorial service was held for Josh Palacio on Friday of that week, in the gym where his sneakers had pounded the floorboards. Brock Rapoza gave Josh's parents a basketball signed by all his teammates, and the mayor, Ruth "Wally" Richardson, read a letter from Governor Tony Knowles, emphasizing the importance of curbing Alaska's familial violence and understanding its causes. Josh's mother, Claudia Palacios, admitted that her son was taken away before she had entirely figured him out. "Joshua was a puzzle and all of you have pieces... because each one of you now have those pieces, you'll always be part of our family."

Despite all these efforts, the weeks and months following the shootings were difficult for everyone. A year later, Velda Miller looked back and characterized that time as "hazed over with fear, anger, tears, extreme shock, and intense sadness... the confusion, as a parent, of letting my children go to school each day yet the frustration of not feeling safe, and of the unanswered question of 'why?'"

On February 27, Evan Ramsey was formally indicted on two counts of first-degree murder, three counts of first-degree attempted murder for shooting at two police officers and the student, Shayne McIntyre, and nineteen counts of third-degree assault.

Evan was not among the 16 who testified that day. He was being held at the Cook Inlet Pre-trial Facility in Anchorage on half-a-million dollars bail, and it was simply too difficult and expensive to fly him back and forth to the courthouse with the kind of security detail warranted by his crime. During his March 6th arraignment at the Bethel Court, he phoned in his "not guilty" plea.

As the trial date approached, the Bethel public defender turned the case over to Wally Tetlow, an Anchorage public defender with more homicide experience. Earlier that year Tetlow had defended an Anchorage high school sophomore who had murdered his parents while they slept. Tetlow asked for a three month postponement in order to familiarize himself with over 1,100 pages of documents and to make a variety of motions including a change of venue. His preparation was further hampered by budget cuts, an understaffed office, and the unavailability of the defense investigator.

Evan agreed to waive his right to a speedy trial, believing that the postponement would enhance the preparation of the case. Assistant Attorney General Renee Erb argued that the trial be kept as scheduled. "We have a whole community of Bethel and a number of victims who need to have this matter closed," she told the press. Furthermore, postponing the trial to the winter months would make travel to and from Fairbanks or Anchorage difficult for the expert witnesses who were expected to testify. Judge Wood found on the side of the defense and delayed the trial to December 21.

During a change-of-venue hearing in October, Wood ruled that Evan could not get a fair trial in the Kuskokwim Delta. The town of Kotzbue was rejected because travel would be too expensive and security too difficult to enforce; and Anchorage and Fairbanks, because their different demographics might make assembling a jury of peers impossible. Eventually the judge chose Dillingham, a predominantly Yup'ik town 175 miles to the southeast, in an area even more barren and isolated than Bethel.

The trial began on January 26, 1998, almost a year after the shooting. Troopers stood guard at Dillingham's little courthouse and everyone was required to pass through a metal detector. Because of Dillingham's skewed age distribution, the jury was exceptionally young, with half the members being under 35 and several of them teenagers. Tetlow believed that this worked against Evan, since younger jurors would be less sympathetic. Planeloads of Bethel residents jammed into the tiny courthouse to watch the proceedings. Absent was Evan's family. His brothers attended one day to testify but during the rest of the trial he was alone.

In his opening argument, Tetlow told the jury that Evan's crime was really a suicide attempt, prompted by a history of physical, emotional, and sexual abuse, and therefore he should be convicted of manslaughter, rather than first degree murder, greatly reducing his sentence so he might one day leave prison and enjoy whatever shred of life was left to him. His intent was to injure students, creating a situation where the police would have to kill him. Renee Erb countered that it was a planned, malicious attack on students whom Evan disliked, just that and nothing more. She presented, as evidence, one of the letters Evan had written before the killings. During the next five days, 25 witnesses recounted, again and again, the harrowing minutes when Evan stalked the school with a shotgun. Many of them spoke in the flat, soft cadences that are characteristic of the Eskimo dialects. There was a terrible sadness about the proceedings. One reporter commented, "There are moments when the 12 people sitting in the jury box of this borrowed courtroom seem to be the only people—except for the lawyers and the judge—not crying." Brock Rapoza testified that Evan and Josh had been in several fistfights, and recounted the story about Evan menacing them with a metal pipe. In another instance, while standing in the lunch line, Evan had aimed a racial slur at Josh. While such slurs are common banter among adolescents, and sometimes even terms of endearment, Evan had intended it hatefully.

Tetlow, in contrast, presented his case in one day, and called only three witnesses: Evan's two brothers, John and William, and Kathryn Fritch, the mother of one of Evan's friends. Mrs. Fritch told how Evan had confided in her twice during the spring of 1995 and again in the winter of 1996, that he was thinking about killing himself because the students picked on him, because his brother was "into his stuff all the time," and no one cared about him. "He just didn't want to be here anymore . . ." Mrs. Fritch told the courtroom. "I watched him become unhappier and unhappier." The final testimony came from the nurse at the Yukon Kuskokwim Correctional Center, who had interviewed Evan after he was apprehended to determine if he was suicidal. Evan told her that he was not suicidal at that time, that he had never attempted suicide, and that he hadn't considered suicide in more than a year. Tetlow tried to have the testimony suppressed but the judge allowed it. The judge also disallowed testimony of Evan's sexual and physical abuse. Tetlow swore he would appeal on this account. While Evan was present in the courtroom throughout the trial, he was never called on to testify.

> . . . the 17-year-old sat silently, staring down at the defense table before him as his attorney tried to save him from a life in prison. Wearing a blue oxford shirt and jeans, his legs shackled, his hair now grown out and slicked back, the impassive Ramsey seemed strangely peripheral to the courtroom drama deciding his fate around him.

The jury took five hours to reach a verdict. Evan was found guilty of two counts of first-degree murder, one count of attempted murder, and 15 counts of assault. He was acquitted of one of the murder charges and of an assault charge. The *Tundra Drum* wrote ". . . there was a general sense in Bethel more of nodding acknowledgement than of relief."

James Randall's case came to trial in September of 1998 in Anchorage and went on for six weeks. Because he was a juvenile, information about the proceedings, other than the charges and the verdict, were kept confidential. Jurors were deadlocked regarding the first-degree murder charge, but convicted him of two counts of second-degree murder. Matthew Charles had pled guilty to the lesser charge of negligent homicide and testified against James. Because they were tried as juveniles, they were released at the age of 19, in 2002.

During the same week—a year after the killings—Bethel Regional High School, in response to requests by the students and faculty, held a day-long celebration of the lives of Josh Palacios and Ron Edwards. School began at 10:00 AM with a private candle-lighting ceremony, which was followed by workshops in yoga, beadwork, poetry writing, and other expressive arts, crafts, and activities. Some rooms were available for students to talk through their feelings about the victims of the shootings with selected teachers and staff. Later that day helium balloons were released with messages for Edwards and Palacios. At noon a memorial service, open to the community, took place in the gym, followed by a potluck. The day ended with a concert featuring local musicians.

The families of Ron Edwards and Josh Palacios sued Evan in civil court in April of 1998, seeking unspecified monetary damages for wrongful death. While Evan had few assets, Myron Angstman, the lawyer representing Claudio Palacios, explained that they were pursuing the case because she was having difficulty learning about events that had led to the slaying of her son, and the discovery process that precedes a lawsuit would force the information to come to light. Eventually the insurance company reached a settlement with the plaintiff. Both families sued the Golden Eagle Bus Company, claiming that the driver should have noticed that Evan had a rifle down his pants leg. The school bus company, owned by Alaska Senator Lyman Hoffman, a Bethel native, and Bob Herron, the school board president, offered to settle for $1,102,500 at the insistence of their insurers. Finally the Edwards family sued Matthew Charles. Matthew's attorney argued that the boy was not responsible for his actions because of his Asperger's Disorder. When the Edwards family learned, 15 minutes into the jury's deliberations, that they might find in favor of Matthew, they dismissed the case, worried about the expenses they might accrue if court costs and legal fees were awarded to the defendant.

Hours after the shooting, Susan Hare went on sick leave. In the months that followed, Lucy Crow, a board member, wrote a commentary piece for the *Tundra Drum* calling for Hare's resignation. A disgruntled former Bethel resident placed an ad in another issue, criticizing Hare in strong language. During the second week of March, Hare changed her official status to "administrative leave for an indefinite period of time," stating that she felt that the board no longer wanted her to serve and she was investigating other career paths. She had held her position for 14 years in an era when three or four-year terms were not uncommon.

Wilson Naneng, the boy who had stopped Evan from committing suicide many years before, was among those in the library who watched the killings without raising a hand. During the following months he became consumed with guilt that he could have stopped Evan from bringing the shotgun to school. He gnawed at his hand until the skin was raw and cut his arms with knives. While competing in the state academic decathlon in Anchorage, he returned to his hotel room and tried to hang himself with his belt. Friends intervened at the last moment. Later, he described the conflicting emotions that had driven him to this. "I felt betrayed by Evan and I felt some guilt that I should have stopped it. I felt as though I had been shot myself. When I talked about Evan, it was like he was dead. I felt like I had lost a brother."

The sentencing took place on December 1, 1998, in a makeshift courtroom set up in the multipurpose room at the Yup'ik Cultural Center. Attendees included a camera crew and producer from *60 Minutes* who were filming the proceedings for a special on the "school shooter phenomenon." Carol Ramsey was the first witness. In order to support the diagnosis of Evan's depression, she had to publicly acknowledge her neglect, her drinking, and the fights with her boyfriends. She left the stand, sobbing. Reyne Athanas testified that she had lost the ability to trust people and to do creative artwork. Rodney Thomas, Josh Palacios' father, gave Evan a sermon about accepting Christ as his savior, along with a bible. "I've forgiven you a long time ago," Thomas said. "I've never hated you because that's not the love of Jesus." One of the police officers whom Evan had shot at that day testified by phone, calling Evan a "monster" who should be locked up, and Renee Erb said that he had committed "murder with a black heart." When Evan's turn finally came to speak, he said in a voice so soft it could hardly be heard, "I'm so sorry."

Evan was sentenced to a 210-year term. Judge Wood, admitting that rehabilitation was a possibility, structured the sentence so that Evan will be eligible for parole in 52 and a half years, in 2050, when he is 70 years old. He is currently incarcerated at Spring Creek Correctional Center, Alaska's only maximum-security prison, in the barren, snowy mountains of Seward. Because Spring Creek is one of the few facilities in the U.S. that allows journalists to interview prisoners, and because he is articulate and appealing in a bad puppy-dog kind of way, Evan Ramsey has become the poster boy for school shooters. Whenever a TV news show or news magazine decides to do an article on the subject, a reporter is dispatched to Alaska to interview him. He has appeared on *60 Minutes II* and on MTV; he has been interviewed by the *San Diego Union-Tribune* and by *Time* magazine; and he was the subject of a series of six articles in the *Boston Globe*.

During these interviews he is invariably asked about the motive for his crime. He told *San Diego Union-Tribune* reporter Jenifer Hanrahan, "There were a couple of people I wanted to kill. At the time there was two people I hated, hate as in the way Hitler hated the Jews." When Steve Fainaru, of the *Boston Globe*, asked why he killed Ron Edwards, Evan responded, "I don't remember. I think it was one of those little things. I thought he was an asshole but not one of those assholes that you'd really want to hurt." He told Carol Marin of *60 Minutes II*, "My main objective of going into the high school was to check out, to commit suicide."

Despite his media exposure, Evan is rarely visited. During his May 2001 interview with the *San Diego Union*, he confessed that he had seen no one since his mother had paid him a surprise visit on New Year's Day, six months ago. His father, currently living in Anchorage, wheelchair bound and without a car, hadn't visited in two years, and his older brother, John, was not permitted to visit because he was on parole, having recently completed a sentence for armed robbery. Evan does, however, receive volumes of mail and email. One group of writers is the social scientists, professional and amateur, who are curious about what *really* motivated his crime.

[To Evan Ramsey]
I would like to know more about why you shot up a school. I am doing a school project and I kind of like to have an idea to go on while I am researching. I would really appreciate, all information you could give me. Sincerly

Sydney Coon

P.S. Just so you know I dont think any less of you as a person because i am sure you had a good reason to do it. [Author's spellings and punctuation retained]

Another group is young women who find Evan interesting. After Whitney from Greenville, North Carolina, saw him interviewed on MTV, she wrote him a letter confiding that she too felt like an outsider, and sent him pictures of herself that she had taken in the mirror. After corresponding for some time, they decided to get married, and, as of May 2001, she was planning a move to Seward to be near him. Weddings are performed at Spring Creek but conjugal visits are not permitted.

CHAPTER 4

CASE 9: LUKE WOODHAM

Socialization into Extreme Violence

> How shall we comfort ourselves, the murderers of all
> murderers? What was the holiest and mightiest of all
> that world has yet owned, has bled to death under our
> knives.   NEITZSCHE, from *The Parable of the Madman*

PRIOR TO JOINING A SATANIC CULT, killing his mother, his ex-girlfriend, and her best friend, and wounding a half-dozen other students, Luke Woodham had never been in trouble with the law or with school authorities. He was an A and B student and a valued employee at Domino's Pizza, where he worked after school. A neighbor recalled a single public act of defiance, performed repeatedly. Luke's mother, Mary Anne, took pride in her lawn— she was an avid gardener—but had trouble getting Luke to mow it. When, after being coaxed, badgered and threatened, he finally emerged from his room to do the job, he would mow one or two strips in the lawn, or cut a square section in the middle of the yard so it resembled a punk haircut in reverse, and retire, leaving his mother livid.

Luke's father, John P. Woodham II, moved from Newton, Mississippi in 1965 to the town of Pearl, an hour south on I-20, to escape the influence of his family. Pearl had a reputation as a safe, pleasant, fast-growing, God-fearing community. The town had been planned without a downtown shopping area to deter teens from hanging out. Stores and services were clustered in strip malls at the edge of town. At the time of the shooting, Pearl had a population of 22,000—mostly evangelical Christians—41 churches, no bars, and very little crime.

In 1967, John married Mary Anne, whose bubbly personality balanced his quiet and reserved demeanor. She was a blonde with a good figure, who favored pink workout suits. They were considered a striking couple: attractive, well-dressed, and well-groomed. John got an accounting job and Mary Anne enrolled in a local college where she earned a two-year degree in education. After graduation she worked part time as a substitute kindergarten teacher, often cross-examining her students to learn if they had been abused or neglected with a fervor which other teachers found excessive and some-times embarrassing. She gave up her job in 1973 with the birth of her first child, John P. Woodham III, and resumed teaching when he started kinder-garten. Neighbors recall her being over-protective, and compulsive about the timing and execution of his meals, bath, and daily prayers.

Although Mary Anne tried to get pregnant again immediately, seven years passed before she gave birth to Luke Timms Woodham. John Jr. was jealous of his new brother and, according to Luke, often punched him while he was napping, or tripped him in the backyard when others had turned their backs. When Luke tried to hit back, John would hold him at arm's length, infuriating him. When the boys visited other children's homes, they would become aggressive if they didn't get their own way. Invitations to play dates became infrequent, and neighbors with children kept their distance. In an attempt to provide Luke with companionship, his parents bought him a number of pets, and he spent hours in the backyard caring for them and confiding in them. In kindergarten Luke was teased and bullied because he was plump and wore thick glasses to correct his extreme near-sightedness. His mother kept his hair cut in bangs and dressed him in shorts year-round.

In the mid 1980s, John Sr., who had worked for years at the City of Pearl Audit Office, was promoted to Assistant Comptroller, an important job with a good salary, in the neighboring county of Madison. A short time later he was fired for poor performance. He became listless and depressed, holing up in his home, retreating to his small study, refusing to help with parent-ing or domestic chores. The marriage, which had always been fraught with conflict, became unbearable. In 1987 he walked out on his wife and children and rarely returned to visit. Luke was seven years old, in second grade.

Luke stated, after the shooting, that despite the conflict between him-self and his brother, and between his parents, his life had been easygoing before his father's departure. The event was catastrophic as far as he was concerned. Mary Anne ran the home by herself, washing, cooking, cleaning, driving the boys to school and appointments, and arriving at work—a bet-ter-paying job as a receptionist—by 8:00 AM every morning. John Jr. was spending as much time as possible away from home, leaving Luke to pro-vide for their needy mother. She delegated more and more chores to him, which he refused to complete. She also sought to make him her confidant and a source of emotional support, a role he refused, discouraging her sometimes intimate questions about how she should proceed with her life with a curt "yes" or "no."

Mary Anne's behavior during this period often veered toward the sadis-tic. On one occasion, soon after the separation, Luke scraped some uneaten food into the garbage. Mary Anne, who couldn't bear to see food wasted, picked all the pieces out of the garbage and made him eat each one. On another occasion she caught him smoking one of her cigarettes and forced him to smoke two packs in succession, until he threw up on the floor. She would regularly inspect his bedroom, withholding allowance if the room wasn't spotless. On one occasion, when he failed to clean the room, Mary Anne collected all his clothes and toys and dumped them in the trash. He retrieved them but she made him put them back in the trash. Although Luke was not yet in high school, she would go out on overnight dates with a variety of men, behavior he found difficult to reconcile with her presentation of herself as a devout Christian churchgoer. During her overnights, she would often leave him alone, a situation he preferred to being babysat by his brother, who might become aggressive and pummel him. While she was away he would forage through the kitchen, satisfying his hunger with bags of chips and cookies.

Luke entered Pearl High School in September of 1995. He was at least 20 pounds overweight and wore thick, large-framed glasses that dominated his face. He was called "fat," "chubby," "chunky," and other insulting names, and was frequently beaten up. He would shuffle through the halls, comforting himself with bags of chips and cookies, and gazing at the floor. When he did make eye contact with another student, he would stare aggressively, which, on more than one occasion, resulted in his snack food being torn from his hand and crushed underfoot. Rick Brown, a senior during Luke's freshman year, and an aspiring minister, believed that reports of his persecution by classmates were exaggerated. Other students, he said, were ridiculed far more harshly.

Newman remarks, "School shooters are not all loners and they are not all bullied, but nearly all experience ostracism and social marginality. For some of these boys . . . it's the perception of marginalization, despite evidence to the contrary, that matters most."

Life at home was no more welcoming. Mary Anne scolded him for not completing his chores, harangued him about his grades, and encouraged him to be more like his brother John, who had been "Mr. Popular" in high school. Other SR shooters, such as Michael Carneal (Case 10), Kip Kinkel (Case 12), Dylan Klebold and Eric Harris (Case 13, discussed in Chapter 5 of this book) had popular older siblings, who, by contrast, emphasized their own sense of social failure and isolation at home.

Luke later said of his relationship with his mother, "I guess I really didn't have much of one. . . . We never really got along. And she always deserted me and left me out. I guess it just wasn't really good." He perceived his problem with her as one of alienation and exclusion. *She deserted him and left him out.* His father had done the same, years earlier. The situation was no better at school. In the introduction to this book, I wrote of how Durkheim (1897/ 1952) had linked suicide to alienation. Abraham Maslow (1987) ranked "belongingness," as he referred to alienation's opposite, as one of mankind's essential needs. If Luke, or any of the other SR shooters, had felt a sense of belongingness anywhere, at home or at school, they probably could have endured their alienation. For an adolescent, even one close relationship with a mentor may be sufficient to reject suicide or a negative identity.

A former classmate, Ben Timberlake, recalled a single incident when Luke retaliated to being bullied. The semicircular drive in front of the high school was known as "Freshman Loop" because those who didn't have cars were dropped off there by their parents. Every morning when Mary Anne dropped Luke off, she would kiss him on the cheek as though he was a little boy. When a school bully suggested that Luke had an incestuous relationship with her, he lost control and attacked him. "Luke went completely crazy," Ben Timberlake recalled. "We never saw him like that before and I tell you that other kid would have been seriously injured if we hadn't all pulled Luke away."

Here again is the impulsivity which is characteristic of the dramatic personalities. There is no record about whether kids ever teased Luke for the fun of watching him blow up, as they did Evan Ramsey; most likely he struggled over the years to keep his temper in check rather than give bullies the satisfaction of making him appear a fool. The crack about incest was more than he could bear, not because he was actually having an incestuous relationship with his mother (although the possibility exists), but because he was battling his attraction to her and her provocative behavior toward him. After his father and older brother abandoned the family, Luke found himself living alone with an attractive, overtly sexual woman, who turned to him for the emotional support previously provided by her husband. This is a parallel situation to that of Brenda Spencer, whose mother and older siblings left her and her very needy father living alone together for several years during the onset of her puberty. It is also similar to the case of Barry Loukaitis (Case 7), whose mother confided in him in a manner so inappropriate that an expert witnesses at his trial labeled it "emotional incest."

An important aspect of identity formation is coming to understand one's own sexuality and how one will relate sexually to others as an adult. Incest, physical or emotional, short-circuits this process, leaving the survivor skeptical of ever becoming a sexually functional adult. First-person accounts of incest, such as *The Kiss*, help us understand the sense of shame and secrecy, the fear of insanity, and the suicidal and homicidal impulses that accompany this experience.

As the year progressed, Luke spent more time in the isolation of the library, reading philosophy and literature. At home, he would escape to his room to play his guitar and write songs and poetry. He began to believe that his intellect was superior to those of his classmates and that his ideas were of value simply because "no one would think like I did." While it is true that no two people think exactly alike, the idea that one's differentness in intellectual pursuits, physical appearance, or talents (such as the singing example recounted below) might be analogous to greatness is the illogical leap of the narcissist.

William Dodson, the district superintendent, was quoted as saying that Luke and his friends were of "higher then average intelligence students," but Rick Brown, who knew Luke very well by then, was less impressed. "People see somebody read some book on philosophy and think, well, they must be a genius."

Mrs. Valerie Neal, Luke's freshman English teacher, asked the class to describe in their journals how he or she would spend a day as Mrs. Neal. Luke wrote:

> If I could spend a day as Mrs. Neal I would be very nice to Luke Woodham and pass him for the year. Then I would knock the crud out of the "omniscient dork" for putting junk on my computer,
>
> Then I would go crazy and kill all the other teachers. Then I would slowly and very painfully torture all of the principals to death.
>
> Then I would withdraw all of my money from the bank and give it to Luke Woodham. Then I would get all of the other teachers and principals bank account numbers, withdraw all of the money and give it to Luke Woodham.
>
> Then I would do acid. Then I would get a gun and blow my brains out all over the dog-gone room and leave my house to Luke Woodham.

This sample sounds more like the work of a ten-year-old than an adolescent. The vocabulary is small, the sentences, short and singsong. Luke doesn't seem to understand the meaning of "omniscient." What is most surprising is the number of homicidal, suicidal, and antisocial acts he describes in four sentences. For another assignment, "write about an incident that upset your parents," Luke made up a story about killing a man and his dog, robbing a phone booth, torturing clergy and desecrating a church, and robbing a bank and killing the tellers. Mrs. Neal chose not to bring either paper to the attention of the school's counseling services, perhaps because she was afraid of him, or wished to have as little to do with him as possible.

At the end of the year Luke learned that he would have to repeat the ninth grade, an extraordinary wound to narcissism based on intellectual superiority. Despite the hours he had spent reading, he had not applied himself to his schoolwork, or so he rationalized it to himself. The reader can better understand his rage by considering a similar kind of narcissistic wounding that occurs publicly on the popular television show *American Idol*. At the start of each season a few contestants perform who have no stage presence or singing ability. Their auditions are embarrassing to everyone but themselves. Eventually one of the judges, usually the Englishman Simon Cowell, interrupts their performance to ask, barely cloaking his disbelief, if they really imagine that they have a chance of winning *American Idol*. They invariably reply, "Yes, because my singing is unique," or "Yes, because no one else sings the way I do," as if this quality is of value to the world. Simon bluntly disabuses them of the notion, explaining that they are completely without talent and better suited for a less glamorous profession. At first they appears confused and disoriented, as though the ground has been snatched from under them. They may argue with Simon and refuse to leave the audition room. When they have had a few minutes to regroup and digest what has occurred, they explode with anger, making derisive hand gestures at the camera, and attacking the competence of the judges with language that is unacceptable on the airwaves. The fragile structure of their narcissism has been publicly attacked. The trophy on the mantle is revealed as a sham, the problem in the basement exposed. They may fume about the incident for weeks or months before returning to their old selves. Nothing is learned from such lessons; they protect themselves by continuing to believe that the show is unfair and the judges inept.

One of the few teens who showed Luke any kindness in the fall of that year was Lea Ann Dew, who lived a few streets away, and sometimes gave him a ride to school, sparing him the humiliation of the Freshman Loop and his mother's displays of affection. When Luke decided he wanted to go to the prom, and his mother agreed on the condition that he could find somebody to drive him, Lea Ann Dew offered to be his chauffeur and his date. They danced together, talked together, and socialized with other students. Afterwards they went out to eat at the Waffle House, after discovering that Shoney's was too full to seat them.

In February of 1996, while watching the evening news, Luke saw a story about a Washington state high school student named Barry Loukaitis (Case 7), who had killed his algebra teacher and two classmates, and held the rest of the class hostage. While previously, the inspiration for SR shooting had been found in novels such as *Rage*, the music video of the Pearl Jam song *Jeremy* and the movie *The Basketball Diaries*, all of which include glamorized depictions of SR shootings; now, because of their increasing frequency and mortality, SR shootings had become lead stories on TV news and on newspaper front pages. They had entered the mythology of adolescent bad-boy behavior and were discussed in the lunch room and after school. Like the serpent Ouroboros, who consumes his own tail, the phenomenon could now feed on itself.

Luke's second stint as a freshman began in September of 1996. It was during this time that he met Christina Menefee. Like himself, Christy's parents had divorced when she was little. Initially she had lived with her mother and her new stepfather in Louisiana. In 1992, following a fight with her stepfather, Christy had moved in with her stepmother and her father, Robert, an electrician, who was stationed at the naval base in Jacksonville, Florida. In the summer of 1996, Robert was discharged from the Navy and got a job offer in Pearl. An important factor in his decision to move was the buzz about it being a safe place to live. Christy and Luke had something else in common: they both owned small menageries. Christy had a hamster, a dwarf rabbit, and a white terrier named Fluffy, who followed her around the house. She had wanted to be a veterinarian but when she learned that their duties occasionally included euthanizing animals, she decided to pursue meteorology, which she hoped to study at the University of Oklahoma. She took ROTC, and wore an enameled "Taz," the voracious Tasmanian Devil character from Looney Tunes, around her neck on a leather thong. Like Luke's mother, she cultivated a rose garden in the backyard.

Luke approached her at a time when she had just moved to Pearl and knew few other students. She may have found his gentle, soft-spoken manner appealing. Her father, asked to explain the attraction, said, "Christy was always for the underdog." For whatever reason, she agreed to go out with him. For their first date, a trip to the movies, Mary Anne chauffeured them and was waiting outside when the picture let out. When Luke went to see Christy at her home, his mother insisted on coming along. Her parents mistakenly interpreted her hovering as an old southern custom of which they'd been ignorant. When Luke and Christy sat together on a love seat, his mother interrupted to question whether they should be so close. Luke wrote an essay in his journal, "The Day Something Good Finally Came in the Mail," about his happiness at being with her.

On October 1, 1996, after three dates spread over the period of a month, Christy told Luke that she could no longer date him but wanted to remain friends. She had told a girlfriend after only a week or two that Luke was getting "too controlling." He would get mad at her if she failed to call him at a certain time every day, or walk with him to class. She also mentioned that it was embarrassing going on dates with his mother. He had kissed her on the cheek but never on the lips.

Furious with Mary Anne, whom he held at least partially responsible for the break-up, he tried to avoid her whenever possible. At home, he remained locked in his bedroom, inscribing lyrics about lost love and suicide in his notebooks. Some days later Luke received a letter from Christy saying that she was in love with somebody else. It included an attractive picture of herself. In the weeks that followed, Luke threatened suicide twice, telling friends of Christy's that he would use guns from his dad's collection. Both times he was dissuaded, once by Christy herself, and once by a classmate named Jack. While suicide, as I have mentioned, is disturbingly common among teens, and a stock component of teenage romance since well before Shakespeare's *Romeo and Juliet*, suicide threats following a relationship comprised of three dates and a kiss on the cheek suggests a teen who is over-dramatizing his life, and over-emphasizing his own importance in the world. It is not clear whether anyone discussed these incidents with adults or whether any adults intervened. John Kendrick, the associate director of the Resource Center Network, an agency that provides counseling and casework services to at-risk families in the county, admitted that the Woodhams were known to them, as were Luke's behavioral problems. Services had been offered and the family had declined, but he could say no more because of the laws of confidentiality.

After their breakup, Luke began working at Domino's Pizza. He was soon considered an exemplary employee. "He always kept to himself," according to Glenn Davis, the area supervisor. "Always been a good worker, always said, 'yes sir, no sir,' got along with his fellow team members. He was thinking about going into our assistant manager's program when he turned 18." He soon became friends with another Dominos employee, Donald Brooks, Jr., or "Donnie," who enjoyed role-playing games (RPGs) like Dungeons & Dragons. Donnie told Luke about an RPG group he belonged to led by a Pearl High School senior named Grant Boyette.

Grant Boyette was the son of deeply religious couple who were members of the founding board of a local Baptist church. He often wore a dress shirt and tie to school because he considered it the Christian way to dress. He was very thin, sported a fine moustache, and kept his hair closely trimmed. "Grant always looked kind of foxy," a fellow student said. "He'd squint his eyes at you if he didn't agree with what you said and then you'd feel him drilling into your mind, trying to work out where you were coming from." Grant and his friends would always make a show of praying before they ate, whether in the school lunchroom or at Pizza Hut, dazzling classmates and community with their sanctity. The lunchroom would fall silent when they bowed their heads, and then the hubbub would return after their "amen." Church members, family friends, and former teachers agreed that he was an intelligent and well-behaved student who regularly attended church and Sunday school. Billy Baker, a Sunday school teacher at Crossgates Baptist Church, regarded Grant as somebody who "seemed to have his head screwed on pretty good. . . . He knew a good bit about scripture." Those who knew him better knew that he lived a double life. Rick Brown, who had known Grant from sixth to tenth grade, explained Grant's predilection for Satan and Hitler, even while he was singing his praises to Jesus.

> If he couldn't be accepted by us, he wanted to be accepted by someone, so he prayed to Satan for power, influence, and money . . . Grant liked Adolph Hitler a whole lot and admired some of his tactics—the way he could control people, the way he could manipulate people.

Killing seemed to preoccupy Grant as a means of problem-solving. Later on, when Luke and the others had gotten to know each other, and Luke explained his sadness and bitterness over his rejection by Christy, Grant told the group, "He should just kill her and be done with it so he won't have to see her again." In the days before the shooting, Grant encouraged Donnie Brooks to kill his father after he had grounded him for stealing his credit card and running up a big debit. Troy Parker, a Pearl High student and one of the original members of their group, told how one day he had been complaining about his mother, and Grant had advised him, "You just need to go out and kill her." Troy, refusing to believe Grant was serious, had laughed off his advice. He also described Grant's habit, while standing around the commons, of pointing out students he didn't like and riddling them with bullets from an imaginary machine gun, while muttering, "You're dead, motherfucker!" and chuckling to himself. Troy left the group in December of 1996 because "It started seeming serious and at the same time I was getting old. It all seemed kinda juvenile." Prior to meeting Luke, Grant had played RPGs with boys his own age, but they had dropped out of the circle, complaining that his relentless love affair with evil had made gameplay tedious. Grant wanted to play his own kind of game with characters who were well-known criminals, whom Grant would put into horrible circumstances and force to commit horrifying acts.

He reasoned that younger, more impressionable teens would be more likely to go along with it, and looked for recruits from the freshman and sopho-more classes.

At this time Donnie, Luke's coworker at Domino's Pizza, introduced him to Grant, and both boys were welcomed into the group. Other group mem-bers included Justin Sledge, 16, who Luke knew from a classics class they had taken together, and Luke's two friends from freshman year, Wesley Brownell, 16, and Daniel Lucas Thompson, 15. Justin, who suffered from Lupus, was an outspoken athiest, and often reminded Pearl's bible-thump-ing community of the fact. Wesley, the gentlest of the group, wanted to be a veterinarian and had worked as a kennel assistant for a local vet. Later, when Grant and Luke, and perhaps some of the other boys, began practicing magical spells and evoking demons, Wesley was kept ignorant about it. The final member of the group, Delbart "Alan" Shaw, 17, was the only boy who had been in trouble with the law. A neighbor had caught him blowing up mail boxes with explosives made according to recipes culled off the Internet. His parents had gotten divorced when he was nine, and for years he had been passed back and forth between his mother, his father, and a grandmother in Louisville.

Becoming part of a role playing group was a dubious honor. In many high schools, RPG players, like Goths, are those rejected by other social groups. Although RPG players are typically smart, computer savvy, and have a rich fantasy life, the activity of pretending to be a character with spe-cial powers—a mage, or wizard, or rogue—is uncomfortably close to those make-believe games where a child of a much younger age can be anyone he likes and have any power or ability, as long as the other children agree to it. In adolescence the emphasis should be on developing real-world identities and competencies. Jocks must practice and excel in sports. It is not enough to pretend to be a great baseball player who can hit a home run every time he comes to bat. Members of the French club must become flu-ent in French. It is not sufficient to pretend to speak a foreign language. This may be what District Superintendent William Dodson meant when he said that Luke and the other members of the group ". . . were apparently students that didn't have an identity, however, and they tried to make their identity themselves."

By December Grant and Luke had formed the closest bond of the six. Grant wanted to be thought of as "The Father," even, at one point, insisting that members of the group call him by that title. For Luke, who had lost his father when he was five, this older teen, with his sympathetic way of listen-ing, his revolutionary ideas, and his willingness to lavish attention on Luke, was irresistible. Rick Brown believed that Grant's fondness for Luke was a result of the perception that the younger boy's malleability. "Luke was a social recluse all his life. . . . He would be easy to control and easy to manipulate." Grant also admired Luke's bookishness, and the glib way he could coin aphorisms. Some of his favorite were, "This country was built on the blood of others and shall be destroyed in the blood of others," and "God is only a shallow concept made up by fools looking for something to believe in."

In the winter of 1996, Grant and Luke began to study the *Necronomicon*, (Simon, 1980), which had been brought to their attention by Wes Brownell. The *Necronomicon* is a mythical grimoire or spell book first described by H.P. Lovecraft, the Victorian writer of horror stories. Ed Simon, a contemporary writer, created the book, using Lovecraft's description as a blueprint. It is beloved by RPG players as a source for props. Chunks of its high-faluting pseudo-medieval rhetoric, rewritten in a calligraphic hand or typed in a Gothic font, made blasphemous books and occult diaries that could be used in game play. While the book is an acknowledged hoax, gamers have created rationales for the legitimacy of its spells. Luke himself took it seriously, referring to it as ". . . a bunch of spells and a bunch of history and stuff like that. Love spells and spells that can kill people and things like that." They also read Anton LaVey's *Satanic Bible*, a tract on self-indulgence and hedonism with a sprinkling of information about spells and rituals.

The more they found themselves powerless and without competencies in the real world, the more they were drawn to a make-believe world, where influence was achieved without talent, labor, or wealth. Having spent hours discussing how gratifying it would be to put curses on the people they disliked, they decided to try casting a spell. Luke had a classmate named Danny whom he disliked because "He would always talk down to me and he tried to use me any way he could. . . ." One night in January of 1997, in a room lit by candles, they inscribed a pentagram on the floor. While Grant was chanting the spell, Luke suddenly had a vision—not of Danny, but of Danny's best friend, Rocky Brewer. This puzzled him until, two nights later, Danny appeared at the door of Luke's home, tearful and distraught. He told Luke that Rocky was dead; he had been killed trying to sprint across State 25, a four-lane highway, to buy beer. Luke knew immediately that the death was attributable to their spell. It had worked indirectly, hurting Danny by killing Rocky. This event convinced Luke that Grant had supernatural powers. From then on, whenever Grant wanted anything done, he and Luke would cast spells and evoke demons to do their bidding.

"The Kroth," as Grant had decided to call the group (he sometimes referred to it as the "Fourth Reich") met frequently, often at Luke's home, to discuss their plans to amass power and money. Grant told the other boys that he had an AK47, that he always carried a revolver, and that he had access to weapons and cash. He used a variety of slogans to bond them together: "We cannot move forward until all our enemies are gone," and, "If you are not with me, you are against me. If you are against me, you are dead." Together, they planned a takeover of Pearl High School. They would set fires with home-made napalm, cut the phone lines, kill certain students and faculty, and after-wards flee to Louisiana, then to Mexico, and finally to Cuba via a hired boat.

On Tuesday, April 8, Luke stayed home from school. Grant came over to the house as he often did, and they began to talk about the "beauty of death." They decided to see how Luke's dog, Sparkle, would respond to a beating. A neighbor who lived one house away later described to the police how he had watched through the cracks in the fence as the two boys chased the little dog around the backyard. He saw Luke catch her and hold her while Grant beat her with a stick until she was howling with pain and could barely walk. That night he told his wife about the incident and offered his opinion that Grant—not Luke—would one day kill a man. On several occa-sions during the week that followed, Luke's older brother John noticed that the dog was limping and asked Luke to take him to the vet. Luke declined for fear that the vet would recognize the nature of the bruises. On Saturday, April 12, at about 2:00 PM, Luke called Grant to come over and help him dispose of the dog. They beat Sparkle again, put her in a garbage bag which they sealed within a second bag and a third, and sealed that within an old book bag. Despite their efforts, the dog could still be heard whimpering. They carried the bag about a half mile, to a pond in a deserted wood, where they killed her in a sadistic, drawn-out manner. A cavalier description appears in Luke's journal:

> On Saturday of last week, I made my first kill. The date was April 12, 1997, about 4:30 pm. The victim was a loved one. My dear dog Sparkle. Me and my accomplice had been beating the bitch for a while and last Tuesday I took a day off from school just because I didn't want to go. . . . I took the night stick and hit her in the shoulder, spine, and neck . . . I'll never forget the howl she made, it sounded almost human, we laughed and hit her more . . .

Although Luke describes himself as delivering the death blow, he later said that it was Grant who had done it, and Grant who had made him write it down that way.

Mary Anne believed that Sparkle had simply run off. John thought Luke might have been involved and tried to broach the subject, but Luke was evasive. Donnie Brooks, a regular visitor prior to the killing, stopped coming around about then. Sparkle's slaying may have scared him, but another event took precedence: he had been grounded for the unauthorized use of his father's credit card. Wes Brownell also began to distance himself from Luke, screening his phone calls and refusing to return them. Grant, however, continued his daily visits. Now he took on the title of "Master of High Demon Activity." Alan Shaw became "Commander and Chief (Explosives)," because of the skill he had demonstrated in blowing up mail boxes. Luke was "The Assassin." He would receive communications through a demon, whose arrival Grant would predict.

In Chapter 1, I described a biological theory of violence proposed by Jonathan Pincus (2001) and Dorothy Otnow Lewis (1998), which suggests that most homicides are committed by people who have been abused as children, are paranoid, and have some kind of damage to the frontal lobes or gray matter of the brain that results in disinhibition. The process of socialization into violence undergone by Luke Woodham under the tutelage of Grant Boyette, and other SR shooters such as Evan Ramsey, Michael Carneal (Case 10) and Dylan Klebold, suggests an alternative theory of the origin of individual violent behavior, a process of *socialization* into extreme violence that has been described by Lonnie Athens (1992), a professor of criminology at Seton Hall University. The two theories—Pincus-Lewis, and Athens—represent the polar extremes of biological versus environmental etiology, between which psychological theory has oscillated over the centuries. The Pincus-Lewis theory admits some amount of environmental influence in that childhood abuse is a precondition, but the Athens theory dismisses the influence of any biological component.

According to Athens, a sequence of experiences must be completed before a person achieves the state where he chooses a violent solution to a problem. This can be informal and spontaneous or, in the case of street gangs or military organizations, carefully planned and fine-tuned over years or decades. The first experience is that of being forced, physically, into submission, as when a bully threatens to keep twisting the candidate's arm until he "gives up," or when a father beats a child until he "learns a lesson," or "promises to behave." The experience results in anger, humiliation, a hunger for retribution, and an understanding that people can and will communicate through the infliction of physical pain rather than words. (When we encourage children to "use your words" we are trying to discourage precisely this kind of acting-out behavior.) All of the 13 cases reviewed for this book were abused by their parents or bullied by schoolmates. Luke Woodham was bullied from a very early age by his older brother and his mother, and later by his schoolmates.

The second experience in Athens' theory is the witnessing of a close friend or family member being abused, as when a crowd of children observe a member of their clique being bullied without intervening, or when a child is forced to watch his father beat his mother or a sibling, or overhear such an ordeal, but is unable to intercede on her behalf. The emotional and psychological toll of being a bystander to bullying has become a subject of study over the last few decades. Bystanders suffer from guilt over the vicarious satisfaction they might have gotten from the bullying and from their own reluctance to intervene. They may suffer survivor guilt, believing that they should have been the victims. While people assume that getting beat up is more hurtful than observing it, both experiences can be devastating. "The worst part of both . . ." Athens writes, "is the twisted feelings and thoughts which can linger on in a disordered state . . ." long after the experience has ended. The reaction of Wilson Naneng, who witnessed the Evan Ramsey shooting, is an example of how seriously a bystander can be affected. Naneng was consumed with guilt because he had done nothing to stop the shootings, and also experienced survivor guilt. While trying to deal with these feelings, he expressed violent impulses *toward himself*, rather than against others, cutting himself with knives, gnawing at himself, and attempting suicide by hanging.

The third experience is falling under the influence of a violence coach, a close friend, parent, parental figure, or other influential member of the candidate's immediate social network who advocates violence as the most reliable way of attaining what one wants, of settling disputes, of maintaining one's dignity, and gaining the respect of others. It is advocated as the best problem-solving strategy, superior to discussion, mediation by an adult, transferring the problem to enforcers of adult justice such as teachers or police, and so forth.

The existence of a second teen playing this kind of role was suggested by the *New York Times*, in a study conducted on the anniversary of the Columbine High School shooting. The *Times* staff, examining a database of 100 rampage shootings that occurred over a 50-year period, found that, unlike adult rampage killers who operated in isolation and secrecy, school-age rampage killers often had peers ". . . goading, sometimes even collaborating" in their crime.

In SR shootings, the violence coach is often an older and seemingly more savvy adolescent who may be motivated by a desire to express his own aggression through a proxy. The peer who plays the role of the violence coach is often difficult to identify *post hoc*. After the shooting he may "forget" that he had any association with the crime; he may admit that while he encouraged the candidate to commit a multiple murder, he had been joking all along; he may argue that threatening to shoot people is a common form of hyperbole and camaraderie in their clique, or that he never believed the candidate would go through with it.

In the case of Luke Woodham, Grant Boyette played the violence coach. He was older, charismatic, worldly, and successful—at least relative to the other members of the group. He taught Luke that the best solution to any problem, from his girlfriend jilting him to his mother's refusal to lend him the car, was murder. In the case of Evan Ramsey, James Randall encouraged him to redirect his suicidality—his aggressive impulses toward himself—into aggression toward classmates and teachers. While Randall did not endorse violence as the best solution for every eventuality (as far as we know), he did suggest that a multiple murder would make Evan world famous, solving the problem at hand, namely creating significance in a life that seemed little more than an exercise in human misery. In the case of Wayne Lo, he and his friends often discussed shooting other students and advocated violence as a solution to a range of problems. In the case of the Columbine High School shooting, discussed in the next chapter, Eric Harris appears to have coached Dylan Klebold through acts of escalating violence. The fact that Harris chose to participate in each of these acts, including a final act of suicidal violence, did not diminish his role as violence coach. In the case of Michael Carneal (Case 10), a group of boys, some older and more sophisticated, who played role-playing games and believed in the occult, hinted that Michael could join their group if he killed students in the morning prayer group. Violence would solve the problem of social isolation.

And what about Brenda Spencer? Did the Christmas gift of a rifle and ammunition from her father constitute violence coaching?

While according to Athens, the first three experiences—abuse, the witnessing of abuse, and being coached in violence—may occur in any sequence, the next experience, a crisis of identity, must follow. I have discussed Erikson's contention that the primary crisis of adolescence is laying the foundation of an adult identity. Adopting an identity that justifies or even glamorizes extreme violence as a way of righting the wrongs a child has endured, offers an ameliorative way of thinking about previous indignities, as well as providing hope about the future. (e.g., *Never again will I have to experience the shame of doing nothing while I am bullied, or observe another being bullied. The next time it happens, I will hurt or kill the aggressor. When people see who I have become, they will treat me with respect.*) Models for these violent identities are always available, in the real-life presence of tough neighborhood teens and adults, and in the glamorized criminals of movies, TV shows, rap songs, and music videos. Because adopting such an identity means violating society's norms, and putting at risk one's "physical safety, freedom, and psychological well-being," the candidate does not make this decision lightly. He reflects on it at length, as one might consider any voluntary, profound life-change. When the decision to engage in violence is made, it is a kind of awakening. The candidate decides to initiate his first violent event (and in the case of SR shooters, his last outside prison walls), but only

> . . . if he deems it absolutely necessary for the well-being of his body and mind and if he believes he has at least some chance of success . . . the subject has now reached the plateau in his development where he is ready and willing to injure badly or even kill someone, should the proper circumstances arise.

For nearly all SR shooters, this crisis takes the form of a period of introspection, sometimes more than a year in duration, during which time the candidate fills journals with soul-searching, immerses himself in media that suggests violent yet glamorous role possibilities, and spends hours on the phone with friends processing his future plans and the advisability of violence as a coping strategy.

The violent event is, in the cases described in this book, the SR shooting; and the candidate is assured of success because, as we have seen time and again, the process of sneaking a gun into a public building and opening fire on unarmed, unsuspecting children requires neither intellect, nor courage, nor cunning. There are further stages to Athens' scheme of socialization into violent behavior, but for SR shooters, these stages take place after incarceration or are avoided by suicide and, as such, are beyond the scope of this book.

Late at night, while Luke was lying in bed, the demons would appear to him, often exhorting him to kill. They came in two types: one satanic, hunched over, dressed in red cloaks, with spikes jutting from their bald heads and glowing eyes; the other angelic, airy and beautiful to behold. If he believed that the demons were illusions caused by the play of light in his room, a colored bulb refracted by a hanging bauble; or if they were the visions that sometimes accompany the descent into sleep—*hypnogogia*, they are called—they would be hallucinations, and of minor concern; but if he believed that the demons were actual beings bringing assignments from his spiritual master, that would be evidence of psychotic thinking, a condition that usually draws attention to itself, and makes survival outside of a psychiatric hospital difficult or impossible.

If Luke had experienced a break with reality, no one noticed or called attention to it, but there might have been reasons for that. He avoided his mother and brother when possible. He spent most of his time with Delbert Shaw, who may have shared his crazy beliefs, and Grant Boyette, who pretended to share them in order to accomplish his own ends. During Luke's infrequent appearances at school, he was so odd, disagreeable, and generally frightening that his teachers kept their distance. As for any others he might have come in contact with, Luke's psychoses involved only a wrinkle in the consensual reality of Pearl, Mississippi, where visitations by angels and demons were often sensed by the evangelical public, if not actually seen.

Donnie Brooks had used his father's credit card to purchase a stereo system, a new computer, and parts and accessories for his car. The debt, between ten and fifteen thousand dollars, was a burden for his father, a member of the Pearl Fire Department. Among the punishments meted out was an 8:00 PM curfew for months to come. Grant, furious to learn that his "army" had been reduced by one, decided to kill Donnie's father. He and the others hatched a plan to coat the doorknobs in the Brooks' home with a fat soluble poison of their own concoction that would seep into the victim's blood stream through his skin. It would appear as though his father had suffered a heart attack and nobody would be the wiser. When Donnie realized that they were serious, he got scared. After hearing about the killing of Sparkle, he believed that Luke would do anything Grant suggested. It was one thing to fantasize about revenge, another to kill one's father, particularly since, aside from the credit card theft, he and Donnie had a pretty good relationship. On June 11, 1997, Donnie made an appointment with a Rankin County Youth Court officer, and told him all about the Kroth, the names of the members, and the plot against his dad. The confession had an evangelical quality.

> Where I went wrong is I stopped following God. My life had hit an all time low. Instead of asking God for help, or my friends and family for help, I listened to [others] . . . that would be interested in my soul in exchange for money or whatever I wanted. I said no. But things got worse and Satan got me when I wasn't looking.

It is unclear whether the court took any action, whether information about the cult traveled beyond the walls of youth court.

That summer, Luke, buoyed by his new position of importance with the Kroft, tried to rekindle relations with Christy Menefee. According to Christy's friend, April Evans, Luke began stalking her and on several occasions threatened "to put a bullet" in her head if she didn't date him. Christy didn't take his threats seriously.

When school began again in September, Grant was visiting so often that Luke left the door unlocked for him, to his mother's displeasure. Around 7:00 PM on Sunday, September 28, Lucas Thompson dropped by Luke's house. They ordered a "bunch of pizzas" and Luke described how he was going to kill his mother so he could take her car to school. He would use his brother's gun to shoot Christy and some others. No exit strategy was needed. "I figure I'll be in a shootout with the cops," he told Lucas, "and die."

On Tuesday, November 30, Luke asked his mother if he could borrow the car. When she refused, citing the usual reasons—that Luke had miserable eyesight and no driver's license—he ran up to his room, slammed the door and remained there the rest of the day and night. That evening he called Lucas and whispered that he was going ahead with it. With a knife, he replied when Lucas asked him how he would do it.

It was dark when the alarm woke him at 5:00 AM the next morning, October 1, the one-year anniversary of his breakup with Christy. He crept down to the kitchen and slid the butcher's knife out of the drawer. Returning to his bedroom, he took a pillow and, on impulse, his aluminum baseball bat. As he emerged from his room, he was surprised to see his mother, whom he had assumed would still be asleep, dressed in her pink jogging outfit, walking toward the kitchen. In his confession, he said that he sneaked into her bedroom and killed her in her sleep, but the evidence showed unmistakably that he first attacked her in the hall. She broke free of him, ran back to her room and tried to shut the door. She was a strong woman, only 50, five-foot-eight and 145 pounds, but Luke forced his way in, knocking over an ironing board. He smashed some of the furniture with the bat while Mary Anne huddled on the bed. He stabbed and bludgeoned her repeatedly. She fought for her life and pleaded for mercy. Finally he suffocated her with the pillow. The coroner's report described a crushed jaw, a brain contusion, seven stab wounds, and eleven slashes to the body. A rape kit done after Luke's arrest showed that intercourse had not taken place.

Nine months later Luke told a jury that the morning of the murder he had been awoken by visions of red-cloaked demons with glowing eyes. He told the court that he recalled taking a knife, a baseball bat, and a pillow to his mother's room while hearing the voice of an older teenager in his head, goading him on. He had no recollection of killing her. "I just closed my eyes and fought with myself because I didn't want to do any of it. When I opened my eyes, my mother was lying in her bed, dead."

After the murder, he cleaned the blood stains off the walls, washed his jeans and bloody towels in the washing machine, showered, and cleaned and bandaged the knife cuts he had gotten on his hands during the struggle. In the bedroom, he composed a last will and testament five pages in length.

> I, Luke Woodham, being of sound mind and body, will to Grant Boyette my books. To Lucas Thompson: My guitar and amplifier and their equipment . . . I also leave my writings of philosophy and poetry to Grant Boyette. They are parts of me and must be published as pieces of my life. Also, to Grant Boyette, I will all my cassette tapes.

He justified his crime as revenge for being teased.

> Throughout my life I was ridiculed. Always beaten, always hated. Can you, society, truly blame me for what I do? Yes, you will, the ratings wouldn't be high enough if you didn't, and it wouldn't make good gossip for all the old ladies.
>
> I am the hatred in every man's heart! I am the epitomy [sic] of all evil! I have no mercy for humanity, for they created me, they tortured me until I snapped and became what I am today!

He exhorted his imagined audience to hate, encouraged self-improvement through education, and evoked Nietzsche.

> Hate until you can't hate anymore. Then learn, read poetry, books, philosophy books, history books, science books, autobiographies and biographies. Become a sponge for knowledge. Study the philosophy of others and condense the parts you like as your own. Make your own rules. Live by your own laws. For now, truly, you should be at peace with yourself. Live your life in a bold new way. For you, dear friend, are a Superman.

Like other school rampage killers, he found it important to leave written documentation of his sanity.

> I am not insane. I am angry. This world shit on me for the final time. I am not spoiled or lazy, for murder is not weak and slowwitted. Murder is gutsy and daring.

The statement about murder being "gutsy and daring" caught the fancy of the print media and was widely quoted.

People like me are mistreated every day. I do this to show society "push us, and we will push back." I suffered all my life. No one ever truly loved me. No one ever truly cared about me.

I only loved one thing in my whole life and that was Christina Menefee. But she was gone a way from me, I tried to save myself with [name redacted], but she never cared for me.

As it turns out she made fun of me behind my back while we were together. And all throughout my life I was ridiculed. Always beat on, always hated.

The document continues in the vein for several more pages, ending, "Wednesday 1, 1997, shall go down in history as the day I fought back."

Having completed his will, or "manifesto" as the press referred to it, he called Grant to tell him of the kill. They were interrupted by a call-waiting beep. It was Lucas, wanting to know if Luke had done what he had vowed to do. Luke replied in the affirmative, in a voice that was teary and less determined than the night before.

Luke got his father's .30-.30 Marlin hunting rifle from the attic, and filled the pockets of his trench coat with shells. Because Mary Anne wasn't available to drive him to school, he had to drive himself. He had little experience behind the wheel. Several early-rising neighbors heard his tires squealing as he over-accelerated, and saw him backing erratically out of the driveway, crushing shrubbery and nearly crashing into a fence.

Luke arrived at Pearl High School at 7:55 AM, parked in front of the main entrance and sat in the car, watching the teenagers crowd into the building. Many of them were coming from early morning prayer meetings and carrying bibles under their arms. After a few moments he got out of the car with four of his notebooks and walked into the Commons, a large, open area bounded by the cafeteria on one side and administrative offices on the other. There, by design or coincidence, he found Justin Sledge and gave him the notebooks of his writings, making him promise to pass them along to Grant Boyette. Later Justin told the court that he guessed what Luke was planning then and there, because of his odd behavior, and fled to the library for protection, shepherding some of his close friends along with him, and muttering oblique warnings about their safety.

Luke returned to his car, put on the trench coat and hid the rifle in its folds.

Chip Smith, a substitute teacher, was talking to Christy Menefee and her best friend, Lydia Kaye Dew, Lea Ann Dew's younger sister, about visiting the Mississippi State Fair, which was in session that week. "I heard a 'boom'," Smith said, "and she [Christy] dropped. She was alert and still talking about going to the fair. She was trying to talk to someone else, I don't know who. Then she stopped and her eyes rolled back in her head."

Luke turned to Lydia Kaye and shot her in the head. Lydia was a competitive weight lifter who could bench press 110 pounds, and was known affectionately to her friends as "Taz" because, like Christy, she loved the Looney Tunes character. Her parents remembered her ability to see the best in people and her forgiving nature. Her stepfather, Mike Long, said of her, "She'd probably be the first one to hug Luke's neck and say, 'I know you didn't mean to do it.' That was the kind of person she was."

Many had thought, at first, that the gun was some kind of joke. Now they knew it was not. Luke moved through the Commons, firing randomly while students and teachers hid or fled. Some screamed, some wept. Others stayed silent, hoping not to draw his attention. Assistant principal Joel Myrick described Luke as being utterly calm and composed, shooting, ejecting the spent shells, and thumbing fresh rounds into the side port of the rifle as he proceeded. Because his eyesight was poor, and he had never handled a gun before, the carnage was less than it might have been.

Deekpika Dhawan was standing next to Christina and Lydia when they were shot. In her frenzy to get away, she ran into a wall, at the same time experiencing a sharp pain in her left shoulder. She reached the girls' bathroom, where she huddled, crying. Not until the shooting had stopped did she realize that her arm was awash in blood. She was treated and released from Methodist Medical Center in Jackson on the same day. Two days later, she was still deeply disturbed. Every time she closed her eyes, she saw the same sequence of images: "I see his face, I see black, I see the rifle, I see Christina falling on the floor." She admitted that she was terrified of returning to school.

Jerry Safley, a linebacker on the Pearl High Pirates who had turned 17 the day before, was wounded in both legs while shielding his girlfriend from gunshots. According to several witnesses, Luke shot him and then hurried over to apologize. With his poor eyesight, he had mistaken him for Kyle Foster, the mayor's son, a tight end on the football team, whom he had intended to shoot because, according to different sources, he was a high profile target who would garner attention, or because they had gotten into a pushing match in September, or because he was a typical, popular "Johnny Footballer," as jocks are called in that part of he country, and thus a representative of the group who had tormented him all his life. In fact, the mayor's son was stuck in traffic and didn't reach the school until after Luke had been apprehended. Safley was treated at Rankin Medical Center and released the same day.

Alan Westbrook, a senior, heard Luke shout at him, "You turned your back on us," before shooting him in the hip. He fell and couldn't get up. The sensation ". . . was like there were a thousand ants all over my legs." While trying to flee, Denise Magee, a sophomore, was knocked to the floor by a bullet to the left side of her stomach. Joni Palmer, a freshman, was shot in the right hip. Robert Harris, Jr., also a freshman, was shot several times in the left calf, a sensation he likened to being "kicked very hard." Stephanie Wiggins, a sophomore, was shot in the left hip. While surgeons cleaned her wound in the Rankin Medical Center ER, her mother, Laurie Brown, paced the hallway waiting for news. "This is a nightmare," she said. "Every morning I tell them I love them, I hug them and tell them to do good. This was just like any other morning at home." Some of the wounded were discharged the same day. Miraculously, all were back at their homes by Thursday.

When Luke ran out of shells and had to reload, another student, Jason Barton, tackled and tried to subdue him. Luke, who was bigger, pulled free and fled the building.

Assistant principal Joel Myrick, working in his office off the Commons area, had been a commander in the National Guard, and recognized the sounds coming from the commons as rifle shots. First he herded students into his office and locked them inside, then he went after the shooter. Reluctant to confront Luke empty-handed, Myrick ran out to the parking lot, took the .45 caliber pistol out of the glove compartment of his truck, and loaded one bullet. On his way back, he saw Luke leaving the building at a rapid walk, and shouted for him to stop. Luke looked back, then hurried to his mother's car. He gunned the engine and tried to drive away, almost colliding with Justin Barnett, a junior, who was just arriving. Justin described what happened next:

> This white car was spinning out and going crazy. I stopped and put my car in reverse . . . I was blocking the road. His tires were spinning. He shot straight backward. He was trying to find a way out, and the only way was going through the grass. But he couldn't get any traction . . .

Myrick ran to the driver's side of the car. "I could see that he still had both hands on the steering wheel," Myrick said, "so I knew he wasn't holding a weapon. I told him to put his hands up and get out of the car, which he did . . . I told him to lie down on the ground. I pulled his jacket over his head and put my foot on his back. I kept him like that until the police arrived a few minutes later."

While they waited, Luke pleaded for leniency by reminding Myrick that he had delivered a pizza to him the night before, and had discounted the price.

Myrick was astonished by the inappropriateness of the remark. He asked Luke, over and over again, why he had gunned down other students.

"I've been wronged," Luke replied. "The world has wronged me and I just couldn't take it any more."

"Well, wait until you get to Parchman," Myrick said, invoking the legendary Mississippi Delta prison.

While Myrick was praised for his courage, and for saving lives—there were still unfired rounds in the rifle—he also received a mild scolding from Jim Hemphill, spokesperson of the State Department of Education, who reminded the public that it was "against the law to have a gun on any campus in any school district." Bill Dodson, the district superintendent, said, "We feel all right about it, since he had it in his car (sic)." Later, when Myrick was interviewed by the press, he recalled that he didn't regularly keep his pistol in the glove compartment. He had put it there in preparation for a weekend visit out of town and had forgotten to remove it. In fact a careful reading of the law revealed that adults could legally keep guns in their cars on a school campus as long as they refrained from "brandishing" them.

As Roy Dampier, the arresting officer, was driving Luke to the station house, he noticed him removing the tape from his palms. How had he gotten those cuts on his hands?

"Killing my mom," Luke responded in a low voice, without much emotion.

Police were immediately dispatched to Luke's home, where his mother's body was found, a blood-soaked pillow over her face, her chest and arms covered with stab and slash wounds.

At the station house Luke was charged with three counts of murder and six counts of aggravated assault. He was taken to a day room for questioning. Having waived his rights to a lawyer, he wrote a statement in his own hand describing his actions that morning from the time he left home until the time of his arrest. He accurately recalled the order of events, whom he had shot, and the circumstances of his arrest. The handwriting deteriorated as he wrote, and his signature at the bottom of the page was almost illegible. After mug-shots were taken, he agreed to a videotaped interview. The camera shows him sitting in front of the office doorway, barefoot, his left ankle resting on his right knee, his hands folded in his lap. He is wearing dark pants, a dark t-shirt over a light t-shirt, and glasses with black frames and thick lenses. He describes killing his mother in a matter-of-fact tone. But when the investigator asks him why he did it, and he must explain that she never loved him, that she called him "fat" and "stupid" and "lazy," and swore he would never amount to anything, his voice catches in his throat, his eyes fill with tears, he struggles to find the words. Later in the interview, the questioner probes to determine if Luke was psychotic. Irked, he replies, "I am not insane, sir. I knew what I was doing. I was just pissed at the time."

The students had been scheduled to take standardized tests that day, those tests schools give at regular intervals to evaluate teaching effectiveness, but the principals of the junior high and the high school decided to cancel ". . . because there was too much activity." High school students were sent home as were junior high students, so they could be with their families. When the students finally took the test a few weeks later, their scores had declined a half point, or ten percent, from the prior year (Pearl used the "Iowa" tests which are scored on a scale of one to five). It is not unusual for traumatic events to significantly impact learning outcomes. Such declines help us understand why poor urban children living with constant violence score lower on such tests than those in non-violent neighborhoods.

That night four of the Baptist churches in the community held special services for teens and adults. "The service really calmed me," said one 14-year-old girl whose sister's best friend had been killed. "I am feeling a lot better about it all now." Another student felt less angry afterwards, and was glad she had attended. In the days to come, people softened the edges of their anger and grief by planting memorial trees, donating blood, installing plaques with the names of the deceased in front of the school, and adorning the "Pearl High School" sign with poems, stuffed animals, and balloons in a style of extemporaneous memorializing that was made familiar by the adornment of the fence surrounding the Oklahoma City Federal Office Bulding following its 1995 bombing.

Luke Woodham was the lead story on *NBC Nightly News* that evening. The shooting, nine months after the Evan Ramsey shooting, 21 months after the Barry Loukaitis shooting (Overview, Case 7), and 24 months after the Jamie Rouse shooting (Overview, Case 6), suggested an escalating pattern of violence. Incidents were occurring more closely together and claiming more victims. Newscasters were talking about an "epidemic," using the word in its loosest sense, since there was no real statistical evidence of contagion; no understandable cause, course or cure; no known risk factors. The Pearl NBC affiliate received requests for coverage from NBC, CNN, and the BBC. The print media was more conservative; the *Boston Globe* and the *Washington Post* both placing the story on page three of the first section, and the *New York Times* relegating it to page 12, but devoting four columns and a multi-column picture to the subject.

On Thursday morning, the day after the shooting, a note was found pinned to the entrance of the school, a computer printout with a variety of

Gothic-style fonts, and a vertical lightening bolt page center, not unlike the symbol used by the Nazi SS but pointing downward.

CHRISTINA
They took Alan, Wes, Justin, Donnie
Lucas, Grant, and Luke.
This is what happens.
We told you not to leave A1 Or
There's be some shit.
They've removed ¼ of our army, but
They'll pay soon enough.
THE END IS NEAR ... APOCALYPSE NOW.
Sincerely,
The Alliance of the
Immortalz
Think what you want-Lydia was no accident

The note, with its implication that the carnage might continue, shocked and demoralized the community. The night before, Merrell Jolly, the Woodham's observant and talkative neighbor, had called the district attorney, a man named John Kitchens, about Grant Boyette's daily visits to the Woodham home and the killing of Sparkle. Police had found satanic posters in Luke's room and occult writings. Students, during their counseling sessions, had spoken in hushed tones about a group of boys that cast spells and tortured animals, and grief counselors had encouraged them to pass the information along to the police. The more Kitchens heard, the more certain he became that he was investigating the work of a cult, but despite the wealth of information being unearthed, he was not ready to make an arrest.

The school was closed for the rest of the week, with plans to resume classes on Monday and restore the routine as soon as possible. Grief counselors, imported from local hospitals and mental health agencies, met with children in the high school gym during the hiatus. An article in the local paper helped parents recognize the symptoms of trauma in their children. Be good listeners, the article advised. Encourage them to talk and let them know it is okay to attend counseling, should they desire it.

Justin Sledge fell into the role of Luke's apologist. He appeared on the *WLBT-Channel 3 News* out of Jackson, and on the nationally syndicated news show, *Hard Copy*. He spoke to the local paper, the *Clarion-Ledger*. He told the media that the shooting was not the result of a failed romance, or a parents' messy divorce, but rather a society that "put down the thinkers and the true geniuses of the world and replaced them with men whose strength is physical strength and physical abilities." Thursday night he interrupted a candlelight vigil that was being conducted in front of the school. Four hundred people listened, first in amazement, then in irritation, and finally in anger as Justin began a "disruptive, rambling monologue," using "emotionally charged language," defending his friend and blaming society. "Things have to change," he told the crowd. "My friend did this under my nose. He went mad because of society. We, as a society, must change." While a minority appeared interested in what Sledge had to say, most were relieved when he left. Students felt "he had no business justifying what Luke did," and accused him of just wanting attention. Roy Balentine, the Pearl High principal, though tempted to press charges for disturbing the peace, gave Sledge four days suspension instead.

Unlike the other homes in Pearl, which were festooned with blue ribbons in memory of Christy and Lydia Kaye, Luke's home was cordoned off with the yellow tape of a crime scene. Bright-colored wax pooled on the driveway where candles had burned all night in memory of Luke's mother, Mary Anne. A pink ribbon-trimmed wreath that stood in the front yard read, "In remembrance of Mary Anne Woodham," and was signed "Kwick as a Wink," the nickname of a friend whose identity was not made public.

Monday morning seven police officers and several pastors from the community churches were stationed around the school, welcoming returning students. One of the teachers stood at the entrance, encouraging students to take the last few steps over the threshold. While some students had dropped by for counseling on Thursday and Friday, others had kept their distance and remained wary and undecided. Latasha Tucker, a senior, said, "I've got butterflies in my stomach. I'm scared to go in. I'm afraid it could happen again." Another senior, Aretha Ruffin, admitted that she was "shaking" and felt the need for more security, including metal detectors. Brook Cannon, another senior, said "I don't want to be here. It's too weird for me."

Teachers kept to the regular schedule as planned but many left time for open discussion of the shooting. Survival needs, such as food, shelter, and *safety*, must be attended to before people can concentrate on higher needs, such as learning, and students did not yet feel safe. On the other hand, being in school provided a stable, structured, familiar environment, and let them join in a community of grieving. The value of this was reflected in the high attendance figures: only 100 of the 1,039 students were absent, slightly more than average, although a number of students found themselves too discomforted to finish the school day. According to the protocol for the day, they signed out early and left the campus with a parent. The missed days were made up at the end of the semester by adding an extra hour on seven consecutive school days, rather than losing a holiday, or adding a day at the end of the year.

Monday evening, Grant Boyette, Donnie Brooks, Jr., and Justin Sledge were arrested at their homes. The next morning Wesley Brownell, Lucas Thompson, and Delbert Shaw were arrested during their first period classes and led away in handcuffs. They were accused of conspiring to murder students at Pearl High School. Grant Boyette and Donnie Brooks were also charged with plotting to murder Donnie's father.

The latter charge was made despite Donnie's confession the previous June, suggesting that Kitchens and his office had never been informed of it. This does not necessarily reflect poor police work as much as the inherent difficulty in determining the importance of one relatively innocuous interview among hundreds of others that may have involved offenses such as child abuse, domestic violence, rape, and murder. There was no implication of police negligence, Kitchens told a press conference when the original report surfaced, since Donnie's confession contained no information about the Pearl High School shooting or anything else that suggested anyone was in eminent danger. Donnie's attorney pointed out that no attempt had been made on his father's life, and that his father "fully supports him and stands by him and doesn't believe the charge."

All six boys pleaded not guilty. Bail was set at one million dollars per charge because of the serious nature of the crime, the risk of flight, and the protection of the community as well as the protection of the suspects themselves.

The string of arrests reignited the fears of the community. A local journalist described it eloquently: "If Wednesday's shooting rampage . . . saddened the community, the latest arrests may have broken its collective heart and stolen what was left of the town's innocence." Lea Ann Dew said, "I'm scared of everything. I don't know who else was in the group and if there are any left." Bill Buckley, a parent of a Pearl student, said, "It is a terrible situation. You don't realize who is involved or if there are more. The only thing to do is pray." Jeaneen Rocha, whose four children attended Pearl schools, admitted that she was scared. "I don't feel in my heart that this is the end of it." School officials tried to be reassuring but many of the parents felt that classes had been resumed prematurely and that students could not learn in an atmosphere of such fear and uncertainty.

This news of the Kroth, with its aura of satanism and the supernatural, rocketed the case back into the national media. *NBC Nightly News* ran a two-minute segment. CNN covered the story periodically throughout the day on Tuesday, and *CBS Morning News* reported it on Wednesday. The *New York Times* printed a quarter page story—"Southern Town Stunned by Arrests in Murder Plot"—on page 16 of the first section on Thursday, October 9. The *National Enquirer* interviewed Pearl residents for a four-page spread on "Kids Who Kill."

In a preliminary hearing, Boyette's attorney painted a benevolent picture of the Kroth as a group of kids who banded together because they had the common experience of being picked on and excluded. They played *Star Wars* role-playing games and Boyette was the Game Master because of his charisma and fertile imagination. While Boyette may have encouraged Luke to cause trouble at school, he never imagined the boy would go this far. Members of the community vouched for the rest of the group. Lea Anne Dew described them as "gung-ho Christians" with the exception of Justin Sledge. Donnie Brooks, Jr. was particularly well-liked by the neighbors. None of them had a bad reputation expect Delbert Shaw, who was "in and out of trouble." Even he seemed to have a good side. While he had blown up the neighbors' mail boxes, he had repaired each and every one of them.

On Thursday night, October 9, following an hour-long meeting between Kitchens and Donnie's attorney, his bond was suspended and he was freed on his own recognizance. On Friday, Wesley's lawyer spent the day wrangling with Kitchens, and by evening Wesley had been released on a $50,000 bond. Shaw was released on Saturday, October 11, on a $3,000 bond, but was re-arrested a week later, in the middle of the night, for driving erratically with beer in the car. Justin Sledge was released on Tuesday, November 25, on a $50,000 bond. While free on bail, the boys were barred from speaking to the media or to the other defendants, returning to school, or leaving the state. Lucas Thompson, because he was a minor, was transferred to Youth Court jurisdiction and moved to the county's youth detention center, where subsequent proceedings were confidential. Two months later, on December 16, Circuit Judge Robert Goza released Grant Boyette on a $75,000 bond, but because of a technicality Grant was back behind bars by the end of January.

Pearl became intrigued by satanism and cults. The *Clarion-Ledger* ran articles explaining how parents could tell if their sons or daughters were involved in cult activities, and the town government hired William Reisman, an authority on the subject, to conduct a seminar for Pearl parents.

Three months after Luke's shooting, Michael Carneal (Overview, Case 10), a student at Heath High School in Kentucky, brought a gun to school, and shot at a student prayer circle in the lobby, killing three girls and wounding five. This case had much in common with Luke's: it occurred in a small Christian community; among the victims were females who were perceived as having rejected the shooter; and the shooter was, or longed to be, a member of a group of outcasts who imagined they had supernatural powers. This group exploited him for their own amusement and as a proxy expresser of their rage. Principal Ballentine called his Kentucky counterpart to commiserate, prepare him for what lay in store, and describe how his community had responded to the crisis. The Pearl High student council sent Heath High a check for $650, and constructed a four-foot by three-foot wooden sympathy card signed by a number of students, bearing messages such as "Be strong and hang in there. We know exactly what you're going through." Coincidentally, both schools had a pirate for their mascot.

When teens returned to Pearl High School in the fall, they found that the program had been enriched with a conflict resolution curriculum, taught for ten minutes each day during the first two weeks of school, as well as a program in sensitivity training, to make students more aware of their environment, and to encourage them to tell teachers if their classmates were engaged in risk-taking behaviors such as using drugs, or carrying a weapon. In addition to fire drills, they had to participate in lock-down and evacuation drills, so they could respond quickly to other types of threats and emergencies.

Luke underwent a month-long psychiatric evaluation at the Mississippi State Hospital at Whitfield in December and returned to jail on January 22. His IQ was determined to be 115, in the high normal range. Dr. Chris Lott, a clinical psychologist who worked for the hospital, and frequently served as an expert witness in Mississippi cases involving insanity defenses, said of him, "It was my opinion that he was fabricating. It's a little bit stronger than exaggerating. I just didn't believe that he actually ever suffered from a delusional belief such that he saw demons or believed that demons were adversely influencing him." Dr. Michael Jepsen, a psychologist from Santa Fe, New Mexico, who had been hired by the defense, said that Luke was "a very psychologically disturbed youngster whose disturbed thinking and distorted reality left him helpless to judge the appropriateness of his own behavior, to appreciate the implications of his conduct, or to conform his conduct to the requirement of the law." Based on testing, he diagnosed Luke as having a borderline personality disorder (BPD). The reader will recall that this, like the narcissistic personality disorder, is one of the "dramatic" cluster described in Chapter 3. All the diagnoses within a cluster share certain characteristics—the lack of empathy for others, the tendency to over-dramatize a situation, behavior that is erratic and impulsive—yet they differ in emphasis, or "essential features" as the DSM refers to them. The essential features of the narcissistic personality disorder are "a pervasive pattern of grandiosity, need for admiration and lack of empathy," while the essential features of BPD are "instability of interpersonal relationships, self-image, and affects, and marked impulsivity. . . ." It should be noted that clinicians tend to use these diagnoses somewhat freely, often based on a gut response to the patient—a "flavor"—rather than a strict reliance on the DSM. The DSM acknowledges that the cluster system "has serious limitations and has not been consistently validated," so it is more of a measure "by thumb" than some finely calibrated caliper. Based on the available documentation for this case, Luke seems more narcissistic than borderline, but Dr. Jepson was probably privy to information that inclined his diagnosis toward BPD.

"It was my belief," Jepson told the court, "that Luke had been able to conceal his thinking and emotional difficulties by his isolation, essentially in retreating into his own head and not getting around situations that generated strong emotions. He was essentially a loner and used that as a way of trying to conceal his emotional problems."

Luke would be tried twice, the first time for the murder of his mother, the second for the deaths and the havoc he had caused during his shooting spree. Both trials were moved to the Neshoba County Courthouse in Philadelphia, Mississippi, because of the difficulty of finding an uncontaminated jury in Pearl, where nearly everyone knew someone who was personally involved in the incident. The first trial was scheduled for April 27, 1998, then postponed to June 1 because of the volume of forensic evidence, the number of witnesses to be prepped, and the sheer complexity of what had transpired.

During the five days of testimony, Luke was depicted by the defense as the psychologically damaged dupe of puppet-master Grant Boyette, and by the prosecution as a craven bloodthirsty killer. Doctors Lott and Jepsen presented their expert testimony regarding his sanity. Luke, who had seemed cold and remorseless in his television interviews, wept frequently during the trial, and sobbed when, during his closing argument, Assistant District Attorney Tim Jones said of him, "He's mean. He's hateful. He's bloodthirsty. He wanted to kill her. Murder was on the boy's mind." As if by divine will, a sudden thunderstorm crashed down on the courthouse during the jury's deliberation, knocking out the power and plunging them into semi-darkness. When the jury returned, less than three hours later, the spokesman read the verdict by the shafts of daylight that filtered in the courthouse windows. The insanity defense was rejected. Luke was found guilty of first-degree murder and sentenced to life imprisonment. As he was being led in manacles to the waiting patrol car, he called to the crowd of reporters, "I'm going to heaven now. Everything happens for a reason. It's God's will." Afterwards, one of the jurors, an elderly woman, exclaimed through her tears, "I never, never want to do this again."

Luke returned to trial on the following Monday, June 8, 1998, for the school shooting charges. He carried a bible with him and told the press outside the courthouse, "I have something to live for now." He claimed to have experienced a religious conversion in jail. Now he carried a bible with him everywhere and often quoted scripture, favoring passages about redemption.

Luke's lawyers proposed that they skip over descriptions of the shooting, including evidence that Luke himself fired the gun, and move directly to the discussion of his sanity, arguing that the emotions evoked would compromise the jurors' ability to reason clearly. Judge Richardson rejected the proposal, emphasizing the importance of them hearing the story from beginning to end, in all its emotional intensity.

One after another, students took the witness stand and described the events of the day. One of them likened it to a horror movie. Those who were wounded recounted their surgeries and physical therapy, their pain and fear. The arresting officers testified to Luke's apparent clarity about his acts. He was "pumped" on adrenaline, Detective Roy Dampler testified, but "calm and observant . . . he guessed we were going to lock him up in Parchman for the rest of his life for this. Then he laughed and said, 'Or the loony bin.'" One of the Rankin County sheriff's investigators answered questions about the Kroth, acknowledging that Grant Boyette had ordered Luke to kill other students, and that Luke had done as Grant commanded.

Doctors Lott and Jepsen again debated Luke's sanity, recapitulating their testimony from the previous trial. That afternoon, against the recommendations of his attorneys, Luke took the stand. He talked about how his life had deteriorated after his parents' divorce, how he felt like an "outcast" at school, how Christina Menefee had been the first person to ever accept him, and how he had been devastated by her rejection. "I didn't eat," he told the court between sobs. "I didn't sleep. I didn't want to live. It destroyed me." He told how Grant Boyette had lured him into his group, and had led him to believe that through the use of the occult, he could get Christy back, or wreak vengeance on her. He spoke of the car crash as a defining moment: "One second I was some kind of broken-hearted idiot, and the next second I had power over many things. My mind didn't know how to take it."

Shiela Henry, Christy Menefee's biological mother, drove up from her home in Louisiana to watch the trial. "He doesn't look like someone who killed somebody," she said when she saw Luke. "He looks like a kid off the street." She recalled thinking, *That's the little boy who thought he was God and took my child from me.* She reminded people that, contrary to reports in the press, Christy was never Luke's "girlfriend."

Of the members of the Kroth, only Grant Boyette, still being held in custody, could be located. He took the stand but invoked his constitutional right to remain silent during questioning.

The prosecution completed their case by showing the videotaped confession where Luke stated, "I knew what I was doing, I was just pissed at the time."

After five hours of deliberation, the jury found Luke guilty of all charges and gave him a life sentence for each murder plus twenty years for each of the seven aggravated assaults, 140 years altogether, all sentences to be served consecutively.

"I'm sorry for the people I killed and the people I hurt," he told those gathered in the courtroom. "The reason you don't see any more tears is I have been forgiven by God. If they could have given the death penalty in this case, I deserve it." Of Grant Boyette, he said, "He told me to kill my mom. He told me I had to get the gun and the car and go to school and get my revenge on Christy and cause a reign of terror."

Three days after his conviction, Luke was sent to the Central Mississippi Correctional Facility in Rankin, the processing and classification center for all the state's criminals, where he received a battery of psychological and physical tests, and then on to the state penitentiary at Parchman, the only maximum security facility in the state of Mississippi. This was the notorious Parchman Farm Prison of song and story, where Bukka White wrote the blues, where southern lawmen put a scare into Freedom Riders from up north while they awaited trial, where Vernon Presley served three years for forgery while his son Elvis was in diapers. There he would spend the rest of his life.

On Wednesday, July 22, Judge Robert Goza dismissed conspiracy charges against Delbert Shaw, Wesley Brownell, and Donald Brooks. Kitchens explained that "handling conspiracy cases is like walking through a minefield. I'm not saying these people are not involved in this, but it would not be the right thing to do to prosecute the case at this time." The pleasure of being freed was tinged with resentment. Brownell's lawyer, Wayne Milner, said that his client had been ". . . subjected to public scorn, criticism, ridicule, and hatred. I think it's a shame that he had to go through something like this. . . . He had absolutely nothing to do with any kind of crime or any attempt to hurt anyone." A few days before Christmas, 1998, a grand jury, after listening to a taped interview where Luke stated that Justin Sledge had nothing to do with the killings, refused to indict him for the accessory to murder charge. He was free of all criminal charges. "The isolation, fear, and utter hatred directed toward me were the things I remember most," Justin said afterwards. "Friends and school peers turned their backs on me, and I realized that a conviction in the eyes of my friends was a prison in itself." Justin, now 18, chose not to return to Pearl High for his senior year.

Of the Kroth, only Grant Boyette remained. His trial was moved to Warren County and postponed because of construction work on the courthouse and a busy trial calendar. It was rescheduled for February 28, in Biloxi, but at the last moment Grant, now 21, struck a deal with the prosecutors and changed his plea to guilty of conspiracy. Grant was sentenced to six months in a Regimented Inmate Discipline (RID) program to be followed by a five-year prison sentence. RID, a prison-based, boot-camp style program for young offenders, was supposed to teach respect for the law and self-discipline. If Grant completed it successfully, he could serve his five-year sentence as supervised probation outside prison walls. He could attend college, or seminary, marry, hold down a job, and live the life of a free man. "We would have liked to have had a better case . . ." Richard Mitchell, Rankin County's new district attorney said, apologizing for the brevity and leniency of the sentence. "We were having to rely on the word of a three-time convicted murderer . . . It's not very often that you can send a person to prison for talking."

Although the members of the Kroth were free, their parents remained entangled with the law. In 1998, Kaye Long, Lydia Dew's mother, filed a lawsuit naming the parents of Kroth members and the Pearl Public School District as defendants and claiming that they had been negligent in allowing her daughter's killing.

Robert Menefee couldn't go on living in Pearl because so many places and people reminded him of Christy. In the summer of 1998, he and his wife moved back to Florida. Later, Robert and Christy's lawyer, Robert Schwartz, promoted legislation that would allow prosecutors to seek the death penalty for any action that resulted in multiple homicides. It was to be called "Christy's Law." Parents who have lost a child to violence often pursue the passage of a law or policy that might prevent other parents from suffering the same kind of anguish, as a way of making sense of their loss.

At Parchman, Luke was imprisoned in a six-by-nine-foot cell in the notorious unit 32-C building. The building housed 1,000 maximum-security inmates including those on death row. There was no television or radio and little ventilation. Every month he was rotated to a new cell to foil attempts to tunnel out. The toilets often backed up, spilling sewage into the cells. But the main issue in the summer of 2000 was the heat. It was one of the hottest summers in Mississippi history and the plain box of a building was set out on a field of sun-baked clay with no trees or shrubs for shade. The prisoners' only relief came from electric fans purchased at the prison commissary. On May 28, as a result of two convicts using heat generated from an electrical outlet to form scraps of plastic into a handle for a tool used to facilitate their escape, Robert Johnson, the corrections commissioner, ordered all electrical outlets removed, rendering the fans useless. Prisoners began a hunger strike and when the warden refused to meet with them, they purposely stopped up the plumbing, forcing the toilets to overflow the cells and run into the corridors. The protesters were maced, beaten, and thrown in the "hole." The ACLU and other human rights groups brought the predicament to the attention of the public, and finally, on June 1, 2000, in response to outraged editorials, letters, and phone calls, Luke and more than 800 other inmates were moved to 400 cells in unit 29, which had been recently renovated. There he remains under more tolerable conditions, filing appeals and responding to torrents of mail from alienated teens around the country, many of whom find him heroic.

CASE 13: ERIC HARRIS AND DYLAN KLEBOLD: EVENTS LEADING TO THE COLUMBINE SHOOTING

Stigma / Relocation Stress

BACKGROUND OF THE KLEBOLD FAMILY

DYLAN BENNET KLEBOLD WAS DESCENDED on his mother's side from the Yassenoffs, a family of Russian-Jewish heritage who immigrated to the United States in the 1880s. Two cousins, Leo and Frank, settled in Columbus, Ohio in the first decade of the 20th century, and attended Ohio State University where Leo played for the Buckeyes and was named All-American. After a successful career in real estate, he devoted himself to philanthropy, establishing scholarships in art and technology, and endowing a chair in Jewish studies at Ohio State. When he died, he left most of his personal fortune, more than 13 million dollars, to a foundation established in his name. The local Jewish Community Center, the largest in Ohio, also bears his name.

Leo's son Milton (Dylan's grandfather) married Charlotte, a gentile who observed the Jewish traditions and, like the rest of the family, belonged to Temple Israel, the local Reform congregation. They raised their daughter Susan (Dylan's mother) and her siblings in the Jewish faith. Frank Yassenoff and his son, Solly (Skip), also married gentiles.

Susan Yassenoff, her older sister Diane, and her younger brother Philip grew up in Bexley, one of the most desirable suburbs of Columbus and the home of other well-known philanthropic Jewish families. A neighbor who knew them well described them as "wonderful, warm, and caring. The kids had a terrific family life." Susan graduated from the elite Columbus School for Girls in 1967 and went on to Ohio State University, where she majored in art education.

Dylan's paternal grandfather, William Klebold, worked as a sales manager with the Buckeye Brewing Company as a young man. His first son, Donald, was born in 1931. William later bought a hardware store in Holland, a working-class suburb of Toledo, with an apartment in the back for the family. He remarried, and Thomas, his second son (Dylan's father), was born in 1948. William died when Thomas was only 11 and Donald took over the task of fathering him. They moved to Sylvania, a more affluent suburb. Thomas graduated from Sylvania High School and went on to Wittenberg University in Springfield, Ohio, before transferring to Ohio State, where he met Susan.

Tom began his college studies as an engineering major, but later switched to art, and graduated with a major in sculpture. The couple married in 1971 in Columbus, the year Susan graduated, and they lived briefly in Bexley before moving on to Milwaukee, where Tom earned a master's degree in geophysics from Marquette University. A job with Phillips Petroleum necessitated a move to Oklahoma in the mid '70s. Later he worked for another Oklahoma-based oil company, Conoco. In 1980 Conoco moved the family to Lakewood, a suburb of Denver, where their first son, Byron was born. Dylan was born three years later. Thomas Klebold's love of literature, and perhaps a bit of pretension, was evident in his decision to name his sons after his favorite poets, Lord Byron and Dylan Thomas. Thomas started his own consulting firm but abandoned it when low oil prices ruined the market. In a mid-life career change he founded a mortgage management company, Fountain Real Estate. The success of this venture allowed him to move the family to Littleton, about ten miles to the south, to a newly-constructed home of wood and glass nestled at the base of a dramatic outcropping of rock. Susan Klebold rose from director of disability services at a local community college, where she found job placements for blind and disabled students, to a management position in Denver's state-wide community-college system. Their elder son, Byron, was popular and played varsity football. The Klebolds seemed to be successful at whatever they chose to do. One of Tom Klebold's hobbies was tinkering with old BMWs, and three of the five cars in the driveway were vintage BMWs, including Dylan's black 1982 model in which he commuted to school.

When they settled in Littleton, the Klebolds joined St. Philip Lutheran Church. Despite this, Susan continued to refer to herself as a Jew, and Dylan and his family held a Passover Seder on April 1, nineteen days before the shooting. Dylan, being the youngest, had the honor of asking the Four Questions, a pivotal part of the Passover ceremony, the dialogue between the father and the youngest son that begins, *Why is this night different from all other nights?* After the shooting, Dylan was given a Lutheran funeral, demonstrating the family's public or external commitment to the faith, if not their personal enthusiasm for it.

While observing antithetical religious practices is not uncommon among mixed-faith marriages, it has its ill-effects, particularly for adolescents who are struggling with the interlinked issues of integrity and identity. It often results, as Rabbi Jeffrey Goldwasser has written (2007), in feelings of guilt over behaving like an apostate (embracing two different belief systems, each of which forbids the other) or anger at one's parents for encouraging hypocritical behavior (*go through the motions, you don't have to mean it*) and self-contempt for obeying them.

In the videotaped self-interviews referred to as the "basement tapes," because Dylan and Eric recorded them in the Harrises' basement during the months before the shooting, Dylan complains that his extended family, his grandparents, uncles, and aunts, and older brother—but never his parents—treated him like an outcast.

Which side of the family was he referring to?

Was it the Yassenoffs who rejected him because he belonged to an Episcopal congregation? Or the Harrises, because he observed the Jewish traditions? Or did one or both sides of the family scapegoat him for reasons that had nothing to do with religion?

Whatever the case, confusion regarding religious affiliation does nothing to clarify an adolescent's struggle to find a religious identity, nor to build a sense of belonging to a particular group. Alienation, a sense of belonging, and the association with suicide have been discussed in previous chapters.

By nearly all accounts, Tom and Sue Klebold were attentive parents. Her cousin, Skip Yassenoff, said of her, "She was a nice, normal person." While he didn't talk to her frequently, the last few times he had phoned her she seemed to be ". . . the same sweet Susan I had known." Brooks Brown, a friend of Dylan's from kindergarten and chronicler of, and apologist for, Dylan's life and deeds, recalls Tom and Susan attending every game, assembly, and other activity that Dylan was involved in from first grade on. If Dylan and Byron both had activities at the same time, Tom would attend one and Sue the other. Tom, a liberal, supported gun control laws and both parents discouraged violence of any form in their home. "Dylan told me once," Brown wrote, "that he wasn't allowed to have any toy guns in the house. As we got older, his mom worried about the level of violence in the video games we were playing." James Garbarino, an authority on youth violence, was approached by the Klebolds' attorneys in June of 1999 following the publication of the book *Lost Boys: Why Our Sons Turn Violent and How We Can Save Them*. He and his sometimes writing partner, Claire Bedard, spent many hours with the Klebolds, conducting interviews that eventually inspired them to write their next book, *Parents Under Siege*. While their agreement with the Klebolds prohibited them from disclosing details about the interviews because of pending lawsuits, they did describe them in generalized terms.

> Sitting with Tom and Sue Klebold and their remaining son, Byron, in their home in the wake of the Columbine shootings was more than enough to reinforce our profound humility. Here were two loving and intelligent parents, who cared for their two boys, who spent time with them, and looked after them, yet who had lost their second-born son . . .
>
> . . . we can assert without a doubt that they [Dylan's parents] are good parents—attentive, involved, and loving...

Following an editorial about Columbine on the fifth anniversary of the shooting, Tom Klebold contacted its author, the *New York Times* columnist David Brooks, and apparently engaged him in a long telephone conversation. Following it, Brooks wrote another column describing Tom and Sue Klebold.

> They are a well-educated, reflective, highly intelligent couple (Dylan was named after Dylan Thomas). During our conversation they discussed matters between themselves, as well as answering my questions. Their son, by the way, is widely seen as the follower, who was led by Eric Harris into this nightmare.
>
> The Klebolds describe the day of the shootings as a natural disaster, as a "hurricane" or a "rain of fire." They say they had no intimations of Dylan's mental state. Tom, who works from home and saw his son every day, had spent part of the previous week with Dylan scoping out dorm rooms for college the next year.
>
> When they first heard about the shootings, it did not occur to them that Dylan could be to blame.
>
> They feel certain of one thing. "Dylan did not do this because of the way he was raised," Susan said. "He did it in contradiction to the way he was raised."

The day after the killings, nineteen of their neighbors left a sign on their gate saying, "Sue and Tom, we love you. Call us."

In the basement tapes Dylan says that his mother and father "always taught me self-awareness and self-reliance. I always loved you guys for that . . . I'm sorry I have so much rage . . . you can't understand what we feel, no matter how much you think you can." At another time Dylan described his relationship with his parents as "better than most kids," and characterized them as supportive, loving, dependable, and trustworthy.

Don Fleming, whose daughter was one of the shooting victims, was among their few critics. He grew incensed after reading a flattering portrait of them in the David Brooks' editorial. "For as highly educated as . . . [the Klebolds] are," Fleming wrote in response, "they thought this couldn't happen to their son. They're elitists. They thought this was something white trash would carry out." He stated that the Klebolds' and the Harrises' clueless state regarding their sons' lives was itself a form of bad parenting. Like Fleming, parents across the nation have expressed incredulity that the Klebolds and the Harrises could have lived in the same house with their sons and remained oblivious to their midnight forays, their construction of pipe bombs and grenades, and the accumulation of weapons and ammunition taking place under their noses. Fleming also criticized them for not acting more assertively when their son and Eric Harris were arrested for burglarizing a van a year before the shooting.

DYLAN KLEBOLD

Dylan Klebold, stretched out on the autopsy table, was 74.5 inches and weighed, 143 pounds. The coroner's report describes him as a "well-developed, well-nourished . . . white male appearing consistent with the stated age of 17." In his yearbook picture his hair is parted down the middle. He has a broad nose and a pleasant smile. In scraps of video tape from that period collected by the Jefferson County sheriff's office, he seems funny and glib, and reminds me of the character, Jeff Spicoli, played by Sean Penn in *Fast Times at Ridgemont High*.

Following his death, Dylan's parents told the police that he had been a gentle boy and had never shown any signs of having a violent nature. Dylan's uncle, Donald Klebold, said of him, "He was a very, very fine boy. He was very bright." About a year before the assault on the high school, Dylan and Eric broke into a parked van and stole some electrical equipment. Sue Klebold, asked to provide a description of her son for a professional psychosocial assessment prior to sentencing, sounded understandably peevish:

> Dylan is introverted and has grown up isolated from those who are different in age, culture, or other factors. He is often angry or sullen and [his] behaviors seem disrespectful and intolerant of others . . . [He] stays in his room constantly.

Randy Brown, Brooks' father, recalled Dylan in first grade. "[He] was the sweetest, cutest kid you'd ever meet. He was really shy, though, and it would take him fifteen or twenty minutes to warm up to us every time he came over, even though we knew him and we were close to him." Judy Brown, Brooks' mother, recalled Dylan as being an introverted, sensitive child who worried too much about what people thought about him. "As Dylan got older, he never told his parents he was being teased. Never. He kept it all inside." When he did express his anger, it could be sudden and frightening. Brooks recalled a schoolyard fight with Dylan in second grade. Although he had known Dylan for over two years, "that fight was the first time I ever saw Dylan's temper. Because Dylan internalized things so much, he would let his anger build up within him until one little thing finally set it off. When that happened it was like an explosion."

Dylan's school history, as related by Brown, is a story of a pathologically shy boy being bullied, the bullying growing worse by the year, achieving a kind of *Lord of the Flies* intensity by high school. Also disturbing is Brown's description of a second grade teacher scapegoating Dylan and himself, and the corrupt practices in assigning students to a middle school program for the academically gifted. Such events, unimportant though they may seem in retrospect, contribute to a child's cynicism about the workings of the adult world.

Dylan first met Eric Harris at Ken Caryl Middle School, the ambience of which Brown likened to ". . . a prison yard. . . . You find a gang of people to hang out with so that the other 'gangs' leave you alone. . . ." They became friends based on their mutual enthusiasm for computers, video games, and baseball, but they did not become inseparable until high school.

ERIC HARRIS

Eric Harris at 17 was five foot eight and a half inches and between 135 and 140 pounds according to the coroner's report. He kept his hair close-cut, in a military style. In photographs his face is narrow and he has a cynical, even caustic expression. In adolescence, he was drawn to the works of ideologues like Ayn Rand, Nietzsche, and Hitler, and embraced the gamut of fascist and racist ideas (despite the fact that his closest friend was half-Jewish). Senior year he took first period bowling (in lieu of gym) and he would shout "Heil Hitler!" whenever he rolled a strike. He had studied German for years, and was a fan of German techno/metal, particularly the bands Rammstein and KMFDM. Brooks Brown, who had known him since seventh grade, told *Time* magazine, "Eric was an incredible individualist.

Charismatic, an eloquent speaker, well-read, the kind of guy who could bull-shit for hours about anything and be witty and brilliant."

The Harris family had lived in the Denver area for generations. A pro-file in the *Rocky Mountain News* described them: "[Spread across] south Denver and the city's southern suburbs, they are nurses and business own-ers, retired state employees and homemakers. And they are well thought of by neighbors and acquaintances. Solid folks, some quite affluent. No violent pasts." Eric's grandfather worked for more than 20 years as a valet at the Brown Palace, one of Denver's grand old hotels. Wayne Harris, Eric's father, grew up in a small, well-kept house on South Lafayette Street in Englewood, a working-class suburb of Denver. He graduated in 1966 from Englewood High School, and spent three years as a business major at the University of Colorado. Then he changed his career path and transferred to Metropolitan State College, from which he graduated with a degree in avi-ation maintenance management. On April 17, 1970, he married Kathy Pool at the First Presbyterian Church of Englewood. Kathy had grown up in a brick home in southeast Denver's modest Virginia Village neighborhood. Her father ran the Hilltop Hardware store on Holly Street and later worked for the Colorado Department of Transportation as a warehouse supply offi-cer. Neighbors held them in high regard. Former classmates interviewed by the *Rocky Mountain News* remembered Kathy as a nice girl and an average student. She belonged to the high school ski club and played hostess for the school's PTA fashion show.

Following their marriage, Wayne joined the Air Force, and he and his family began a series of relocations that were pretty typical for an armed forces family, first to Fairchild, Washington, where he piloted refueling tankers; then to Wichita, Kansas, where his two sons were born, Kevin in 1978 and Eric on April 9, 1981. Following a promotion to research and test pilot, he was reassigned to Wright-Patterson Air Force Base in Ohio, to iron out kinks in the still experimental B-1 bomber; then, in August of 1989, to Wurtsmith Air Force Base in Oscoda, Michigan, where he worked as an air-craft commander and instructor; then to Plattsburgh, New York, because Wurtsmith was scheduled to be closed because new long-range weaponry had made it redundant; and finally, in 1993, following his retirement at the rank of Major, with two meritorious service medals and two Air Force com-mendation medals, back to Colorado, to Littleton, only four miles from South Lafayette Street, where he had grown up.

The Harrises bought a home on South Reed Street, a "J" shaped cul-de-sac in a sprawling development of attractive brick and clapboard homes with patios perfect for barbecues and lawns surrounded by cedar fences.

While this was a development, it was not a community; after the shooting some residents expressed surprise to learn that the Harrises lived in such close proximity. Kathy worked as a caterer for a company called Everything Goes, and Wayne, beginning in 1995, was employed by FlightSafety Services Corporation, a defense department contractor in Englewood, Colorado that produced sophisticated training simulators for the Air Force. These simulators involved mock-ups of jet cockpits with computer monitors where windows would have been, displaying challenging situations a pilot might encounter while flying. The product bore many similarities with the first-person shooter games which absorbed so many evenings of his son's life.

Eric thought a great deal of his parents. He repeatedly apologized for what he was planning to do. "My dad's great and my mom's so thoughtful. . . . It sucks that I'm doing this to them." Those who had fleeting contact with Kathy and Wayne Harris admired them. Eric's teachers and coaches praised them for consistently attending parent-teacher conferences, and little league games and practices together. Wayne was a Scout leader, coached his sons' sports teams, and was on the board of the property owners association in Oscoda; Kathy volunteered at middle school, on one occasion making special shirts for Halloween. Friends of Eric's recalled how comforting his home was, how tidy and well-organized, how both parents were usually home, and Kathy always had sandwiches for them. Neighbors in the South Reed Street development praised the industrious way that all the Harrises kept the property in shape, the walks shoveled, the lawn tidily mowed, and the leaves raked, and the way they helped neighbors in a pinch.

After the shooting, Wayne Harris declared that family and friends would speak to no one about their son, their family, or the events leading up to April 20, 1999. He did not find it necessary, as did the Klebolds, to hunt up authorities like James Garbarino or opinion makers like David Brooks to bare witness to their good qualities. Tom and Sue Klebold wanted people to know that they were intelligent and loving parents; Wayne Harris wanted people to keep quiet, and even though this was one of the biggest news stories of the decade, people honored his request. He clearly knew how to give and enforce orders.

Eric attended first and second grade in Beavercreek, a comfortable middle-class suburb of Dayton, Ohio; and third, fourth, and fifth grade in Oscoda, Michigan, a wilderness on the banks of Lake Huron, much appreciated by outdoorsmen. Bonnie Leach, his fifth grade teacher, remembers him as being small for his age, and bright, an A student. She described him as "the perfect little fifth grader . . . adorable." This period, from age eight to 11, was probably the happiest of Eric's life. While describing his Oscoda friends during the making of a basement tape when he was 17 and had already decided to end his life, he began to cry and turned off the camera out of shame at this incongruous display of weakness and sentiment. Eric started sixth grade in Plattsburgh, New York, a city north of Albany, on the edge of Adirondack State Park, and an hour's drive from Montreal. Kris Otten, who identified himself as Eric's best friend during this period, remembers frequent sleepovers at Eric's house They would play computer games together, dive off the couches into piles of pillows in the basement, and build snow forts. "The Eric Harris . . . [that committed the shootings] was not the kid I knew in New York," Otten said.

In the fall of 1993, Eric, now 12, entered Ken Caryl Middle School, his fifth relocation in seven years, and his fifth new school community counting preschool in Wichita. (Moves within a neighborhood don't necessarily involve changing communities.) Linda Pollack, who lived on West Elmhurst Avenue, in another part of the development, recalls Kevin and Eric as "terrific boys... pleasant, clean-cut, respectful toward their parents." They were unlike kids in neighboring homes, she went on, who smoke, drank, and threw parties while their parents were on vacation.

America is a mobile society. Half of the entire population relocates—moves and registers a new address—at least once every five years. How such moves are experienced by children depends on their age, the developmental task at hand, and the intensity and number of the stressors they must juggle. The younger child may experience relocation as a disintegration of his or her world, analogous to death, while for the teen, it will mean the loss of a peer group, a parental sabotage of efforts to construct an adult identity. The idea that children are resilient and possessed of a special ability to "bounce back" from the stress of moving is a myth propagated by a culture that has had to accept social instability in the service of economic survival. Children suffer the same stress as adults when they move, only worse because they are not in control of their fate. In a study of adolescent stressors, fifteen-year-olds were asked to rank 37 stressors in order from worst to least, and placed relocation seventh, worse than divorce but not quite as bad as physical abuse. The more moves they've endured, the worse the stress, with six moves constituting a kind of tipping point. Wood and his colleagues found that children ages six to 17 who had experienced six or more relocations were at serious risk for developing behavior problems. They were 77 percent more likely to have four or more behavior problems than children who had moved less frequently.

Eric had an additional risk factor: a congenital disorder called *pectus excavetum* or "funnel breast," a condition where the sternum is sunken into the chest. In an era when boys yearn to look like American Gladiators with large chests and taut abdominal muscles, *pectus excavetum* creates the opposite topology: a sunken chest and a protuberant potbelly. The ill-effects are not only cosmetic; in extreme cases, the fallen sternum restricts the inflation of the lungs, making prolonged exertion difficult, and leaving the child easily exhausted. Pressure on the heart may cause cardiac arrhythmia or tachycardia, or, in extreme cases, a heart murmur. Medical textbooks emphasize that children with this condition are reluctant to appear bare-chested in public and are often ridiculed by their peers for their unusual appearance, and poor physical endurance.

Surgeons have differing opinions regarding the best age for correcting the problem, but most agree that 13 is ideal, and soon after Eric's 13th birthday, he underwent the first of two operations, having a bar or "strut" inserted beneath his sternum to support his chest in a convex shape. The strut is usually removed in a second operation performed six to 12 months later, after the bones have knit and the convex shape of the chest has become stabilized. I believe that Columbine investigators have overlooked or minimized the ramifications of this condition, both physical and psychological, in understanding Eric Harris' compulsion to punish his schoolmates and end his own life. Brooks Brown wrote that Eric was teased whenever he took off his shirt. "It wasn't that noticeable—it was just sunken in a bit. . . ." But this was *after* the operation; *after* his chest had been reshaped. Brooks hadn't known him prior to that. Who knows how much worse the declivity had been before the operation? The Governor's Report on the Columbine High School shootings relegates the *pectus excavetum* to a footnote explaining his rejection by the Marines. Other accounts don't mention it at all, and Eric himself *never* refers to it in his journals or in the six hours of basement tapes, or anywhere else to my knowledge, although he does mention that throughout his childhood he was constantly teased for being the "scrawny white kid."

Some children tolerate *pectus excavetum* with little emotional scarring, depending on the support from their parents, teachers, and community. We can imagine a child with this deformity—we'll call him "Joey"—entering first grade. Joey's mother alerts the teacher to the way he is "different" from the other boys and how the difference must be discussed intentionally and with tact. She has read up on the subject, and made copies of informative articles downloaded from the Internet. The teacher, inspired by the mother's industry and love for her child, vows to be a first-class advocate. She rehearses how she will introduce the subject to her class when the opportunity presents itself. One day, during a "shirts and skins" basketball game, the students begin to comment on Joey's sunken chest. Like all differences of this kind, it is a source of anxiety, and some of them cope with it by ridiculing him. However, because the teacher is well-prepared, she can end the teasing before it starts, and, when the students return to the class room, lead a discussion on the subject, weaving in biology, and issues of disabilities and diversity. She can even, in a kind but firm manner, make it known that she will have a zero tolerance for teasing in her classroom. Thanks to her attentiveness, the kids get to know Joey and grow accustomed to him looking the way he does. It becomes *no big deal*. But what happens if Joey frequently changes schools? Does his mother have the patience to repeat the process every time he changes schools? After all, she has another son to take care of, a husband with a military career, and even dreams and aspirations of her own.

Eric was perpetually the new kid on the block; his *pectus excavetum* made his playmates anxious and they dealt with it by ridiculing him; and the physical frailty that accompanied the disorder made him easy pickings for schoolyard bullies. As a result, he was constantly, brutally teased. He dealt with this aggression in a common way, by internalizing the disdain of those who bullied him. This is a common defense mechanism called "identification with the aggressor." We've seen this before, in the cases of Wayne Lo and Luke Woodham. Early on in his life, Eric Harris *split off* the damaged part of himself, the imagined source of his weakness, the declivity of his chest. It became unmentionable in conversation, in his journals, in the six hours of basement videotapes, in the sprawling diatribes of his website. Meanwhile he cultivated the supposedly "strong" part of himself, embracing ideologies that celebrate the powerful and leave the weak in the dust. He became, in his imagination, German speaking, Hitler worshipping, the creator of unimagined damage with guns and bombs and fire, the one who could strike terror into people's hearts, and make the streets run red with blood.

Maybe—and this is conjecture—what had kept him optimistic about his future prior to the operation was the possibility that afterwards he would look like a normal kid, perhaps even an athlete with a good-looking body, which in turn would make him acceptable. But then, after the operation, he discovered that he was still the same person—still bullied, still excluded—it came as a terrible blow to him, dashing his hopes, and making him cynical. The reader will recall that this age is, developmentally, all about the formation of a future identity. To learn that the future will be no better than the past is a crushing realization. Eric repeatedly rails against the jocks, threatening to kill them by the score; but secretly he envies them, he wants to be one of them. When, during the library massacre, after killing a boy who is developmentally delayed, several girls, and one of the schools' two black students, he finally comes across an athlete, a jock, an *Aryan* man, he lets him leave the building unharmed. He is a Robin Hood in reverse: he kills the weak, and lets the strong go free.

COLUMBINE HIGH SCHOOL

In 1995, Eric and Dylan were among the five hundred students entering the freshman class at Columbine High School. Although this was a public school, they and their classmates were unusually affluent. The average home price in Littleton was over $200,000 in 1999 and the median income of Littleton parents was almost twice that of the rest of the nation. The school had high academic standards, small classes, and a student to teacher ratio of about twenty to one. Most of the graduates went on to college. The physical plant had just undergone a 15 million dollar renovation, and its 75 classrooms provided 250,000 square feet of space. Frank DeAngelis had been principal for three years and a faculty member for 19 years before that.

Dylan's brother Byron was starting his junior year. Tall, good-looking, popular, and athletic, he left footprints that Dylan could never quite fill. Although Byron and Dylan had been very, very close as children, they had grown apart in adolescence. Like many of the other Columbine athletes, Byron made fun of his younger brother, "ripped" on him and, in Dylan's own words, "added to the rage." Eric's brother, Kevin, was also a junior, and also excelled socially and athletically. He kicked for the school football team, the Rebels. Friends and neighbors repeatedly characterized him as the ideal son, and Eric mentions admiring him (or perhaps damning him with faint praise) because he was "motivated."

In high school Eric began to display a dramatic, passive-aggressive, vindictive side to his personality not evident to his middle school teachers. He invited a girl named Tiffany Typher, with whom he rode the school bus, to the homecoming dance. She went with him, but refused to date him again. A normal 15-year-old boy might have chalked it up to experience, or gotten angry for a while before letting it go. Eric arranged for her to discover his "dead" body following a mock suicide. He splashed his head and a rock with fake blood left over from Halloween, lay down on the ground, and struck a pose that suggested that he had bashed in his own head with the rock. He was so amused by Tiffany's horrified reaction to the tableau that he lost control of himself and began to laugh. Tiffany called him immature and stomped off. This was parasuicide in its purest, most unambiguous form, an act that resembled suicide in order to draw concern and attention, but that could never result in death.

During freshman year, Eric's and Dylan's circle of friends included Zach Heckler, Nick Baumgart, and Brooks Brown. They were acquaintances from elementary school and middle school, and they were, all of them, enchanted by computers. They gathered often in the school library to surf the Internet on the library computers, a relatively new pastime in 1995. At times they would become so rowdy they would be asked to leave. Having a clique also afforded them some protection against the bullying, which, according to Brooks Brown, had reached a remarkable intensity in the high school.

> At lunchtime the jocks would kick our chairs, or push us down onto the table from behind. They would knock our food trays onto the floor, trip us, or throw food as we were walking by. When we sat down, they would pelt us with candy from another table. In the hallways, they would push kids into lockers and call them names while their friends stood by and laughed at the show. In gym class, they would beat kids up in the locker room because the teachers weren't around.
>
> Seniors at Columbine would do things like pour baby oil on the floor, then literally "go bowling" with freshmen; they would throw the kid across the floor, and since he couldn't stop, he'd crash right into other kids while the jocks pointed and giggled . . .
>
> One guy, a wrestler who everyone knew to avoid, liked to make kids get down on the ground and push pennies along the floor with their noses. This would happen during school hours, as kids were passing from one class to another. Teachers would see it and look the other way.

Was Brown exaggerating?

Apparently not. Eight months after the shooting, Regina Huerter, director of Juvenile Diversion for the Denver District Attorney's Office, prepared a report on bullying at Columbine for the Governor's Columbine Review Commission. Interviews with 28 parents and 15 current and former students confirmed that bullying at the high school was sadistic in nature, frequent, and often went unpunished because the bullies were the jocks, the heroes of the high school, while the bullied were the "outcast" groups at the bottom of the social ladder. Teachers actually admitted to a fear of losing their jobs. Frank DeAngelis, the principal, and most of the deans and assistant principals at Columbine High School, had been coaches or had coaching backgrounds and were biased toward athletes. In the same report she stated that Eric and Dylan were perceived as loners and "were often the brunt of bullying and ridicule," most of it involving shoving, pushing, and name-calling. People who associated with them were also bullied, making it a liability to be in a social relationship with them. One girl reported being smashed into a locker and called a "fag lover" by a notorious bully, after she had been seen talking to Dylan. In another incident, "people surrounded them in the Commons and squirted ketchup packets all over them, laughing at them, calling them 'faggots.' That happened while teachers watched. They couldn't fight back. They wore the ketchup all day and went home covered with it."

In sophomore year, Dylan found a niche for himself in the theater department, doing tech work for student productions. He and some friends would huddle together in the light booth during plays, following the sound and lighting cues and sometimes getting drunk. He was also involved in video production for the school's TV news network and helped maintain the school's computer server. At home, he spent hours online, playing first-person shooter games such as *Doom II* and *Quake*, surfing the Internet and visiting chat rooms. His online name was "voDKa," because he drank vodka, and his initials were embedded in the middle of the word. When questioned by adults, he denied drinking, but the accounts of his friends suggest that he drank often in school and at home.

During this time he met Robyn Anderson, who was dating a boy in the theater department, and would later become one of Dylan's closest friends. She had just moved to the area and perceived him as a "rough guy" with a warm heart. Following the shooting, when she was asked by the police if she had been his girlfriend, Robyn replied that he "was never the type to get a girlfriend," and believed that Dylan had never had a girlfriend. Later in the same interview, explaining how they had the money to buy the weapons and ammo, she stated, "They both [Eric and Dylan] worked and neither one spent money on anything including girls since they really did not date." Responding to a question by the police, she stated that he was not gay.

As well as she knew Dylan, she may have been wrong; she seemed to have had an uncanny ability to overlook the obvious. A fictionalized cinematic account of the Columbine High School shootings, *Zero Day*, depicts characters based on Eric and Dylan as exploring homosexual feelings for one another, while the characters around them seem convinced of their homosexuality. Whatever the case, suicide pacts such as that which existed between Dylan and Eric suggest tremendous intimacy. Like religion, physical appearance, professional aspirations, and social milieu, gender preference figures importantly in creating an identity. The culture of Columbine High School was homophobic, as the previously described bullying incidents would suggest. Being part of the culture themselves, Eric and Dylan had internalized the homophobia, as evident in the rants which Eric posted

186 | JONATHAN FAST

on his website. Eric Houston (Case 3) was an example of an SR shooter who was gay and had internalized the homophobia of his community, causing him deep distress, and contributing in a fundamental way to his SR shooting. The additional developmental difficulties experienced by GLBT teens is evident in their suicide attempts, which are two to three times as frequent as attempts among heterosexual teens.

During the spring semester, Dylan began to explore his thoughts in a journal. On the cover he wrote: "Fact: People are so unaware . . . well, ignorance is bliss, I guess . . . that would explain my depression." He wrote in his journal, "It's interesting, when I'm in my *human form* [italics mine], knowing I'm going to die, everything has a touch of triviality to it." In his senior-year essay on Charles Manson, he wrote, "Although *still on Earth*, [italics, mine] they [Mickey and Malory Knox, antiheros of the film, *Natural Born Killers*] live by their own morals. . . ." The delusion that he had grasped a facet of reality that had eluded others weaves its way through his writings. He seems to have believed that while this deeper understanding made him more vulnerable to the travails of being human, it also promised a higher form of existence after death.

He wrote about being an outcast, of being depressed, and hating his life. He suspected that people were conspiring against him. He considered asking someone to buy him a gun so that he could shoot himself, and also imagined how it would feel to go on a killing spree. In a more sentimental mood, he described his "first love," a person whom, in all likelihood, he never told of his affection. He named several girls with whom he had fallen in love but never spoken to. His journals included an unsent letter to one of them.

Unlike Dylan, Eric was never involved in theater or any other extracurricular activities. His only outside interest was in computers and computer gaming. "The Harris's study is in the front of the house," Randy Brown recalled, "and every time I went by, he was there [using the computer]. It was uncanny." Eric spent many hours of computer time creating new levels for *Doom II*, an improved version of the computer game described in Chapter 4, and sharing the levels with friends and other gamers online. One of many post-Columbine myths was that Eric had created a level that was a simulation of the attack on the high school: two assassins with many weapons and unlimited ammo, moving along a floor-plan of the high school, firing at fleeing humans who could not shoot back. In reality the levels he created were more mundane: a hockey rink, where assassins slid around on ice, another where participants were forced to fight with fists, rather than weapons; and other levels with science fiction themes. Some of these survive on the Internet, but they do so as curiosities, as criminal memorabilia, rather than works of particular artistry, fun, or ingenuity. Eric was frequently online, visiting discussion groups for *Quake* and *Doom*, engaging in *Doom* deathmatches, posting the levels he had authored for downloading, and publishing odd humor, apocalyptic rants, and descriptions of the mischief he had committed and the mischief he had planned.

During sophomore year, Dylan and Eric began associating with a cluster of students referred to as the Trench Coat Mafia (TCM). The TCM consisted mostly of older teens who espoused Goth or punk culture, dressed in black, colored and cut their hair in unusual ways, worshipped Wicca or Satan, believed they might be vampires or wizards, enjoyed heavy metal or death metal music, and otherwise encouraged others to believe that they were in some way gifted or unusual and not simply the school's social detritus. The folklore of the group's christening was this: one boy's mother bought him a black trench coat, and his friends, liking the look it, got their mothers to buy them the same garment. Some jocks, seeing them sitting together at lunch one sweltering day in their black trench coats, remarked that they looked like a "trench coat mafia," and the name stuck.

Chris Morris was among the leaders of the group, to the extent that such groups have leaders. He had been adopted at the age of five by a couple who divorced soon afterwards, and his childhood had been a barefoot hike along a rocky path made worse by his own violent temper, over which he had gained some control by high school. Robyn, who had dated him for a month during sophomore year, described him as "gentle," sometimes "hyper," occasionally funny, and "off in his own world. . . . He did his own thing and . . . if he didn't want to go to class some days he just would not go." He wore a letter "A" patch on his jacket which stood for "anarchy." After school Chris worked at Blackjack Pizza, a few blocks south of the high school. Sensing the commonality in their charismatic styles, nihilist humor, and subcutaneous rage, Chris took a liking to Eric, and helped him get a job at Blackjack Pizza. After Eric was hired, Dylan applied, and soon the three of them were elbow deep in pizza.

During down time at Blackjack, Dylan and Eric talked, got involved in pranks, and became inseparable friends. Most of their mischief took place in the alley behind the store. They would cover a mound of dry ice (obtained from a nearby Baskin Robbins) with a vinyl traffic cone borrowed from a construction site, holding the cone down while the pressure from the melting ice mounted, and then letting it go, to see how far their homemade missile would fly. More often their activities involved fire and explosives. They set off fireworks in the alley, and started a fire in the dumpster that blazed out of control, necessitating a visit from the fire department. They set fire to aerosol cans, once in a mop sink and another time in an oven, to see if they would really explode as the label warned, and what kind of damage they would do. Later in the year, after they had begun building pipe bombs, Dylan brought one into work. He was written up for it and soon afterwards quit, but was later rehired when the store needed workers. It's unclear to what extent Chris Morris took part in these diversions.

REBEL MISSIONS

During the winter of their sophomore year, Eric and Dylan, in the company of select friends, began undertaking "Rebel Missions," named after the school football team, the Rebels, and reflecting Eric's sense of irony as well as his longing to be a team member like his brother. He adopted "REB" as a nickname for his covert nighttime and online activities. He, voDKa, and four other friends—KIBBz, Excaluber (sic), Jester, and Imaginos (their real identities have not been made public)—would stage acts of mischief and vandalism on neighboring homes, and then Eric would boast about it on one of his websites:

> Ok people, Im gonna let you in on the big secret of our clan. We aint no god damn stupid ass quake clan. We are more of a gang. We plan out and execute missions. Anyone pisses us off, we do a little deed to their house. Eggs, teepee [toilet paper unrolled in the trees around the house], superglue, busyboxes [a homemade device that provides a perpetual busy signal], large amounts of fireworks, you name it and we will probly or already have done it. We have many enemies in our school, therefore we make many missions. Its sort of a night time tradition for us.

By the winter of 1997, Eric had posted descriptions of six Rebel Missions. The first involved setting off firecrackers. "[W]e put an entire assortment of very loud fireworks in a tunnel, and lit them off at about 1:00 AM. Thus mission was part of a rebellion against these assholes that shot one of our bikes one day." In mission two they vandalized the home of Nick Baumgarten, no longer among Eric's friends. After the mission, they would get drunk, "Not with whimpy beer . . . [but with] hard liquor. Aftershock, Irish Cream, Tequila, Vodka, whiskey, Rum and sometimes a few shots of EVERCLEAR [a brand of pure grain alcohol available in 190 proof and illegal in many states]." They did not get drunk after the fourth mission because of ". . . this person named Brooks Brown who tried to narc on us.

Telling my parents that I had booze and shit in my room. I had to ditch every bottle I had and lie like a fuckin salesman to my parents." Later attacks went beyond adolescent pranks. On Halloween Eric and Dylan hid in the shadows of a roof top and fired BBs at two children who were trick or treating, a scene they described gleefully to friends in the lunchroom on more than one occasion.

The falling out between Eric Harris and Brooks Brown occurred about midway through sophomore year. Although he was now 16, Eric still didn't have his driver's license. His brother had gone off to college and, in order to avoid the humiliation of riding the school bus, he had arranged for Brooks and another boy, Trevor Dolac, a friend from the debating club, to take turns driving him to school. Brooks was compulsively late and Eric, who was compulsively punctual, would spend every trip scolding him. One morning when Brooks was particularly late, Eric called to find out where he was. Hoping to avoid the predictable helping of verbal abuse, Brooks told Eric to find a ride with somebody else. It was too late for Eric to catch the school bus so he got a ride in his dad's truck. On the way to school, they passed Brook's car. Eric's dad pulled over, figuring that his son would rather ride to school with his friends. No sooner had Eric climbed into the back seat than he began berating Brooks. Brooks vowed that he would never drive Eric to school again.

In return, Eric gave Brooks the silent treatment. Brooks heard from mutual friends that Eric was insulting him behind his back and plotting revenge. A few days after Rebel Mission Two, an attack on Nick Baumgart's house which included the hurling of uncooked eggs, the unrolling of toilet paper, and application of superglue to doors, Eric told Nick that Brooks Brown was responsible for the mischief. Nick told his parents, who contacted Brooks' mother, Judy Brown. Because Brooks had been at home, grounded, on the night in question, Eric's deceit was revealed and Eric was livid. A few days later, when Brooks drove by the school bus stop, Eric threw a chunk of ice at the car, cracking the windshield. Brooks told his parents, and then knocked on Eric's door and told his mother:

> Your son's been sneaking out at night. He's going around vandaliz-
> ing things. He's threatened people. And just now he broke my wind-
> shield. He's got liquor in his room. Search it. He's got spray paint
> cans in his room. Search it. Eric's fucked up and you need to know
> about it.

Mrs. Harris wanted him to stay and confront Eric, but Brooks fled. When he returned home, his friend Trevor was waiting for him. After cracking Brooks' windshield, Eric had struck Trevor's car with a second piece of ice, denting the trunk. Trevor, in revenge, had stolen Eric's backpack, which, in the confusion, had been left behind at the bus stop. It was time, Mrs. Brown decided, for both boys to confront Eric. With the backpack and the boys in the car, she drove to the bus stop where Eric was still waiting. "Eric, I've got your backpack," she told him, having made sure the car doors were locked, and the window only barely opened, "and I'm taking it over to your mom's. Meet us over there." The intensity of Eric's anger shocked them all. His face turned beet red and, in Judy Brown's words:

> He just went crazy. I started to pull away slowly and he wouldn't let go [of the car door handle]. I said, "back away from the car. We'll meet you at your mom's." He didn't listen. He just kept screaming, "Give me my backpack!" We were all scared.

When Judy, Brooks, and Trevor arrived at the Harris home, Kathy Harris was standing in the driveway. Judy told her what had happened and her eyes welled with tears. Judy, who recalled Kathy Harris as "a very sweet, a very nice lady," immediately gave her the book bag without even thinking of looking inside it. That evening, Kathy, with Wayne on the extension, called Judy. Wayne insisted that his son's threats lacked any substance.

> He said, "This is just kids' stuff. The truth is, Eric's afraid of you." I [Judy Brown] said, "Look, your son isn't afraid of me—he came after me at my car." And he said, "My son said that he is afraid of you." He didn't want to hear that his son had done anything wrong.

The next day, Brooks heard from friends at school that Eric was still threatening him. When he got home, he told his mother, who called the police. An officer stopped by their house and listened to their story. The officer agreed to visit the Harrises, who lived a few blocks away, and, at the very least, let Eric know that his acts would have consequences. Later that night, Judy got a call from Wayne Harris. He was bringing Eric over to apologize. She arranged to confront the boy alone.

> Eric came over and stood in our doorway, and he just had this fake tone to his voice . . . "Mrs. Brown, I didn't mean any harm, and you know I would never do anything to hurt Brooks . . ." I let him finish but I could see right through the act. And then I said, "You know, Eric, you can pull the wool over your dad's eyes, but you can't pull the wool over my eyes."

That seemed to surprise him. He said, "Are you calling me a liar?" And I said, "Yes, I am. And if you ever come up our street, or if you ever do anything to Brooks again—if I ever even see you on our street again—I'm calling the police."

Regarding his reaction, Judy Brown said, "I don't think anyone had ever confronted him like that before… Maybe he had gotten away with it for so long, manipulating people that way, that he was stunned when it didn't work."

JUNIOR YEAR

By junior year, Dylan, Eric, and their clique were often in trouble. Dylan regularly swore in front of his teachers. He and Eric and a friend were suspended for hacking into the high school server and stealing locker combinations. Dylan said that they "opened a locker or two to test to see if [the] list was current," but friends knew that he had intended to leave a threatening note in the locker of an "enemy." Dylan stole a laptop from the school and his father made him return it. Eric was given a one-day in-school suspension for scratching the locker of a student with whom he was angry. He also had to pay $70 to have the locker repaired.

In the fall of their junior year Eric and Dylan produced a short film for their marketing class called *Hit Men for Hire*. In this *Pulp Fiction*-influenced video, they offer their services as protectors to marginalized, bullied, fragile students not unlike themselves. They roam the hallways of the high school corridors in black dusters, cool sunglasses, and ferocious attitudes, pretending to execute school athletes with toy guns. A desperate student is willing to go to any lengths to stop the bullying.

"I'll pay anything!"

"All right. It's twenty dollars a day in school. You know we can't have any weapons on school grounds."

"Th-that's fine! I'll—I'll get 'em off the property!"

"All right. We'll protect you on school (sic). Take away any bullies that are pickin' on you. Whatever. And off school grounds we could relocate this person. That'd be a thousand dollars."

"Thank you SO much!"

In the basement tapes, Eric and Dylan express their hopes that generations of future fans will interpret *Hit Men* and other recent activities as "foreshadowing" the Columbine shootings, but it is probably more accurate to understand it, along with the basement tapes, the journals, and the essay on Charles Manson, as narcissistic self-promotion of the type we have seen in previous cases. They are assembling their "press kit."

THE VAN BREAK-IN

One night in January, Eric and Dylan parked in a lot near Deer Creek Canyon Road to listen to a new CD. They were driving the '86 gray Honda Civic which Eric's parents had given him as a reward for finally passing his driver's test. When they grew tired of the music, they got out of the car, set off some fireworks and broke some bottles on the ground. They noticed a white van parked nearby. After deciding that the owner had left it there for the night, Dylan smashed in the side window with a rock, and opened the door from the inside. They took a briefcase, a pair of sunglasses, and about $400 worth of electrical equipment. A few miles down the road, they parked again so they could examine their spoils at their leisure. Officer Tim Walsh, on patrol that night, found their behavior suspicious and, after watching them for a few minutes, approached the car, and shined his flashlight at Dylan's face. Officer Walsh asked where they had gotten the electronics. On the side of the road, Dylan replied. On further questioning, they confessed to robbing the van and were taken into custody. Later, in his statement, Eric laid the blame on his closest friend. "Dylan suggested we should steal some of the objects in the white van," he told the police. "At first I was very uncomfortable and questioning with the thought." The boys claimed that a parking ticket on the windshield led them to believe that the van was abandoned. Sentencing was postponed until April.

Eric's mother, growing ever more concerned about his behavior, took him to see a psychologist. Eric openly admitted his feelings of anger, depression, and suicidal thoughts. The Harrises' family doctor prescribed Zoloft, later changing over to Luvox, presumably because of side-effects. Luvox is an SSRI, a selective serotonin reuptake inhibitor, a class of medications that includes Prozac, Zoloft, and Paxil. News stories had begun to surface about adolescents who had committed suicide while taking an SSRI-type medication, but among most psychiatrists it is considered among the safer and more effective medications for depression.

Peter Breggin, the author of *Talking Back to Prozac*, and other anti-SSRI advocates have suggested that the shooting was a result of an SSRI-inspired mania. The argument is unconvincing because Eric's plan to assault to the high school predates his use of the medication. "The doctor recommended antidepressant medication which seems to have helped," Sue Harris told a juvenile court intake worker, during Eric's assessment. "His mood is more upbeat." The intake worker concurred. "He said that he is feeling better now that he is on medication." His improvement in mood may have coincided with the onset of Luvox treatment but the cause, more likely, was the increase in energy and focus that is common among those who have chosen the course of suicide and see an end to their suffering.

The intake worker and Eric both identified anger as a central issue.

> Eric said that he has problems with anxiety and allows his anger to build up until he explodes. Eric said that when he gets really mad he punches walls. He is seeing a therapist once or twice a month, the family also meets with him on occasion. Eric says he has thought about suicide a couple of times but never seriously, mostly out of anger.

In the same intake, Eric described himself:

> [I] often get angry at almost anything I don't like. People I have no respect for trying to tell me what to do. People telling me what to think. I have too many inside jokes or thoughts to have very many friends or I hate too many things.

The Klebold family began seeing a therapist at some point, but the stimulus was not only Dylan's criminal behavior but problems with his older brother, Byron, who had gone to live with a friend after being expelled from the house for using drugs. Although Byron had graduated high school the year before, his future seemed uncertain. He was not attending college. At the time of the shootings, he was working in a custodial function at a car dealership, keeping the cars sparkling and the snow shoveled off the tarmac.

One morning toward the end of junior year, March of 1998, while students were rushing through the hallway, Dylan slipped Brooks a scrap of paper with a web address scribbled across it, one of Eric's websites, he explained. Brooks *had* to read it, and also promise never to tell Eric who it was who alerted him to it. That evening Brooks accessed the website, and found, among the homicidal rants, white supremacist rhetoric, swaggering accounts of "rebel missions," and instructions on how to make pipe bombs, this unnerving passage:

> God I can't wait till I can kill you people. I'll just go to some downtown area in some big-ass city and blow up and shoot everything I can. Feel no remorse, no sense of shame. Ich sage FICT TU! I will rig up explosives all over a town and detonate each one of them at will

after I mow down a whole fucking area full of you snotty ass rich
mother fucking high strung godlike attitude having worthless piece
of shit whores. I don't care if I live or die in the shootout, all l want
to do is to kill and injure as many of you pricks as I can, especially a
few people. Like Brooks Brown.

On other pages, Eric had posted Brooks' phone number, a list of things
Eric hated about him, and a reward for anyone who would hunt him down
and kill him. Unknown to Eric, this latest posting had gained notoriety,
even beyond the Brown household. The Simon Wisenthal Center, which
regularly trawls the waters of the Internet for hate group postings, had
come across it. Concerned by its vicious racism, they had saved a copy in its
archives, where it remained, forgotten, until weeks after the shootings.

On March 18, 1998, the Browns again called the police. This time, the
officer who had responded to the van break-in came to the Brown home.
They gave him printouts of the webpages, reviewed the history of antago-
nism between the boys, and discussed the pipe bombs and Eric's homicidal
threats. Mostly Randy Brown voiced his concern for his son's safety. The
deputy filed a suspicious incident report. When Randy and Judy Brown
returned to the sheriff's office a week later, they talked to a Detective Hicks,
who seemed genuinely concerned. Members of the bomb squad, who also
met with them, recalled a pipe bomb explosion they had investigated earlier that month that resembled one of the bombs Eric described on his website. "Pazzie [one of the pipe bombs; Eric had named them as one might
name pets] was a complete success and it blew dee fuck outa a little creek
bed. Flipping thing was heart-pounding gut-wrenching brain-twitching
ground-moving insanely cool!" While Hicks was uncertain, because of the
ambiguous wording, whether they could prosecute Eric for threatening
Brooks' life, he assured the Browns that they could and would prosecute him
for building and detonating an incendiary device.

At the beginning of April, rumors spread through the high school that Eric
and Dylan were in trouble with the police. Judy and Randy Brown, assuming
that this was in response to the threats on their son's life, breathed a collective
sigh of relief. In fact, it had nothing to do with it. Although the JCSO had
begun paperwork for a warrant to search the Harris home, the search was
never conducted. There was no further investigation. The case was dropped,
the records lost or destroyed, accidentally or intentionally, then or later on
after the shooting. When Littleton residents eventually learned how close
JCSO had come to uncovering the plot, how lackadaisical or corrupt police
work had led to the deaths of their sons and daughters, they were outraged.

The rumors were about Eric and Dylan's sentencing for the van break-in. Because this was a first offense and non-violent, they had been referred to a "juvenile diversion program," which consisted of fines, counseling, anger management classes, and a community service assignment. Eric took his website offline at this time. He wrote a letter of apology to the owner of the van explaining how disappointed he was in himself for his actions. An account of his arrest, written for a school assignment, probably captures the tone and sentiments of that letter:

> As I waited, I cried, I hurt, and I felt like hell. . . . My parents lost all respect and trust in me and I am slowly regaining it. The experience showed me that no matter what crime you think of committing, you will get caught, that you must, absolutely must, think things through before you act.

Now, in a journal he had begun in the open squares on the left side of his school day planner, he recorded his private thoughts.

> Isn't America supposed to be the land of the free? How come if I'm free, I can't deprive a stupid fucking dumbshit from his possessions if he leaves them sitting in the front seat of his fucking van out in plain sight and in the middle of fucking nowhere on a Fri-fucking-day night?

The journal became a place for him to vent his anger, and plan his assault on the high school, which would take place a year from then.

> Sometime in April me and V will get revenge and kick natural selection up a few notches. . . . We will be in all black. Dusters, black army pants, and we will get custom shirts that say R or V [Reb or voDKa] in the background and NBK in the front in a smaller font. . . .
>
> Then get totally prepared and during A lunch we go and park in our spots. With sunglasses on we start carrying in all our bags of terrorism and anarchism shit into our table. Being very casual and silent about it, it's all for a science/band/English project or something. . . .
>
> We use bombs, fire bombs and anything we fucking can to kill and damage as much as we fucking can. . . . I want to leave a lasting impression on the world.

NBK refers to the Oliver Stone film, *Natural Born Killers*, with which Dylan and Eric had became obsessed. In November of his senior year, Dylan wrote a pretty good 12-page paper about Charles Manson; with hindsight, however, it was more of an opportunity for him to ruminate about *Natural*

Born Killers, and how the world would think of Eric and himself following their crime and their deaths. Consider the following paragraph:

> [*Natural Born Killers*] portrayed the main two characters who, at the point between innocent teenagers and experienced adult, defy society, and get lost in their own little world, killing, and robbing whoever (sic) they come across. Although *still on Earth*, [italics, mine] they live by their own morals, beliefs, and at the end of the film, expose the media and law for its flaws.

While he and Eric made a point of distancing themselves from previous SR shooters, they had both fallen pray, like Barry Loukaitis (Case 7) and others before them, to the weird homicidal ideology of the film. The following speech, delivered by Mickey Knox after he and Malory, his wife and partner in homicide, have cold-bloodedly murdered 48 men and women (52 by the end of the movie) expresses the kernel of it. He is being interviewed by Wayne Gale, the host of a fictional TV show called *American Maniac*.

> You'll never understand. Me and you, Wayne, we're not even the same species. I used to be you . . . then I evolved. From where you're standing, you're a man. From where I'm standing, you're a ape. I'm here . . . I'm right here . . . and you . . . you're somewhere else, man. You say why? I say why not?

The concept of "natural selection" as a justification for killing people whom they deemed inferior, "you humans" as they repeatedly put it, occupied an important place in their ideology. In the basement tapes, Dylan wonders "what ever happened to natural selection?" On his webpage, Eric described natural selection as ". . . the best thing that ever happened to the earth. . . . Getting rid of all the stupid and weak organisms. . . ." When the Columbine 1998 yearbook came out in April, Eric and Dylan were no longer shy about sharing their rage. Eric wrote in one girl's yearbook, "Natural selection needs a boost, like me with a shotgun." Dylan wrote in Eric's yearbook: ". . . the holy April morning of NBK . . . killing enemies, blowing up stuff, killing cops!! My wrath for January's incident will be godlike. Not to mention our revenge in the Commons." Eric wrote in Dylan's notebook, "God, I can't wait till they die. I can taste the blood now—NBK." Eric went through his own yearbook, page by page, writing "worthless," "die," and "beat" under practically every picture and, when he tired of this, slashing each with an "X." In his journal, Eric wrote, "It would be great if God removed all vaccines and warning labels from everything in the world and let natural selection take its course." During the rampage, Eric wore a t-shirt with "Natural Selection" printed across the front.

SENIOR YEAR

In the beginning of their senior year, Brooks discovered that he was in two classes with Eric, third hour and fourth hour Creative Writing (Columbine had "hours" rather than periods). Knowing how uncomfortable it was to be the focus of Eric's hostility, he decided to offer an apology. Oddly, Eric, who was known for holding a grudge forever, accepted. He, Brooks, and Dylan, who was also in his fourth hour class, became friends, often cutting Creative Writing together, as a group. Brooks found Eric transformed, slower to anger, and responding to harassment with philosophical indifference. On one occasion some football players drove by, yelled an insult, and threw a bottle that shattered at Dylan's feet. "Don't worry about it," Dylan responded, "It happens all the time." In a second incident, an anonymous source, most likely a student with a grudge against them, told authorities that Eric and Dylan were carrying drugs in school, and they were publicly searched and humiliated. They shrugged the episode off. In Creative Writing class, Eric was more open and expressive. A piece he wrote in response to an assignment on "personification," about a wedding between a shotgun shell and a shotgun, and how the couple gave birth to "pellet babies," left the class helpless with laughter. Other essays seemed to convey that he had "worked through many of his issues." Mental health workers are familiar with this phenomenon. Often people who have made the decision to commit suicide have a brightening of mood, an elevation of energy. The end is in sight; their suffering is finite.

There were many more warnings of what was to come.

As is the practice with most high schools, when the picture of the graduating class was taken, the photographer shot one "serious" picture and one silly picture, where students could cross their eyes, pretend to strangle one another, pull their t-shirts over their heads, and so forth. Eric, Dylan, Brooks, Zach Heckler, and Robyn Anderson were standing together, and Eric suggested that for the silly picture, they pantomime firing guns at the camera. "It seemed like a funny thing to do," Brooks recalled. "I never thought twice about it."

Nate Dykeman watched Eric and Dylan detonate a pipe bomb on Super Bowl Sunday, January 1998. He told no adults. Eric's father found one of the pipe bombs in a box with sundry bomb-making materials, and confiscated it, but later returned the box. On another occasion a clerk from Green

Mountain Guns called Eric's house and told him, "the clips are in," his father responded that it must be a mistake, he hadn't ordered any clips, and that was the end of that. In an essay for Creative Writing, Dylan described a trench coat-garbed assassin who shot and killed bullies outside a bar. A co-worker at Blackjack Pizza recalls Eric remarking that he would use his pay-check to buy more propane tanks; that he already owned seven but planned to purchase nine more; that he hoped to have thirty by April 20. The co-worker told no adults. Nichole Markham, Chris Morris's girlfriend, saw Eric and Dylan standing in the cafeteria, studying a piece of paper. When they wouldn't tell her what it was, she playfully pulled it out of their hands, and saw that it was a diagram of the lunchroom that they had drawn, which included the placement of security cameras. According to Brooks, Eric and Dylan would now sit together in the back of the classroom and ask each other, "Can I shoot that guy?"

On January 23, 1999, 22-year-old Philip Duran, who worked with Eric and Dylan at Blackjack Pizza, introduced them to Mark Manes at a gun show. Manes, a computer technician with a history of drug dealing and addiction, claimed he could get them a TEC DC-9 assault pistol for $500. That night Dylan brought him $300. Eric and Dylan scraped together the rest of the money and Philip Duran delivered it to Manes. During the shoot-ing, Eric would wield this weapon.

The Tanner Gun Show, "the Rocky Mountain Region's best monthly gathering," was held one weekend each month at the Denver Merchandise Mart Pavilion, off Interstate 25 in north Denver. Dylan and Eric visited the show on a Saturday and found the weapons they wanted, but were turned away by dealers because they were not yet 18. On Sunday they called Robyn Anderson, who was already 18, and convinced her to go back to the show with them. By senior year she was among Dylan's closest friends, along with Eric, Zach Heckler, and Chris Morris. She took calculus with Dylan, called him about three times a week, occasionally visited him at Blackjack Pizza to formalize plans for the weekend, and often went midnight bowling with him and other friends on Friday nights at the AMF Belleview Lanes. Nine months after the shooting, testifying before a House Judiciary Committee in support of a bill to expand background checks on all gun show sales, she described buying guns for Eric and Dylan.

> While we were walking around, Eric and Dylan kept asking sellers if they were private or licensed. They wanted to buy their guns from someone who was private—and not licensed—because there would be no paperwork or background check. At one point Eric was inter-

ested in a gun from a licensed dealer. The dealer asked me if I would fill out some paperwork and I said, "No, I didn't feel comfortable with that." I didn't want to put my name on something that I wasn't going to have control of.

They bought guns from three sellers. They were all private. They paid cash. There was no receipt. I was not asked any questions at all. There was no background check. All I had to do was show my driver's license to prove that I was 18. Dylan got a shotgun. Eric got a shotgun and a black rifle that he bought clips for. He was able to buy clips and ammunition without me having to show any I.D. The sellers didn't write down any information. . . . When I look back at it, I think I was kind of naive . . .

The three guns Robyn purchased were a Stevens 12-gauge double-barreled shotgun, a Savage-Springfield pump action 12-gauge shotgun, and a Hi-Point model 995 carbine rifle (the "black" rifle), each from a different dealer. While a regular shotgun needs to be reloaded after every shot, the pump action can be fired five times before reloading. She also purchased four ten-round clips for the carbine and 250 nine-millimeter rounds to fill the clips; 15 twelve-gauge slugs, 40 shotgun shells, and two switchblade knives. There was no haggling. She paid cash, five or six hundred dollars altogether, which the boys had given her. Robyn was not surprised that they had the money because "they both worked and neither one spent money on anything including girls since they really did not date." She, in turn, gave the goods to Eric and Dylan. Colorado law allows adults to transfer ownership of long guns to juveniles, protecting a rite of passage in many states where hunting is common, the passing of a rifle from father to son at puberty.

After the gun show, Dylan dropped Eric at his house, transferring two guns to the trunk of his car. Eric went up to his room and wrote in his journal:

Well folks, today was a very important day in the history of R[eb]. Today, along with VoDKa and someone else who I won't name, we went downtown and purchased the following: [he lists the weapons, the knives and ammo]. We . . . have . . . GUNS! We fucking got em, you sons of bitches! HA! HA HA HA! Neener! Booga Booga. Heh. It's all over now. This caps it off, the point of no return . . .

Dylan, with the third gun in his trunk, drove Robyn back to his house so they could study calculus together. When they got to his bedroom, he tried to hide the shotgun in the bottom drawer of his dresser, but it was too long. He later told her that he had sawed down the barrel to make it fit in the drawer, a statement she accepted at face value. (Part of the fun of Robyn Anderson seems to have been her remarkably good-natured gullibility. In another incident, Chris Morris, having just returned from a trip out of state, told her he had been attending a national conference of the Trench Coat Mafia. She believed him.) In fact, sawing off the barrel of a shotgun creates a wider spray of pellets, making it more lethal, a fact commonly known in Colorado and other states where people hunt game and guns are more commonplace. Robyn agreed to keep the weapon purchases secret because Eric and Dylan were underage and could get into trouble—not because they planned to harm anyone. They had promised her that the weapons would be used only for target shooting. When the authorities cross-examined her after the shooting, they found the degree of her naiveté difficult to accept.

> When asked if she had second thoughts about why they were purchasing these guns since they did not sound like outdoor hunters, she replied she did not know about Dylan since he lived in the mountains and there were deer outside his home.

She said that her father owned a gun, kept it in the house, but never used it. Many people she knew collected guns that they never fired. When they continued to press her on this point, she responded that had she

> . . . known about this thing occurring [the assault on the high school] she would not have gone to school [on April 20, the day of the shooting] nor would she have returned back to the school after lunch with Monica, one of her closest friends . . . she would not have driven into the parking lot and put herself and her friends in that type of situation . . . she would have told the authorities . . . she would not have sat in her car in the parking lot and asked Monica the question of who is so stupid and retarded as to do this type of thing [the assault on the high school] sixteen days prior to graduation.

They tested the guns at Rampart Range, a section of the Pike National Forest about 35 miles southwest of Denver. In a videotape of the occasion, recorded using the school's equipment, Dylan is wearing his long black coat and a baseball cap turned backwards, his hair bushing out from under it like a clown. Eric wears his favorite KMDC cap turned backwards and a blue windbreaker. Mark Manes is there in a black leather motorcycle jacket and jeans, his long hair in a ponytail, appearing authoritative about the guns and how to fire them. A girlfriend, Jessica Miklich, curses enthusiastically about the power of the firearms. Philip Duran, ill-at-ease with the whole escapade, stays out of the picture much of the time. Dylan and Eric try out the shotguns, which are now sawed down at the barrel for more spray, and at the stock, to make them easier to conceal. Their violent kick abrades the skin between thumb and index finger, and the boys display their wounds to the camera like badges of honor. During the attack on the high school they will protect their hands with leather gloves, sharing a single pair because Dylan is left-handed. They use wooden bowling pins for targets, wedging them into the "V" between a low tree bough, resting them on branches, or propping them against tree trunks. The most striking aspect of the video, aside from peculiar air of festivity, is the difficulty they have hitting anything. Even when they aim at the tree trunks, they fire ten or fifteen shots before one finally scars the bark. When they hit a bowling pin, they are so delighted that they bring it close to the camera and point out the holes, using terms like "entree wound" and "exit wound" as though it were human. They discuss taking the pins home as souvenirs.

In the beginning of February, Eric and Dylan received an early discharge from the juvenile diversion program because of their exemplary behavior. The termination report on Eric described him as "a very bright young man who is likely to succeed in life," and Dylan as "intelligent enough to make any dream a reality, but he needs to understand hard work is a part of it."

In March, Eric and four other unidentified teens, one of them a girl, visited the Dragon Arms gun shop in Colorado Springs and tried to buy an M-60 machine gun and a pistol with a silencer. Eric "was doing all the talking," according to the store owner, Mel Bernstein. He refused to sell the guns to Eric because he was under 18. When the girl volunteered that she was 18, he threw them out. "They were real mopey, like punk kids with the makeup on, like punk rockers," Bernstein said. Although the Dragon Arms surveillance tape was given to the JCSO, the teenagers on it were never identified.

Eric and Dylan began recording the basement tapes to document their final month of preparation. The tapes remain unreleased to the public, but have been viewed and described by journalists and investigators selected by the JCSO. The first tape, almost two hours long, was recorded on three separate occasions in March. In the opening sequence Eric and Dylan face the camera posed like vintage-era gangsters, Dylan sitting in a tan recliner chewing a toothpick, Eric in the other seat, cradling the sawed-off shotgun in his lap, drinking straight from a bottle of Jack Daniels and grimacing as it burns his throat. The second tape, about 22 minutes in length, was recorded on two separate occasions on April 11 and 12, 1999, and the third tape, 40 minutes in length, was recorded on eight separate occasions, the first early in April, the last, April 20, 1999, the morning of the shooting.

The content of the basement tapes falls into three categories. First, they document their sadness and anger about the way they were treated during childhood. Eric describes moving around the country with his family, from one military base to the next, starting over from zero, socially, at every location. He recalls how classmates made fun of him, his face, his hair, and his choice of shirts (but never his sunken chest, the aspect of his physique most likely to elicit teasing). He was always "the scrawny white kid." Dylan speaks of his anger toward his brother, Byron, who humiliated him time and again. He complains that his extended family, his grandparents, uncles, aunts—but never his parents—treated him like an outcast. He even recalls being snubbed by the "stuck-up" kids at the Foothills Daycare Center, which he attended when he was three years old!

The self-pity turns easily to rage, and they revel in their hatred for every race including their own, for their enemies, and for the friends who didn't do enough to defend them.

"I hope we kill 250 of you," Dylan says. "It will be the most nerve-wracking 15 minutes of my life, after the bombs are set and we're waiting to charge through the school. Seconds will be like hours. I can't wait. I'll be shaking like a leaf."

Eric agrees. "It's going to be like fucking *Doom*," he says, referring to the video game. "Tick, tick, tick, tick . . . haaa! That fucking shotgun is straight out of *Doom*." They assure each other that their murderous rampage will endure in the daydreams and nightmares of the public. They talk about creating a "revolution of the dispossessed" (a term Marx coined to describe the serfs during the Russian Revolution), about being ghosts who would haunt the survivors, create flashbacks, and eventually "drive them insane."

The second topic was their skill at deceiving people. They gloat over how easily they fooled their parents. Dylan remembers a time in his room, when he was trying to conceal his sawed-off shotgun beneath his leather duster. His parents walked in and noticed nothing. Eric remembers his mother spotting the handle of his gun sticking out of his gym bag and assuming it was his BB gun. "I could convince them that I'm going to climb Mt. Everest, or I have a twin brother growing out of my back," he boasts. "I can make you believe anything." Eric mockingly describes the conversation he imagines his parents would have after he was gone: *If only we had reached them sooner, found the tape, searched their rooms, asked the right questions. . . .*

The third area involves a variety of narcissistic beliefs, some of them bordering on the delusional. There is quasi-Nietzschean talk of evolution to a higher level of existence ("above human"). They believe that their lives will become art, and that their killings will constitute some kind of "masterpiece," bringing them fame and inspiring people all over the world to anarchical and revolutionary behavior. In recent months they had filled their lives with "a lot of foreshadowing and dramatic irony" to enrich the biographical movie that they were certain would be made after their deaths. They believe that top Hollywood talent will vie to direct it, and they argue about whether Stephen Spielberg or Quentin Tarentino could better adapt it for the screen. They emphasize the originality of it. They are not simply copying what had happened in Oregon and Kentucky, they insist, evidently unaware of the many SR shootings that had preceded theirs. Their shooting will be different because of the scale of it, the violence, the brutality, the drama.

Finally, they document their cleverness in preparing the bombs, procuring the weapons, and planning the event. They take the camera on a guided tour of Eric's bedroom, showing off their armory. The video tape displays 21 pipe bombs, most of them six-inch segments of galvanized steel pipe packed with gunpowder and laced with nails and BB pellets; and 29 "crickets" or "grenades," small bombs fashioned from the kind of CO_2 cartridge used in seltzer bottles. The videotape shows a coffee can full of what the boys call "gunpowder," probably the slow-burning, unstable "black powder" used in fireworks and antique firearms, as opposed to the highly explosive "smokeless powder" of modern munitions. By the time they attacked the high school, they had constructed 27 pipe bombs, and 48 "crickets." Seventy-six of the devices were later found in and around the school, 13 rigged to blow up their cars. Eight more pipe bombs, of which they were particularly proud, remained in their homes as souvenirs. There were 11 one-and-a-half gallon propane bombs and two 20-pound propane bombs, created from the kind of propane tanks used in outdoor barbecues. Seven red plastic gasoline cans of various sizes were filled with 40 gallons of jellied gasoline, a crude form of homemade Napalm. Some of these containers would later be attached to the propane bombs as detonators. The videotape shows them performing dress rehearsals, and records a trip in Eric's car to buy supplies for the assault.

On another part of the tape, Dylan acknowledges the help of Mark Manes and Philip Duran, thereby assuring their conviction as accomplices.

> I'd like to make a thank you to Mark and Phil. I hope you don't get fucked. We used them. They had no clue. . . . Don't blame them. And don't fucking arrest them. . . . Don't arrest any of our friends, or family members, or our coworkers. They had no fucking clue.

Although Mark Manes and Phil Duran cooperated with authorities, they were both charged with illegally providing a handgun to a minor and possessing an illegal or dangerous weapon (the TEC DC-9 was made illegal by the Brady Act of 1994). They both pleaded guilty. Manes was sentenced to six years in prison, and Duran received a four-and-a-half year sentence. They were the only people charged with crimes related to the shooting.

On the tapes, the boys speak of April 19, the fourth anniversary of the bombing of the Oklahoma City Federal Building and the sixth anniversary of the Branch Davidian conflict in Waco, Texas, as the day for the assault on the high school. Why they rescheduled it for April 20 is not known. April 20 was Hitler's birthday (his 110th, were he alive). Four-colon-twenty (4:20) is the California criminal code defining punishment for possession of marijuana, and many pot-smokers had decided to skip school that day in observance of the unofficial "National Marijuana Day." April 20 was "free cookie day" in the lunchroom, which would mean a larger turnout and the potential for more fatalities. They may have thought Robyn Anderson would be absent on the morning of the 20th because of her class schedule (as it turned out, she attended school that day).

Throughout this period, they were scrupulous about concealing their homicidal and suicidal plans, pretending that they would live into adulthood. Eric talked about how he couldn't wait to turn 18 so that he could legally purchase guns. Dylan, accepted at the University of Arizona, told his parents that he planned to major in computer science. The family drove to Arizona together to visit the campus and help Dylan choose a dorm room. Sue Klebold described those days to Judy Brown:

> She was so excited about how Dylan was doing. Dylan was picking out his room and he was looking at the girls and talking about them; it was something he'd never really done before. He would nudge his dad and say, 'Ooo, she was gorgeous; did you see her?"
>
> She said she was so happy that Dylan was on his way. She asked him, "Are you sure you want to take off like this, to a big college? Do you maybe just want to break away slowly instead?" But he wanted to go. He picked out a dorm room that was going to be near the cafeteria. He talked about how great the campus was. He was excited.
>
> He loved computers and now he was going to computer school. He was planning on going to the prom. It was so unlike him, seeing him coming out of his shell like this. It seemed like he was happy, like he was finding his way. . . . And all the while, he was planning this massacre.

Eric applied to, and was rejected by, several colleges. Two weeks before the assault on the high school, he tried to enlist in the Marines. During his initial screening, Eric told the interviewer, Staff Sergeant Mark Gonzales, that he was not currently taking any drugs. Ten days later, during a home visit which Eric did not attend, Kathy Harris told Gonzales that Eric was taking Luvox. Gonzales promised to see how this might affect his eligibility. Two days later he left a phone message for Eric, but the call was never returned. In fact, Eric would have eventually been disqualified on three counts: because he was taking an antidepressant, because of his *pectus excavitum*, even though it had been partially corrected, and because he had lied during the interview. Eric wrote in his journal about how he would have been a good marine if only he had been given "a reason to be good."

The senior prom was scheduled for April 14, barely a week before the shootings. Suffering an attack of shyness, Eric asked a girl in his video production class to play Cyrano and invite Brandi Tinklenberg to be his date. "I hadn't planned on going to the prom," Brandi recalled. "It was late notice. It was nothing against Eric. He was always really sweet to me." Previously, when she walked into class, Eric would smile and say hello, but after she turned him down, he refused to look at her. On the day of the shootings she skipped school to visit a tanning salon, and for years afterwards wondered what would have become of her if she had attended school that day and crossed Eric's path. Eric asked some other girls to the prom, who also refused, and finally invited a girl over to his house to watch a movie.

After Dylan let drop that he had never been to a school dance, Robyn urged him to take her to the prom. He agreed, reluctantly, as a favor to her. Dylan picked her up at her house so her parents could take pictures of her in her prom dress and him in his tux. At their next stop, Kelli Brown's home, they met up with a group of ten friends and drove to the prom together in a stretch limo rented for the occasion. After a few hours at the dance, they returned to Kelli's house, changed out of their prom clothes, and drove as couples to the Columbine "after-prom" party. The theme was "New York, New York," and the major attraction was a gambling casino with blackjack tables and roulette wheels. Robyn chauffeured Dylan, perhaps because he had been drinking. There Eric caught up with them, and he and Dylan and Chris Morris spent most of the night at the "casino," gambling with play money. At around 3:00 AM they grew tired and Robyn drove Dylan back to Kelli's house, so he could pick up his tuxedo. She left him at his doorstep around 3:45 AM.

On April 18, in the middle of the night, Dylan completed his math homework along with eight pages of personal writings and drawings. "About

26.5 hours from now," he wrote on a sheet of notebook paper, "the judgment will begin. Difficult but not impossible, necessary, nervewracking & fun. *What fun is life without a little death?* It's interesting, when I'm in my human form, knowing I'm going to die. Everything has a touch of triviality to it."

The following night, Eric met with Mark Manes to buy 100 rounds of ammunition for the TEC DC-9.

Was he going shooting that night, Mark asked?

Eric replied that he might be going shooting tomorrow.

CHAPTER 6

CASE 13: THE SHOOTING AND THE AFTERMATH

Grieving / Memorializing

W HILE THE WEATHER AROUND DENVER often had a rainy chill that time of year, Monday, April 20, 1999, was sunny, the sky clear. The air was warming up after months of winter. Eric and Dylan recorded their activities for that morning in their day planners.

Dylan's read:

Walk in, set bombs at 11:09, for 11:17
Leave
Drive to Clemente Park. Gear up.
Get back by 11:15.
Park cars. Set car bombs for 11:18
get out, go to outside hill, wait.
When first bombs go off, attack.
have fun!

And Eric's:

5:00 up
6:00 meet at KS
7:00 go to Reb's house
7:15 he leaves to fill propane
         I leave to fill gas
8:30 Meet back at his house
9:00 made d. bag set up car
9:30 practice gearups
Chill
10:30 set up 4 things
11:    go to school
11:10 set up duffel bags
11:12 wait near cars, gear up
11:16 HAHAHA

Their schedules were organized around the moment when the boys imagined the cafeteria would be most crowded: 11:17 AM, or so Eric had calculated after spending hours in the cafeteria watching the students come and go. While Dylan wrote openly about "bombs" and used words like "attack," Eric avoided self-incriminating language and even referred to himself in third person—"go to Reb's house"—perhaps to further obscure his complicity in case something interfered with his suicide plan and he found himself in the courtroom, facing a possible prison sentence. Dylan's shorter, less complex list may have reflected a limited capacity to carry out complicated plans, or an unwillingness, on Eric's part, to trust him. "Having fun"—how little they had, how much they imagined others had, how often they perceived others as interfering with their own fun—is a recurring theme in their journals and in the basement tapes. In his last and only journal entree for 1999, Eric wrote, "I hate you people for leaving me out of so many fun things."

At 6:15 AM on the morning of April 20, Eric Harris appeared at his first-hour bowling class wearing ordinary school clothes and "not acting strange," according to classmate Jessica Rosecrans. After bowling, he drove to an open field east of Wadsworth Boulevard, about three miles south of the school, and left two backpacks jammed with pipe bombs, aerosol canisters, and small propane tanks, all set to be detonated by a timer. By scheduling these bombs to explode concurrently with the bombs in the cafeteria, they hoped to divert the deputies, and create an air of catastrophe and confusion. This was probably one of the "4 things" Eric planned to do at 10:30. A second thing, most likely, was videotaping their goodbyes. At some time between 10:30 and 11:00 AM, they went to Eric's house. He held the camera while Dylan spoke.

> It's about half an hour before our little judgment day. Just know that I'm going to a better place than here. I didn't like life too much, and I know I'll be happier wherever the fuck I go. So I'm gone.

Then Dylan taped Eric:

> I just wanted to apologize to you guys for any crap. To everyone I love, I'm really sorry about all of this. I know my mom and dad will be just fucking shocked beyond belief.

That morning Brooks Brown dragged himself out of bed and drove himself to school as he did every morning. He didn't notice anything out of the ordinary until third hour, when Eric failed to appear for Chinese Philosophy. A test had been scheduled that would account for a third of their semester grade and to miss it was to fail the course. During fourth hour, Creative Writing, both Dylan and Eric were absent. Again, this seemed strange. While they often cut Creative Writing, they always invited at least one of their friends from class, Becca Heins, Nate Dykeman, or Brooks himself, to join them. Becca and Nate were both in class that day and neither of them knew where Dylan and Eric had gone. After class, Brooks stepped outside for a cigarette. From his vantage point overlooking the south parking lot, he could see Eric's gray Honda pull into somebody else's space in the junior parking lot. It was ten minutes after 11:00.

"What the hell's wrong with you, man?" Brooks demanded, running up to the car. "You weren't in third hour, today. You missed the test!"

Eric gave him a look he couldn't decipher and laughed. "It doesn't matter any more. Brooks, I like you now. Get out of here. Go home."

Brooks recalled him pulling a light blue gym bag out of the back seat as he spoke. He was wearing a white t-shirt imprinted with the words, "Natural Selection," black fatigue-style pants, and black combat boots. The accretion of details gave Brooks a queasy feeling. On the basis of this and nothing more, as he states in his account of the shootings, he turned his back on Eric and began to walk quickly away from the school. He crossed the parking lot to Pierce Street, the four-lane, north-south road that ran by the school, at a quickening pace as he felt more and more certain that something awful was about to happen. He heard a succession of loud *cracks*, which he assumed were caused by nail guns at a nearby construction site, then the wailing of police sirens. He was a self-described ugly boy, six-foot-four inches tall, and probably the sight of him running hysterically from one house to the next, banging on doors and demanding to use a telephone, scared people into hiding. Eventually someone opened the door to him and gave him a phone. Brooks called his father and told him about his suspicions that Eric was planning an act of violence against the school, which was consistent with the rants they had read about—and tried to warn the police about—on his website. Some friends of Brooks who were driving by in their jeep picked him up and, using one of their cell phones, he joined the legions of 911 callers flooding the lines that morning. Police and fire engines were converging on the school and helicopters were circling overhead. A wave of hysteria was sweeping through the neighborhood fuelled by radio reports, unfounded, that the shooters had left the school and were prowling the streets looking for victims.

A student named Aaron Wright recalled seeing Eric carrying a duffel bag along the path that led to the cafeteria at about 11:15 AM. Its weight was apparent in that he lugged it with both hands. Another student, Sarah

Slater, who testified before the governor's commission, recalled noticing, at a few minutes after 11:00, a blue duffel bag on the cafeteria floor, at the base of a supporting column, barely worthy of notice among all the other student backpacks piled around it except that it blocked her way. She asked her friends if it belonged to any of them. She couldn't move it out of the way with her foot because of its weight, so she stepped over it. Soon a second duffel appeared alongside it, although nobody actually witnessed either bag being brought into the school. According to an FBI computer simulation, had the explosives in the duffels exploded at 11:17, as Eric and Dylan had intended, the explosion would have compromised the structural integrity of the school, bringing down the roof, killing more than a thousand and making it the worst school disaster in history. Those who survived would have fled, past Eric, stationed outside the west entrance of the school, or Dylan, stationed outside the east entrance, and been cut down like targets in a shooting gallery.

Eric returned to his car, the back seat of which was crammed with more explosives, two 20-pound propane tanks, 20 gallons of gasoline, and an assortment of pipe bombs, and set the detonator, jerry-rigged from a clock, for 11:47, by which time the parking lot would be crowded with unsuspecting deputies and rescue workers. He left the clock face-down to conceal the detonation time from anybody peering in the windows. According to Rick Young, a bomb technician from Littleton Fire Rescue, the bombs never detonated because of the unpredictable nature of fireworks powder, and "a very simple electronic failure," the details of which he refrained from sharing lest other amateur bombmakers benefit from the knowledge. One of Dylan's car bombs detonated that night around midnight because he had confused AM with PM.

Eric dressed in a long black duster, a backpack filled with pipe bombs, and a utility belt with pouches stuffed with shotgun shells. His capacious pockets bulged with crickets and 9mm clips. He had a match striker taped to his forearm to light fuses, and he wore a black leather glove with the fingers cut off, to protect his skin from the sawed-down shotgun's kick. He and Dylan carried seven knives between them. While students overheard them talk about stabbing victims, the coroner reported no such wounds.

Dylan had parked his BMW in the southwest senior lot in a space that was not his own. His car was also filled with explosives and set to detonate at the same time as Eric's. He stood now on a hill at the other side of the parking lot, armed with the pump shotgun and the TEC semiautomatic, waiting for the explosion, the fleeing students. He was wearing a t-shirt with the logo of the heavy-metal band Wrath, black cargo pants, and black combat boots, a red medallion with a hammer and sickle on the left boot. He too wore a full-length black duster, a back pack, a utility belt, a match striker, and the other glove from a set he had shared with Eric. During the autopsy, the coroner would discover "a large caliber, copper-jacketed bullet" in the toe of the right boot, just in case he should find himself without ammunition to end his own life.

Eric and Dylan waited. Eleven-seventeen came and went but nothing exploded. Realizing that the first phase of the attack had failed, they rallied at Eric's car and presumably decided to launch a commando-style assault on the school. Concealing their weapons under their dusters, they ran across the lot toward the cafeteria, and up the steps paved into the hillside, following the curve of the building. From the top of the steps they could see the school's west entrance, the southwest lot, the athletic fields to the west, and the north lawn where, because it was the first nice day in weeks, students were picnicking.

Inside the cafeteria, students who happened to be gazing out the window at that moment saw the gunmen and reportedly heard one of them shouting, "Go, go!" They watched in horror as they drew their weapons from under their dusters and fired repeatedly at Rachel Scott and Richard Castaldo, who were sitting on the lawn and eating their lunch.

During an appearance on NBC's *Dateline*, Rachel's mother told this story: after Richard Castaldo's first surgery—he had undergone seven surgeries for a bullet that struck his spinal cord—he told Mrs. Scott that the first shot had only wounded Rachel. The gunmen had approached her and asked her if she believed in God. When she said, "Yes," they fired three additional shots that killed her. Dylan had known Rachel in middle school, and was aware that she was an evangelical Christian. After subsequent surgeries, Richard no longer remembered her testifying to her faith, only that she had survived the initial shooting. He left the hospital in the end of August of 1999 and remains confined to a wheelchair.

A school custodian named Jay Gallatine routinely monitored the security tape of the cafeteria. Puzzled by the students crowding the windows and their looks of distress, he contacted Neil Gardner, the community resource officer, on his two-way radio. "Neil, I need you in the lunchroom, quick," Jay said, in a panicky voice. Usually Neil and his friend, a school security guard, had lunch in the faculty lounge but that day the cafeteria was serving teriyaki, which they both disliked. They bought sandwiches at a nearby Subway and parked on the south side of Clement Park.

Back at the school, three students, Daniel Rohrbough, Sean Graves, and Lance Kirklin, emerged from a side door, at the bottom of the steps. They were heading for Clement Park for a smoke between classes and were unaware of the shootings, the panic in the cafeteria, and the two gunmen watching them from the top of the steps. Eric took off his trench coat in deference to the warm day, aimed the carbine, and fired down on them. Daniel fell first. Lance tried to catch him but then toppled as he himself was shot. More bullets struck Sean, and all three boys lay on the ground wounded.

Five other students sitting on the west lawn, realizing what was going on, sprinted for the shelter of an athletic storage shed. Dylan and Eric opened fire and wounded two of them, Michael Johnson and Mark Taylor. Mark collapsed, unable to move. He had been shot eight times in the chest, arms, and leg. Michael, although bleeding profusely from a leg wound and other injuries, reached the storage shed. The other three students escaped uninjured.

Dylan started back down the stairs. He came up behind Daniel Rohrbough, who had regained his footing and was limping toward the cafeteria entrance, and fired a shotgun blast into his back, causing him to bleed to death. He was left lying on the sidewalk overnight because law enforcement agents couldn't identify the body. His parents, who suspected the worst, were not allowed to see if it was their son lying on the concrete walkway. Their suspicions about their son's death were not confirmed until the following morning, when they read about it in the newspaper. Later they were misinformed that their son had been the victim of friendly fire, an unnecessary mistake that caused them additional heartbreak and took over a year to untangle.

Approaching the already seriously wounded Lance Kirklin, Dylan fired a shotgun blast into his face. Over the next four months Lance was wheeled into the operating room six times for reconstructive surgery. His jaw and face were rebuilt with bone and tissue grafts from his leg, and titanium alloy. He did not eat solid foods again until August. He tried to return to school the following year but was unable to maintain regular attendance.

Sean Graves had taken a bullet in the neck and three more in the abdomen. One had bounced off a hip bone and fractured a vertebra. With his hands and arms, he pulled himself halfway into the cafeteria side entrance, propping open the door with his body. "I can't feel my legs," he told a teacher, Christina Redmerski. After months in the hospital he could walk short distances with the help of a cane to keep balance.

Dylan entered the cafeteria, stepping over Sean's body, and looked around, probably trying to determine why the bombs hadn't exploded yet. He left the cafeteria and rejoined Eric at the top of the hill.

At a minute or two before 11:21, some of the diversionary explosives left in Wadsworth Field, the pipe bombs and one of the aerosol cans, exploded, but the noise and the grass fire were enough to attract attention. The dispatcher sent a deputy to investigate and the fire department was also notified.

Anne Marie Hochalter had been sitting on the curb in the parking lot with some friends. When they saw the gunmen, they rose and ran across the lawn, hoping to reach the cafeteria. Eric shot at her again and again. A bullet in her spine paralyzed her for the rest of her life. One of her friends, Jason Autenrieth, dragged her out of the line of fire, to the shelter of the cafeteria's outside wall. Witnesses reported Eric and Dylan shouting, "This is what we always wanted to do. This is awesome!" They shot at students standing near the soccer field but missed them even though they were only a few yards away. Between shots they hurled pipe bombs and crickets onto the roof of the school, into the parking lot, and toward the grassy hillside.

At 11:23 AM the 911 dispatcher got a call reporting Anne Marie's shooting. ". . . a female down in the south parking lot" the caller reported. "I think she's paralyzed." Neil Gardner and the school security officer, still on route to the school and stopped by a red light at the corner of Fair Street, also heard the dispatch. The gravity of the situation began to sink in; he turned on the sirens and lights and stomped down on the accelerator. As they approached the school, they got a call on the two-way radio from Mr. Horvath, the dean of students: "Neil, I need you in the school, there's been a shooting." When they reached the school they were greeted by a plume of white smoke from an exploding pipe bomb.

Eight months earlier, following the Kip Kinkel shooting (Case 12), the Secretary of Education and the U. S Attorney General had released a landmark document, "Early Warning, Timely Response: A Guide to Safe Schools," which suggested that the best way for a school to deal with a crisis was to have a "school safety plan" in place, a brief document drafted with the help of local fire department and law enforcement agencies suggesting a course of action to follow during a crisis, and designating duties for staff. Columbine High School did not have a safety plan and this contributed to the chaotic nature of the response. There was no schoolwide policy about who to call, or what to do in a crisis.

Custodians Jon Curtis and Jay Gallatine; William "Dave" Sanders, who taught business courses and coached girls' basketball; and teachers Cheryl Lucas, Judy Kelly, and Monette Park, moved through the cafeteria, telling students to take shelter under the tables. Readers in their 50s and 60s may recall crouching under their school desks when they were little children in anticipation of Soviet missile strikes. It may have seemed just as pointless in the Columbine cafeteria that day but students complied; the time stamp reads 11:22:56 (hours: minutes: seconds). Around 11:24:00 something explodes—not the 20-pound propane tanks, more likely a cricket or a small pipe bomb, but it's enough to stampede the students. At 11:24:08 we can see them charging out of the cafeteria. At 11:25:35 the cafeteria appears empty but for a few stragglers injured in the crush. Four hundred and eighty-eight teens had evacuated the enormous room in 27 seconds or less.

The gunfire was coming from the west, so the panicked students ran east, up the staircase, along the central corridor, and out the east exit by Pierce Street. About 40 students took refuge in the choir room, while others barricaded themselves into offices and classrooms. While students knew that guns were being fired and bombs were exploding around them, they remained uncertain about the scale of the attack. Many witnesses described a gang of as many as eight assailants, of which Eric and Dylan were two, and provided detailed descriptions of the other killers. Columbine critics such as Russ Kick and Dave McGowan remain convinced that the assault on the high school involved other gunmen and may have continued until 3:00 PM that afternoon, three hours after Eric and Dylan committed suicide. Reports from the JCSO and the Governor's Report agree that there were only two gunmen. Some of the testimonies of witnesses were redacted by the JCSO to exclude the names of several other students who were identified as participants in the shootings. On the transcripts, they appear as black rectangles, inked in with a heavy hand. Although such redactions are often made to protect the identities of innocent people who have been wrongly identified, these particular redactions remain confusing and provocative, particularly in the light of the rest of the Jefferson County police work.

Patricia Nielson, another teacher, had been assigned to "hall duty." Looking out the double doors of the west lobby she saw a student dressed in black, holding a gun.

What was this all about? she asked a boy she didn't know, Brian Anderson, who happened to be standing beside her. Brian said that he recognized the boy from his video production class. They were probably making a movie. It was probably a cap gun. Cap gun or not, Mrs. Nielson didn't think it appropriate for him to have it at school and she was going to tell him so. As she approached the double doors, Eric leveled his carbine and fired. The glass shattered, pelting her with fragments of metal and glass, abrading her forearm, shoulder and knee. Shards were buried in her neck and back. "Dear God! Dear God! Dear God!" she screamed. Another shot shattered more glass, sending shards into Brian Anderson's chest. Brian and Mrs. Nielson fled toward the school library.

THE LIBRARY

Rather than eating a lunch at 11:15, so early that it seemed like a continuation of breakfast, Austin Eubanks preferred to go to the library and study with his friends, Corey DePooter, Makai Hall, and Dan Steepleton. Soon after they had settled in at a back table, they heard a distant hammering sound which Corey insisted was gunfire. After a few more volleys, the other boys were also convinced. Suddenly Patricia Nielson ran into the library yelling, "Where's Ms. Keating? Where's Ms. Keating?" Ms. Keating was the librarian. "That guy has a gun," she said. Brian Anderson followed a moment later, hunched over, with blood on his shirt. Using the phone at the front counter, Ms. Nielson called 911. Her reporting of the incident in a shrill, shaking voice is preserved on tape, punctuated in the background by gunfire and thunderous explosions. She interrupted her own call to shout at the students, who were standing around, gaping, "Everyone get under the table, get under the table!"

Neil Gardner had only now reached the school parking lot. He saw Eric standing on the lawn some 60 yards away, firing the carbine at the west doors where Patty Nelson had stood moments before. Then Eric saw him and turned and fired ten rounds at his car—none hit their mark—before the gun jammed. While he was trying to fix the mechanism, Gardner returned fire. Eric spun around as though hit, but then got off another round and escaped into the high school. Gardner got back in the car and radioed the dispatcher, reporting that shots had been fired inside the school and requesting help. He didn't follow Eric into the school.

Eric and Dylan stood just inside the west entrance, where the hallway that ran east-west, past the auditorium, met the hallway that ran north-south, past the library. Laughing, intoxicated by their newfound power, they fired down one hallway and then the other. Stephanie Munson, a junior, shot in the foot, fell to the floor and crawled to cover. At the south end of the library corridor, where the staircase descended to the cafeteria, Dave Sanders stood, just beyond their view and unaware of their proximity, herding students toward the Pierce Street exits. Now that most of the cafeteria students were out of harm's way, Sanders and a student turned the corner to the east-west corridor and started for the library, to evacuate the students there. Finding themselves face-to-face with the shooters, they turned and ran. The student escaped unharmed but Sanders was shot twice from behind by Eric, once in the torso, partially severing a vein, and once in the neck and head, cutting the carotid artery. He fell forward, then managed to get up on his hands and knees and, with the help of another teacher, reached the storage closet of a classroom in the science wing. Blood, pouring from his mouth, marked his passage. Some 30 students who had taken refuge there turned the closet into a make-shift ICU, balling up their shirts to make a bed for Sanders and covering him with wool blankets (required inventory in every science room). Students, including two Eagle Scouts with first-aid training, tried to staunch the bleeding but admitted later that they had never been trained to deal with gunshot wounds. Dave said, "I'm not going to make it. . . . Tell my girls I love them," referring to his two adult daughters. A teacher made a sign in blue marker which she held up at the window, "1 bleeding to death," a gesture which, because of its simplicity, humanity, and desperation, quickly became part of the iconography of Columbine. Another teacher called 911 repeatedly to report his deteriorating condition. Students snapped the legs off a table to improvise a gurney so they could carry him out of the school, but the 911 operator, falling back on protocol, kept urging them to leave him where he was and wait for professional help. The SWAT team arrived at 2:42—Eric and Dylan had killed themselves at noon—radioed for paramedics, waited for a half an hour and, when the paramedics still had not arrived, decided to move Dave closer to an exit. By the time the paramedics arrived, he had bled to death.

By now over 1,000 law enforcement officers and emergency medical personnel from Arapahoe County, Lakewood, Arvada, and other neighboring communities had converged on the high school. Some of them had to park as far as a mile from the school because of the congestion. On Wadsworth, a fire engine was dousing the flames of the earlier explosion. In the six local hospitals, emergency codes were being announced over the speaker systems, while medical workers readied their operating rooms, checked blood supplies, and prepared for incoming ambulances.

Eric and Dylan continued to prowl the library hallway, shooting randomly, hitting the walls and the ceiling and breaking windows. They reached the spot where Dave Sanders had stood minutes before and began pulling pipe bombs from their backpacks, lighting them and hurling them down the cafeteria stairwell, hoping to ignite the big propane bombs below. The cafeteria surveillance tape shows a pipe bomb exploding in the region of the propane bombs. The blaze is quickly extinguished by the sprinkler system.

In the library, Austin Eubanks and his friend, Corey DePooter, took shelter under a table in the far corner of the library. Austen crouched, and Corey lay on his stomach with his legs sticking out. Two more students, Peter Ball and Jennifer Doyle, huddled alongside them. They heard more gunshots. An explosion shook the floor. Austin stuck his head out for a moment and Patti Nielson shouted, "Get down!"

As Eric and Dylan approached the library, a student named Lisa Kreutz recalled overhearing one of them asking the other, "Are you still with me? We're still doing this, right?" It seems likely that Eric was seeking reassurance of Dylan's commitment to the next phase of the plan. That they could still experience uncertainty after the killing of Dave Saunders, Rachel Scott, and Daniel Rohrbough, and the wounding of so many others, strains belief. Athens might suggest that once you have made the decision to engage in extremely violent behavior, issues such as proximity to the victim and degree of interpersonal violence are no longer of much consequence. You turn the corner and that's that. A wealth of research indicates that among witnesses and victims of violence, the more proximal to the offender, the worse the trauma. It seems likely that killers also share this dynamic despite the psychological advantage of being in control of the situation, nominally at least. Killing at a distance, as when a bombardier drops bombs over a city obscured by clouds, is a very different experience than killing a man in hand-to-hand combat with a knife, to give an extreme example. I assume Eric and Dylan had already made some kind of plan to enter the library and kill people at close range, in a leisurely, premeditated manner, and the prospect of this probably frightened them as much as it thrilled them. The majority of the killing they would do that day—the predatory, calculated murder of ten classmates— would be done in the library, in the next few minutes.

They burst into the room, demanding that everyone get up, or, according to other witnesses, that students wearing white caps or baseball caps get up. Such caps were part of the jock "uniform."

At that moment, 56 students, two teachers, and two librarians occupied the room.

When no one responded to the command, one of the gunmen said, "Fine, then I'll start shooting."

Eric "racked" the shotgun and fired twice at sophomore Evan Todd, who was standing near the front counter. Todd dove behind the counter, avoiding the brunt of the blast, but a splinter from the shattered counter stuck in his eye and buckshot peppered his back. Strolling toward the library's west window, Dylan casually shot Kyle Velasquez, who was seated at a row of computers, in the back of the head, killing him. He was a special-needs student, developmentally delayed— the result of a stroke suffered in infancy—and possibly the only student in the library who hadn't grasped the importance of taking cover. Although he was big, six feet tall and 230 pounds, he behaved like a little boy, accompanying his mother when she ran errands, helping his father wash the car and cut the lawn.

Dylan and Eric then set down their backpacks and reloaded their weapons. Dylan took off his duster, as if settling in for the long haul. At this point Mrs. Nielson dropped the phone, leaving the 911 connection open, and took refuge under a desk. During the next seven and a half minutes, police dispatchers could hear Dylan and Eric move around the room, taunting and executing students and sparing the lives of others according to their whim. They could hear the screams, the crying, the pleading, and the explosions of gunfire so loud it made their ears ring. After the shootings, people were incensed to learn that authorities had listened to their children being executed without intervening. The JCSO countered by explaining that they had performed their job according to protocol; they had secured the perimeter of the school so that the killers could not escape. Later they released a video of the high school corridors demonstrating what a confusing place it was—a veritable maze, they suggested—to track down an assailant. This did not address the fact that they knew where the killers were, what they were doing, and precisely how to get at them. Sharp shooters even had them in their sights at certain moments during the library occupation but were warned not to fire.

Patrick Ireland, who was crouched under a table with Daniel Steepleton and Makai Hall, recalled one of the gunmen saying, "This is for all the shit you put us through." Daniel recalled them saying something about "the four years of bullshit you put us through." Dylan shot at the table where the three of them were crouched, wounding all of them.

Steve Curnow and Kacey Reugsegger were hiding under a computer table on the south side of the library. Eric killed Steve with a single shot to the neck, and opened a massive wound in Kacey's shoulder. Steve Curnow was, at 14, the youngest victim of the shooting, a passionate soccer fan, and one of those kids who had seen *Star Wars* so many times that he could recite the dialogue along with the actors. When the new *Star Wars* film, *The Phantom Menace*, premiered a month after the shooting, *Star Wars* fans around the country organized a Go-to-Star-Wars Memorial Day in his remembrance.

Cassie Bernall was huddled under another table. Harris rapped twice, said, "Peek-a-boo," placed the shotgun muzzle to her head and killed her execution style. Misty Bernall, Cassie's mother, wrote a book about her daughter's death called *She Said Yes: The Unlikely Martyrdom of Cassie Bernall* that related an alternative account of the killing, as told by a student identified only as "Josh." Josh admits that he ". . . did not see her at all but . . . says he will never forget what he heard as he crouched under a desk about 25 feet away":

I couldn't see anything when those guys came up to Cassie, but I could recognize her voice. I could hear everything like it was right next to me. One of them asked her if she believed in God. She paused, like she didn't know what she was going to answer, and then she said yes. She must have been scared, but her voice didn't sound shaky. It was strong. Then they asked her why, though they didn't give her a chance to respond. They just blew her away.

Another unidentified student remembers Cassie under a table, her hands clasped in prayer. Other library survivors have questioned whether it was Cassie, or another student with a similar voice, who was killed for her sincere answer. The identity of the speaker is less important than the courage displayed in the face of relentless hate. Prior to her tragic death, Cassie Bernall had put her life back on track through acts of love and faith; that is of importance.

When Eric fired the shotgun at Cassie, he lost control of the weapon and, during the recoil, the butt struck him in the face, breaking his nose. Bree Pasquale, a student who was sitting on the floor, exposed, because there was no more room under the tables, recalled that Eric seemed dazed from the blow, and blood poured from his nose. When he recovered his wits, he asked Bree if she wanted to die. Patrick Ireland drew attention to himself by trying to aid a wounded student nearby. Dylan shot him twice in the head and again in the foot, wounds he remarkably survived.

Dylan discovered Isaiah Shoels, one of Columbine's 16 black students, sheltered under a table with Matthew Kechter, and Craig Scott, Rachel Scott's older brother. All three were popular athletes, but Dylan was only interested in Isaiah. Although Isaiah was only four-foot-eleven, and Dylan was six-foot-two, he could not pull him out from under the table. He called for Eric, who joined him, leaving Bree Pasquale alive.

"Josh," the source of the Cassie Bernall story, describes what happened next.

They went over to Isaiah and taunted him. They called him a nigger before they killed him. [Eric killed him with a shotgun wound to the chest.] Then they started laughing and cheering. It was like a big game for them . . .

Dylan fired on Matthew Kechter, inflicting a lethal chest wound. Kechter, a 210-pound sophomore, played offense and defense on the football team, lifted weights, and was an A student. While he was jock—one of the few jocks they actually killed— he was only junior varsity, well-behaved and studious.

He was not representative of the jocks they envied so, the ones who got special treatment from the teachers, worshipful glances in the halls, dates with the prettiest girls. Craig Scott, lying in the expanding pool of Matthew's blood, pretending to be dead, was overlooked in the carnage.

Eric threw a CO2 cartridge, which rolled under a table where Makai Hall, Daniel Steepleton, and Patrick Ireland were crouching. Makai grabbed it and threw it to the south end of the library where it exploded without harming anybody. Eric jumped up on a row of bookshelves and began shaking them and swearing. They shot at the books. Paper and cardboard exploded and for a moment the air seemed to be filled with confetti.

At this time Austin Eubanks heard one of the gunmen say, "We're going to blow up the library," and they began to hurl pipe bombs. Lisa Kreutz remembered hearing windows breaking and students screaming. Austin Eubanks recalled fire alarms clanging, the air thick with smoke, and an atmosphere of confusion.

Dylan shot out the display cabinet near the front door. He turned the TEC-9 at the nearest table and, firing as fast as he could, shot Mark Kintgen, a student with cerebral palsy, in the head and the shoulder. Under the next table, a single one of his bullets penetrated Lisa Kreutz's wrist and lodged in Valeen Schnurr's body. A final volley of shots killed the third girl under the table, Lauren Townsend, captain of the girl's varsity volleyball team, member of the National Honors Society, straight A student, and candidate for valedictorian of the senior class.

Eric kneeled beside a table where two girls were cowering in terror. "Pathetic," he said, peering at them, but let them live.

While he and Dylan were standing at an empty table, reloading, Val Schnurr began to cry aloud "Oh my God," or "Oh, God help me!"

Intrigued, Dylan asked her if she believed in God.

She grew confused, denying and then confirming it, trying to anticipate the "right" answer.

Why?

Because it was what her family believed.

Dylan mocked her but let her live.

Eric fired under another table, wounding John Tomlin and Nicole Nowlen. When John tried to crawl away, Eric taunted him about trying to escape and Dylan kicked him and shot him repeatedly, inflicting wounds that would be fatal. John liked to work on cars and had driven to Mexico to help build a house for a poor family. Kelly Fleming, who wanted to be a published author one day, was Eric's next victim, slain by a shot in the back that killed her instantly; Eric continued to fire at the table behind her, again hitting Lauren Townsend, who was already dead, and Lisa Kreutz, and wounding Jeanna Park in the knee, the shoulder, and the foot.

It was now 11:37. Again Eric and Dylan paused to reload at a table in the center of the room.

"Identify yourself," Eric commanded, noticing a student hiding beneath a table. It was Dylan's friend, John Savage. John asked him what they were doing.

"Killing people," Dylan responded.

Did they plan to kill him? John Savage asked.

Dylan replied that he would be allowed to live because they liked him. He left the library unharmed.

Eric fired under a table, killing Daniel Mauser, a smart, owlish, blond boy with glasses, shooting him in the face. They crossed the library, firing randomly at the students huddled under the tables. Dylan pointed the TEC-9 at Austin Eubanks and his friends and sprayed them with bullets. Austin realized that he had been shot in the right hand, injuring his index and little finger, and his left knee. He saw blood on Jenny Doyle's left arm. Corey DePooter had his eyes shut and was moaning. Austin noted that there was "a lot of blood on his back." His ears rang from the gun's report. He played dead, resting his head against Corey's red backpack.

Several witnesses reported Eric and Dylan discussing how shooting had lost its thrill. Knifing people might be more fun, Dylan suggested. He had always wondered how it would feel to stab somebody. Later the authorities found seven knives between them but no evidence of their use, no blood stains or stab wounds.

As they were leaving the library, Dylan confronted Evan Todd, their first library victim, and berated him for being one of the jocks whom they detested. Evan replied that he had nothing against either of them, and he did not want to make trouble.

"You don't know what trouble is!" Dylan shouted.

He turned to Eric. Should he kill Todd?

Eric, possibly still disoriented from the blow to his head, did not seem to comprehend the question and Todd walked away unharmed.

As a parting gesture, Dylan shot a television and hurled a chair at a computer terminal on the main counter behind which Patti Nielson was hiding.

It was 11:42. During the previous seven and a half minutes, they had shot 22 students, killing 10 and wounding 12 more. Despite the clanging of the fire alarms, almost all the witnesses described it as eerily quiet after the gunmen had gone. Students avoided each other's eyes. After a few minutes, when they felt sure that Eric and Dylan wouldn't return, they began to straggle out an emergency exit. Austin Eubanks held Corey's wrist but could not find his pulse. He grabbed Dan Stapleton by the arm and helped him leave. Todd Adams saw Mark Kintgen, the student with cerebral palsy, being jostled by the crowd, and picked him up and carried him to safety. Only Lisa Kreutz and Patrick Ireland were unable leave because of the gravity of their injuries. Patrick Ireland, drifting in and out of consciousness, eventually made his way to a broken window and leaned out. Two SWAT team members, catching sight of him, drove their armored truck under the window and, climbing onto the roof, caught him as he lunged through the glass. The photograph and the video of the rescue were reprinted and replayed countless times in the months to come.

Lisa Kreutz lay gazing at the underside of the table until she was rescued by SWAT crew, combing through the wreckage at 3:22, and transported to Denver Health Medical Center. Patti Nielson crawled out from under the counter and hid in a cupboard in the library break room for the next four hours until the SWAT convinced her it was safe to leave.

After leaving the library, Eric and Dylan shot out a window, exchanging gunfire with Neil Gardner and other officers and SWAT team members. They moved down the library hallway and east along another hallway that ran by the science wing, peering through windows of locked classrooms, making eye contact with students and teachers, and then moving on. The JCSO described their movements at this point as "directionless." They fired into empty rooms. They taped a Molotov cocktail to the door of a storage closet and detonated it, starting a small fire; after they moved on, a teacher who had been hiding nearby extinguished it. Returning to the library hallway, they tossed more bombs down the stairwell, into the cafeteria. One or more of them exploded, blowing out a row of windows, but failing to ignite the big propane bombs.

At 11:44 the security tapes showed them back in the cafeteria, Eric kneeling like a sharp-shooter, resting his rifle on the stair rail, and firing at the duffel bags. Dylan walked right over to them and began tampering with the detonators, perhaps hoping to set them off manually. Somebody hiding in the cafeteria, identified by the sheriff's report only as "a witness," heard them remark, "Today the world's going to end. Today's the day we die." As they were departing, the ignition device for one of the big bombs, a container of flammable liquid, detonated, creating a small explosion, a burst of flames quickly extinguished by the overhead sprinklers. Deputy fire marshal Rick Young later told the Columbine Commission that "had it not been for the defective fusing of the explosive devices, particularly the two propane tanks, the death toll at Columbine High School would have exceeded a thousand."

Eric and Dylan's approach to the east side of the building was heralded by shots and explosions of increasing volume in the background of two 911 calls, one dialed by a school secretary, the second by a school security officer hiding in the administrative office. The gunmen were firing shots everywhere, it seemed, in the office, into the ceiling, and in the art hallway, the callers reported. Their movement appeared increasingly random and purposeless.

At 11:56 they returned to the cafeteria a final time, surveying the damage, and observing the police response in the parking lot. According to the sheriff's reports,

> Their images, captured once again on the cafeteria's security cameras, show a defeated posture. The bombs did not explode, the sprinkler system put out the fire caused by the gasoline and fuel explosion, and the damage seemed to be minimal compared with their original plan.

Returning to the library, deserted now but for the bodies of their victims, they stood at the window and fired more shots at the law enforcement officers in the parking lot. Sometime between 12:02 and 12:08 they approached the table beneath which lay the lifeless bodies of Matthew Kechter and Isaiah Shoels. They lighted a Molotov cocktail, which they placed on the table. The fuse burned down, the bottle broke, the flaming gasoline spilled out, starting a small fire, and setting off a smoke detector overhead. Crime scene specialists believe that Eric and Dylan killed themselves sometime between the moment they lighted the fuse and the time the smoke detector sounded. Lisa Kreutz, still lying semiconscious under a table, could not distinguish between the sounds of their suicide shots and the general cacophony, nor could Patti Nielson and three library staff, still hiding in the break room. Patrick Ireland, who was lying on the library floor unconscious, did not awake until around 2:30.

The forensics experts found no evidence inconsistent with a double suicide. A rumor circulated among Columbine students that Dylan and Eric had counted to three and then shot each other. An alternative story was that Dylan, coming to his senses at the last moment, had refused to kill himself and Eric had executed him. The story shows, if nothing else, the extent of the sympathy for Dylan, and the perception that he had been duped by his manipulative, charismatic friend. Six months after the shooting, when the basement tapes were screened for a select audience, public opinion became less sympathetic because of the savage emotions Dylan displayed.

The autopsy reports of both boys were sealed by a judge following the killings. Eric's report was released in response to a lawsuit filed by the *Rocky Mountain News*, but Dylan's remained sealed by the request of his parents. It too was eventually released, confirming that Dylan had taken his own life. The confusion stemmed from the fact the entry wound was on the left temple, and investigators had been under the mistaken belief that he was right handed. When people shoot themselves in the head, because they can't see what they're doing, they typically press the gun barrel against their skin for kinesthetic feedback regarding its position. The proximity of the barrel creates lacerations, because of the gas escaping the muzzle, and an aureole of soot, as a result of the powder being fired so close. This is referred to as gunshot residue or GSR. Intermediate, or close-range gunshot wounds, as would have resulted from Eric executing his friend, "show a wide zone of powder stippling, but lack a muzzle imprint and laceration. The area of powder stippling will depend upon the distance from the muzzle." Dylan's entrance wound showed the characteristic abrasion and residue, and no stippling.

Eric's autopsy revealed that he had a therapeutic level of Luvox in his blood, refuting speculation that he had stopped taking the medication prior to the shooting, and laying a foundation, however insubstantial, for a lawsuit against the Swiss pharmaceutical company, Solvay, which developed and manufactured it. Aside from the Luvox, the toxicology report indicated no evidence of alcohol or other drugs in their systems.

By 12:30 SWAT teams were moving cautiously from one classroom to the next, searching every desk and backpack, collecting and defusing pipe bombs, and liberating students in hiding. As students left the high school they were directed across the lawn to a holding area where they were frisked, questioned, and offered medical care. From the triage center across the street, they were taken by ambulance to one of the local hospitals, or bused to Leawood Elementary School to be reunited with their parents. In some photographs we see the students leaving the school in lines with their hands clasped over their heads, as if they were the prisoners. While the circumstances of the shooting seem pretty obvious in retrospect, at the moment and for several days afterwards, deputies remained confused about the number and identity of the shooters. At 4:00 PM they found Eric and Dylan's bodies and at 4:30 declared the incident over. The sheriff's office estimated 25 casualties. The entire school was taped off as a crime scene, the bodies of the deceased left where they had fallen, some of them overnight.

The relief that parents waiting at Leawood experienced at being reunited with their teenage sons and daughters is difficult to describe. As the hours wore on and the buses grew less frequent, a pall fell over those parents who were still waiting. Some of them accepted the fact that they would never see their child again, while others kept hoping that it was a case of missed communications, or confusion about the assigned meeting place.

Throughout that day and the next, crime scene analysts picked through the rubble, collecting spent shells, analyzing blood traces, and gingerly defusing unexploded devices. On the evening of the 20th, while specialists were transferring the bombs into a trailer, one was accidentally detonated but no one was hurt because the technicians were wearing protective suits. Once photographs had been taken and distances measured, bodies were removed from the crime scene and transported to the Jefferson County Coronor's Office to be formally identified and autopsied.

Students who survived reported a heightened awareness of their mortality. Columbine student Aaron Welsh realized ". . . I could have been one of the students who didn't make it out alive . . . I started to wonder how I would be remembered. . . . Would they say I lived my life to the fullest?" Others, like Janelle Behan, described demonstrations of group solidarity—"There were people I hardly knew, comforting me and hugging me"—and surprising mobilizations of strength and courage: "There was a group of six boys who literally saved all our lives. . . . It was kind of funny because many of these boys are thought of as goofy kids in everyday life." Others reported experiencing reconciliations with their families, and a renewed appreciation of life. Survivor guilt was everywhere. Rachel Goodwin, a friend of Lauren Townsend, wondered why her life had been spared. "Why Lauren? What did she ever do in her life to deserve such a fate? Why not me?" Some students simply could not tolerate the sadness and sense of loss. "Even during the first weeks . . . there were others who were eager to 'get over all the fuss' and move on."

Rachel Scott's Honda and John Tomlin's pickup truck, discovered the next day in the Clement Park lot, became spontaneous shrines for grieving classmates. John had started saving for that truck when he was 14. Students found comfort in being near the vehicles, in decorating them with bouquets of flowers, notes, and poems (often sealed in baggies to protect them from the weather) and blue and white balloons (the colors of the high school and of the Columbine flower). Adults erected a canopy over the car, as they did some of the other makeshift shrines, to protect them from Denver's wettest April in 100 years. Clement Park remained the locus of the mourning. In imitation of the wall around the Oklahoma City Federal Building, a wall of two-by-fours and latticework was erected. People from around the nation and around the world—as many as 200,000 according to the Foothills Park and Recreation Department—came to pay their respects and leave stuffed animals, crosses, angels, candles, bouquets, photographs, ribbons, and the omnipresent blue and white balloons. Soon an entire acre was covered with objects arranged so densely that it was difficult to find a place to walk between them.

At one end of the park, a mound of dirt displaced from a construction project, dubbed "Rebel Ridge" by the students, rose twenty feet in the air to overlook the park and the high school, now boarded up like an abandoned factory. During the first week of May, Greg Zanis, a woodworker from Chicago, traveled to Littleton and, on his own initiative, erected 15 rough-hewn crosses, six feet high, in a row across the length of the ridge. Thirteen were for the victims, two for the killers. Eric and Dylan's names were written on their crosses in a different font to distinguish them from the rest. Pictures of the crosses set against the bleak Colorado sky, often with mourners huddled beneath them, seemed to capture the grief and despair of the moment. Some of the people who visited the Ridge were upset to be reminded of the killers in this way. Some wrote angry messages on the crosses of the killers—"evil bastard" on Eric's—while others encouraged forgiveness. On Friday morning, Rich Petrone, Daniel Rohrbough's stepfather, destroyed the two crosses that represented the killers. The next morning somebody had put up two smaller crosses to take their place. This question of inclusion or exclusion of the killers in the grieving rituals, of expressions of rage versus forgiveness for their unthinkable crimes, would be played out again and again in months to come.

On May 10th a candle started a fire in Clement Park which spread, burning the items surrounding it and the canopy that sheltered it before the fire department got it under control. The next day, one month after the shootings, the Colorado Historical Society began the lengthy task of boxing up all the memorial objects for posterity. Volunteers joined together to clean up the park from the refuse and wear of hundreds of thousands of visitors. The crosses were removed from the ridge for environmental reasons, but that was not quite the end of the dispute. In mid-September, 15 ten-foot-tall sycamores were planted by members of Littleton's West Bowles Community Church to commemorate the dead. On Sunday, September 26, during a rally outside the church, Rich Petrone cut down two of the trees. He said that the church could "honor murderers, but they're not going to honor Dan with them." He was accompanied by Al Velasquez, Kyle's father. Earlier, West Bowles church had sent a letter to the Rohrbough family informing them of the plan to plant the trees and stating that "hate is our true enemy." Members of the youth group propped up the two sawed down trees. Police made no arrests.

Parents of the deceased had to plan funerals for children who had overnight become nationally known. Ministers and funeral directors helped with the logistics of scheduling 13 funerals over the next nine days (classes would resume on Friday, April 30) in such a way that a mourner who was so inclined might attend all services, as well as non-funerary Sunday morning services. They expected that crowds might exceed a thousand. John Tomlin's funeral was held on Friday. Rachel Scott's huge funeral was on Saturday. Bruce Porter, a visiting minister who presided, was criticized for trying to co-opt the tragedy to promote a right-wing religious agenda. Later that week, during an appearance on Pat Robertson's television show *The 700 Club*, Rev. Porter stated, "Prayer in schools was officially reestablished on April 20, 1999, because it was accompanied by bombs and shootings. It is always the blood of martyrs that acts as rocket fuel for the church." On Sunday evening, Kelly Fleming and Dan Mauser had a joint funeral service at a local Catholic church in the late afternoon. The funerals of Dave Sanders, Lauren Townsend, Cassie Bernall, and Dan Rohrbough were scheduled consecutively for Monday, at one-hour intervals with a one-hour break for lunch; services for Kyle Velasquez, Corey DePooter, and Matthew Kechter took place Tuesday; and the community grieved for Steve Curnow on Wednesday. The final service, that of Isaiah Shoels, was held on Thursday, at noon. Five thousand mourners attended. A reporter from the Associated Press remarked that, "Many in the crowd appeared exhausted."

While this was the sixth school shooting in 18 months, the American public had not tired of such spectacles. CNN's broadcast of Rachel Scott's funeral received the highest ratings of any show ever aired on that network.

On Sunday, April 25, a memorial service was organized by Governor Bill Owens, whom *USA Today* characterized as "a young Republican with close ties to his state's religious right." Sixty-five thousand people amassed in the Bowles Crossing Theater parking lot, a shopping mall across the street from Clement Park, to mourn the deceased and pray for the wounded. Vice President Gore and General Colin Powell joined the Reverend Franklin Graham, the son of Billy Graham, and local pastor, Gerald Nelson, to conduct the memorial service. Governor Owens read a necrology, releasing a white dove into the air for each name. The word "columbine" is derived from the Latin, *columbinus*, meaning "dove-like." The names of the killers were not included. Four Air Force F-16s flew overhead in a "missing man" formation.

While the service represented the faith of the majority of Littleton residents, representatives of other denominations, and of other races, were upset at being marginalized or excluded. Neither blacks, nor Hispanics, nor Jews, nor non-fundamentalist Christians were represented in an event that had been publicized as a ceremony to comfort *all* the people of Colorado and of the nation. Jews were particularly offended by a story told by Reverend Nelson about one of two women imprisoned in a Nazi concentration camp during World War II, who supposedly survived because she had accepted Christ as her savior. Others were troubled by the collaboration of the federal government and right-wing evangelicals, and how this impacted on the separation of church and state.

On Friday, April 30, two thousand emotionally battered Columbine students made their way over to Chatfield High School to finish out the last month of school. Columbine's facilities were too badly damaged to serve the students, and even if it had been possible to make superficial repairs in that short period of time, many of the students were too traumatized to re-enter the building. Even after the Chatfield athletic department had limed a great heart on their football field, containing the name Columbine High School, not all students felt welcomed. Eric and Dylan's close friends, Brooks Brown, Nate Dykeman, Zach Heckler, and perhaps a dozen other students were asked not to return to school. They were offered passing grades in all subjects and a diploma in return for simply staying home. Brooks, who had been failing several courses, wrote that it was ". . . an offer I couldn't refuse." While the administration would not provide a reason, the decision to exile the clique was probably more protective than punitive. Brooks described people muttering "murderer," behind his back and occasionally shouting it to his face from a passing car. He writes in his memoir that he had become another victim of Columbine; his social life as a Littleton teenager was over as surely as if he had taken a bullet himself.

The JCSO did little to dispel the rumor of Brooks' involvement. Soon after the shooting, when information became public about the reports the Brown family had made regarding Eric's homicidal threats against their son and the failure of the JCSO to intervene, Sheriff Stone smarmily suggested, during an appearance on the *Today Show*, that criticism of the investigation was "a smokescreen" to divert attention from Brooks' possible complicity in the shootings.

The public grew more incensed as information leaked out about Eric and Dylan's other antisocial activities during the years before the shooting, the complaints filed against them, the reports of attempts to buy weapons, the pipe bomb exploded in an empty field, the vandalism, the burglary, the homicidal threats, the racist rants on the website, and repeated warnings of a massacre. Why had nothing been done? For the Brown family, uncovering the truth became a personal crusade. They found that the JCSO investigation file of Eric's website had vanished in its entirety. The draft search warrant of Eric Harris's home came to light in April of 2001, but only after CBS News went to court to force its release. It had been filled out but never submitted to a judge.

In the winter of 2000, then-Governor Bill Owens formed a commission to study and report on the shootings. The alleged purpose was to identify lessons that would reduce the likelihood of its recurrence, and improve medical and law enforcement response, but the public clearly hoped for a document that would set the record straight regarding JCSO's actions before and during the shootings. Although JCSO had courted the media, providing access to records and leaking evidence to *Time* magazine, they refused to help the commission with anything beyond the most superficial information, "on the grounds that civil litigation was pending against the sheriff and other Jefferson County officials, commenced by victims and their families," and that "several of the defendants would be prejudiced in the course of that litigation were they to provide the data sought by the commission." By this time, JCSO was involved in ten separate lawsuits involving the shootings. The Denver police department also refused to cooperate, canceling their scheduled appearances before the commission without explanation. However, the FBI, the Arapahoe County sheriff's office, the Lakewood police, the Arvada police, and other agencies, cooperated fully. The commission's final report stated that the sheriff's report, circulated on CD-Rom and through their website, contained "inaccuracies and omissions."

In September of 2004, a grand jury report, prepared in response to ongoing public outcry, revealed that Sheriff Stone, District Attorney Dave Thomas, County Attorney Frank Huftless, and Sheriff's Lieutenant John Kiekbusch had met clandestinely in the days after the shooting to decide how they would explain their failure to act on the search warrant that was written in response to the threat on Brooks Brown's life, and how they would handle press inquiries regarding that document. A report by Colorado Attorney General Ken Salazar, released at the same time, revealed that Kiekbusch had "ordered the destruction of a 'pile' of Columbine records and that key documents were purged from the computer system at the sheriff's office in the summer of 1999."

Eleven families of slain and injured victims sued Jefferson County, charging that, had the sheriff's office responded more professionally, their children might still be alive. They complained about the JCSO's attempt to conceal the history of Eric and Dylan's antisocial behavior, their failure to intervene during the library shootings, and their decision to keep paramedics out of the building for an excessive amount of time, resulting in the death of Dave Sanders. Families also sued the school district. Some documents suggested that school personnel had known how dangerous Eric and Dylan were and should have done something to prevent the crime. As is frequently the case in crimes of this sort, the failure to communicate information (about violent class essays, about criminal acts, about psychiatric problems, about the adolescent's medical and psychiatric history) prevented the crisis from being averted. This is a particularly thorny problem because of the confidentiality that surrounds psychiatric treatment, as well as the confidentiality of juvenile justice proceedings. These same communications issues were revisited during the recent Virginia Tech shooting (April 16, 2007), where numerous warning signs and a history of serious mental illness were suppressed, resulting in the deaths of 32 students and professors. On the other hand, many adolescents go through a period of "experimenting" with criminal behavior and subsequently become adults who are valued by society; by the same token, many who suffer mental illness make outstanding contributions to our culture. Life is difficult enough without early experiences of psychiatric and behavioral problems branding the individual like the mark of Cain.

In November of 2001, the lawsuits against the JCSO and the school district—all except that of Dave Sanders' family—were summarily dismissed because the county and the school district were protected by government immunity. "Holding police officers liable in hindsight for every injurious consequence of their actions would paralyze the functions of law enforcement," U.S. District Judge Lewis Babcock stated. Many families appealed the decision and later, in June of 2002, settled for $15,000 apiece from the county and another $15,000 from the school district. Dave Sander's lawsuit was allowed to proceed because the circumstances seemed so egregious. Members of the Sanders family claimed that police gave "repeated false assurances that help would be there in ten minutes." Police had prevented paramedics from going to aid Mr. Sanders even though they knew his location, the gravity of his condition, and that the shooters were no longer a threat. When the lawsuit was settled for 1.5 million dollars in the summer of 2002, some were relieved to have it over, but others were frustrated by the plaintiff's agreement to keep confidential all evidence and testimony that had been uncovered during the discovery process. Another lawsuit that was allowed to proceed was that of Patrick Ireland, who came to be known as "The Boy in the Window." His was the last of the lawsuits to be settled, in

March of 2004, with Jefferson County paying him $117,500.

A number of families, perhaps as many as 36, filed lawsuits against the Harrises and the Klebolds, claiming that they had the responsibility and the opportunity to prevent the slayings; they also sued those who had supplied Eric and Dylan with guns. The insurance companies offered a settlement of 2.85 million dollars to be divided among the plaintiffs in the summer of 2002. Among the six families who refused to settle were the Shoelses.

> Race played a pivotal role in their decision. Isaiah Shoels and his two siblings constituted three of the 16 black students in a school of 1,965. An eyewitness reported one of the gunmen remarking, "Look, there's the little nigger," before killing him. "Should that be the last thing you have to hear before the last breath leaves your body?"

While living in Littleton, the Shoelses had repeatedly been the victims of hate crimes involving vandalism of their home and car.

Dave Sanders' family, Mark Taylor, and three other Columbine families sued Solvay, the pharmaceutical company that manufactured Luvox, the effects of which, they alleged, had predisposed Eric toward his shooting spree. Eventually all but Mark withdrew their claims. By the fall of 2002, Mark had established a career as a motivational speaker, touring the country and talking about his experience at Columbine. Lisa Van Syckel, a New Jersey housewife whose adolescent daughter had a violent reaction to an SSRI (but not Luvox), heard about his campaign and donated $31,000 to keep the lawsuit afloat. Solvay settled with them in February of 2003 in return for a donation of $10,000 to the American Cancer Society.

Dave Sanders' wife and two step daughters sued 11 video game manufacturers and Time/Warner, producers of *The Basketball Diaries*, a film in which an alienated high school student, played by Leonardo DiCaprio, dreams of dressing up in a black duster, drawing a shotgun from under his black duster and killing a number of classmates. Dylan and Eric had watched it on several occasions. The lawsuit alleged that the producers should have known that their products could have led to an event like the assault on Columbine. They also suggested that the video games were "defective" because they taught Eric and Dylan to shoot but did not teach them the responsibilities or consequences of using guns. "Setting aside any personal distaste, as I must," U.S. District Judge Lewis Babcock wrote, dismissing the lawsuit in March of 2002, "it is manifest that there is social utility in expressive and imaginative forms of entertainment, even if they contain violence."

The annual convention of the National Rifle Association, which was scheduled to take place the weekend following the shooting, April 30, May

1 and 2, in Denver, was stripped down to bare bones. The three hundred-odd exhibitors, ranging from *Soldier of Fortune* magazine to the Rocky Mountain Elks' Foundation, were told to cancel their travel plans. Only an annual members meeting, as required by New York State not-for-profit statutes, where the NRA is incorporated, was conducted. Charlton Heston, president of the organization, said in a planned statement, that "the tragedy in Littleton . . . calls upon us to modify our schedule to show our profound sympathy. . . ." No "festive" events, he promised, would be conducted. Protestors, among them many Columbine students and parents, marched from the state capitol to the Adams Mark Hotel, where the convention was taking place. They formed a human chain around the hotel, and waved placards that read "Shame on the NRA" and "NRA, Pusher of Child Killer Machine." Tom Mauser, father of shooting victim Daniel Mauser, carried a banner that read, "My son died at Columbine, he'd expect me to be here today." He spoke to the crowd about the absurdity of a society where a child can easily obtain a TEC-9, an automatic weapon designed with no purpose beyond committing mayhem. When President Clinton gave his State of the Union address in January of 2000, Tom Mauser was invited to sit in the gallery. After this, Mauser took a year-long leave from his job with the Colorado Department of Transportation to serve as director for political affairs for SAFE (Sane Alternatives to the Firearms Epidemic) Colorado, a not-for-profit lobbying organization. He remains a passionate and articulate anti-gun activist to this day.

At the time of the shootings, three firearm related bills were being debated in the state congress, all aimed toward relaxing controls over guns and facilitating their sales. SB 84 simplified the process of getting permits for concealed weapons, SB 205 limited the freedom for local governments to litigate against gun manufacturers, and a third bill gave state laws precedence over local ordinances in case of a conflict. Responding to a slough of negative emails and calls from constituents, the sponsors of the bills agreed to have the legislation scrapped or tabled. Representative Gary McPherson, a Republican from Aurora, spoke for all legislators when he said it was done "out of deference to the victims and their families. Now is not the time to have this debate."

At this time a variety of firearm control bills initiated during previous school shootings were lying dormant in the Republican-controlled Congress. There were bills requiring gun owners to use lock boxes or trigger locks, bills requiring gun show dealers to conduct background checks on buyers before selling firearms, bills regulating Internet guns sales, and reinstating the five-day waiting period before the purchase of a handgun. The week after Columbine, President Clinton proposed, as part of an omnibus anticrime package, reviving the previous gun legislation and adding new laws, including background checks on the sales of explosives, and a lifetime ban on gun sales to those who had committed violent crimes as juveniles. He proposed federal child access prevention (CAP) laws. CAP laws held parents responsible for gun crimes committed by their children. Furthermore, any adult who allowed a child access to a gun that was subsequently used in a crime would be held criminally liable and pay a $10,000 fine. The sixteen states that had already adopted CAP laws reported a 23 percent reduction in fatal unintentional shootings, demonstrating the utility of such laws beyond any question.

The juvenile justice bill debated in the Senate the following month, which had already been in development for two years, was one sponsored by Orin Hatch, a Republican from Utah. Gun control measures were hotly debated, in particular the need for background checks at gun shows. The final vote, a fifty-fifty split, was resolved by Vice President Gore. In the Republican-dominated House, gun-control legislation was trimmed to the bone and funds were redirected toward toughening prosecution of younger teens, mandating prison sentences for violent teens, and banning those under 18 from purchasing excessively violent or sexual computer games. Democrats criticized their opponents for trying to maintain the appearance of cracking down on crime without confronting gun control, which they considered the core issue. Henry Hyde, a Republican from Illinois and Chairman of the House Judiciary Committee, insisted that, "What happened in Colorado and Georgia will not be remedied by passing new federal gun laws." He blamed the homicides on a decline in cultural values.

Eight months after the legislation had been proposed on March 7, 2000, the Department of Justice published a report called *Kids and Guns*. Seventy percent of juvenile homicides between 1980 and 1997 involved guns, the report stated, and the rise in homicides from the mid-1980s to 1993 was gun-related. The gun homicide rate in the U.S., it pointed out, was higher than in the 25 other industrialized countries of the world *combined*. Clinton used the report as a call to action to the House, where the gun control legislation remained in a logjam. At about this time Clinton also proposed a $10 million budget initiative for "Smart Gun Technology," which would assure that a gun could be fired only by its legal owner. This initiative did not arise from concern about school shooters or adolescent violence. During the 1990s, 57 police officers had been slain by their own weapons in the hands of others, and the FBI was promoting the development of Smart Guns as a remedy. The Department of Justice partnered with Smith & Wesson and FN Manufacturing, the producers of the M16 machine gun and other military weapons, to study different approaches to the problem.

One would imagine that an event like Columbine would mobilize a country around gun control. Following the massacre of school children in Dunblane, Scotland, in 1996, Great Britain banned handguns, buying back weapons from their owners. During the next two years gun-related crime in that country decreased by 17 percent. However, in fairness, handgun-related homicides were already relatively rare in Great Britain, and there was no romance with guns as there is in this country, no mythology like ours of the "Old West" glorifying gun fighters and gun play. While individual states continue to pass CAP laws, and laws requiring background checks for unlicensed vendors at gun shows, *none* of the gun-control legislation proposed after Columbine became federal law.

Most of the parents of victims banded together in a project to board up the library and build a new one, new classrooms, and an atrium open to the sky. They met as a group two or three times a week to socialize, provide mutual support, and strategize about the 3.1 million dollars they had to raise to complete the project. During an appearance on the *Today Show* to mark the one-year anniversary of the assault on the high school, Dawn Anna, Lauren Townsend's mother, acting as spokesperson for the group, described a sense of haste to get the renovation underway. "Because of the outdoor classrooms, it has to be built during the summer. Once we take care of the children, we can deal with our own grief which we have been pushing down."

Meanwhile Littleton civic leaders led a campaign to create a permanent memorial site on the southeastern side of Clement Park. They dealt with the usual issues of creating a memorial: pleasing a great number of people with diverse tastes and ideas; issues of scale; of accessibility; of incorporating symbols that had been important to the community, such as the blue and white ribbon; and of creating something that would make the human spirit soar rather than cripple it with grief and gloom. In an attempt to satisfy everyone, the design may have become baroque:

> The interior of the memorial is an oval stone outer wall softened by a grove of trees in the center and low native plantings around the edges. . . . As the memorial elements are revealed, the visitor notices the inner Ring of Remembrance, and the outer Ring of Healing. At the core of the memorial, an intimate grove of trees grows out of an oval of intricate landscape and stone paving. . . . This low elegant wall

of stone invites you into a circle of stories. The stone is etched with words that are individual narrative remembrances of the deceased victims; remembrances crafted from interviews of the victim's family and friends. . . . An intricate ribbon design fills the center space and hugs the Ring of Remembrance. The tails of the ribbon, inscribed with the phrase "Never Forgotten" frame a connection to the outer Ring of Healing becoming a symbolic link between the community and the deceased.

The cost of the memorial was estimated at three million dollars, two and a half for the construction and another half-million for the mainte- nance endowment, but following the downturn of the economy, and the tragedies of September 11th and Hurricane Katrina, the scale of the proj- ect was reconceptualized, the budget trimmed to 1.5 million. President Clinton, who had felt a personal concern about SR shootings since the 1998 incident in Jonesboro, Arkansas, within spitting distance from Little Rock and where he had sat as governor for 12 years, raised several hundred thou- sand dollars for the fund through personal appearances. On April 24, 2007, the Columbine Memorial Fund announced that it had successfully reached its goal and construction began. The memorial was dedicated on Friday, the 21st of September, 2007, bringing a degree of closure to this terrible event.

CHAPTER 7

REDUCING THE INCIDENCE
OF SR SHOOTINGS
AND SCHOOL VIOLENCE

T HE RESPONSE TO A CRISIS such as a school shooting is sometimes con-
ceptualized as having three dimensions: prevention (how it can be
prevented); intervention (what to do while it is occurring to minimize damage and loss of life); and postvention (how to help the survivors deal with
what has occurred and regain their pre-crisis level of functioning). In this
chapter I will discuss the current thinking regarding crisis response as it
applies to SR shootings. I will begin with a review of the primary strategies
(those specific to identifying and preventing a school shooting) and secondary strategies (those that reduce school violence in general). Then I will discuss interventions and postventions. The chapter ends with a short history
of gun technology and gun control.

PRIMARY PREVENTION STRATEGIES

IDENTIFYING A POTENTIAL SR SHOOTER

Identifying an SR shooter before the shooting takes place is the most
appealing form of prevention. People whose knowledge of criminology is
derived from television and movies—and this group includes most legislators, educators, and policy mavens—may believe that it is simply a case of
developing an accurate profile, as the FBI has done with serial killers.
Consulting firms, preying on school administrators' fears, have offered violence prediction services, with and without specially designed software to
enhance the credibility of the enterprise. I have two responses: First, the FBI
does not *ever* use its profile of serial killers to predict who will commit a
crime; it uses them to winnow down the suspects *after* a crime has been
committed. Currently, predicting crimes before they are committed is the

purview of science fiction, and it is hard to imagine how such predictions could ever be accomplished without sacrificing some of our most basic constitutional rights. The following paragraph from the FBI report on SR shootings explains (scraping the fender of Nonsense while trying to squeeze into too tight a space) that even if you could predict a violent incident, you couldn't.

> Reliably predicting any kind of violence is extremely difficult. Predicting that an individual who has never acted out violently in the past will do so in the future is still more difficult. Seeking to predict acts that occur as rarely as school shootings is almost impossible.

An earlier report from another branch of the government presents a list of risk factors for identifying SR shooters (social withdrawal; excessive feelings of isolation and rejection; feelings of being picked on and persecuted, etc.), but concludes with the caveat: "Such signs, may or *may not* indicate a serious problem."

The quest for identity that lies at the heart of adolescence may take on bizarre forms. I recall teenage boys who came to school in tuxedos, or the camouflage costumes designed by the army for desert warfare, and girls who, ducking into the lavatory when they arrived at school, would change from the modest clothing in which their mothers had sent them, into garb more appropriate for sex workers. High schools make pariahs of those who are unusually pierced, shaved, dyed, or draped. It is easy to imagine the stigma of "potential school shooter" being added to the burden of criticism already weighing down these tormented souls. While SR shootings remain rare events, teen suicides do not.

THREAT ASSESSMENT PROTOCOL

Even though one cannot identify a would-be school shooter, or predict when a shooting might take place, it is still possible to avert an SR shooting using an approach known as "threat assessment protocol."

Four months after Columbine, the National Center for the Analysis of Violent Crime, a division of the FBI, held a five-day symposium on preventing school shootings. One hundred-and-sixty law enforcement agents, school administrators, psychiatrists, and mental health professionals converged on Leesberg, Virginia, among them well-known authorities such as Dewey Cornell, Park Dietz, James Garbarino, and Robert D. Hare. From their analysis of 18 FBI case histories of school shootings or foiled attempts, they identified threat assessment as the key tool in avoiding a school shooting. "Without exception, these kids will tell you what they are going to do beforehand," was their consensus. The FBI refers to such communications as "leakages," and they can be verbal, or take the form of drawings, journal writings, videos, or school essays. Consider Harris and Klebold's video production, *Hit Men for Hire*. Leakage may also occur when the shooter tries to solicit the help of friends or classmates in obtaining weapons, or perpetrating violence. Leakages may take the form of a cry for help, an expression of inner conflict, or a boast. Dependence on leakages creates a secondary problem: re-socializing adolescents to recognize leakages for what they are and share them with school authorities and law enforcement agents. To snitch on a peer runs contrary to one of the most deeply embedded norms of adolescence, but the culture may be changing. Since Columbine, many potentially serious school rampage shootings have been thwarted by students who had heard of the plans and warned adults. In 2001 school shootings were averted at New Bedford High School in New Bedford, Massachusetts; at Southside High School in Elmira, New York; at Royal Valley High School in Hoyt, Kansas; at Monument High School in Twentynine Palms, California; and in other locations.

At the same time the National Threat Assessment Center, a branch of the Secret Service, was also studying the problem. An examination of 37 school shootings, from 1974 to 2000, led them to a similar conclusion: that school shootings could best be avoided by attending to the leakages. Because the Secret Service has expertise in threat assessment, they concentrated on this particular form of leakage. Two of their publications provide school teachers and administrators with a practical, structured approach to analyzing threats on the school and those who work or study there.

These publications distinguish between four kinds of threats. A direct threat is a specific act against a specific target, made in an unambiguous manner. "I am going to put a bomb in the gym." An indirect threat is, in some manner, vague and ambiguous. "I could kill everybody in this school, if I wanted to." A veiled threat implies, but does not explicitly threaten violence. "The school would be better off without you." A conditional threat is the kind often seen in kidnappings or extortion. "If you don't pay me a million dollars, I will burn down the school."

The study identifies four factors in threat assessment. The first is the threat's level of detail. A threat is more likely to be real when the details, such as the identity of the victim, the motivation, the means by which it will be carried out, and the time and place are specific and plausible. Consider the following: "I got the combination to my dad's gun locker and next Wednesday, after the game, I'm going to show everybody who's the dangerous one around here." This is a detailed and specific threat, and one that should elicit grave concern. A second factor is plausibility. A threat may be detailed and specific, yet implausible. A student who threatens to detonate one hundred pounds of plutonium in the auditorium during Wednesday lunch poses a low risk since plutonium is almost impossible to obtain, expensive, difficult to transport, and to detonate. A third factor is whether the student making the threat is under unusual stress, such as the divorce of parents, a failing grade on a paper or in a course which might lead to the loss of a scholarship or other grave circumstances, a break up with a girl-friend, a public humiliation of some kind, or an arrest that might result in a felony. One must remember that adolescents vary greatly, as individuals, in their response to such events. While one student may be relieved or indifferent to a break-up with a girlfriend, another may be plunged into a profound depression by the loss, or experience the rejection as a narcissis-tic wounding that threatens his entire sense of himself. A fourth factor is the character of the student making the threats. At one extreme, the threat may come during a flare-up, from a boy who is rarely in trouble, but who loses his temper after being provoked. At the other extreme, the student who has posed the threat may be known for his violent behavior, or have a history of encounters with the law. He may have made and carried out threats of vio-lence in the past.

SECONDARY PREVENTION STRATEGIES

ANTI-BULLYING PROGRAMS

We have seen how all of the SR shooters have been victims of bullying. Many of them have also been bullies. It is common for children who have played the former role to want to experience the latter. Anti-bullying pro-grams benefit vulnerable children by lessening their experience of humilia-tion and alienation from their classmates. Educators are always talking about the importance of school as a socialization tool, yet few schools have comprehensive anti-bullying programs. Bullies can turn school into a living hell that their victims remember from a very early age. In the basement tapes, Dylan Klebold recalled being excluded in daycare, when he was three; and Kip Kinkel being bullied when he attended preschool in Spain, at the age of four. Nearly every case in this book involves bullying, and the obvious chain of causation, from bullying to humiliation to rage to revenge, made this one of the first characteristics of school rampage shooters to be identified.

While America's interest in bullying is relatively recent, Norway and Sweden have been concerned about the problem since the late 1960s. Dan Olweus, a Norwegian psychologist at the University of Bergen began publishing scientific research on this subject in 1973. He has conducted major research studies in Norway and Sweden, including longitudinally tracking his original panel of victims and bullies whom he first interviewed in 1970. While the bullying discussed in this book has been what Olweus refers to as the direct sort, he also recognized "indirect bullying," involving ". . . indirect ways of harassment such as slandering, spreading of rumors, and manipulation of friendship relationships." This is the kind of bullying we usually associate with girls. American authorities refer to it as "relational bullying," or "relational aggression," and it has been explored in popular books such as *Odd Girl Out* and *Queen Bees & Wannabes*. It is just as serious a problem as direct bullying, if not more so because of its subtlety.

Olweus has found from his longitudinal study that bully/victim identities remain stable over time, or at least until the participants graduated from high school or college and joined the working world. In 1993, re-interviewing his original panel who were now 23, he found that, while the former bullying victims no longer perceived themselves as such, many were depressed and suffered from poor self-esteem.

The American version of Olweus' bullying prevention program (the Scandinavian version differs in a few minor regards) is implemented in the classroom, throughout the school, in the home, and also, ideally, in the outside community. First the school forms a Bullying Prevention Coordinating Committee to oversee the program. They are trained in the philosophy of the program: zero tolerance for bullying behavior, immediate and consistent response to situations involving bullying, and a system of uniform, fair, appropriate, and immediate punishments for bullying incidents and rewards for its cessation. An anonymous questionnaire, developed by Olweus, is used to determine the nature and extent of bullying in the school. The program begins, for the community, with a full-day conference, during which the school's bullying statistics, derived from the questionnaire, are shared in order to give teachers, parents, and students a sense of the nature and the magnitude of the problem. The goal of the conference is to create a long term, detailed plan of action, in which everyone is invested. Schoolwide anti-bullying rules and consequences are agreed upon at this time. Parents are encouraged to make the culture of their home more or less consistent with the anti-bullying culture at school. Teacher presence is increased in parts of the school that are typically unsupervised, such as the playground, the lunchroom, and hallways between classes. The Olweus questionnaire is used again later in the school year, as a post-test to determine what progress has been made. The program demands attentiveness, self-scrutiny, consistency, detachment, and dogged attention to detail. There are no magic tricks to it, no silver bullet.

CHARACTERISTICS OF NON-VIOLENT SCHOOLS

"Early Warning, Timely Response" includes a list of the characteristics of schools which experience little violence. This is useful because it provides a vision of what a low-violence school night look like. Tasks involving change, be they institutional or personal, are more easily accomplished if there is a vision of the final product, a model that can be kept in mind during the process of change.

Focuses on academics. Academic achievement is valued; it is assumed that all students are capable of good academic work and socially acceptable behavior. Expectations, academic and behavioral, are communicated clearly and identified as the student's responsibility. The school that focuses on academic achievement is modeling institutional integrity and discouraging cynicism.

Forges links with the family and the community. The school has strong linkages with the community, including local police, mental health agencies, and the faith-based community; and with the families of students. The school supports these families when they express concern about their children and aids them in finding help in addressing troubling behaviors.

Emphasizes social inclusion of all children. Teachers are encouraged to form positive relationships with all students and provide special support when it is needed. Mentoring programs with outside volunteers increase the density of the social networks and improve the chances of students forming positive bonds with adults. Isolated students must be actively sought out and encouraged to develop connections with other students and teachers. Non-violent schools make an effort to promote positive relationships between students and reduce or eliminate bullying.

Promotes equal treatment. All students should be treated equally by the school regardless of ethnicity, gender, race, social class, religion, disability, nationality, sexual orientation, or physical appearance. Sports stars should not be granted favoritism, nor should those who are struggling socially be scapegoated. The school should create a community where all members are equally valued and respected.

Openly discusses safety issues. The dangers of firearms and other weapons should be discussed in school, as well as the consequences of bringing weapons to school. Students should be taught anger management skills and conflict resolution techniques in elementary school and junior high school. Mediation teams should be available to resolve disputes.

Promote a climate where students can share their concerns with adult authorities. Schools should create systems for students to report their concerns about possible incidents of violence ("leakages," in FBI jargon) anonymously or in a manner where they will not fear retribution.

Offers extended day programs. Programs, such as tutoring, mentoring, cultural arts, community service clubs, and homework help, before and after school have been shown to reduce violence. At the most rudimentary level, these programs serve a babysitting function. Most adolescent crime and teen pregnancy occur between the time school is dismissed and the time when parents return from work. Extended day programs also have a positive effect in building community, creating mentor-type relationships with adults, fostering ego strengths, and improving academic skills.

Assists students in making the transition to adult life and the workplace. Work-study programs, apprenticeships, and vocational skills all help students find a place in adult society. This is the vocational aspect of creating an adult identity. American high schools, which excelled in providing vocational support when America was a manufacturing economy, have been slow to figure out how to address the needs of an information and service economy, and our children have suffered as a result.

THE SCHOOL AS FORTRESS

A final category of violence reduction strategies involves stationing guards or "community resource officers" around the school; making students pass through metal detectors, or be scanned with wands; adding surveillance cameras or increasing their number; searching packages and book bags, or insisting that book bags be made of transparent plastic; reducing the number of entrances and exits to the school; having the principal carry a gun; and putting up fences around schools. Professional educators typically hate these kinds of controls. One often hears them referred to as "school as a fortress" measures since they evoke prisons, making students feel that they are under surveillance, and teachers, that they are jailers.

INTERVENTION

The second phase of crisis response, intervention, refers to the school's response to an SR shooting, terrorist attack, ecological disaster, or other crisis. The keystone of the intervention is the response plan, or "safety plan," as it is more commonly referred to, a document created and implemented by an interdisciplinary crisis response team selected from the school and the community. The safety plan specifies how teachers, school administrators, students, parents, policemen, firemen, emergency workers, and others will respond collaboratively to a variety of crises that could take place in or around the school. The plan coordinates the actions of seasoned responders, and provides those with less crises experience with specific, effective tasks so they are less likely to panic, become paralyzed with fear, or respond in a way that jeopardizes others. Because they also know what *not* to do, conflicts, role duplications, and bottlenecks are avoided.

While the school's response to a rampage shooter will differ from its response to a hostage-taking terrorist, a fire, or a natural disaster, they will share three common elements: First, the safety of the students must be maintained through evacuation of the building or through containment in the classroom, a process known as "lockdown," depending on the nature of the threat. While a speedy evacuation of the building is called for in the case of fire or flood, a lockdown is considered the best strategy if rampage killers or terrorists have entered the building. A school may have to spend money equipping classrooms with locks. In the absence of frequent lockdown drills (and I know of few schools that practice lockdown drills, frequently or otherwise), school personnel may forget the emergency codes, and substitute teachers may be ignorant that such codes exist. In some cases the evacuation must be tailored to the crises. For example, if a bomb is discovered in the school, the evacuation should proceed in stages starting with the students most likely to be harmed: those in the rooms nearest the device.

Second, a quick and foolproof communications system must be available to teachers in their classrooms. This could be an intercom, a telephone, or a cell phone in an "emergency kit." A cell phone presents additional problems because batteries must be kept charged, and operation may be unreliable in some suburban and rural areas. In the last few years, SR shootings have occurred more frequently on college campuses, environments which create a whole different set of problems, since the locus of responsibility for the students' moment-to-moment whereabouts is no longer the teacher, but the student him or herself. In recent years universities have been implementing alert systems that allow them to text message student cell phones if a shooting or other crisis is taking place. A recent survey showed that at Virgina Tech, where 27 students and five faculty members were killed in a shooting in April of 2007, four out of ten students had failed to sign up for service. Campus safety experts attributed their disinterest to "feelings of invincibility and reluctance to give out personal information," as well as an aversion to paying text-messaging fees. Some universities have tried to get around this by providing students with cell phones that are preprogrammed to receive emergency alerts. Abilene Christian University in Texas has gone so far as to issue every incoming freshman an iPhone (adolescent America's most coveted gadget at the time of writing) presumably preprogrammed to receive school alerts. Videos of its impeccable operation, posted on YouTube, show a students being warned of an approaching tornado.

Third, a means of securing immediate external support from police, hospital, or rescue teams, must be available. A telephone or intercom may suffice. Safety experts have also discussed a "panic button" of the sort installed behind the counter in banks, but this seems out of place in a school room and a source of potential trouble.

All school personnel must be trained to understand the safety plan and what role they will play in a crisis. Protocols must be practiced so that they can be executed smoothly in times of confusion. *Early Warning, Safe Passage* recommends a brief manual, pamphlet, or flipchart be provided to all staff and teachers to remind them of their responsibilities since no one would be expected to remember the protocols or search through a safety plan while students' lives are in jeopardy. Some school systems have developed a "crises response notebook," or "emergency kit" containing updated school floor plans, class rosters, lockdown protocols, a list of staff members serving on the crisis response team, and of staff members certified in first aid. In addition, the emergency kit might contain a cell phone and a portable radio.

POSTVENTIONS

Postvention refers to those services that are provided after the crisis to help the students, the school, and the community deal with their grief and eventually return to a pre-crisis level of functioning.

A child's response to a crisis such as a school shooting will vary depending on age, prior experience of trauma, and the stability of his or her home-life, among other factors. Younger children may exhibit sadness, fear, anger, or shame. They may show internalizing symptoms, such as insomnia or loss of appetite, somatic symptoms such as stomachaches and headaches, or externalizing symptoms such as fighting, or destroying property. They may become withdrawn or clingy and school work may deteriorate in quality. Substance abuse, sexual acting out, and delinquency are common in older children. The reader will recall Monika Selvig, who was shot in the stomach by Brenda Spencer when she was eight, and began using alcohol and drugs at 13. She attributed 15 years of alcoholism and drug addiction to her refusal to discuss her experience of the shooting. There will likely be survivor guilt, as in the case of Evan Ramsey's friend, Wilson Naneng, who gnawed and cut at himself, and tried to commit suicide because of his guilt about not having prevented the shooting.

Teachers and staff are often so busy attending to the needs of their students that they neglect their own needs. This can lead to difficulty fulfilling professional obligations, accelerate "burn-out," and create and aggravate a variety of emotional and cognitive problems. Adult teachers, therapists, and rescue workers sometimes must be reminded to participate in debriefings, and other kinds of grief work, lest problems develop later. For many years the American Red Cross insisted that all Disaster Mental Health Services volunteers debrief in groups before returning home from a deployment.

After the crisis, school should be reopened as soon as possible, to provide comforting routines, an opportunity for students to confront their fears of returning to the scene of the violence, and to provide a familiar setting where they can process what has occurred. Students who are too fearful to enter the building should be provided with tutoring outside the school, alone or in groups, until graduation, or a time when they are ready to reenter the school. Being "forced to face your fears," a popular piece of folk wisdom, may help some children but only heightens the trauma for others, and it is better to err on the side of caution. Schools invariably close down for a few days to a week after the crisis so that the community can attend funerals and memorial services, and also so the school can clean up and repair the destruction. Usually, by the time the students return, the classrooms and hallways are pristine, as though the crisis had never taken place. This seems like a good idea, intuitively, but who knows what it suggests to children? That parents can make anything go away like magic? That we deal with a crisis by making it appear as though it had never taken place? The issue is thought-provoking but moot since few parents would send a child back to a classroom with bullet-riddled and blood-stained walls.

The crisis response team should keep a list of local helping professionals and have a means of reaching them quickly. A "phone tree" where a member of the clergy mobilizes other clergy, a representative of a family agency contacts his colleagues, and so forth, is useful. They, in turn, should organize a variety of forums, public and private, where everyone can publicly and safely discuss what they are feeling and thinking. Such forums provide the opportunity to share sorrows, articulate ideas and "normalize" feelings that may seem inappropriate or shameful. Funerals and memorial services are often open to the community and attended by thousands. It is important that people have an opportunity to say their final goodbyes in a public ceremony, express their love for the deceased, and pledge to remember him or her. People also find solace in grief projects that involve handicrafts. The project may be a communal effort, like the Thurston Healing Quilt created after the Kip Kinkel shooting (Overview, Case 12), or the work of an individual, like the crosses put up by the carpenter who visited Littleton after Columbine. Memorial walls like the ones at Heath High following the Michael Carneal shooting (Overview, Case 11) and at Columbine, provide an opportunity for people to join a "community of bereavement," to use a term coined by Edward Linenthal, and express themselves by leaving objects of reassurance such as keepsakes, personal messages, teddy bears, poems, and pictures. Others find meaning in their losses by writing about them, as Misty Bernall and Brooks Brown did after Columbine, or through social action, like Columbine parent Tom Mauser, who became an outspoken gun control advocate.

Counseling, individual and group, should be made available as soon as possible and should remain available as long as needed. For some, symptoms may emerge months or even years after the crisis (hence the diagnosis "*post* traumatic stress disorder") and funds and professional help must still be available at that time. The shooter's trial and the various civil lawsuits may also be considered part of the postvention in that they satisfy the needs of the victims to tell their stories publicly, and to provide a sense of closure and the knowledge that justice has been done. By the same token, postponement and rescheduling of these events may retraumatize the victims or prolong their discomfort.

GUNS AND GUN CONTROL

Regardless of our beliefs about the advisability of gun control laws, it is a simple fact that school shootings are impossible without guns that are affordable, available, easy to load and fire, and capable of firing many rounds within a few seconds. Thus, the issue has a technological dimension which is important in understanding why SR shootings, as we now know them, did not occur during the first half of the 20th century.

It is instructive to imagine the Jonesboro case (Overview, Case 11) as it might have taken place just prior to the time of the Civil War. Andrew Golden, 11, and Mitchell Johnson, 12, decide they are going to attack their school (in those days, a one-room school house). The most destructive weapons at hand are their homemade slingshots. They collect a bag full of small stones to use as ammunition. Mitchell hides in the bushes while Andrew runs into the school house, shouting, "Indians!" The students rush for the door. As they emerge into the sunlight, a pebble comes flying at them, and then another. Being hit feels like a bee sting, only worse, and leaves a nasty welt. Perhaps one student is hit in the eye and loses his vision. The attack ends when the constable sneaks up behind Mitchell, grabs him by the collar, and lifts him into the air. Both boys are taken to the jail house and their parents are notified. They receive a beating from their fathers, and are made to apologize, and perhaps pay a compensation to the parents of the boy whom they half-blinded. Their sling shots are confiscated and their chores, doubled. It sounds almost like an episode out of *Tom Sawyer*.

Had Mitchell and Andrew been absolutely determined to lay their hands on a firearm of some kind, they might have gone to a local tavern, waited until a hunter fell into a drunken stupor, and stolen his rifle, which was likely to be a flintlock. Flintlocks emerged around 1630 and remained in vogue perhaps 250 years. The mechanism of the flintlock was ingenious: pulling the trigger released a hammer holding a piece of flint, which struck a piece of steel called the *frizzen*. This generated a spark which ignited a bit of black powder held beneath it in a pan, which in turn ignited the powder in the barrel, which drove the bullet, a lead ball, out the muzzle. Let's say Andrew's grandfather had been a hunter (incidentally, he had), giving Andrew the opportunity to watch him prepare the gun for firing often enough to know the routine: begin by half-cocking the hammer (hence the expression, "Don't go off half cocked"); pour a measure of gunpowder down the barrel (and it had to be just the right amount lest the gun explode); wrap the bullet in a small piece of cloth or paper (to give it a tight fit), and ram it down the barrel on top of the gunpowder, using a ramrod; place an additional pinch of powder in the flintlock's pan, and snap the frizzen in place.

Then aim, fully cock the hammer, and squeeze the trigger.

Assuming the day was dry, the flint sharp, the powder correctly measured, and the bullet neither too tight nor too loose in the barrel, there was a good chance that the gun would fire, but the odds of hitting a target at several hundred feet, human or otherwise, without considerable practice, were slim, and by the time they had prepared the gun to fire a second bullet, the constable would have put a stop to the dangerous prank. The percussion cap, invented in 1825, provided a reliable substitute to the flint and made possible handguns with revolving bullet chambers such as the Colt "Walker" and the "Dragoon." Even though they were mass-produced, less than 10,000 existed in 1850, and their owners guarded them like jewels.

Even if the boys had been able to steal one, the guns were ungainly—over four pounds in weight—and difficult to manipulate.

Automatic pistols with ammunition magazines were invented in 1893 and by the turn of the century, they had been adopted by armies around the world. Such weapons were light, simple to operate, and could quickly fire eight or more rounds without reloading, assuming the mechanisms didn't jam (even today some police prefer revolvers to automatic pistols because the automatics tend to jam). As the carrying of concealed pistols became more common, several states tried to pass "pistol bills," to control their sales and license their owners. Legislation addressing social problems often follows awful events. A revolver concealed in a pocket handkerchief was used to assassinate President McKinley in 1901. The following year the South Carolina legislature banned pistol sales to anyone except sheriffs and "special deputies" (a group which included Ku Klux Klan members). In 1910 William Jay Gaynor, the mayor of New York, was wounded and eventually died from a handgun wound and a year later the state passed the Sullivan Act, which gave police the discretionary power to issue licenses permitting civilians to carry concealed weapons.

I referred before to the automatic pistol, which fired each time the trigger was pulled without needing to be constantly reloaded. With long guns, the term "automatic" has a different meaning: a weapon that will continue to fire as long as the trigger is held down. Until World War I, the reloading of long guns was time-consuming. With the best of the bolt-action rifles, such as the Lee-Enfield, highly trained British soldiers could fire 15 rounds per minute or a bullet every four seconds. Untrained shooters would take longer. The Gatling gun, a "machine gun" developed during the Civil War, could fire a continuous stream of bullets at an enemy, but it was the size of a small cannon, had to be moved on wheels, and required a team to fire it. The first machine gun which a single soldier could carry into battle, the Thompson sub-machine gun, was demonstrated to the public in 1920. Although originally developed for the Army, the "Tommy Gun" quickly became a favorite of Chicago's prohibition era gangsters. Because it used pistol ammunition, it was considered a short-range weapon. While the stream of bullets was deadly, it would not have reached from the trench where Mitchell Johnson and Andrew Golden lay in wait, to the schoolyard at Westside Middle School, where children were about to emerge for a fire drill. The first federal gun law, the National Firearms Act, passed by Franklyn Delano Roosevelt in 1930 was an effort to limit the use of the Tommy Gun and other favorite gangster guns and devices, such as sawed-off shotguns, silencers, and guns concealed in walking canes.

Opponents to gun control often cite Hitler's legislation of 1938, which banned civilians from owning firearms, as the basis of their objections. Had guns been available to the Jews, they argue, they might have fought off Nazi tyranny. In fact the law in question, the Law on Firearms and Ammunition, was initially passed by the Weimar government in 1928 in order to disarm the nascent militias that had been forming around the country, including the "brownshirts" who later became the Nazis. Hitler simply extended the law in 1938, at a time when his National Socialist Party already exercised tyrannical power throughout Germany.

The first fully automatic rifle, portable, like the Tommy Gun, but capable of firing real rifle ammunition, was developed by the Germans during World War II. Gas pressure from the exploding cartridge ejected the spent shell and forced a new shell into the firing position in the rifle's chamber. Legend has it that Hitler himself dubbed it the *sturmgewehr* or assault rifle, a term that continues to be used to this day. Such weapons could also be fired in semi-automatic mode, conserving ammunition by firing one bullet with each squeeze of the trigger. These weapons became immensely popular among military forces around the world and proliferated rapidly. Soon the United States, the Soviet Union, England, Isreal, China, and other countries were manufacturing assault weapons in great number for their own armies, and to sell to other countries. After the assassination of President John F. Kennedy, the *New York Times* identified the murder weapon as a "cheap, foreign, war-surplus military rifle . . . one of hundreds of thousands of cast-off weapons of foreign armies that are now available to mail-order customers of American gun dealers." A Senate subcommittee reported that of the million guns being bought and sold by mail annually, 25 percent were falling into criminal hands. Senator Thomas J. Dodd introduced federal gun control legislation but it was defeated by "hysterical opposition by a small but well-organized minority." Officials of the National Rifle Association, who supported the bill, had their lives threatened by more fanatic members of their own association.

On August 1, 1966, Charles Whitman, 25, having failed as a marine and as a college student, climbed to the top of the tower at the University of Texas at Austin with several rifles and began a sniper attack on the students and faculty strolling through the plaza. He killed 14 people and wounded many others before he was killed by law enforcement officials. The following day President Lyndon B. Johnson, a Texan, urged a revival of Dodd's gun control law.

> What happened is not without a lesson: that we must press urgently
> for the legislation now pending in Congress . . . [Senator Dodd's]

gun control bill would not prevent all such tragedies. But it would help reduce the unrestricted sale of fire-arms to those who cannot be trusted in their use or possession. How many lives might be saved as a consequence? (Semple, 1966)

The revised bill banned interstate sale of small firearms, regulated interstate sale of rifles and shotguns, barred sale of pistols and revolvers to people under 21, banned over-the-counter sales of small firearms to out-of-state purchasers, and restricted the importation of surplus military arms. The NRA found this version of the bill too restrictive and lobbied against it. It took two more years and two more assassinations, Martin Luther King in April of 1968 and Robert Kennedy in June of the same year, before legislators could summon the nerve to defy NRA lobbyists and pass what has become the core of federal gun control legislation, the 1968 Gun Control Act. In addition to the provisions described above, the legislation required serial numbers on all guns; prohibited mail-order sales of firearms and ammunition; decreed that a long gun purchaser must be 18, and a handgun purchaser 21; increased penalties for those carrying and using firearms in crimes of violence or drug trafficking; prohibited the possession, sale, and manufacture of new assault weapons (but allowed gun owners to keep the assault weapons owned at the time the bill was enacted); prohibited the sale of parts or "conversion kits" that could be used to convert semiautomatic weapons to fully automatic firing capacity; and required that all gun dealers be licensed. An exception was made for private parties who sold their wares at gun shows, the infamous "gun-show loophole" that made it possible for Robyn Anderson to purchase weapons for Dylan Klebold and Eric Harris without having to fill out paperwork; paperwork which, as she stated before a House Judiciary Committee in support of a bill to expand background checks on gun show sales, would have deterred her.

Each case study in this book recounts attempts at the state and federal level to pass gun control legislation in the wake of a tragic shooting. The number of firearms in this country and their availability increase every year. In the year 2000, over three thousand young people were killed by firearms. One thousand seven hundred and seventy-six were murdered, 1,007 committed suicide, and 193 were victims of gun-related accidents. We have seen the problem of firearm availability approached from a variety of perspectives: a ban on all guns, or all hand-guns, or all assault weapons; gunlockers, trigger locks, and other mechanical devices to prevent children from getting their hands on weapons; the extension of liability to the parents of the shooter, or whomever the child obtained his weapon from; waiting periods, so hot-heads can cool off; background checks, to keep guns out of the hands of criminals and lunatics; and the registration of all guns and the licensing of all gun owners, so weapons could be traced back to their owners. Gun control opponents cite examples of crimes with firearms committed in states where controls were already in place. They argue that people kill people, not guns; that the U.S. Constitution gives them the right to bear arms; and that if guns are outlawed, only outlaws will have guns. They talk about protecting their families from gun-toting burglars and forming militias in case a fascist leader comes to power. Fighting back is an appealing idea, hard to counter. No one wants to be a victim. Perhaps the best response is the following statement about the British ban on handguns, passed after the massacre of 16 kindergarten children in Dunblane, Scotland:

> Many applauded this move, seeing it as conveying a message about the kind of society Britain wants to be, a message reflecting the belief that the widespread ownership of handguns is not compatible with a sane, civilized or safe society.

REFERENCES

INTRODUCTION

9   In fact, government studies (see, for example Dwyer, Osher, & Warger, 1998).

9   Regarding the deaths of teenagers, accidents are the primary cause (33 deaths per hundred thousand teens), then homicides (9.5 deaths per hundred thousand), and suicides (7.3 deaths per hundred thousand) (Hoyert, Kung, & Smith, 2005).

9   Yet in a national poll of 409 teenagers conducted following the Columbine High School shootings, a third believed that a similar incident would occur in their own high school (CNN, 1999a).

11   "This is a wound that is so deep, you can't measure it in terms of weeks, months, or even years to heal. It is something I will never be over, and I don't think many who were there will."(Anderson, 1993, August 17, p. A8).

11   Some researchers call this "variation along the dependent variable," (King, Keohane, & Verba, 1994, p. 129)

11   Hans Eysenck a well-known British psychologist, suggested a multi-dimensional theory of criminal behavior over forty years ago (Eysenck & Eysenck, 1964)

11   the teaching of evolution (former Representative Tom DeLay, Rep TX as quoted in Clines, 1999)

11   the teaching of values curriculums (Schlafly, 1999)

11   ignorance of the Ten Commandments (Representative Robert B. Aderholt, Rep AL, as quoted in Mitchell & Bruni, 1999)

11   or even the bleak architecture of the suburbs (Kunstler, 1999)

12   criminologist Lonnie Athens' term (1992)

12   Such murders are often called "affective," the human equivalent of the fight or flight response seen in animals (Meloy, 1997)

12   Mass murders, "the intentional killing of multiple victims by a single offender within a 24 hour period of time" (Meloy, 1997, p. 326)

12   "set and run" killers, those who set bombs and disappear, such as Ted Kaczynski, the Unabomber; and "pseudo-commandos," those who are preoccupied with fire-arms and military garb, and plan and deliberate extensively before they act (Dietz, 1986)

13   A research effort conducted by the *New York Times* (Fessenden, 2000)

13   A report prepared by a special investigative team organized by the Secret Service, (Vossekuil, Fein, Reddy, Borum, & Modzeleski, 2002)

13   A report prepared by a special investigative team organized by the Secret Service, released a few months after the *New York Times* study, found that SR shooters were often bullied. (While the final version was not published until 2002, preliminary findings were published in 2000.) (Vossekuil, Reddy, & Fein, 2000)

13   . . .attackers felt persecuted, bullied, threatened, attacked, or injured by others prior to the incident. A number of attackers had experienced bullying and harassment that was longstanding and severe. In those cases the experience of bullying appeared to play a major role in motivating the attack at school… (I)n a number of cases, attackers described experiences of being bullied in terms that approached torment. They told of behaviors that, if they occurred in the workplace, would meet the legal definitions of harassment." (Vossekuil et al., 2000, p. 7)

13   Other studies of SR shooters (Dwyer et al., 1998; Newman, Fox, Harding, Mehta, & Roth, 2004; O'Toole, 2000; Vossekuil et al., 2002)

13   Katherine Newman, a Princeton sociologist, and her colleagues identified five conditions common to SR shooters (2004)

1300   Second, he suffers from psychosocial problems—learning disorders, psychiatric disorders, dysfunctional families, and the like—that "magnify the impact of the marginality" (p. 229)

14   The literal truth is that places with more guns have higher rates of adolescent suicide, homicide, and injury than places with fewer guns (Grassel, Wintemute, Wright, & Romero, 2003; Miller, Azrael, & Hemenway, 2002; Wiebe, 2003, and others)

14   Statistical formulas are likely never to be useful for predicting infrequent instances of targeted violence such as school or workplace homicides, because the base rate is so low that, mathematically, high rates of accuracy are nearly impossible. (Borum, Fein, Vossekuil, & Berglund, 1999, p. 4)

14   Seeking to predict acts that occur as rarely as school shootings is almost impossible. This is simple statistical logic: when the incidence of any form of violence is very low and a very large number of people have identifiable risk factors, there is no reliable way to pick out from that large group the very few who will actually commit the violent act. (O'Toole, 2000, p. 3)

14   are more likely to provide the deep and comprehensive understanding necessary for theory building (Strauss & Corbin, 1990)

14   "grounded theory" (Glaser & Strauss, 1967)

14   The criteria used to select cases was built upon that suggested by Deitz (1986)

14   and Meloy (1997)

16   cheap, foreign-made, "assault" rifles such as the Uzi, the Kalishnakov, and the Chinese SKS flooded the American market (Ellis, 1986)

16   A school shooting occurred in Alberta, Canada eight days after Columbine (CNN, 1999b)

16   More than 25 school shootings have occurred since then, most of them in the United States but more and more often in other countries such as Germany (BBC News, 2002, April 26)

16   Bosnia (BBC News, 2002, April 29)

16   Argentina (Associated Press, 2004, Sept. 28)

16   and even Finland (CNN, 2007, Nov. 7)

16   "a theory is a systematic and formalized expression of all previous observations, and is predictive, logical, and testable" (Wikipedia contributors, 2007, 24 Dec.)

1   *The Discovery of Grounded Theory* (Glaser & Strauss, 1967)

17   The central crisis of adolescence is forming the foundations of an adult identity (Erikson, 1963)

17   Baumeister (1986)

18   as Durkheim (1897/ 1952)

18   Athens (1992)

19   This kind of ceremony seems to be a throwback to something very ancient and primitive, where the supplicant plays the part of a god, and indulges in a forbidden or privileged activity prior to his own execution or banishment from the tribe (Eliade, 1954/1974)

20   *The Truth behind the Deaths at Columbine* (Brown & Merritt, 2002)

20   *Child's Prey* (2001)

An Overview

24   Could it be that people don't want to see what they have done to others? Or are they just simply so confident that it never even occurs to them? (David, 1997)

25   I do feel very sorry for the victims, and their families, but we lost someone too. I wasn't close to Tony, I am closer to his brothers age, but I still love him. (Anonymous, 1997)

29   I realized what hell life was... I have been serving 11 years of hell." (Mueller, 1995, February 16, p. B1).

29   Why? Because they don't pat you on the back for what I am planning." (Breed & AP, 1993, April 23, p. B1; Mueller, 1995, February 10, p. A1)

31   I just didn't see anybody I could trust. I didn't see myself being any other way than I

was. I didn't see no alternative to it: I thought it would always be like that. (Meyer, 2000, April 22, p. 32)

32   [He became] ...real quiet, clammy, and then cussing at everybody... Some days he was fine, but other days you just couldn't talk to him." (Kimbrough, 1997, August 27, p. 3).

33   Killing a bastard that deserves to die,
Ain't nothing like it in the world,
But he sure did bleed a lot.
(Poems entered into record at Loukaitis hearing, 1996, April 19, p. 7)

33   If he didn't remember my life, he was going to remember my death. (Caputo, 1996, September 27, p.1).

34   When asked why she had done this, she replied, "because I told him everything." (Kimbrough, 1997, September 9, p. 1).

35   Students later described him "laughing, just going crazy." (Marquez, 1997, February 27, p A7).

36   Evan was sentenced to a 210 year term with a possibility of parole at the age of 70, in 2050. (Evan Ramsey's case is described in detail in Chapter 3).

38   I don't take stuff from teenagers or parents and I am seriously mad at the world... (Adams, 1998, December 18, ¶2)

38   I went home and cried yes I admit it I cried. (Adams, 1998, December 18, ¶20)

38   "...been clean for a year now." (Adams, 1998, December 18, ¶20).

39   "an English project—props for a play." (Bartleman, 1998, June 24, p. 14A).

40   said one psychologist who interviewed Michael before the trial. (Harding, Mehta & Newman, 2003, p. 149).

42   On one occasion, while serving detention for refusing to remove his cap, he was asked to write an essay about his behavior. One sentence: "I have a pellet gun and I am not afraid to use it" (Heard, 1999, June 6, ¶25)

42   Cathy O'Rourke, a neighbor and friend from the Minnesota trailer park, said that Mitchell had told her that the whole thing was a "big misunderstanding" (Associated Press, 1998, April 1, ¶20)

43   "He just meant to scare them, I guess. But then something went terribly wrong." (Associated press, 1998, April 6, ¶3).

44   "I thought he was bragging, like always. I didn't think he was going to hurt anybody really." (Associated Press, 1998, March 30, ¶7).

46   Steve Williams, a fellow teacher, thought she was kidding. "What have you been hit with, a firecracker?" She replied, "I've been shot; get me out of here." (Waite, 1998, April 5 ¶27, 28).

46   "I said, 'Get up, Brittany,' and she said, 'I can't.' When I looked down, there was blood on her legs." (Davis & Porter, 1998, March 26, ¶40)

47   "The older one hesitated . . . We had to shout two or three times to get them to raise their hands off the ground." (Davis & Uyttebrouck, 1998, March 26, ¶36).

47   "Both of them just said, 'I don't know. I just don't know.'" (Davis & Uyttebrouck, 1998, March 26, ¶41).

47   However, sheriff's deputy Terry McNatt, said that he overheard one of the officers asking Mitchell why he had done it, and him responding, "Andrew was mad at a teacher. He was tired of their crap." (Heard, 1999, March 27, ¶5).

48   Our thoughts and prayers are with the victims, their families, and the entire Jonesboro community." (Davis, 1998, March 25, ¶60).

48   Lawrence Graves, spokesman for the state attorney general's office, said, "...for all practical purposes, at age 18 they walk." (Fullerton, 1998, March 27, ¶6).

49   "I try to find answers. If I didn't have this [gun control advocacy], I'd probably turn into myself and withdraw and not wake up in the mornings." (Cofer & Heard, 1999, March 21, ¶77).

49   "he stares gloomily out into the juvenile cell block. The sleeves of his too long orange prison shirt extend past his hands when he walks." (Heard, 1998, May 18, ¶2).

50   "This is not a comfortable environment," he told the press, "but this is not a motel. It's a jail." (Heard, 1998, July 22, ¶34).

50   filed a wrongful death suit alleging that Mitchell Johnson and Drew Golden had shown ample evidence of antisocial behavior and had a "propensity to commit acts which could normally be expected to cause injury." (Harris & Associated press, 1998, August 11, ¶3).

50   "technologically feasible and economically practical" and to omit them made the weapons "defective products" that were "unreasonably dangerous." (Harris & Associated press, 1998, August 11, ¶10).

50   The complaint against Remington Arms Company, now operating as Sporting Goods Properties, Inc., was dismissed because of "intervening factors," (Heard, 1999, May 10, ¶4),

51   Nobody had a clue that he was going to do this... Only a handful of people knew that he had any kind of fascination with guns and bombs. (Betina Lynn, a student assistant in Kip's Spanish class, as quoted in McCown, 1998, July 30, ¶26).

53   During a pre-trial neuro-psychiatric assessment conducted by Jonathan Pincus, a neurologist whose work is discussed in Chapter 1, the boy "described the gun-drenched culture of his family, the verbal abusiveness of his parents, and his sense of loneliness and being threatened." (Pincus, 2001, p. 9).

55   When she warned Faith and Bill about their son's activities, they had nothing more to say than, "Thank you for telling us." (Dietz, 2000, December 15, ¶9).

55   He was understandably disturbed and warned store employees, who, according to police reports, told him to ". . . mind his own business." (Barry Reid as quoted I Dietz, 1999, February 15, ¶16).

55   It was black and white and it was, like, wavy. From one way it looked black, and from one way it looked white. It was weird." (Casey Guinan, a friend of Kip's, as quoted in Kirk & Boyer, 2000f, ¶191).

55   Why? Why did God just want me to be in complete misery? I need to find more weapons. (Kirk & Boyer, 2000b, ¶19)

56   I don't know who I am. I want to be something I can never be. I try so hard every day. But in the end, I hate myself for what I've become. (Kirk & Boyer, 2000b, ¶5)

57   My head just doesn't work right. God damn these VOICES inside my head. I want to die. I want to be gone . . . (Kirk & Boyer, 2000b, ¶3)

59   "It took weeks for him to make eye-contact with me," she said, "and even longer to say something. When he finally did, it was 'I am so sorry.'" (Kristin Kinkel's letter to judge, 1999, November 4, ¶8).

59   one student said. "It gave you the most vivid picture of what happened." (Dietz, 1998, May 27, ¶13)

59   Another student said of the whiteness, "You don't even want to step on it, like it's forbidden territory." (Dietz, 1998, May 27, ¶14)

60   A bullet hole was hidden behind a campaign poster on the cafeteria wall; but the scars on our tender hearts could not be so easily concealed . . ." (Harvey, 1998, May 27, ¶7).

60   It's starting to get more normal again, seeing all my friends. The teachers are a good support." (Landan Shaw as quoted in Bishop, 1998, March 26, ¶5).

60   "I keep feeling like Kip's in my room and putting a gun to my head." (Dietz, 1998, May 27, ¶3).

60   ". . . only way to get over this is have our grieving period and get back to normal school life as soon as possible." (Dietz, 1998, May 27, ¶29).

60   So Ben will live through other people." (Hartman & Foster, 1998, May 26, ¶8).

61   he quoted from First Corinthians, "then that he lays down his life for his friend. If Mikael hadn't been standing where he was, someone else would have died." (Bjornstad, 1998, May 27, ¶9).

61   They recalled him as a tinkerer, a computer nut, a Trekkie, a card shark and a student who was "easy to teach and eager to please." (Bjornstad, 1998, May 27, ¶11).

61   "He would do it in the middle of class just to see me crack up." (Bjornstad, 1998, May 27, ¶15).

62   Bill Morrisette, now a state Representative, spoke for many when he said, "A scab has been ripped off a wound that is now bleeding again." (Steves, 1999, April 22, ¶4).

62   ". . . I offer my plea of 'guilty' freely and voluntarily, of my own accord, with a full understanding of the charges and of the rights that I am giving up by this plea." (From

Kip Kinkel's Plea Petition, 1999, September 24, ¶6).

62   Oregon State Constitution (1996)

62   who called it "cruel and unusual punishment," and "shocking in the moral sense to all fair-minded persons." (State public defender files notice . . . , 1999, December 8, ¶3).

63   If there's a word bigger than overwhelming, that would be it . . . It's going to be years before I'll even be able to feel it, to feel what happened. (Kirk & Boyer, 2000a, ¶80,81).

CHAPTER 1

65   This is the "flying below the radar," behavior noted by Newman and his colleagues (2004)

66   called, "Off the Pig." (Newsreel Film Collective & Black Panther Party).

66   curriculums, is called, "Law and Order: The Policeman is Our Friend—Off the 'Pig.'" (Larkins, 1971).

67   Abbie Hoffman's book, *Steal This Book* (1971/2002)

67   3. ". . . deliberately destroyed others' property." (American Psychiatric Association, 2000, pp. 90, 91)

68   and that such labels encourage people to think of themselves as criminals or mental patients (Harwood, 2005).

68   These criticisms are well-founded, but the DSM IV-TR also has real value in that it represents the current "paradigm" of psychiatric science in the Kuhnian sense (1962)

68   ($140,638.88 in 2007 dollars according to the Consumer Price Index) http://data.bls .go/cgi-bin/cpicalc.pl

69   She told friends that her "battle plans" included turning the garage into a fortress and digging a hideout tunnel in the backyard. This kind of planning and publicizing of the event are characteristic of all school shootings. (Newman et al., 2004; O'Toole, 2000; Vossekuil, Fein, Reddy, Borum, & Modzeleski, 2002).

69   Brenda may have thought she would do the same. Newman and her colleagues refer to this as "following a cultural script," (Newman et al., 2004, p. 150)

76   They found that the damage involved the left and right prefrontal cortices in a pattern that, as confirmed by the most current research, "causes a defect in rational decision making and the processing of emotion." (Damasio, Grabowski, Frank, Galaburda, & Damasio, 2004, p. 21).

76   Several well-conducted studies by Adrian Raine, a researcher at UCLA, and his colleagues, using modern imaging techniques such as the PET (Positron Emission Tomography) scan, have confirmed the association between antisocial, violent, and predatory behaviors and frontal lobe damage and deficits. (Raine, 2002; Raine, Lencz, Bihrle, LaCasse, & Colletti, 2000; Raine et al., 1998).

76   A theory developed by Jonathan Pincus and Dorothy Otnow Lewis suggests that some disinhibiting form of brain damage is one of three precursors to most homicidal behavior, the other two being childhood abuse and paranoia. (Lewis, 1998; Lewis et al., 1985; Lewis, Pincus, & Bard, 1988; Pincus, 2001).

77   Although surveys have confirmed that epilepsy is two to four times more common among violent offenders, (Treimen, 1986)

77   My view... [is that] brain damage, not epilepsy, increases the chances of violent behavior. Brain damage, especially in limbic areas, can cause paranoia, and frontal damage can cause disinhibition. Paranoia and disinhibition are significant precipitators of violence, especially when combined with a history of childhood abuse. Limbic and/or frontal damage can also cause seizures, but seizures themselves rarely cause violence. Though the presence of seizures can be indicative of brain damage, it is the brain damage, not the seizures, that disinhibits. (2001, pp. 209-210)

78   Research by Lewis and her colleagues, (see, for example Lewis, Yeager, Swica, Pincus, & Lewis, 1997)

78   by James Chu (Chu & Dill, 1990)

78   and by other respected scientists (McLean, 2004)

78   The DSM IV-TR (APA, 2000)

79   "...cruel and unusual punishment and... "deliberate indifference" to the health needs
      of inmates. Among the cases... were instances of untreated or poorly treated pul-
      monary and cardiac problems, hypertension, sickle-cell anemia, and cancer. Attorneys
      also attributed at least two prison deaths to the poor quality of health care, including
      the case of a mentally ill woman with gastrointestinal problems. Confined naked to a
      prison cell, the woman ingested her own body waste and eventually died of untreated
      pancreatitis and starvation. (Talvi, 1999)

82   Victims [of incest] report a fear of abandonment, fear of not being believed, fear of
      punishment, and fear of being blamed for allowing the incestuous activity to occur and
      continue... (Herman & Hirschman, 1977)

82   While the child may not be able to take direct action in response to the incest, she may
      express her anxiety indirectly through [acting out behaviors]. The older child may act
      out by engaging in delinquent behavior or running away. (Herman & Hirschman,
      1977)

CHAPTER 2

83   He might have been the protagonist of a modern-day Horatio Alger story, an exem-
      plar of the Asian-American "model minority (Yen, 2000)

84   Wayne attended Lewis and Clarke Middle School and started Billings Central Catholic
      High School in the fall of 1989, where he was the only Asian among 340 students (Yen,
      2000)

84   While the Los were not Catholic themselves, their thinking ran thus: America is a
      Christian country, and nothing could be more Christian than Catholicism. (J. Kenton-
      Walker, personal communication, August 27, 2003)

84   April Coolidge, who managed The Great Wall, said that Wayne was "fun to be around,
      nice, polite. He never seemed depressed. He seemed to like his school, he really did...
      [the shooting] comes as a shock to us, if that helps explain his character at all." (Gorov
      & Roche, 1992, December 16, p. 38.)

85   The frequent and prolonged history of physical and sexual abuse committed by a par-
      ent or parent substitute has been pervasive and extreme among the 150 or so murder-
      ers I have seen. It has been the life experience of 94 percent of all the murderers I
      examined in a consecutive five-year period and reported in 1995. Extreme abuse was
      also pre..sent in the histories of thirteen of the fourteen individuals Dr. Lewis and I
      examined who were on death row for homicides committed before they were eighteen
      years old and in fifteen condemned murderers we had examined just before scheduled
      executions. (Pincus, 2001, pp. 67, 68)

85   Similarly, in Athens' 1992 qualitative study of 110 convicts who had committed
      extreme violence (which may or may not have involved murder,) 100 percent had been
      victims of childhood abuse. Quantitative researchers (Smith & Thornberry, 1995; C. S.
      Widom, 1989; C.S. Widom, 2001; Zingraff, Leiter, Myers, & Johnsen, 1993)

85   Parenting practices are, unless closely scrutinized, inherited from generation to gen-
      eration. (Van IJzendorn, 1992)

86   We were very sorry to see that he left because we lost a very valuable member of the
      symphony." (Gorov & Roche, 1992, December 16, p. 38).

86   According to Gary Gaudreau, one of Wayne's teachers at Billings Central Catholic
      High School, he did very well during the first semester of his freshman year, but in the
      second semester there was a "buildup... of tremendous stress, tremendous anxiety."
      (Gibson, 1999, p. 206).

86   Additional stress came in the form of his parents' high expectations for him. "Our
      whole hope is our two boys," C.W. once told a reporter (Glaberson, 2000a).

86   Asian Americans of this era were considered "the model minority," a term defined by
      legal scholar Rhoda Yen as "a non-white group that has achieved economic success and
      social acceptance through hard work and conservative values." (Yen, 2000, p. 2).

87   It's no wonder that the median income of Asian and Pacific-American families is much
      higher than the total American average . . . (Reagan, 1984)

87   *Fortune* magazine ran a headline describing Asian Americans as "America's Super
      Minority." (Yen, 2000)

87 [T]hreats to cultural identity, powerlessness, feelings of marginality, loneliness, hostility and perceived alienation and discrimination remain unredressed and hidden under the veneer of the model minority myth. Both social and psychological forces to conform to the model minority stereotype place an inordinate amount of pressure on Asian Americans. (Days Sandhu, as quoted in Morrissey, 1997)

87 Some psychiatric disorders, such as bipolar disorder, and schizophrenia, often begin this way, during adolescence, but the behavior also falls well within the limits of normal teenage acting-out. William Glaberson (Glaberson, 2000a),

88 I was really into this Mormon chick but she won't give me the time of day so being pathetic I said I would kill myself and she called the cops on me! So the Aspen police shows up and asks me if everything is ok. So that's that. (Lo, 2007)

88 In the Glaberson interview Wayne complains of feeling "Taiwanese in Montana, Montanan in Massachusetts." (Glaberson, 2000b).

88 Anne Coulter, a critic of liberalism sometimes given to hyperbole, described Bard as a "Safe Streets program for traitors and lunatics." (2003).

88 While the Billings Central Catholic High School prohibited sexual behavior and drug use, a member of the Simon's Rock counseling staff said nonchalantly of the incoming students that ". . . when they come here there's a lot of acting out—sex, drugs. They're trying things on for size." (David Reed, as quoted in *Friends of Lo Receive Counseling*, 1992, December 18, p. 1C.)

89 I guess I was the jock, so it was a reverse Columbine. From an interview on the Wayne Lo website ("Zach", 2007)

89 In the spring of 10th grade, Wayne asked a young man named Robert Schork, a Simon's Rock graduate who was tutoring him in economics, if he could borrow his car and drive to Pittsfield to buy a gun. "No way in hell," Robert responded. (Etkind, 1994, January 20, p. A4).

90 Erikson called this poor solution to the crises of identity formation, a "negative identity." (Erikson, 1968, pp. 172-173).

90 This, a common psychological defense mechanism among the abused, is called "identification with the aggressor (Freud, 1967)

90 "It's not like we haven't been afraid of Wayne and his friends," said a senior named Ziadee Taekheir, 20, from Portland, Maine. (Pratt, 1992, December 16, p. A1).

90 "My friends and I had been talking daily about how scary he is." (Gorov & Roche, 1992, December 16, p. 38.)

90 He would target African Americans one time and then Jews or homosexuals another time . . ." (Gibson, 1999, p. 159).

91 But then years later when she appeared on the A&E [Arts & Entertainment Channel] documentary "Rampage Shooters," she claimed she left SRC because of me! (Lo, 2007)

92 He told Floyd, "If I'd known you were going to throw the whole book at me, I would have gotten my money's worth. I have the power to bring the whole school down to its knees." (Etkind, 1994, January 133, p. B1.)

93 Wayne had previously scheduled a meeting with the dean for 11:30 to discuss his transfer, a regular practice for college-bound students. The dean would have an opportunity to question him at that time. (McGrory, 1992, December 25).

94 "Anyone adding to this book, God will add to him the plagues mentioned here. Anyone taking away from this book, God will take away his tree of life. Amen. God be with you." (Lo's last exam gave cryptic warning, 1994, January 12, C4.)

94 "That stuff is for my dad's gun at home..." he said, equivocating, "but maybe it's not." (Gibson, 1999, p. 229.)

95 According to Jared, "He changed his mood. He got very serious. I had never seen him that serious. He said, 'Because I don't care anymore. I don't want to live.'" (Lo's Friend testifies about 'Last Supper', 1994, January 13, C5.)

95 In an alternate account, it was another friend, someone on the periphery of the click named Jeremy Robinson, in whom Wayne confided. (Gibson, 1999),

96 I opened the door to talk to him and he stuck the barrel of the gun through the door.

. . . I tried to push the door shut. He shot twice. I finally got the door closed . . . he pushed the gun barrel through one of the windows and shot two more times . . . (Etkind, 1994, January 13, p. B1)

96   I was calm when I went on the shooting. I thought I was on a mission from God. I know, it sounds ridiculous now, but I actually believed it then. I wasn't nervous or disorganized. I was calm but with a lot of anger. I just shot at anything that moved in front of me. The plan was to attack Simon's Rock College so I guess I succeeded. I didn't really have a step by step plan as to who or where I was going to shoot at. ("Zach", 2007).

98   . . . the room exploded with gunfire, Everyone… went down. Glass was flying, the gun banging, bullets zinging around. Tom McElderry was shot in the leg. Rose was on the floor with the phone, still trying to call for help. Kids were screaming. Rob ran out the back door and through the woods to get help at the guard shack. (Gibson, 1999, p. 81)

98   . . . [I] felt a pressure in my side. I curled up and rolled into a nearby hallway. I lay there and I wasn't sure what had happened… [Friends] were telling me I was shot. I took a look and said 'It looks like it just grazed me,' but I was told, 'Nope there's a hole in the other side.' (Lahr, 1994, January 14, p. B1)

98   I heard an explosion and noticed that I was suddenly sitting on the ground. I first thought a firecracker had gone off. I looked down at my legs and noticed that I was bleeding from two holes in each of my thighs . . . I could tell my heart [was] beat[ing] because with each heart beat, more blood came out. (Lo called 911 after shootings, 1999, January 14, C4)

99   Her liver and intestines had been torn by the bullet and her pelvis shattered. In her distress, she mistook the officer for the killer and began screaming, "Please stop, please don't shoot me again, please, please…" (Gentile, 1992, December 18, pp. A1, A8).

99   "One of the students," she said. "Wayne Lo." (Gentile, 1992, December 18, p. A8.)

99   "I'm killing people. I'm fucking shooting people." (Gibson, 1999, p. xx)

100   "I'm the person who shot the people at Simon's Rock…" he said, and added, "the people at Simon's Rock needed to be taught a lesson." (Etkind, 1994, January 15, p. B1.)

100   Wayne obeyed. They pulled off his knit cap "to see what he looked like," (Gentile, 1992, December 18, p. A8),

100   "I think one of the reasons he stopped shooting was because he got disgusted with the gun," an officer suggested several days later. (Gentile, 1992, December 18, p. A8).

100   When they arrived at the stationhouse, Wayne asked an officer, "What did I do tonight?" (Etkind, 1994, January 20, p. A1, A4).

101   This nonsense word appears in the Stephen King novel, *The Shining* (1977) as well as the film adaptation, (1980)

103   "I couldn't believe it," his father later told the court. "It was a shock to me… I looked at him. He was different. It seemed to me to be a different soul inside. It was not Wayne." (Father: Lo had 'different soul inside,' 1994, January 25, p. 1B.)

103   When Lin-Lin visited him in the jail the following week, she concurred. "The Wayne I saw there was not the son I have. I look at him and he looks empty." (Mother: jailed Lo 'empty,' 1994 January 28, p. C4.)

103   She asked him, in Mandarin, "How do you feel now?" He replied, also in Mandarin, "My mind is peaceful." (Etkind, 1994, January 28, p. B1.)

104   Money to pay for expert witnesses, psychiatric assessments, and the like, had to be granted by the court, but this proved no impediment to the attorneys presenting the strongest possible case for Wayne. (Janet Kenton-Walker, personal communication, August 27, 2003).

104   Mental disease or defect does not otherwise constitute a defense." (U. S. Congress, 1984).

104   In fact it was probably not necessary as the insanity defense is used in less than two percent of all felony cases, and fails in 75 percent of those cases. (Linder, 2001).

104   While narcissistic personality disorder is arguably a mental illness—it is listed in the DSM IV-TR (A.P.A., 2000)

105   Responses to a Rohrshach test were "characterized by a lot of aggression . . . and grandiosity of a religious type." (Etkind, 1994, January 26, p. B1.)

105   He testified that Wayne was suffering from a "psychotic disorder with command hallucinations and paranoid delusions of grandiosity" and "paranoid schizophrenia" that "interfered with his ability to appreciate the criminality of his acts." (Gibson, 1999, p. 208.)

105   The next expert for the defense, Dr. Albert Gaw, a psychiatrist fluent in Mandarin who served as an advisor on cross-cultural issues for the DSM III-R, (the edition of the DSM used between 1987 to 1994),

105   A delusion is a "fixed, false belief that is resistant to reason or confrontation with fact" (*Random House Unabridged Dictionary*, 2006)

105   For example, Revelations was written to the churches in Asia. Wayne said, 'I am Asian, therefore Revelations is being written to me.'"

106   (Gibson, 1999, p. 210.)

106   As for Wayne's statement that he had copied out Revelations in order to appear crazy, Dr. Gaw admitted that it was "a very significant statement and that it bothered me . . . I felt it was inconsistent." (Etkind, 1994, January 28, p. B4.)

106   No one believed in UFOs, Wayne said, but if you had been abducted by one, you couldn't help but believe in them after that. The experience of being commanded by God was the same. He had never even believed in God, but when God had come to him he had been powerless to resist, powerless to conceive any other reality than that which had issued the command. (Gibson, 1999, p. 255)

106   Dr. Profit was particularly struck by Wayne's need to take control of the conversation during their 20 hours of pretrial interviews, a behavior also noted by Glaberson (2000b)

107   During the trial, C.W. had apologized personally to the families of each of the boys killed or maimed by his son. Evelyn David, Mathew David's mother, probably echoed the pity felt by many of those in the courtroom when she said, "I feel badly for the Los. It's a dreadful experience. They lost their son. I still have my son." (Gentile, 1994, February 4, p. A4.)

107   After the trial, Wayne told friends that he was angry at his attorneys. He believed that he was perfectly sane, ("Zach", 2007; Glaberson, 2000b; Lo, 2007),

108   "Who's to say if this guy might have thought twice if we'd had a death penalty." (McGrory, 1992, December 17, p. 37.)

108   In an attempt to work through his grief, Galen Gibson's father, Gregory, spent seven years investigating the details of his son's murder, a journey of discovery that he later made into a book called *Gone Boy, a Walkabout*. (Gibson, 1999).

108   Anger was the fuel for what I did. I wanted to teach those people [Simon's Rock administration] a lesson and I think I did my job. Anger can be empowering, but if you maintain it past its usefulness, it becomes sick. [Writing the book and the lawsuit] . . . transformed me from being just some poor schlub. I could do something. I could write it down. I could record and analyze it. It made me realize I'm not just a victim, I'm an agent. (Galen as quoted in Higgins, 2001, April 19, p. B1)

109   Wayne wrote back that "he accepted full responsibility for his crimes. He regretted them more than words could say. . . . he was sorry for what he had done." (Gibson, 1999, p. 273.)

109   Amiable, with smooth, slightly dimpled cheeks and a sparkling intelligence, Wayne Lo often spoke with disarming frankness. He was also manipulative, controlling, and so eager to portray himself in a positive light that it was sometimes impossible to believe he thought he was telling the truth. (Glaberson, 2000b)

109   He insisted that he had never been mentally ill. "Personally I am, I guess you could say, a proud person. I would like to think that I have control of myself, that I am not impaired in any way." (Butterfield et al., 2000, April 12, A1.)

110   Zach and Wayne are very easy to deal with. Honest, friendly, and very eager to get your items out as fast as possible. It's just not possible to find murderabilia at a lower price anywhere else on the Internet. (Gilks as quoted in "Zach", 2007)

CHAPTER 3

111 He accused Murkowski and his colleagues of torching his apartment, wrote threatening letters to the senator, and vowed to "go to war." (Bingham, 1997, February 27, p. A6).

112 "That's when I started drinking," she said. "I didn't know what else to do." (Fainaru, 1998, October 18, p. A1.).

112 The only beautiful thing he can think of is his cat, which died: and it hurts when he cries." (Fainaru, 1998, October 18, p. A1.)

112 "My mom was always messing things up," he said of her. (John Ramsey as quoted in Toomey, 1998, February 3, p. A1).

112 Eventually Carol and her sons found themselves in Napakiak, a village of about 350 on the Kuskokwim River, where half of the adult population was unemployed. (U.S.Census, 2000).

113 They had their jackets but no hats or gloves. So we gave them breakfast and in the morning washed them and called DFYS [Department of Family and Youth Services]." (Janna Hulse as quoted in Fainaru, 1998, October 18, p. A1.)

113 "When she's sober she's the type of person you wouldn't mind hanging around with," he said of her. (Evan Ramsey quoted in Fainaru, 1998, October 18, p. A1.)

114 Remembering the incident, Sue Hare said, "You always think the thing that's bad is the worst thing that'll ever happen... And then you live a little longer." (Sue Hare quoted in Fainaru, 1998, October 18, p. A1.)

115 "It was a bird gun. I don't think I even connected the fact that you can kill a person with a gun that you use to shoot birds." (Fainaru, 1998, October 18, p. A1.)

115 "He went to a cliff, got in the water, and was planning to wade out to sea and drown himself." (John R. Smith, PhD, as quoted in Marin, Pelley, Grodin & Simon, 2001.)

115 He called up a close friend, Wilson Naneng, and said, "You've got five minutes to get over here or I'm going to shoot myself." (Evan Ramsey quoted in Fainaru, 1998, October 19, p. A1.)

115 "I didn't really tell anybody about that," Wilson explained, "because of how friends are." (Fainaru, 1998, October 19, p. A1.)

115 According to his fellow students, Evan was "more an object of ridicule than a source of fear." (Marquez, 1997, February 27, p. A6).

115 Students would often provoke him just to see him explode. "Kids made fun of him," Sharin Mojin, 14, said. "He would do one of his things and kids would call him a 'spaz'." (Marquez, 1997, February 27, p. A6).

115 Donald Ramsey said of his son. "He's slow to anger, but when he angers he blows up." (Bell & Shinohara, 1997, February 20, p. A1.)

116 "He'd blow his top and just go off. His mind would shut off. He wouldn't listen to anybody." (Shinohara, 1997, February 21, p. A1).

116 Once he threw around the chairs in the library, "actually picked them up and winged them around the room." (Myron Angstman as quoted in Bell & Shinohara, 1997, February 20, p. A1.)

116 He described Evan as ". . . freaking out. It was like he snapped or something." (Fainaru, 1998, October 18, p. A1.)

116 This kind of impulsivity is the most common underlying factor of the narcissistic, antisocial, and borderline personality disorders. (Looper & Paris, 2000).

116 The teens in question do not "snap" under pressure, fly into an uncontrollable rage, grab a gun, and shoot other students. (Vossekuil, Fein, Reddy, Borum, & Modzeleski, 2002).

117 "We were just talking. He had just woke up; I could hear him crunching on a bowl of cereal . . . I just called to let him know I got out of prison." (Hunter, 1997, February 20, p. A1.)

117 "It was just, 'You know I love you, don't you, son?' And he told me, 'I love you too, dad.'" (Fainaru, 1998, October 19, p. A1.)

117 While all unsuccessful suicides resemble parasuicides, they are differently motivated and are associated with different psychological conditions, the former with mood disorders

and alienation, the latter with narcissism and a taste for excessive dramatics. (Suominen, Henriksson, & Suokas, 1996; Tsoi & Kua, 1987; Wai & Heok, 1998; Welch, 2001).

118   The three boys spent hours walking the boardwalks, smoking unfiltered Camels with marijuana mixed in, and playing *Doom*. (Carmack, 1993).

118   I am not suggesting that playing *Doom* causes teenagers to commit SR shootings. An overwhelming body of research suggests it does not. (Freedman, 2002).

119   Evan accused James of suggesting an SR shooting. "He said that my face and name would go across the world. He said I'll become famous . . . He said I should live the fame." (Fainaru, 1998, October 19, p. A1.)

119   Evan had not completed his assignment, which was to create a yearbook pictorial on special needs students, and she asked him what he was planning to do about it. "I don't know," he replied. (Ramsey quoted in Fainaru, 1998, October 19, p. A1).

120   Finally she went to the school social worker, Jacqueline Volkman, who had just been hired that year. "The problem was," Volkman said later, "I wasn't even sure who he was; I had to have someone point him out to me." (Volkman quoted in Fainaru, 1998, October 19, p. A1.)

120   The fact that she didn't know Evan in a school of only 450 students, did not reflect on her lack of competence or industry, but rather on Evan's ability to "fly beneath the radar," (Newman, Fox, Harding, Mehta, & Roth, 2004)

120   For almost 20 years this remained the only tax-supported high school for the region's native children. In 1966, overwhelmed by the number of native children seeking high school educations, Alaska began construction of six regional high schools, each with its own dormitory, in an explicit attempt to destroy the culture of the small villages, which were believed to "retard the development of rural folk into a disciplined and reliable workforce." (Training Corporation of America, 1967, section IV, pp. 11-12)

121   These towns are very poor places to locate high schools for [native] village children . . . boarding schools for middle class children both in the other states of the U.S. and in England have traditionally been placed in rural areas... Yet, in Alaska, the absurdity is that children are taken from small villages and placed in regional towns which usually have much higher rates of social problems than the surrounding villages. (Chapter two: Bethel Regional High School, Klienfield & Bloom, 1973)

122   "Almost every village with an unused building larger than a broom closet pushed ahead with a high school program." (Cotton, 1984, p. 30).

122   "He told me I'd have to be a fucking moron if I didn't know how to fire a gun," Evan said. (Ramsey as quoted in Fainaru, 1998, October 19, p. A1).

122   He called James, crying, and talking about killing himself. "It's either them or me," he said. (Fainaru, 1998, October 19, p. A1).

122   He said, "Go up to the library. Something really bad is going to happen tomorrow." I asked him, "What do you mean something bad's going to happen?" He said he would let people know on the bus and let them know out loud in the lobby. I said, "Is it going to be like a fight?" And he said, "Yes." . . . somebody was going to get hurt. He said, "I'd like to tell you more, but I just can't." Then Sue told him he had to go to bed. (Naneng quoted in Fainaru, 1998, October 19, p. A1)

123   I have thought to myself, what kind of damage can a 12 gauge slug do to a human's internal organs or their head? Well, today I found out and so did everyone else that is in school... No, I am not on drugs... ciggerettes (sic) that's all. I am not really depressed just that the fact that I want people, the world, or maybe just Bethel, to know how mean and cruel the world is or can be. This school has got to get its shit together 'cause there are too many deaths this past 2-3 years . . . (Ramsey as quoted in Fainaru, 1998, October 19, p. A1)

123   Hi, every body! I feel rejected. Not so much alone but rejected . . . I figure by the time you guys are reading this I'll probably have done what I told EVERYONE I was going to do. Just hope 12 gauges don't kick too hard, but I do hope the shells hit more than 1 person because I am angry at more than 1 person. One of the Big [expletive] is Mr. Ron Edwards . . . I was told this would be his Last year, but I know it WILL BE HIS LAST YEAR . . . The main reason why I did this is because I'm sick and tired of being treated this way everyday . . . So I killed a little and killed myself. Jail isn't & wasn't for me, ever. (Ramsey as quoted in Fainaru, 1998, October 19, p. A1)

125   When he came home he would sprawl in his favorite chair, announce that "The captain is in the command module," and turn on *Monday Night Football.* (Fainaru, 1998, October 20, p. A1).

125   The kid came in with the shotgun and everyone was "Whoa." But we have an ROTC program here, and a lot of kids thought it was probably from that, so there was a delayed reaction. Then Josh said, "Hey, that's a shotgun." He stood up and said, "Hey, why do you have the gun here?" He had the gun at his hip and basically aimed at Josh . . . [Josh] just said, "I'm going to get out of here." When he got up, he got shot. (Bell & Shinohara, 1997, February 20, p. A1).

125   "You guys better run!" Evan shouted, firing a shot at the ceiling so it rained plaster on their heads. (Marquez, 1997, February 27, p. A7).

125   Jeffrey Chon, 14, described what happened next. "A lot of kids were like, 'Run, run.' I just started running. The whole school was in tears." (Bell & Shinohara, 1997, February 20, p. A1.)

125   Eric Hodgins, 18, trapped behind a planter in the corner of the room, recalled Evan's pleasure in firing the shotgun. "He was laughing, just going crazy." (Marquez, 1997, February 27, p. A7.)

126   "He just couldn't stop," she said later. "I don't know how to describe it. He looked like he wasn't even there." (Fainaru, 1998, October 19, p. A1.)

127   The terrified boy threw the shotgun off the balcony, crying something like, "I'm done, I don't want to die." (Marquez, 1997, February 27, p. A7.)

127   "Every nook and cranny had a student in it, just petrified." (Marquez, 1997, February 27, p. A7.)

128   I became aware of the shooting as Cheryl, my coworker, yelled for me to come listen to the radio in another office . . . As the voice on the radio told parents to get to the high school to pick up their children, we saw students jumping out of the windows and running across the tundra. [The high school was across the street.] I left TWC immediately and passed many parents driving distraught to the high school . . . I could only get so far in the traffic so I parked off the road and ran searching for my daughter. I asked anybody (sic.) if they had seen her. Finally one person told me she was fine and in the dormitory with the other students. I ran to her, held her and cried with her. I was at a loss for words and all I could do was hold her. (Miller, 1998, February 12, p. 6)

129   I don't think he's trying to emulate the old man, impress the old man, but who can say . . . ?" Growing tearful, he added, "This comes as a total shock to me. This ain't no family tradition." (Hunter, 1997, February 20, p. A1.)

129   "That young man is hollering for help," Evelyn Day told her audience, and this was "his way of getting our attention right now." (Bell, 1997, February 21, p. A1.)

129   A tribal elder had instructed them to use the smoke "to lift you, strengthen you, and protect you." (Marquez, 1997, February 27, p. A8.)

130   "Staff security and student security should be at the top of this school board's agenda," one speaker declared. "Education will have to come second." (Horner, 1997, February 27, p. A18.)

130   He had personally witnessed Evan's pleasure during the shootings. "I saw his eyes and he was enjoying it." (Horner, 1997, February 27, p A18.)

130   "It will be a war zone if this isn't taken care of," said Myron Angstman, a local attorney. (Horner, 1997, February 27, p. A18.)

130   On Friday, 2,000 people, nearly half the population of Bethel, gathered in the school gymnasium to "reclaim the school." (Marquez, 1997, February 27 p. A8).

130   Bob Herron opened the ceremony by welcoming back to school "…our brave faculty and students." (Marquez, 1997, February 27 p. A8.)

130   Les Daenzer, the newly appointed acting principal of the high school told the assembly, "I shudder to think that this is only the tip of the iceberg. There's more out there— I've seen it." (Marquez, 1997, February 27 p. A8).

131   Josh's mother, Claudia Palacios, admitted that her son was taken away before she had entirely figured him out. "Joshua was a puzzle and all of you have pieces… because each one of you now have those pieces, you'll always be part of our family." (Horner, 1997, March 6, p. A1.)

131 A year later, Velda Miller looked back and characterized that time as "hazed over with fear, anger, tears, extreme shock, and intense sadness… the confusion, as a parent, of letting my children go to school each day yet the frustration of not feeling safe, and of the unanswered question of 'why?'" (Miller, 1998, February 12, p. 6.)

132 "We have a whole community of Bethel and a number of victims who need to have this matter closed," she told the press (Associated Press, 1997, July 3, p. 11.)

133 There was a terrible sadness about the proceedings. One reporter commented, "There are moments when the 12 people sitting in the jury box of this borrowed courtroom seem to be the only people—except for the lawyers and the judge—not crying." (Toomey, 1998, January 30, p. A1.)

133 "He just didn't want to be here anymore…" Mrs. Fritch told the courtroom. "I watched him become unhappier and unhappier." (Toomey, 1998, February 3, p. A1.)

133 . . . the 17-year-old sat silently, staring down at the defense table before him as his attorney tried to save him from a life in prison. Wearing a blue oxford shirt and jeans, his legs shackled, his hair now grown out and slicked back, the impassive Ramsey seemed strangely peripheral to the courtroom drama deciding his fate around him. (Spitzer, 1998, February 5, p. 1)

134 The *Tundra Drum* wrote ". . . there was a general sense in Bethel more of nodding acknowledgement than of relief." (Spitzer, 1998, February 12, p. 1).

135 "I felt betrayed by Evan and I felt some guilt that I should have stopped it. I felt as though I had been shot myself. When I talked about Evan, it was like he was dead. I felt like I had lost a brother." (Fainaru, 1998, October 20, p. A1.)

135 "I've forgiven you a long time ago," Thomas said. "I've never hated you because that's not the love of Jesus." (Toomey, 1998, December 2, p. A1.)

135 When Evan's turn finally came to speak, he said in a voice so soft it could hardly be heard, "I'm so sorry." (Toomey, 1998, December 2, p. A1.)

136 During these interviews he is invariably asked about the motive for his crime. He told *San Diego Union-Tribune* reporter Jenifer Hanrahan, "There were a couple of people I wanted to kill. At the time there was two people I hated, hate as in the way Hitler hated the Jews." (2001, May 13.)

136 I think it was one of those little things. I thought he was an asshole but not one of those assholes that you'd really want to hurt." (1998, October 20, p. A1.)

136 He told Carol Marin of *60 Minutes II*, "My main objective of going into the high school (Marin, Pelley, Grodin & Simon, 2001.)

136 [To Evan Ramsey] I would like to know more about why you shot up a school. I am doing a school project and I kind of like to have an idea to go on while I am researching. I would really appreciate, all information you could give me. Sincerly Sydney Coon P.S. Just so you know I dont think any less of you as a person because i am sure you had a good reason to do it. [Author's spellings and punctuation retained] (Coon, 2004)

CHAPTER 4

138 When, after being coaxed, badgered and threatened, he finally emerged from his room to do the job, he would mow one or two strips in the lawn, or cut a square section in the middle of the yard so it resembled a punk haircut in reverse, and retire, leaving his mother livid. (Medgie Swann as quoted in Bellini, 2001, p. 35)..

140 He was called "fat," "chubby," "chunky," and other insulting names (Zimmer, 1997, October 2, p. A1),

140 For some of these boys… it's the perception of marginalization, despite evidence to the contrary, that matters most." (Newman, Fox, Harding, Mehta, & Roth, 2004, p. 242.)

140 Luke later said of his relationship with his mother, "I guess I really didn't have much of one… We never really got along. And she always deserted me and left me out. I guess it just wasn't really good." (Bellini, 2001, p. 33.)

141 For an adolescent, even one close relationship with a mentor may be sufficient to reject suicide or a negative identity (Bernard, 1998; Garbarino, 1999).

141 "We never saw him like that before and I tell you that other kid would have been seriously injured if we hadn't all pulled Luke away." (Timberlake as quoted in Bellini, 2001, p. 41.)

141 Here again is the impulsivity which is characteristic of the dramatic personalities (Looper & Paris, 2000).

141 Incest, physical or emotional, short-circuits this process, leaving the survivor skeptical of ever becoming a sexually functional adult (Herman & Hirschman, 1977).

141 First-person accounts of incest, such as *The Kiss* (Harrison, 1998)

142 "People see somebody read some book on philosophy and think, well, they must be a genius." (Rossilli, 1997, October 29, p. 7A.)

142 Then I would get a gun and blow my brains out all over the dog-gone room and leave my house to Luke Woodham. (Bellini, 2001, p. 48)

144 the inspiration for SR shooting had been found in novels such as *Rage* (King, 1977)

144 music video of the Pearl Jam song *Jeremy* (Pellington, 1992)

144 *The Basketball Diaries* (Goluboff, 1995)

145 "He'd squint his eyes at you if he didn't agree with what you said and then you'd feel him drilling into your mind, trying to work out where you were coming from." (Bellini, 2001, pp. 61, 62.)

146 Billy Baker, a Sunday school teacher at Crossgates Baptist Church, regarded Grant as somebody who "seemed to have his head screwed on pretty good... He knew a good bit about scripture." (Rossilli & King, 1997, October 15, p. 5A.)

146 Grant liked Adolph Hitler a whole lot and admired some of his tactics—the way he could control people, the way he could manipulate people. (Rossilli & King, 1997, October 15, p. 1A)

146 Grant told the group, "He should just kill her and be done with it so he won't have to see her again." (Boyette as quoted in Bellini, 2001, p. 78.)

146 Troy Parker, a Pearl High student and one of the original members of their group, told how one day he had been complaining about his mother, and Grant had advised him, "You just need to go out and kill her." (Troy Parker as quoted in Bellini, 2003. p. 66.)

146 Troy left the group in December of 1996 because "It started seeming serious and at the same time I was getting old. It all seemed kinda juvenile." (Troy Parker as quoted in Bellini, 2001, p. 72.)

147 This may be what District Superintendent William Dodson meant when he said that Luke and the other members of the group "...were apparently students that didn't have an identity, however, and they tried to make their identity themselves." (Sack, 1997, October 9, p. A16.)

148 "Luke was a social recluse all his life... He would be easy to control and easy to manipulate." (Rick Brown as quoted in Rossilli & King, 1997, October 15, p. 1A.)

148 And "God is only a shallow concept made up by fools looking for something to believe in." (Luke Woodham as quoted in Bellini, 2001, p. 68.)

148 In the winter of 1996, Grant and Luke began to study the *Necronomicon*, (Simon, 1980)

148 Luke himself took it seriously, referring to it as "...a bunch of spells and a bunch of history and stuff like that. Love spells and spells that can kill people and things like that." (Woodham as quoted in Bellini, 2001, p. 68)

149 They also read Anton LaVey's *Satanic Bible* (1969)

149 Luke had a classmate named Danny whom he disliked because "He would always talk down to me and he tried to use me any way he could..." (Woodham as quoted in Bellini, 2001, p. 72).

149 "We cannot move forward until all our enemies are gone," and, "If you are not with me, you are against me. If you are against me, you are dead." (Boyette quoted in John, 1997, October 15, p. A1.)

150 Grant came over to the house as he often did, and they began to talk about the "beauty of death." (Bellini, 2001, p. 93.)

150 I'll never forget the howl she made, it sounded almost human, we laughed and hit her more... (Rossilli & King, 1997, October 15, p. 5A)

151 Alan Shaw became "Commander and Chief (Explosives)" (Bellini, 2001, p. 107),

151 but the Athens theory dismisses the influence of any biological component (O'Donnel, 2003; Athens, personal communications, May 10, 2007).

151 The emotional and psychological toll of being a bystander to bullying has become a subject of study over the last few decades (see, for example Coloroso, 2003; Olweus, 1993; Twemlow, Sacco, & Williams, 1996).

151 "The worst part of both . . ." Athens writes, "is the twisted feelings and thoughts which can linger on in a disordered state . . ." long after the experience has ended. (Athens, 1992, p. 44.)

151 The existence of a second teen playing this kind of role was suggested by The *New York Times*, in a study conducted on the anniversary of the Columbine High School shooting (New York Times Reporting and Research Staff, 2000).

151 school-age rampage killers often had peers ". . . goading, sometimes even collaborating" in their crime (Fessenden, 2000, p. 29).

153 Because adopting such an identity means violating society's norms, and putting at risk one's "physical safety, freedom, and psychological well-being" (Athens, 1992, p. 63),

153 . . . the subject has now reached the plateau in his development where he is ready and willing to injure badly or even kill someone, should the proper circumstances arise. (Athens, 1992, p. 60)

154 But things got worse and Satan got me when I wasn't looking. (Bellini, 2001, p. 112)

155 "I figure I'll be in a shootout with the cops," he told Lucas, "and die." (Malone, Riley, Hall & Adams, 1998, December 9.)

157 Always beat on, always hated. (Bellini, 2001, p.128).

158 Then she stopped and her eyes rolled back in her head." (Chip Smith as quoted in King, 1997, October 3, p. 8A.)

158 Her stepfather, Mike Long, said of her, "She'd probably be the first one to hug Luke's neck and say, 'I know you didn't mean to do it.' That was the kind of person she was." (John, 1997, October 3, p. 1A.)

158 "I see his face, I see black, I see the rifle, I see Christina falling on the floor." (King, 1997, October 3, p. 8A.)

159 The sensation ". . . was like there were a thousand ants all over my legs." (Bellini, 2001, p. 134.)

159 Joni Palmer, a freshman, was shot in the right hip. Robert Harris, Jr., also a freshman, was shot several times in the left calf, a sensation he likened to being "kicked very hard." (Bellini, 2001, p. 136.)

159 "Every morning I tell them I love them, I hug them and tell them to do good. This was just like any other morning at home." (Pettus, 1997, October 2, p. B1.)

159 He was trying to find a way out, and the only way was going through the grass. But he couldn't get any traction . . . (Rossilli, 1997, October 2, p. 11A)

159 I pulled his jacket over his head and put my foot on his back. I kept him like that until the police arrived a few minutes later." (Hill, 1997, October 8, p. A1.)

160 "Well, wait until you get to Parchman," Myrick said, invoking the legendary Mississippi Delta prison (King, 1997, October 3, p. A1).

161 Irked, he replies, "I am not insane, sir. I knew what I was doing. I was just pissed at the time." (Bellini, 2001, p. 156.)

161 The students had been scheduled to take standardized tests that day, those tests schools give at regular intervals to evaluate teaching effectiveness, but the principals of the junior high and the high school decided to cancel "...because there was too much activity." (Lindsay, 1997, October 2, p. A11.)

161 Such declines help us understand why poor urban children living with constant violence score lower on such tests than those in non-violent neighborhoods. (Byrd, 2005; Garbarino, 1999; Garbarino, Kostelny, & Dubrow, 1998).

161 said one 14-year-old girl whose sister's best friend had been killed. "I am feeling a lot better about it all now." (Graham, 1997, October 2, p. B1.)

161 Luke Woodham was the lead story on *NBC Nightly News* that evening. The shooting, nine months after the Evan Ramsey shooting (Chapter 3, Case 8)

162 THE END IS NEAR . . . APOCALYPSE NOW. / Sincerely/ The Alliance of the / *Immortalz* / Think what you want-Lydia was no accident (Bellini, 2001, p. 172)

162 He told the media that the shooting was not the result of a failed romance, or a par-

ents' messy divorce, but rather a society that "put down the thinkers and the true geniuses of the world and replaced them with men whose strength is physical strength and physical abilities." (John & Rossilli, 1997, October 8, p. 6A.)

163 "My friend did this under my nose. He went mad because of society. We, as a society, must change." (Rossilli & Kanengiser, 1997, October 3, p. 9A.)

163 Students felt "he had no business justifying what Luke did," and accused him of just wanting attention. (Rossilli & Kanengiser, 1997, October 3, p. 9A.)

163 "In remembrance of Mary Anne Woodham," and was signed "Kwick as a Wink" (John & Rossilli, 1997, October 8, p. 1A & 6A),

163 Brook Cannon, another senior, said "I don't want to be here. It's too weird for me." (Harden, 1997, October 5, p. 1A.)

163 Survival needs, such as food, shelter, and *safety,* must be attended to before people can concentrate on higher needs, such as learning . . . (Maslow, 1987)

164 Donnie's attorney pointed out that no attempt had been made on his father's life, and that his father "fully supports him and stands by him and doesn't believe the charge." (Sack, 1997, October 9, p. A16.)

164 "If Wednesday's shooting rampage . . . saddened the community, the latest arrests may have broken its collective heart and stolen what was left of the town's innocence." (1997, October 8, p, A1.)

164 Lea Ann Dew said, "I'm scared of everything. I don't know who else was in the group and if there are any left." (Lindsay & John, 1997, October 8, p. A1.)

164 You don't realize who is involved or if there are more. The only thing to do is pray." (Kanengiser, 1997, October 8, p. 7A.)

164 whose four children attended Pearl schools, admitted that she was scared. "I don't feel in my heart that this is the end of it." (Kanengiser, 1997, October 8, p. 7A.)

166 "Be strong and hang in there. We know exactly what you're going through." (Message of unity sent to KY schools, 1997, December 18, p. 5B.)

166 I just didn't believe that he actually ever suffered from a delusional belief such that he saw demons or believed that demons were adversely influencing him." (Dr. Chris Lott as quoted in Bellini, 2001, p. 249.)

166 "a very psychologically disturbed youngster whose disturbed thinking and distorted reality left him helpless to judge the appropriateness of his own behavior, to appreciate the implications of his conduct, or to conform his conduct to the requirement of the law." (Bellini, 2001, p. 249.)

167 The essential features of the narcissistic personality disorder are "a pervasive pattern of grandiosity, need for admiration and lack of empathy," (A.P.A., 2000, p. 714),

167 BPD are "instability of interpersonal relationships, self-image, and affects, and marked impulsivity . . ." (A.P.A., 2000, p. 706).

167 The DSM acknowledges that the cluster system "has serious limitations and has not been consistently validated," (A.P.A., 2000, p. 686)

167 He was essentially a loner and used that as a way of trying to conceal his emotional problems." (Dr. Michael Jepson as quoted in Bellini, 2001, pp. 249, 250.)

167 Assistant District Attorney Tim Jones said of him, "He's mean. He's hateful. He's bloodthirsty. He wanted to kill her. Murder was on the boy's mind." (Hughes, 1998, June 6, p. 5A.)

168 he called to the crowd of reporters, "I'm going to heaven now. Everything happens for a reason. It's God's will." (Hughes, 1998, June 6, p. 5A.)

168 Afterwards, one of the jurors, an elderly woman, exclaimed through her tears, "I never, never want to do this again." (Hughes, 1998, June 6, p. 5A.)

168 he guessed we were going to lock him up in Parchman for the rest of his life for this. Then he laughed and said, 'Or the loony bin.' (Hughes, 1998, June 11, p. 7C.)

168 "One second I was some kind of broken-hearted idiot, and the next second I had power over many things. My mind didn't know how to take it." (Hughes, 1998, June 12, p. 13C.)

169 She recalled thinking, *That's the little boy who thought he was God and took my child from me.* (Hughes, 1998, June 10, p. 13A.)

169 "The reason you don't see any more tears is I have been forgiven by God. If they could have given the death penalty in this case, I deserve it." (Hughes, 1998, June 13, p. 2B.)

169 He told me I had to get the gun and the car and go to school and get my revenge on Christy and cause a reign of terror." (Hughes, 1998, June 12, p. 13C.)

169 I'm not saying these people are not involved in this, but it would not be the right thing to do to prosecute the case at this time." (Brown, 1998, July 23, p. 5B.)

169 He had absolutely nothing to do with any kind of crime or any attempt to hurt anyone." (Brown, 1998, July 23, p. 5B.)

170 "Friends and school peers turned their backs on me, and I realized that a conviction in the eyes of my friends was a prison in itself." (Teen says accusation in killings devastating despite innocence, 1998, December 24, p. 10C.)

170 "We were having to rely on the word of a three time convicted murderer . . ." (Brown, 2000, February 9, p. 5A.)

170 We were having to rely on the word of a three time convicted murderer . . . It's not very often that you can send a person to prison for talking." (Payne, 2000, February 12, p. 9B.)

CHAPTER 5

172 A neighbor who knew them well described them as "wonderful, warm and caring. The kids had a terrific family life." (Judy Feiertag, as quoted in Narcisco & Kidder, April 23, 1999.)

173 Dylan, being the youngest, had the honor of asking the Four Questions, a pivotal part of the Passover ceremony, the dialogue between the father and the youngest son that begins, *Why is this night different from all other nights?* (Leppek, 1999).

174 While he didn't talk to her frequently, the last few times he had phoned her she seemed to be ". . . the same sweet Susan I had known." (Columbus Dispatch, Powers, April 24, 1999, p. 3A.)

174 As we got older, his mom worried about the level of violence in the video games we were playing." (Brown & Merritt, 2002, p. 29.)

174 *Parents Under Siege* (2001)

175 Here were two loving and intelligent parents, who cared for their two boys, who spent time with them, and looked after them, yet who had lost their second-born son . . . (Garbarino & Bedard, 2001, p. xviii)

175 . . .we can assert without a doubt that they [Dylan's parents] are good parents—attentive, involved, and loving . . . (Garbarino & Bedard, 2001, p. 8)

175 They feel certain of one thing. "Dylan did not do this because of the way he was raised," Susan said. "He did it in contradiction to the way he was raised." (Brooks, 2004)

175 At another time Dylan described his relationship with his parents as "better than most kids," (Sanchez, 1998a, p. 3)

176 "they thought this couldn't happen to their son. They're elitists. They thought this was something white trash would carry out." (Bartels, 2004, p. 5A)

176 The coroner's report describes him as a "well-developed, well-nourished . . . white male appearing consistent with the stated age of 17." (Galoway, 1999)

176 *Fast Times at Ridgemont High*. (Heckerling, 1982).

176 "He was a very, very fine boy. He was very bright." (Wenzel, 1999)

176 He is often angry or sullen and [his] behaviors seem disrespectful and intolerant of others . . . [He] stays in his room constantly. (Sue Klebold quoted in Sanchez, 1998a, pp. 19, 20)

177 "As Dylan got older, he never told his parents he was being teased. Never. He kept it all inside." (Brown & Merritt, 2002, p. 30.)

177 Because Dylan internalized things so much, he would let his anger build up within him until one little thing finally set it off. When that happened it was like an explosion." (Brown, 2002, p. 32.)

177 to ". . . a prison yard . . . You find a gang of people to hang out with so that the other 'gangs' leave you alone . . ." (Brown & Merritt, 2002, pp. 42, 44).

177 Senior year he took first period bowling (in lieu of gym) and he would shout "Heil Hitler!" whenever he rolled a strike. (Shepard, 1999b, paragraph 17).

178 Charismatic, an eloquent speaker, well-read, the kind of guy who could bullshit for hours about anything and be witty and brilliant." (Pooley, 1999.)

178 And they are well thought of by neighbors and acquaintances. Solid folks, some quite affluent. No violent pasts." (Crowder, 1999, June 21, par. 23.)

179 "My dad's great and my mom's so thoughtful . . . It sucks that I'm doing this to them." (Erickson, 2001, p. 22.)

179 Friends of Eric's recalled how comforting his home was, how tidy and well-organized, how both parents were usually home, and Kathy always had sandwiches for them. (Russakoff, Goldstein, & Achenbach, 2006).

179 development praised the industrious way that all the Harrises kept the property in shape, the walks shoveled, the lawn tidily mowed, and the leaves raked, and the way they helped neighbors in a pinch. (Russakoff et al., 2006).

180 Kris Otten, who identified himself as Eric's best friend during this period, remembers frequent sleepovers at Eric's house (Russakoff et al., 2006)

180 "The Eric Harris . . . [that committed the shootings] was not the kid I knew in New York," Otten said. (Otten as quoted in Russakoff et al., 2006, par. 43.)

180 recalls Kevin and Eric as "terrific boys . . . pleasant, clean-cut, respectful toward their parents." (Russakoff et al., 2006)

180 Half of the entire population relocates—moves and registers a new address—at least once every five years. (Glick, 1993).

180 The younger child may experience relocation as a disintegration of his or her world, analogous to death (Bowlby, 1982)

180 it will mean the loss of a peer group, a parental sabotage of efforts to construct an adult identity. (Raviv, Keinan, Abazon, & Raviv, 1990)

180 fifteen-year-olds were asked to rank 37 stressors in order from worst to least, and placed relocation seventh, worse than divorce but not quite as bad as physical abuse. (Hutton, Roberst, Walker, & Zuniga, 1987).

180 They were 77 percent more likely to have four or more behavior problems than children who had moved less frequently. (Wood, Halfon, Scarlata, Newacheck, & Nessim, 1993)

181 teased whenever he took off his shirt. "It wasn't that noticeable—it was just sunken in a bit . . ." (Brown, 2002, p. 51).

181 The Governor's Report on the Columbine High School Shootings relegates the *pectus excavetum* to a footnote explaining his rejection by the Marines. (Erickson, 2001, p. 18, footnote 37)

181 or anywhere else to my knowledge, although he does mention that throughout his childhood he was constantly teased for being the "scrawny white kid." (Erickson, 2001, p. 22.)

182 This is a common defense mechanism called "identification with the aggressor." (Freud, 1936).

183 Although Byron and Dylan had been very, very close as children, they had grown apart in adolescence. (ABC News, 1999).

183 Byron made fun of his younger brother, "ripped" on him and, in Dylan's own words, "added to the rage." (Erickson, 2001, p. 22).

183 Friends and neighbors repeatedly characterized him as the ideal son, and Eric mentions admiring him (or perhaps damning him with faint praise) because he was "motivated." (Erickson, 2001, p. 22).

184 One guy, a wrestler who everyone knew to avoid, liked to make kids get down on the ground and push pennies along the floor with their noses. This would happen during school hours, as kids were passing from one class to another. Teachers would see it and look the other way. (Brown, 2002, p. 50).

184 Juvenile Diversion for the Denver District Attorney's Office, prepared a report on bullying at Columbine for the Governor's Columbine Review Commission. (Huerta, as quoted in Erickson, 2001, see pages 98-102 and footnotes).

185 They couldn't fight back. They wore the ketchup all day and went home covered with it." (an anonymous student as quoted in Coloroso, 2003, p. xviii.)

185 She had just moved to the area and perceived him as a "rough guy" with a warm heart. (JCSO, 1999b, Robyn Anderson interview, p. JC-001-010624).

185 "was never the type to get a girlfriend," and believed that Dylan had never had a girlfriend. (JCSO, 1999b, Robyn Anderson interview, p. JC-001-010624).

185 "They both [Eric and Dylan] worked and neither one spent money on anything including girls since they really did not date." (JCSO, 1999b, p. JC-001-010626.)

185 *Zero Day* (Coccio, 2003),

186 difficulties experienced by GLBT teens is evident in their suicide attempts, which are two to three times as frequent as attempts among heterosexual teens. (Faulkner & Cranston, 1998; Fergusson, 1999; Garofalo & Wolf, 1998; Hershberger & Pilkington, 1997)

186 Mickey and Malory Knox, antiheros of the film, *Natural Born Killers*] live by their own morals . . ." (JCSO, 1999c).

186 fallen in love but never spoken to. His journals included an unsent letter to one of them. (JCSO, 1999a, par. 15).

186 Randy Brown recalled, "and every time I went by, he was there [using the computer]. It was uncanny." (Brown, 2002, p. 75.)

187 and publishing odd humor, apocalyptic rants, and descriptions of the mischief he had committed and the mischief he had planned. (Shepard, 1999a).

187 "gentle," sometimes "hyper," occasionally funny, and "off in his own world... He did his own thing and . . . if he didn't want to go to class some days he just would not go." (JCSO, 1999bJC-001-010621.)

188 you name it and we will probly or already have done it. We have many enemies in our school, therefore we make many missions. Its sort of a night time tradition for us. (JCSO, 2003, 1997 documents, printout of Harris website by Brown. Misspellings retained.)

188 and lit them off at about 1:00 AM. Thus mission was part of a rebellion against these assholes that shot one of our bikes one day." (JCSO, 2003, 1997 documents, printout of Harris website by Brown.)

188 They did not get drunk after the fourth mission because of "...this person named Brooks Brown (303-972-0602)

189 I had to ditch every bottle I had and lie like a fuckin salesman to my parents." (JCSO, 2003, 1997 documents, printout of Harris website by Brown.)

189 The falling out between Eric Harris and Brooks Brown occurred about midway through Sophomore year. (February, 1997).

189 He's got spray paint cans in his room. Search it. Eric's fucked up and you need to know about it. (Brown, 2002, p. 78.)

190 "Eric, I've got your backpack," she told him, having made sure the car doors were locked, and the window only barely opened, "and I'm taking it over to your mom's. Meet us over there." (Brown, 2002, p. 79.)

190 He didn't listen. He just kept screaming, "Give me my backpack!" We were all scared. (Brown, 2002, p. 79)

190 And he said, "My son said that he is afraid of you." He didn't want to hear that his son had done anything wrong. (Judy Brown as quoted in Brown & Merritt, 2002, p. 80)

191 That seemed to surprise him. He said, "Are you calling me a liar?" And I said, "Yes, I am. And if you ever come up our street, or if you ever do anything to Brooks again— if I ever even see you on our street again—I'm calling the police." (Brown & Merritt, 2002, p. 81.)

191 Maybe he had gotten away with it for so long, manipulating people that way, that he was stunned when it didn't work." (Judy Brown quoted in Brown & Merritt, 2002, p. 81)

191 Dylan said that they "opened a locker or two to test to see if [the] list was current," (Sanchez, April 9, 1998, p. 17)

191 Whatever. And off school grounds we could relocate this person. That'd be a thousand dollars."

191 "Thank you SO much!" (Harris & Klebold, 1998)

192 white van," he told the police. "At first I was very uncomfortable and questioning with the thought." (Bartels & Crowder, August 22, 1999, par. 190.)

192   *Talking Back to Prozac* (1995)

192   advocates have suggested that the shooting was a result of an SSRI-inspired mania. (April 30, 1999).

192   Sue Harris told a juvenile court intake worker, during Eric's assessment. "His mood is more upbeat." (Sanchez, April 9, 1998, p. 18.)

193   The intake worker concurred. "He said that he is feeling better now that he is on medication." (Sanchez, April 7, 1998, p. 4.)

193   He is seeing a therapist once or twice a month, the family also meets with him on occasion. Eric says he has thought about suicide a couple of times but never seriously, mostly out of anger. (Sanchez, 1998b, April 7, 1998, p. 4)

193   People telling me what to think. I have too many inside jokes or thoughts to have very many friends or I hate too many things. (Sanchez, 1998b, April 7, 1998, p. 25)

194   I don't care if I live or die in the shootout, all I want to do is to kill and injure as many of you pricks as I can, especially a few people. Like Brooks Brown. (Brown, 2002, p. 84).

194   Flipping thing was heart-pounding gut-wrenching brain-twitching ground-moving insanely cool!" (JCSO, 2003, Brooks Brown printout of Eric Harris's website.)

195   An account of his arrest, written for a school assignment (11/18/98),

195   The experience showed me that no matter what crime you think of committing, you will get caught, that you must, absolutely must, think things through before you act. (Brown & Merritt, 2002, p. 92)

195   dumbshit from his possessions if he leaves them sitting in the front seat of his fucking van out in plain sight and in the middle of fucking nowhere on a Fri-fucking-day night? (Brown, 2002, p. 92)

195   NBK refers to the Oliver Stone film, *Natural Born Killers* (Tarentino, Veloz, & Stone, 1994),

196   Although *still on Earth*, [italics, mine] they live by their own morals, beliefs, and at the end of the film, expose the media and law for its flaws. (JCSO, 1999c)

196   I'm here . . . I'm right here . . . and you . . . you're somewhere else, man. You say why? I say why not? (Tarentino et al., 1994)

196   killing enemies, blowing up stuff, killing cops!! My wrath for January's incident will be godlike. Not to mention our revenge in the Commons." (JCSO, 1999a).

196   In his journal, Eric wrote, "It would be great if God removed all vaccines and warning labels from everything in the world and let natural selection take its course." During the rampage, Eric wore a t-shirt with "Natural Selection" printed across the front. (Erickson, 2001, p. 22).

197   "Don't worry about it," Dylan responded, "It happens all the time." (Brown & Merritt, 2002, p. 108.)

197   A piece he wrote in response to an assignment on "personification," about a wedding between a shotgun shell and a shotgun, and how the couple gave birth to "pellet babies," (Brown, 2002, p. 108),

197   left the class helpless with laughter. Other essays seemed to convey that he had "worked through many of his issues." (Brown & Merritt, 2002, p. 108.)

197   Often people who have made the decision to commit suicide have a brightening of mood, an elevation of energy. The end is in sight; their suffering is finite. (Grollman, 1971).

197   "It seemed like a funny thing to do," Brooks recalled, "I never thought twice about it." (Brown & Merritt, 2002, p. 115.)

197   On another occasion a clerk from Green Mountain Guns called Eric's house and told him, "the clips are in," (Gibbs & Roche, 1999),

198   According to Brooks, Eric and Dylan would now sit together in the back of the classroom and ask each other, "Can I shoot that guy?" (Brown & Merritt, 2002, p. 119).

199   He was able to buy clips and ammunition without me having to show any I.D. The sellers didn't write down any information. . . . When I look back at it, I think I was kind of naive . . . (January 27, document in support of HB 1242, "The Robyn Anderson Bill," 2000)

199   Robyn was not surprised that they had the money because "they both worked and neither one spent money on anything including girls since they really did not date." (JCSO, 1999b, pp. JC-001-010626.)

199 GUNS! We fucking got em, you sons of bitches! HA! HA HA HA! Neener! Booga Booga. Heh. It's all over now. This caps it off, the point of no return . . . (Brown & Merritt, 2002, p. 117)

200 she replied she did not know about Dylan since he lived in the mountains and there were deer outside his home. (JCSO, 1999b, Robyn Anderson testimony, p. JC-001-010632)

200 she would have told the authorities. . . . she would not have sat in her car in the parking lot and asked Monica the question of who is so stupid and retarded as to do this type of thing [the assault on the high school] sixteen days prior to graduation. (JCSO, 1999b, Robyn Anderson testimony, p. JC-001-010632)

201 In the beginning of February (2/9/99)

201 Dylan as "intelligent enough to make any dream a reality, but he needs to understand hard work is a part of it." (Anton & Ryckman, May 2, 1999, par 43.)

201 Dragon Arms gun shop in Colorado Springs and tried to buy an M-60 machine gun and a pistol with a silencer. Eric "was doing all the talking," (Savidge, Zewe, & Associated Press, 1999, par. 9)

201 "They were real mopey, like punk kids with the makeup on, like punk rockers," Bernstein said. (Savidge et al., 1999, par. 8).

202 physique most likely to elicit teasing.) He was always "the scrawny white kid." (Erickson, 2001, p. 22).

203 And don't fucking arrest them . . . Don't arrest any of our friends, or family members, or our coworkers. They had no fucking clue. (Lindsay, June 24, 2000, par 9)

204 It seemed like he was happy, like he was finding his way . . . And all the while, he was planning this massacre. (Brown, 2002, p. 120)

205 Eric applied to, and was rejected by, several colleges. Two weeks before the assault on the high school, (4/5/1999),

205 "It was late notice. It was nothing against Eric. He was always really sweet to me." (Carnahan, 1999, par. 3.)

206 when I'm in my human form, knowing I'm going to die. Everything has a touch of triviality to it." (JCSO, 1999a, par. 15.)

CHAPTER 6

208 ordinary school clothes and "not acting strange," according to classmate Jessica Rosecrans. (Bartels & Imse, April 22, 1999, par. 17).

208 I didn't like life too much, and I know I'll be happier wherever the fuck I go. So I'm gone. (Dylan Klebold as quoted in Brown & Merritt, 2002, p. 125)

208 I'm really sorry about all of this. I know my mom and dad will be just fucking shocked beyond belief. (Eric Harris as quoted in Brown & Merritt, 2002, p. 125)

209 Brooks demanded, running up to the car. "You weren't in third hour, today. You missed the test!" (Brown & Merritt, 2002, p. 3).

209 "It doesn't matter any more. Brooks, I like you now. Get out of here. Go home." (Eric Harris quoted in Brown & Merritt, 2002, p. 4.)

209 On the basis of this and nothing more, as he states in his account of the shootings, (Brown & Merritt, 2002),

210 a bomb technician from Littleton Fire Rescue, the bombs never detonated because of the unpredictable nature of fireworks powder, and "a very simple electronic failure," (Lowe, 2000, p. A-1),

211 During the autopsy, the coroner would discover "a large caliber, copper-jacketed bullet" (Galloway, 1999)

211 Neil Gardner, the community resource officer, on his two-way radio. "Neil, I need you in the lunchroom, quick," Jay said, in a panicky voice. (Neil Gardner interview, JCSO CR 99-7625, 1999, p. 37).

212 With his hands and arms, he pulled himself halfway into the cafeteria side entrance, propping open the door with his body. "I can't feel my legs," (Erickson, 2001, p. 27)

213 "This is what we always wanted to do. This is awesome!" (gunmen as quoted in Brown & Merritt, 2002, p. 130).

213 ". . . a female down in the south parking lot" the caller reported. "I think she's paralyzed." (anonymous 911 caller as quoted in Erickson, 2001, p. 35.)

213 As they approached the school, they got a call on the two-way radio from Mr. Horvath,
the dean of students: "Neil, I need you in the school, there's been a shooting."
(Horvath as quoted in Erickson, 2001, p. 44.)

213 the Secretary of Education and the U. S Attorney General had released a landmark
document, "Early Warning, Timely Response: A Guide to Safe Schools," (Dwyer,
Osher, & Warger, 1998), Russ Kick (2002) and Dave McGowan (2001)

214 Shards were buried in her neck and back. "Dear God! Dear God! Dear God!" she
screamed. (JCSO, 1999b, p. JC 001-000070).

215 Ms. Keating was the librarian. "That guy has a gun," she said. (JCSO, 1999a, p. JC-
001-000023).

216 Students, including two Eagle Scouts with first-aid training, tried to staunch the bleeding
but admitted later that they had never been trained to deal with gunshot wounds. Dave
said, "I'm not going to make it . . . Tell my girls I love them," (Scanlon, 1999, p. 1A)

217 As Eric and Dylan approached the library, a student named Lisa Kreutz recalled overhearing one of them asking the other, "Are you still with me? We're still doing this,
right?" (Erickson, 2001, p. 30 footnote 75).

217 of interpersonal violence are no longer of much consequence. You turn the corner and that's
that. A wealth of research (See, for example, Roemer, Litz, Orsillo, Elhlich & Freidman,
1998; Schwarz, Kowalski & McNally, 2005; Southwick, Morgan, Nicolau & Charney, 1997)

217 When no one responded to the command, one of the gunmen said, "Fine, then I'll
start shooting." (Erickson, 2001, p. 30.)

218 Patrick Ireland, who was crouched under a table with Daniel Steepleton and Makai
Hall, recalled one of the gunmen saying, "This is for all the shit you put us through."
Daniel recalled them saying something about "the four years of bullshit you put us
through." (Erickson, 2001, p. 30 footnote 76.)

218 When the new Star Wars film, *The Phantom Menace* premiered a month after the shooting (March 19, 1999),

218 "She Said Yes; the Unlikely Martyrdom of Cassie Bernall" (1999)

218 Josh admits that he ". . . did not see her at all but . . . says he will never forget what he
heard as he crouched under a desk about 25 feet away" (Bernall, 1999, p. 12)

219 She must have been scared, but her voice didn't sound shaky. It was strong. Then they
asked her why, though they didn't give her a chance to respond. They just blew her
away. (Bernall, 1999, pp. 12, 13).

219 [Eric killed him with a shotgun wound to the chest.] Then they started laughing and
cheering. It was like a big game for them . . . ("Josh" as quoted in Bernall, 1999, p. 13)

220 At this time Austin Eubanks heard one of the gunmen say, "We're going to blow up the
library," (JCSO, 1999a, JC-001-000026)

221 "Identify yourself," Eric commanded, noticing a student hiding beneath a table.
(Erickson, 2001, p. 32).

221 "Killing people," Dylan responded. (Erickson, 2001, p. 32).

221 He saw blood on Jenny Doyle's left arm. Corey DePooter had his eyes shut and was
moaning. Austin noted that there was "a lot of blood on his back." (JCSO, 1999a, p.
JC-001-000028).

222 The JCSO described their movements at this point as "directionless." (JCSO, 1999c,
par. 2).

222 "had it not been for the defective fusing of the explosive devices, particularly the two
propane tanks, the death toll at Columbine High School would have exceeded a
thousand." (Erickson, 2001, p. 12.)

223 The bombs did not explode, the sprinkler system put out the fire caused by the gasoline and fuel explosion, and the damage seemed to be minimal compared with their
original plan. (JCSO, 1999d)

224 "show a wide zone of powder stippling, but lack a muzzle imprint and laceration. The
area of powder stippling will depend upon the distance from the muzzle." (Denton,
Segovia, & Filkins, 2006).

225 ". . . I could have been one of the students who didn't make it out alive . . . I started to wonder how I would be remembered . . . Would they say I lived my life to the fullest?" (Welsh quoted in Kuntz, 1999, p. D7.)

225 "There was a group of six boys who literally saved all our lives . . . It was kind of funny because many of these boys are thought of as goofy kids in everyday life." (Behan as quoted in Kuntz, 1999, p. D7.)

225 "Why Lauren? What did she ever do in her life to deserve such a fate? Why not me?" (Goodwin as quoted in Kuntz, 1999, p. D7).

225 Some students simply could not tolerate the sadness and sense of loss. "Even during the first weeks . . . there were others who were eager to 'get over all the fuss' and move on." (Bernall, 1999, p. 135.)

226 He said that the church could "honor murderers, but they're not going to honor Dan with them." (Associated Press, 1999, September 27).

226 Earlier, West Bowles church had sent a letter to the Rohrbough family informing them of the plan to plant the trees and stating that "hate is our true enemy." (Associated Press, 1999, September 27).

227 reestablished on April 20, 1999, because it was accompanied by bombs and shootings. It is always the blood of martyrs that acts as rocket fuel for the church." (American Atheists, 1999, par. 13.)

227 A reporter from the Associated Press remarked that, "Many in the crowd appeared exhausted." (Vogt, 1999, par. 10.)

227 On Sunday, April 25, a memorial service was organized by Governor Bill Owens, whom *USA Today* characterized as "a young Republican with close ties to his state's religious right." (Kasindorf, 1999, p. 03.A).

227 The word "columbine" is derived from the Latin, *columbinus*, meaning "dove-like." ("Merriam-Webster online dictionary," 2005).

228 Brooks, who had been failing several courses, wrote that it was ". . . an offer I couldn't refuse." (Brown & Merritt, 2002, p. 171).

229 "on the grounds that civil litigation was pending against the sheriff and other Jefferson County officials, commenced by victims and their families," (Erickson, 2001, p. 7)

229 defendants would be prejudiced in the course of that litigation were they to provide the data sought by the commission." (Erickson, 2001, p. 7).

229 The commission's final report stated that the sheriff's report, circulated on CD-Rom and through their website, contained "inaccuracies and omissions." (Erickson, 2001, p. 7, footnote 7)

229 Kiekbusch had "ordered the destruction of a 'pile' of Columbine records and that key documents were purged from the computer system at the sheriff's office in the summer of 1999." (Salazar, Goodbee, & Langfield, 2004).

230 "Holding police officers liable in hindsight for every injurious consequence of their actions would paralyze the functions of law enforcement," U.S. District Judge Lewis Babcock stated. (CBS News, 2001, par. 4).

230 Members of the Sanders family claimed that police gave "repeated false assurances that help would be there in 10 minutes." (CBS News, 2001, par. 5).

231 "Look, there's the little nigger," before killing him. "Should that be the last thing you have to hear before the last breath leaves your body?" (Belkin, 1999, p. 89).

231 Dave Sanders' wife and two step daughters sued 11 video game manufacturers and Times/Warner, producers of the *Basketball Diaries, (*Kalvert, 1995)

231 dismissing the lawsuit in March of 2002, "it is manifest that there is social utility in expressive and imaginative forms of entertainment, even if they contain violence." (Associated Press, 2002, par. 9.)

232 "The tragedy in Littleton . . . calls upon us to modify our schedule to show our profound sympathy . . ." (Boulder News Staff, 1999, p. 1A).

232 Tom Mauser, father of shooting victim Daniel Mauser, carried a banner that read, "My son died at Columbine, he'd expect me to be here today." (Fish, 1999, May 2, p. 1A).

232 SAFE (Sane Alternatives to the Firearms Epidemic) Colorado, a not-for-profit lobbying organization. (SAFE Colorado, 2000).

232 Gary McPherson, a Republican from Aurora, spoke for all legislators when he said it was done "out of deference to the victims and their families. Now is not the time to have this debate." (Hilliard, 1999, p. 1A.)

233 "What happened in Colorado and Georgia will not be remedied by passing new federal gun laws." (Gay, 1999, par. 6.)

233 Department of Justice published a report called *Kids and Guns* (Bilchik, 2000)

234 "Because of the outdoor classrooms, it has to be built during the summer. Once we take care of the children, we can deal with our own grief which we have been pushing down." ("Today show," 2000, April 20.)

235 The tails of the ribbon, inscribed with the phrase "Never Forgotten" frame a connection to the outer Ring of Healing becoming a symbolic link between the community and the deceased. (Columbine Memorial Committee, 2004, par. 7,8,9)

CHAPTER 7

236 postvention (how to help the survivors deal with what has occurred and regain their pre-crisis level of functioning). (K. P. Dwyer, D. Osher, & C. Warger, 1998.)

236 profile of serial killers to predict who will commit a crime; it uses them to winnow down the suspects *after* a crime has been committed. (see Holmes & Holmes, 1996 for a detailed discussion).

237 Seeking to predict acts that occur as rarely as school shootings is almost impossible. (O'Toole, 2000, p. 3)

237 An earlier report from another branch of the government (K. Dwyer, D. Osher, & C. Warger, 1998)

237 but concludes with the caveat: "Such signs, may or *may not* indicate a serious problem." (p. 6, italics, mine; another close scrape with Nonsense.)

238 "Without exception, these kids will tell you what they are going to do beforehand," was their consensus. (O'Toole as quoted in Kupersanin, 2002, p. 2).

238 In 2001 school shootings were averted at New Bedford High School in New Bedford, Massachusetts; (Ferdinand, 2001);

238 at Royal Valley High School in Hoyt, Kansas; (Norman, 2001);

238 Monument High School in Twenty-nine Palms, California; (Butterfield, 2001);

238 Because the Secret Service has expertise in threat assessment, they concentrated on this particular form of leakage. Two of their publications (Fein et al., 2002; B. Vossekuil, Fein, Reddy, Borum, & Modzeleski, 2002)

239 It is common for children who have played the former role to want to experience the latter. (Olweus, 1993a.)

239 In the basement tapes, Dylan Klebold recalled being excluded in daycare, when he was three; and Kip Kinkel (Overview, Case 12,)

239 from bullying to humiliation to rage and to revenge, made this one of the first characteristics of school rampage shooters to be identified. (Bryan Vossekuil, Reddy, & Fein, 2000).

240 Dan Olweus, a Norwegian psychologist at the university of Bergen began publishing scientific research on this subject in 1973. (1973; 1978; 1986; 1993a).

240 harassment such as slandering, spreading of rumors, and manipulation of friendship relationships." (1993a, p. 19).

240 American authorities refer to it as "relational bullying," or "relational aggression," (see, for example Liepe-Levinson & Levinson, 2005), *Odd Girl Out* (Simmons & Phimister, 2003) and *Queen Bees & Wannabes* (Wiseman, 2002).

240 In 1993, re-interviewing his original panel who were now 23, he found that, while the former bullying victims no longer perceived themselves as such, many were depressed and suffered from poor self-esteem. (Olweus, 1993b).

241 Early Warning, Timely Response (K. P. Dwyer et al., 1998)

243 a document created and implemented by an interdisciplinary crisis response team selected from the school and the community (K. P. Dwyer et al., 1998).

243 First, the safety of the students must be maintained through evacuation of the building or through containment in the classroom, a process known as "lockdown" (K. Dwyer, D. Osher, & C. Warger, 1998)

243   school personnel may forget the emergency codes, and substitute teachers may be ignorant that such codes exist (Cumming, 1999).

243   For example, if a bomb is discovered in the school, the evacuation should proceed in stages starting with the students most likely to be harmed: those in the rooms nearest the device. (Blauvelt, 1999).

243   student cell phones if a shooting or other crisis is taking place. A recent survey (Goodall, 2008)

244   Videos of its impeccable operation, posted on YouTube, show a students being warned of an approaching tornado. (MattMaxwellMedia, 2008).

244   Some school systems have developed a "crises response notebook," (Przygoda, 2000),

244   or "emergency kit" (Brown, 1999)

244   or destroying property. They may become withdrawn or clingy and school work may deteriorate in quality. (Kline, Schnfeld, & Lichtenstein, 1995.)

246   join a "community of bereavement," to use a term coined by Edward Linenthal (1998)

246   or through social action, like Columbine parent Tom Mauser, who became an outspoken gun control advocate. (SAFE Colorado, 2000).

249   one of hundreds of thousands of cast-off weapons of foreign armies that are now available to mail-order customers of American gun dealers." (Franklyn, 1964b, December 6).

249   "hysterical opposition by a small but well-organized minority." (Franklyn, 1964a)

250   But it would help reduce the unrestricted sale of fire-arms to those who cannot be trusted in their use or possession. How many lives might be saved as a consequence? (Semple, 1966)

250   a House Judiciary Committee in support of a bill to expand background checks on gun show sales, would have deterred her. (Gordon, 2000).

250   One thousand seven hundred and seventy-six were murdered, 1,007 committed suicide, and 193 were victims of gun-related accidents. (Centers for Disease Control, 2001).

251   Britain wants to be, a message reflecting the belief that the widespread ownership of handguns is not compatible with a sane, civilized or safe society. (Gun Control Alliance, 2005, par. 1).

BIBLIOGRAPHY

INTRODUCTION

Associated Press. (2004, Sept. 28). 4 Die In Argentina School Shooting: Teen Attack Shocks Argentines Unaccustomed To Such Violence Retrieved Dec 27, 2007, from http://www.cbsnews.com/stories/2004/09/28/world/main646126.shtml

Athens, L. H. (1992). *The Creation of Dangerous Violent Criminals*. Urbana & Chicago: University of Illinois Press.

Baumeister, R. F. (1986). *Identity: Cultural Changes and the Struggle for Self.* New York: Oxford University Press.

BBC News. (2002, April 26). 18 dead in German school shooting. *BBC* Retrieved Dec. 27, 2007, from http://news.bbc.co.uk/2/hi/europe/1952869.stm

BBC News. (2002, April 29). Two dead in Bosnia school shooting. *BBC News* Retrieved Dec. 27, 2007, from http://news.bbc.co.uk/1/hi/world/europe/1958400.stm

Bellini, J. (2001). *Child's Prey*. New York: Pinnacle.

Borum, R., Fein, R., Vossekuil, B. & Berglund, J. (1999). Threat assessment: defining an approach for evaluating risk of targeted violence. *Behavioral Sciences and the Law, 17*(3), 323-337.

Brown, B. & Merritt, R. (2002). *No Easy Answers: The Truth Behind the Death at Columbine*. New York City: Lantern Books

Clines, F. X. (1999, June 17). CAPITOL SKETCHBOOK; In a bitter cultural war, an ardent call to arms. *New York Times*.

CNN. (1999a, April 30, 1999). Poll: One third of teens fear copycat shootings. *CNN* Retrieved Dec. 26, 2007, from http://www.cnn.com/US/9904/30/tee.poll/

CNN. (1999b). Teen charged with murder after Canada school shooting. Retrieved Dec. 27, 2007, from http://www.cnn.com/WORLD/americas/9904/29/canada.shooting/index.html

CNN. (2007, Nov. 7). Teen dead who opened fire on Finnish classmates, police say. *CNN* Retrieved Dec. 27, 2007, from http://www.cnn.com/2007/WORLD /europe/11/07/school .shooting/index.html

Dietz, P. E. (1986). Mass, serial and sensational homicides. *Bulletin of the New York Academy of Medicine, 62*, 477-491.

Durkheim, E. (1897/ 1952). *Suicide: A Study in Sociology*. London: Routledge. .

Dwyer, K., Osher, D. & Warger, C. (1998). *Early Warning, Timely Response; A Guide to Safe Schools*. Washington, DC: U.S.Department of Education.

Eliade, M. (1954/1974). *The Myth of the Eternal Return or, Cosmos and History* (2nd ed.). Princeton: Princeton University press.

Ellis, J. (1986). *The Social History of the Machine Gun*. Baltimore, Maryland: John Hopkins University Press.

Erikson, E. (1963). *Childhood and Society*. New York: W.W. Norton and Co., Inc.

Eysenck, H. J. & Eysenck, S. B. G. (1964). *Manual of the Eysenck Personality Inventory*. London: University Press.

Fessenden, F. (2000, April 9, 2000). They threaten, seethe, and unhinge, then kill in quantity. *New York Times*, p. 1.

Glaser, B. G. & Strauss, A. L. (1967). *Discovery of Grounded Theory: Strategies for Qualitative Research*. New York: Aldine.

Grassel, K. M., Wintemute, G. J., Wright, M. A. & Romero, M. P. (2003). Association between handgun purchase and mortality from firearm injury. *Injury Prevention, 9*, 48-52.

Hoyert, D. L., Kung, H. C. & Smith, B. L. (2005). Deaths: perliminary data for 2003; Leading causes of death among adolescents ages 15 - 19. *National Vital Statistics reports, 53*(15).

King, G., Keohane, R. O. & Verba, S. (1994). *Designing Social Inquiry: Scientific Inference in Qualitative Research*. Princeton: Princeton University Press.

Kunstler, J. H. (1999, June 6). Where evil dwells; Reflections on the Columbine school massacre. Paper delivered at the Congress for the New Urbanism. Retrieved December 2, 2002, from http://www.kunstler.com/spch_milw.html

Meloy, J. R. (1997). Predatory violence during mass murder. *Journal of Forensic Science, 42*(2), 326-329.

Miller, M., Azrael, D. & Hemenway, D. (2002). Firearm Availability and Unintentional Firearm Deaths, Suicide, and Homicide among 5-14 Year Olds. *Journal of Trauma-Injury Infection & Critical Care, 52*(2), 267-275.

Mitchell, A. & Bruni, F. (1999). Guns and schools: The overview; House vote deals a stinging defeat to gun controls. *New York Times*.

Newman, K. S., Fox, J., Harding, D. J., Mehta, J. & Roth, W. (2004). *Rampage: The Social Roots of School Shootings*. New York: Basic Books.

O'Toole, M. E. (2000). *The School Shooter: A Threat Assessment Perspective*. Quantico, VA: FBI, National Center for the Analysis of Violent Crime.

Schlafly, P. (1999, May 12). What Caused Columbine? Retrieved December 4, 2002, from http://www.eagleforum.org/column/1999/may99/99-05-12.html

Strauss, A. L. & Corbin, J. M. (1990). *Basics of Qualitative Research: Grounded Theory Procedures and Techniques* Newbury Park, CA: Sage

Vossekuil, B., Fein, R., Reddy, M., Borum, R. & Modzeleski, W. (2002). *The final report and findings of the safe school initiative: Implications for the prevention of school attacks in the United States*. Washington, DC: U.S. Department of Education, Office of Elementary and Secondary Education, Safe and Drug Free Schools Program; and U.S. Secret Service, Nation Threat Assessment Center.

Vossekuil, B., Reddy, M. & Fein, R. (2000). *An interim report on the prevention of targeted violence in schools*. Washington, DC: U.S. Secret service National Threat Assessment Center

U.S. Dept. of Education

National Institute of Justice.

Wiebe, D. J. (2003). Homicide and suicide risks associated with firearms in the home: A national case-control study. *Annals of Emergency Medicine, 41*(16), 771-782.

Wikipedia contributors. (2007, 24 Dec.). Theory. Retrieved Dec. 28, 2007, from http://en.wikipedia.org/w/index.php?title=Theory&oldid=179973935

OVERVIEW

Attributions for Anthony Barbero (case 1), Eric Houston (case 3), Scott Pennington (case 5), Jamie Rouse (case 6), Barry Loukaitis (case 7), Michael Carneal (case 10), Mitchell Johnson and Andrew Golden (case 11), and Kip Kinkel (case 12). Attributions for the remaining cases follow, arranged according to the sequence of the chapters to which they refer.

ANTHONY BARBERO (Case 1)
Bradford Era (1)

Pettenati, W. (1996). Sniper attack shocked Olean residents 22 years ago today. *Bradford Era*, pp. 1, 10.

New York Times (3)

Kaufman, M. (1974, January 1). Sniper's classmate says guns were 'whole life'. *The New York Times*, pp. 1, 34.

McFadden, R. D. (1974, December 31). 3 killed and 9 wounded by an upstate sniper, 18. *The New York Times*, pp. 1, 6.

Upstate youth in sniper trial a suicide. (1975, November 2). *The New York Times*, pp. 34.

Newsweek (1)

The Pride of Olean. (1975, January 13). *Newsweek*, 27.

Olean Times Herald (20)

Barbaro in court today. (1975, September 29). *The Olean Times Herald*.

Barbaro Trial: Oct. 14. (1975, September 29). *The Olean Times Herald*.

Dec. 30, 1974 . . . Nov. 1, 1975. (1975, November 1). *The Olean Times Herald*.

Funeral services are set for three sniper victims. (1975, January 2). *The Olean Times Herald*.

Graduate Office: Barbaro did not graduate. (1975, July 2). *The Olean Times Herald*.

Hardy, T. S. (1975, January 2). Paint-sprayed picture found in council room. *The Olean Times Herald*.

Hardy, T. S. (1975, January 4). Wounded man trapped by sniper. *Olean Times Herald*, pp. 3.

Schnettler, B. (1974, December 31). Barbaro - was a 'fantastic shot'. *Olean Times Herald*, pp. 2.

Schnettler, B. (1974, December 31). Sniper seized at Olean High after killing 3, wounding 9. *Olean Times Herald*, pp. 1.

Schnettler, B. (1975, January 4). Accused sniper in jail awaiting murder charges. *The Olean Times Herald*, pp. 3.

Schnettler, B. (1975, January 2). Count indicates Barbaro fired 31 rifle shots - Sniper probe continues. *The Olean Times Herald*.

Schnettler, B. (1975, November 1). Sheriff's department ordered to silence. *The Olean Times Herald*.

Sniper case jury will convene. (1975, January 4). *The Olean Times Herald*, pp. 2.

Ward, C. (1974, December 31). Barbaro: loner, scholar - Top rifle team member. *Olean Times Herald*, pp. 1.

Ward, C. (1974, December 31). Barbaro: Loner, scholar, - Top rifle team member. *The Olean Times Herald*, pp. 1.

Williams, P. (1975, November 3). Accused sniper's goodbye notes disclose thnking. *Olean Times Herald*, pp. 1,3.

Williams, P. (1975, October 7). Barbaro trial delayed until Oct. 27. *The Olean Times Herald*.

Williams, P. (1975, October 27). Barbaro trial opens today; Select jury. *The Olean Times Herald*.

Williams, P. (1975, November 5). Remember the good he did, Barbaro mourners are told. *The Olean Times Herald*.

Williams, P. (1975, November 4). Sheriff Hill disclaims knowledge of it: January suicide warning was verbal - to 'a deputy'. *The Olean Times Herald*.

Reader's Digest (1)

Moore, G. (1975, September). Sniper! Get down! *The Reader's Digest*, 69-74.

ERIC HOUSTON (Case 3)

Appeal Democrat (39)

Crawford, D. (1992, May 4). Pride of Linda - Olivehurst will bounce back says principal. *The Appeal Democrat*, pp. A-1, A-8, B-3.

Five Lindhurst shooting victims still hospitalized. (1992, May 4). *The Appeal Democrat*, pp. A-8.

Funeral services set for Lindhurst victims. (1992, May 4). *The Appeal Democrat*, pp. A-1, A-8.

Gobel, P. (1992, May 2). 4 die in school siege. *The Appeal Democrat*, pp. A-1, A-12.

Houston makes brief court showing; to reappear June 16. (1992, June 2). *The Appeal Democrat*, pp. A-2.

Kruger, H. (1992, May 2). A day and night of terror and tragedy: Waiting parents prayed, anguished for safety of kids. *The Appeal Democrat*, pp. A-1, A-12.

Lindhurst reopening. (1992, May 7). *The Appeal Democrat*, pp. A-1, A-12.

Lindhurst seige victim's brother slain. (1993, June12). *Appeal Democrat*, pp. A-1, A-12.

Lindhurst siege came without warning, Yuba officials say. (1992, May 6). *The Appeal Democrat*, pp. A-8.

Sullivan, G. (1992, May 27). Bomb threat forces school evacuation. *The Appeal Democrat*, pp. A-1, A-8.

Sullivan, G. (1992, May 8). Courage of Beamon Hill recalled. *The appeal Democrat*, pp. A-1, A-12.

Sullivan, G. (1992, May 9). Hmong community wary after seige. *The Appeal Democrat*, pp. A-1, A-2.

Sullivan, G. (1992, May 5). Houston kept Brens' grudge to himself. *The Appeal Democrat*, pp. A-1, A-8.

Sullivan, G. (1992, June 26). Lindhurst memorial for slain students, teacher. *The Appeal Democrat*, pp. A-1, A-12.

Sullivan, G. (1992, May 11). Lindhurst reopens: Students, teachers back in class. *The Appeal Democrat*, pp. A-1, A-8.

Sullivan, G. (1992, May 4). Lindhurst seige traumatized bi-county community at large. *The Appeal Democrat*, pp. A-1, A-8.

Sullivan, G. (1992, May 4). Sheriff seeking dealth penalty. *The Appeal Democrat*, pp. A-1, A-8.

Sullivan, G. (1992, May 2). Terror hits peaceful campus. *The Appeal Democrat*, pp. A-1, A-12.

Sullivan, G. (1992, May 6). Wounded students want to finish the school year. *The Appeal Democrat*, pp. A-1, A-8.

Whitman, H. (1992, May 9). Community unites to support Lindhurst. *The Appeal Democrat*, pp. A-1, A-2.

Whitman, H. (1992, May 2). A day and night of terror and tragedy: Wounded students describe nightmare of horrifying ordeal. *The Appeal Democrat*, pp. A-1, A-12.

Whitman, H. (1992, May 19). Gunman had Lindhurst war room: Houston wanted to attack school with 'surgical precision' friend says. *The Appeal Democrat*, pp. A-1, A-8.

Whitman, H. (1992, May 22). Honors begin to pour on Lindhurst hero. *The Appeal Democrat*, pp. A-1, A-12.

Whitman, H. (1992, May 6). A life for a life: Quick thinking Lindhurst high student made ultimate sacrifice. *The Appeal Democrat*, pp. A-1, A-8.

Whitman, H. (1992, June 11). Lindhurst holds emotional ceremony. *The Appeal Democrat*, pp. A-1, A-8.

Whitman, H. (1992, May 8). Lindhurst to return to classes Monday. *The Appeal Democrat*, pp. A-1, A-12.

Whitman, H. (1992, May 15). Lindhurst victim earns silver medal. *The Appeal Democrat*, pp. A-1, A-12.

Whitman, H. (1992, May 7). Lives of Lindhurst victims celebrated. *The Appeal Democrat*, pp. A-1, A-12.

Whitman, H. (1992, May 5). Siege suspect denies murders, other charges. *The Appeal Democrat*, pp. A-1, A-8.

Whitman, H. (1992, May 15). Students, families entitled to state-funded counseling. *The Appeal Democrat*, pp. A-1, A-12.

Whitman, H. (1993, June24). Gruesome testimony heard at Houston trial. *The Appeal Democrat*, pp. A-1, A-2.

Whitman, H. (1993, June 18). Houston courtroom stunned: Defense claims Brens molested seige suspect. *The Appeal Democrat*, pp. A-1, A-12.

Whitman, H. (1993, May 21). May 1 proves unlucky for ex-Lindhurst high hostage. *The Appeal Democrat*, pp. A-1, A-10.

Whitman, H. (1993, May 22). Racially biased jury indicted Houston, defense claims. *The Appeal Democrat*, pp. A-1, A-12.

Whitman, H. (1993, June 26). Students, teachers describe nightmarish Lindhurst seige. *The Appeal Democrat*, pp. A-1, A-10.

Whitman, H. (1993, June 26). Students, teachers tell jurors of Lindhurst seige. *The Appeal Democrat*, pp. A-1, A-2.

Whitman, H. (1993, June 30). Teens tell jury of repeated threats of death by Houston. *The Appeal Democrat*, pp. A-1, A-8.

Whitman, H. (1993, June 29). Witnesses relive deadly hostage ordeal. *The Appeal Democrat*, pp. A-1, A-8.

Whitman, H., & Sullivan, G. (1992, May 6). 'Get on with life,' Brens' dad urges. *The Appeal Democrat*, pp. A-1, A-8.

Los Angeles Times (3)

Gladstone, M., & Ingram, C. (1992, May 2). Man surrenders after terrorizing school crime: Nine are wounded at a Sacramento Valley high school anf gunman holds 60 youths hostage into the night before giving himself up. *The Los Angeles Times*, pp. 30.

Man convicted of murdering 4 in school seige. (1993, July 23). *The Los Angeles Times*, pp. 27.

Morain, D., & Ingram, C. (1992, May 3). School dropout questioned as town agonizes murders: the suspect tells police of his rage against a history teacher, one of the four who died in Olivehurst. Nine people were wounded. *The Los Angeles Times*, pp. 40.

New York Times (1)

Bishop. (1992, May 2). Gunman gives up, ending day of terror at a school. *The New York Times*.

Washington Post (2)

3 youths, teacher are killed in high school hostage- taking; Ex-student frees 20 captives, ends 8 1/2 hour seige. (1992, May 2). *The Washington post*, pp. A2.

Failed student sought revenge in school slayings, officials say. (1992, May 3). *The Washington Post*, pp. A3.

SCOTT PENNINGTON (Case 5)

Daily Independent (45)

Alford, R. (1993, January 22). Carter board hires 9 guards. *The Daily Independent*, pp. 1, 5.

Alford, R. (1993, January 25). Carter schools open: Security guards patrol the hallways. *The Daily Independent*, pp. 1, 10.

Alford, R. (1993, January 21). Students react with fear, anger. *The Daily Independent*, pp. 1, 12.

Alford, R. (1993, January 19). Teen is described as popular, gifted. *The Daily Independent*, pp. 1, 10.

Alford, R. (1993, January 20). Trial as adult sought for teen. *The Daily Independent*, pp. 1, 12.

Alford, R. (1995, February 3). 13 prospective jurors make 1st round of cuts. *The Daily Independent*, pp. 13, 14.

Alford, R. (1995, February 7). 23 possible jurors women: Opening statements expected Wednesday. *The Daily Independent*, pp. 13, 14.

Alford, R. (1995, February 9). Accused was sane, state says. *The Daily Independent*, pp. 1, 10.

Alford, R. (1995, February 23). Closing arguments set. *The Daily Independent*, pp. 1, 10.

Alford, R. (1995, February 20). A dysfunctional family. *The Daily Independent*, pp. 1, 10.

Alford, R. (1995, February 15). Jurors view crime scene photos. *The Daily Independent*, pp. 1, 12.

Alford, R. (1995, March 1). Jury: Guilty but ill. *The Daily Independent*, pp. 1,12.

Alford, R. (1995, March 2). Life, no parole for 25 years. *The Daily Independent*, pp. 1, 10.

Alford, R. (1995, February 2). No deal for Pennington. *The Daily Independent*, pp. 1, 12.

Alford, R. (1995, February 16). No reason given for act. *The Daily Independent*, pp. 1, 12.

Alford, R. (1995, February 28). No verdict reached in murder trial. *The Daily Independent*, pp. 1, 12.

Alford, R. (1995, March 1). Penalty phase proceedings get under way. *The Daily Independent*, pp. 1, 12.

Alford, R. (1995, February 27). Pennington also victim, attorney says. *The Daily Independent*, pp. 1, 10.

Alford, R. (1995, February 22). Pennington isn't faking insanity, psychiatrist says. *The Daily Independent*, pp. 12.

Alford, R. (1995, February 17). Pennington outcast, say instructors. *The Daily Independent*, pp. 1, 14.

Alford, R. (1995, February 8). Pennington trial delayed. *The Daily Independent*, pp. 13, 14.

Alford, R. (1995, February 22). Pennington's memory spotty. *The Daily Independent*, pp. 1, 12.

Alford, R. (1995, February 24). Preparation of instructions delays jury deliberations. *The Daily Independent*, pp. 1, 4.

Alford, R. (1995, February 14). Student testifies about threat. *The Daily Independent*, pp. 1, 12.

Alford, R. (1995, February 18). Student: Pennington a Recluse. *The Daily Independent*, pp. 1, 8.

Alford, R. (1995, February 13). Students continue revelations. *The Daily Independent*, pp. 1, 10.

Alford, R. (1995, February 11). Students describe fatal shootings at East Carter High. *The Daily Independent*, pp. 1, 8.

Alford, R. (1995, February 21). Teen 'wasn't in control'. *The Daily Independent*, pp. 1, 10.

Alford, R. (1995, February 4). Testimony expected to start Wednesday. *The Daily Independent*, pp. 1, 8.

Alford, R. (1995, March 1). Widow knows Marvin Hicks truly a hero. *The Daily Independent*, pp. 1, 12.

Alford, R. (1995, February 10). Witnesses take stand in Johnson. *The Daily Independent*, pp. 1, 14.

Diary entries. (1995, February 16). *The Daily Independent*, pp. 12.

Going on: East Carter must gather the strength to move ahead with task of education. (1993, January 26). *The Daily Independent*, pp. 8.

Hart, K. (1993, January 23). Communities pay last respects. *The Daily Independent*, pp. 1, 8.

Hart, K. (1993, January 21). East Carter High School no stranger to tragedy. *The Daily Independent*, pp. 1, 12.

Hart, K. (1993, January 21). Friday a day of mourning in Grayson and Olive Hill. *The Daily Independent*, pp. 12.

Hart, K. (1995, April 7). Pennington gets life term. *The Daily Independent*, pp. 1, 14.

Hart, K., & Wolfford, G. (1993, January 19). Tragedy in Carter. *The Daily Independent*, pp. 1, 10.

Hetzer-Womack, T. (2003, January 17). East Carter marks 10th anniversary. *The Daily Independent*, pp. 1, 12.

Hetzer-Womack, T. (2003, January 17). A resolution to heal: Tragedy survivor attempts to cope with anniversary. *The Daily Independent*, pp. 1, 12.

Malone, J. (1993, January 20). Guns no oddity in state schools. *The Daily Independent*, pp. 1, 12.

Pennington at-a-glance. (1995, February 16). *The Daily Independent*, pp. 12.

Portfolio samples. (1995, February 16). *The Daily Independent*, pp. 12.

Speaking Out. (1993, January 25). *The Daily Independent*, pp. 12.

Wolfford, G. (1993, January 20). Teacher allegedly targeted: Hicks called a bystander. *The Daily Independent*, pp. 1, 12.

Lexington Herald-Leader (29)

3 schoolmates of '93 killer in Grayson are now officers. (2002, January 20). *Lexington Herald-Leader*, pp. B3.

Breed, A. G. (1993, April 23). Hearing to decide suspect's status in school slaying. *Lexington Herald-Leader*, pp. B1.

Breed, A. G. (1994, August 12). Johnson chosen as Pennington trial site. *Lexington Herald-Leader*, pp. B3.

Breed, A. G. (1995, April 8). Pennington sentenced to life term. *Lexington Herald-Leader*, pp. C1.

Classmates testify in trial. (1995, February 11). *Lexington Herald-Leader*, pp. C3.

Gregory, E. (1994, May 28). Frustrated rage is link in killings. *Lexington Herald-Leader*, pp. A1.

Judge refuses to reduce number of kidnap charges in slayings. (1994, July 14). *Lexington Herald-Leader*, pp. B6.

Langfitt, F. (1989, October 1). KY. police trading force for finesse in hostage crisis. *Lexington Herald-Leader*, pp. A1.

Mueller, L. (1993, January 22). Carter school uneasy despite added security. *Lexington Herald-Leader*, pp. A1.

Mueller, L. (1993, January 23). Sorrow grips Carter County as victims buried. *Lexington Herald-Leader*, pp. A1.

Mueller, L. (1993, April 27). Suspect in slayings to be tried as adult. *Lexington Herald-Leader*, pp. B1.

Mueller, L. (1994, July 2). Carter teen might face execution. *Lexington Herald-Leader*, pp. A1.

Mueller, L. (1994, July 18). Mental state the question in Pennington trial jury selection to begin today for teen accused of killing Carter teacher, janitor. *Lexington Herald-Leader*, pp. B1.

Mueller, L. (1994, July 18). Witnesses still getting counseling. *Lexington Herald-Leader*, pp. B1.

Mueller, L. (1995, February 10). Defense paints teen as insane when teacher, janitor killed. *Lexington Herald-Leader*, pp. A1.

Mueller, L. (1995, February 17). Jurors hear tape of Pennington confession. *Lexington Herald-Leader*, pp. B1.

Mueller, L. (1995, March 3). Jury recommends life term for Pennington prosecutor's call for death penalty rejected: Sentence wold mean no parole for 25 years. *Lexington Herald-Leader*, pp. B1.

Mueller, L. (1995, March 1). Pennington guilty but mentally ill death penalty among sentencing options. *Lexington Herald-Leader*, pp. A1.

Mueller, L. (1995, February 16). Pennington jury to hear confession witness will play tape today as prosecutors end their case. *Lexington Herald-Leader*, pp. B1.

Mueller, L. (1995, February 21). Pennington's parents attend trial for first time. *Lexington Herald-Leader*, pp. B1.

Mueller, L. (1995, February 22). Pennington's sanity focus of testimony. *Lexington Herald-Leader*, pp. C3.

Mueller, L. (1995, February 18). Pennington's teacher was told to contact police, social workers. *Lexington Herald-Leader*, pp. B1.

Mueller, L., & Poore, C. (1993, January 20). Classmates baffled by what enraged Grayson 'whiz kid'. *Lexington Herald-Leader*, pp. A1.

Poore, C., & Mueller, L. (1993, January 21). Move to Carter school was difficult for teen. *Lexington Herald-Leader*, pp. A1.

Poore, C., Mueller, L., & Gregory, E. (1993, January 19). 2 fatally shot at high school in Grayson teen arrested after: Student hostages freed. *Lexington Herald-Leader*, pp. A1.

Suspect in slayings judged not mentally ill. (1993, April 28). *Lexington Herald-Leader*, pp. B1.

Teen indicted in shootings at Carter school 17-year-old charged with kidnapping classmates, killing teacher, janitor. (1993, June 16). *Lexington Herald-Leader*, pp. B1.

Trial postponed for teen accused in school slayings. (1994, March 12). *Lexington Herald-Leader*, pp. C3.

Two Carter schools evacuated because of bomb threats. (1993, March 13). *Lexington Herald-Leader*, pp. C1.

New York Times (1)

Two killed in school shooting in Kentucky. (1993, January 18). *The New York Times*, pp. A13.

People Weekly (1)
Reading, writing, and murder. (1993, June 14). *People Weekly, 39*, 44.
U.S. News & World Report (1)
The tragedy in room 108. (1993, November 8). *U.S. News & World Report, 115*, 41.

JAMIE ROUSE (Case 6)
Giles Free Press (29)
Giles Faces: Giles sad. (1995, November 23). *The Giles Free Press*, pp. 1.
Hargett, S. (1998, March 26). Giles County residents react to Jonesboro, Ark., shooting. *The Giles Free Press*, pp. 1,2.
Keeton, D. (1995, November 23). Richland students remember friend. *The Giles Free Press*, pp. 1, 4.
Keeton, D. (1995, November 16). Richland teachers, students search for answers. *The Giles Free Press*, pp. 6.
Keeton, D. (1995, November 16). Students, parents, teachers deal with aftermath. *The Giles Free Press*, pp. 6.
Keeton, D. (1996, April 11). Scholarship to honor slain Richland teacher. *The Giles Free Press*, pp. 1.
Obituaries. (1995, November 16). *The Giles Free Press*, pp. 8.
Stewart, S. (1995, December 21). Richland shooting: Proceedings to be public. *The Giles Free Press*, pp. 1, 2.
Stewart, S. (1995, November 16). Shooting shatters county. *The Giles Free Press*, pp. 1, 6.
Stewart, S. (1995, November 23). Shooting suspects back in court. *The Giles Free Press*, pp. 1, 4.
Stewart, S. (1996, September 26). Abbott gets 40-year term. *The Giles Free Press*, pp. 1, 3.
Stewart, S. (1996, August 1). Injured teacher testifies. *The Giles Free Press*, pp. 1, 2.
Stewart, S. (1996, June 27). Judge to decide on trial location for Rouse, Abbott. *The Giles Free Press*, pp. 1, 2.
Stewart, S. (1996, July 4). Jury will hear Rouse statement. *The Giles Free Press*, pp. 1, 2.
Stewart, S. (1996, June 13). Motions heard on Abbott case. *The Giles Free Press*, pp. 1, 2.
Stewart, S. (1996, May 9). Murder cases top busy court calender. *The Giles Free Press*, pp. 1, 2.
Stewart, S. (1996, January 4). Richalnd school shooting: Transfer hearing gets underway. *The Giles Free Press*, pp. 1, 2.
Stewart, S. (1996, June 13). Rouse to enter insanity plea. *The Giles Free Press*, pp. 1, 2.
Stewart, S. (1996, January 18). Rouse, Abbott housed in neighboring counties. *The Giles Free Press*, pp. 3.
Stewart, S. (1996, July 4). State wants Abbott attorney removed. *The Giles Free Press*, pp. 1.
Stewart, S. (1996, February 22). Younger Rouse brother convicted. *The Giles Free Press*, pp. 1, 2.
Stewart, S. (1996, July 14). Younger Rouse to remain in custody. *The Giles Free Press*, pp. 1, 2.
Stewart, S. (1996, May 30). Younger Rouse's conviction upheld by circuit court. *The Giles Free Press*, pp. 1, 2.
Stewart, S. (1997, November 13). Dual pictures of Jamie Rouse. *The Giles Free Press*, pp. 1, 2.
Stewart, S. (1997, January 23). Jeremy Rouse denied new trial motion. *The Giles Free Press*, pp. 1, 2.
Stewart, S. (1997, June 26). November 10 set as tentative trail date for Jamie Rouse. *The Giles Free Press*, pp. 1, 2.
Stewart, S. (1997, August 21). Rouse competent judge sets trial date for Nov. 10. *The Giles Free Press*, pp. 1.
Stewart, S. (1997, November 20). Rouse found guilty on all counts. *The Giles Free Press*, pp. 1, 2.
Stewart, S. (1997, December 25). Rouse will spend rest of life in prison. *The Giles Free Press*, pp. 1, 2.
Los Angeles Times (1)
Meyer, R. E. (2000, April 22). When the shooting stops; After Jamie Rouse killed a teacher and a student at his school the questions began. Why did he do it? Could his parents prevented it? A family faces the truth of what their son has done. *The Los Angeles Times*.
Pulaski Citizen (27)
Editorial: What's more important - our image or our children. (1996, January 16). *Pulaski Citizen*, pp. 4.
Hargett, S. (1995, November 28). Crisis team assesses response. *Pulaski Citizen*.
Keeton, D. (1995, November 28). Addressing violence. *Pulaski Citizen*, pp. 1, 2.

Keeton, D. (1995, November 28). School board responds to shooting. *Pulaski Citizen,* pp. 1,2.

Keeton, D. (1996, March 5). Trees planted in memory of slain teacher, student. *Pulaski Citizen,* pp. 1, 2.

Stewart, S. (1995, December 5). Brother of accused Richland shooter taken into custody. *Pulaski Citizen,* pp. 1, 2.

Stewart, S. (1995, November 21). County under seige. *Pulaski Citizen,* pp. 4.

Stewart, S. (1995, December 12). Juvenile detention costing taxpayers. *Pulaski Citizen,* pp. 1, 2.

Stewart, S. (1995, November 21). Second Richland student charged. *Pulaski Citizen,* pp. 1, 3.

Stewart, S. (1996, August 6). Abbott guilty: Trial just beginning: Attorney. *Pulaski Citizen,* pp. 1.

Stewart, S. (1996, October 22). Attorneys to remain on case. *Pulaski Citizen,* pp. 1, 2.

Stewart, S. (1996, February 13). Indictments returned in Richland shooting. *Pulaski Citizen,* pp. 1.

Stewart, S. (1996, January 9). Judge airs concerns. *Pulaski Citizen,* pp. 1, 2.

Stewart, S. (1996, March 19). Richalnd reaches out to grief stricken Dunblane. *Pulaski Citizen,* pp. 1.

Stewart, S. (1996, July 30). Richland shooting case hits court: Abbott trial starts in Maury County. *Pulaski Citizen,* pp. 1.

Stewart, S. (1996, October 29). Rouse declared incompetent. *Pulaski Citizen,* pp. 1.

Stewart, S. (1996, July 2). Rouse, Abbott trials moved to Columbia. *Pulaski Citizen,* pp. 1.

Stewart, S. (1996, January 9). Transfer hearing over. *Pulaski Citizen,* pp. 1, 2.

Stewart, S. (1997, January 14). Abbott denied new trial. *Pulaski Citizen,* pp. 1.

Stewart, S. (1997, November 18). God was in coma. *Pulaski Citizen,* pp. 1, 5.

Stewart, S. (1997, June 24). Hearing tomorrow on Rouse's mental state. *Pulaski Citizen,* pp. 1, 2.

Stewart, S. (1997, September 23). Judge OK's use of cameras in courtroom during Rouse trial. *Pulaski Citizen,* pp. 1.

Stewart, S. (1997, September 16). Media, competent to be dealt with as Rouse trial nears. *Pulaski Citizen,* pp. 1, 2.

Stewart, S. (1997, September 23). Rouse found competent trial will begin November 10. *Pulaski Citizen,* pp. 1, 2.

Stewart, S. (1997, November 11). Rouse trial begins in Columbia: Abbott must testify. *Pulaski Citizen,* pp. 1, 2.

Stewart, S. (1997, November 25). Rouse, vistims fce life after trial. *Pulaski Citizen,* pp. 1, 7.

Trail to air on Court TV. (1997, November 11). *Pulaski Citizen,* pp. 1.

BARRY LOUKAITIS (Case 7)

ABA Journal (1)

Baker, D. (1999). How safe is your 'burb'? *ABA Journal, 85,* 50-56.

Chicago Sun-Times (1)

Dedman, B. (2000, October 15). Examining the psyche of an adolescent killer. *Chicago Sun-Times.*

Columbia Basin Herald (144)

Alexander, K. (1996a, December 9). Family, friends wonder at it all. *Columbia Basin Herald,* pp. 1, 6.

Alexander, K. (1996b, December 12). Hundreds mourn. *Columbia Basin Herald,* pp. 1, 7.

Alexander, K. (1996c, February 5). Tradgedy leaves few answers. *Columbia Basin Herald,* pp. 1, 3.

Alexander, K. (1996d, February 5). Students say murder suspect was a loner. *Columbia Basin Herald,* p. 6.

Alexander, K. (1996e, February 5). Violence in the basin on the rise. *Columbia Basin Herald,* p. 7.

Alexander, K. (1996f, February 6). Barry loukaitis appears on murder charges. *Columbia Basin Herald,* pp. 1, 3.

Alexander, K. (1996g, February 8). Ambulance response time questioned. *Columbia Basin Herald,* pp. 1, 3.

Alexander, K. (1996h, February 21). Loukaitis attorney seeks out of county judge to decide. *Columbia Basin Herald,* pp. 1, 3.

Alexander, K. (1996i, July 29). Violent crime up throughout grant county. *Columbia Basin Herald,* pp. 1, 7.

Alexander, K. (1996j, May 9). Loukaitis residence vandalized. *Columbia Basin Herald,* p. 1.

Anderson, P. (1997a, August 19). Loukaitis jurors quizzed' about guns, insanity. *Columbia Basin Herald,* pp. 1, 3.

Anderson, P. (1997b, August 21). Loukaitis jury whittled down. *Columbia Basin Herald*, pp. 1, 3.

Anderson, P. (1997c, August 28). More students testify. *Columbia Basin Herald*, pp. 1, 7.

Anderson, P. (1997d, September 2). Loikaitis trial delayed by juror illness. *Columbia Basin Herald*, pp. 1, 6.

Anderson, P. (1997e, September 4). Loukaitis confession played in court. *Columbia Basin Herald*, pp. 1, 3.

Anderson, P. (1997f, September 5). Lane: Barry made a choice. *Columbia Basin Herald*, pp. 1, 3.

Anderson, P. (1997g, September 8). Defense to portray the human side of barry. *Columbia Basin Herald*, pp. 1, 3.

Anderson, P. (1997h, September 9). Barry's parents testify about home problems. *Columbia Basin Herald*, pp. 1, 5.

Anderson, P. (1997i, September 10). Tuesday at loukaitis trial. *Columbia Basin Herald*, pp. 1, 8.

Anderson, P. (1997j, September 16). Classmate says barry talked of killing. *Columbia Basin Herald*, pp. 1, 5.

Anderson, P. (1997k, September 25). Courtroom scene closes chapter; the hurt remains. *Columbia Basin Herald*, pp. 1, 3.

Associated Press. (1997, February 3). Caires remembers the day his world turned upside down. *Columbia Basin Herald*, pp. 1, 3.

Associated Press. (1996a, February 7). Family, friends, students gather to remember. *Columbia Basin Herald*, p. 1.

Associated Press. (1996b, November 1). Flurry of motions filed in loukaitis case. *Columbia Basin Herald*, pp. 1, 3.

Baroch, D. H. (1996, February 29). We strengthen all our connections by listening. *Columbia Basin Herald*, p. 4.

Black, D. (1996a, August 15). Loukaitis case better off with new judge. *Columbia Basin Herald*, p. 4.

Black, D. (1996b, February 5). Wounded classmate recovering in seattle. *Columbia Basin Herald*, p. 7.

Black, D. (1996c, February 5). Plenty of confusion in the moments after. *Columbia Basin Herald*, p. 5.

Black, D. (1996d, February 5). Media search everywhere for information, rankle some residents. *Columbia Basin Herald*, p. 5.

Black, D. (1996e, February 5). Counselors say it's a long road ahead. *Columbia Basin Herald*, p. 4.

Black, D. (1996f, February 5). Spiritual leaders answer the call. *Columbia Basin Herald*, p. 4.

Black, D. (1996g, February 15). The town has been transformed. *Columbia Basin Herald*, p. 4.

Black, D. (1996h, February 22). Duty requires being realistic. *Columbia Basin Herald*, p. 4.

Black, D. (1997, January 2). Heroes deserve recognition. *Columbia Basin Herald*, p. 4.

Black, D. (1996i, June 20). Problems in court system led to private defense. *Columbia Basin Herald*, p. 4.

Black, D., & Powell, M. (1996, June 26). Natalie hintz has a few words with hillary clinton. *Columbia Basin Herald*, pp. 1, 3.

Book, frontier shooting share same plot. (1996, April 10). *Columbia Basin Herald*, p. 1.

Caputo, A. (1996a, April 11). Judge yet to decide on closing loukaitis hearing. *Columbia Basin Herald*, pp. 1, 3.

Caputo, A. (1996b, April 16). Loukaitis: Should he be charged as an adult? *Columbia Basin Herald*, pp. 1, 5.

Caputo, A. (1996c, April 17). Testimony suggests loukaitis had plan. *Columbia Basin Herald*, pp. 1, 3.

Caputo, A. (1996d, April 17). Court to hear loukaitis statement. *Columbia Basin Herald*, p. 1.

Caputo, A. (1996e, April 18). Loukaitis confession played in court. *Columbia Basin Herald*, pp. 1, 5.

Caputo, A. (1996f, August 9). Entire loukaitis declination hearing will likely startover. *Columbia Basin Herald*, pp. 1, 3.

Caputo, A. (1996g, August 26). Loukaitis hearing postponed until next month. *Columbia Basin Herald*, pp. 1, 3.

Caputo, A. (1996h, December 9). Steps retraced. *Columbia Basin Herald*, pp. 1, 3.

Caputo, A. (1996i, December 18). Loukaitis defense wants to postpone trial. *Columbia Basin Herald*, pp. 1, 9.

Caputo, A. (1996j, December 24). Barry loukaitis moves to seattle. *Columbia Basin Herald*, p. 1.

Caputo, A. (1996k, December 26). Trial moved: Atmosphere too charged in grant. *Columbia Basin Herald*, pp. 1, 3.

Caputo, A. (1996l, February 27). Local judge to decide loukaitis jurisdiction. *Columbia Basin Herald*, pp. 1, 3.

Caputo, A. (1996m, July 3). Court of appeals opens loukaitis hearing. *Columbia Basin Herald*, pp. 1, 7.

Caputo, A. (1996n, July 10). Meeting with judge closed. *Columbia Basin Herald*, pp. 1, 3.

Caputo, A. (1996o, July 12). Sperline discloses some about closed meeting. *Columbia Basin Herald*, p. 1.

Caputo, A. (1996p, July 31). Loukaitis case: Prosecution, defense want new judge. *Columbia Basin Herald*, pp. 1, 4.

Caputo, A. (1996q, June 24). Judge demotes dano from loukaitis case. *Columbia Basin Herald*, pp. 1, 3.

Caputo, A. (1996r, June 26). Dano wants back on the case. *Columbia Basin Herald*, pp. 1, 3.

Caputo, A. (1996s, June 28). Judge sorts through loukaitis defense team. *Columbia Basin Herald*, pp. 1, 6.

Caputo, A. (1996t, March 5). Judge rules school shooting trial will be open to public. *Columbia Basin Herald*, p. 1.

Caputo, A. (1996u, March 12). Defense motions denied in loukaitis case. *Columbia Basin Herald*, pp. 1, 3.

Caputo, A. (1996v, March 13). More loukaitis motions filed, dano wants out. *Columbia Basin Herald*, pp. 1, 3.

Caputo, A. (1996w, March 15). Dano still defending loukaitis. *Columbia Basin Herald*, pp. 1, 3.

Caputo, A. (1996x, March 15). Judge rules against medicating the suspect. *Columbia Basin Herald*, pp. 1, 3.

Caputo, A. (1996y, March 22). Judge rules loukaitis' statement can be used. *Columbia Basin Herald*, pp. 1, 3.

Caputo, A. (1996z, March 26). Judge sets rules for loukaitis hearing. *Columbia Basin Herald*, pp. 1, 3.

Caputo, A. (1996{, May 31). Hearing to decide if family can afford private counsel. *Columbia Basin Herald*, pp. 1, 3.

Caputo, A. (1996|, May 31). Who pays? *Columbia Basin Herald*, pp. 1, 3.

Caputo, A. (1996, November 5). New charges: Loukaitis pleads not guilty by reason of insanity. *Columbia Basin Herald*, pp. 1, 3.

Caputo, A. (1996~, November 22). Loukaitis denies judges offer. *Columbia Basin Herald*, pp. 1, 3.

Caputo, A. (1996, November 26). Loukaitis trial postponed. *Columbia Basin Herald*, pp. 1, 3.

Caputo, A. (1996, October 8). Loukaitis pleads insanity. *Columbia Basin Herald*, pp. 1, 3.

Caputo, A. (1996, September 13). Prosecutor wants loukaitis parents, attorney to testify. *Columbia Basin Herald*, p. 1.

Caputo, A. (1996, September 17). Loukaitis motion heard friday. *Columbia Basin Herald*, pp. 1, 3.

Caputo, A. (1996, September 20). Judge to decide on loukaitis tapes after declination. *Columbia Basin Herald*, p. 1.

Caputo, A. (1996, September 24). Prosecution: Loukaitis is a calculating killer. *Columbia Basin Herald*, pp. 1, 3.

Caputo, A. (1996, September 25). Insane? Doctor said loukaitis is psychotic and treatable. *Columbia Basin Herald*, pp. 1, 3.

Caputo, A. (1996, September 25). Judge will decide if mental illness matters in hearing. *Columbia Basin Herald*, pp. 1, 3.

Caputo, A. (1996, September 26). Prosecution suggests loukaitis faking illness. *Columbia Basin Herald*, pp. 1, 3.

Caputo, A. (1996, September 27). Loukaitis parents testify about life at home. *Columbia Basin Herald*, pp. 1, 3.

Caputo, A. (1996, September 30). Loukaitis faces murder charges as adult. *Columbia Basin Herald*, pp. 1, 3.

Caputo, A., & Black, D. (1996, April 19). Loukaitis hearing stopped after objection. *Columbia Basin Herald*, pp. 1, 7.

Chavez, K. (1996, March 8). We thank you jon lane and lee caires. *Columbia Basin Herald*, p. 6.

Fritz family files lawsuit. (1996, November 22). *Columbia Basin Herald*, p. 3.

Fritz funeral today. (1996, February 7). *Columbia Basin Herald*, pp. 1, 3.

Funeral for leona caires today in coeur d'alene; fritz buried. (1996, February 8). *Columbia Basin Herald,* p. 1.
Funeral services held for leona caires. (1996, February 9). *Columbia Basin Herald,* p. 1.
Jon lane tells how it happened. (1996, February 5). *Columbia Basin Herald,* pp. 5, 6.
Judge hears motions in loukaitis pretrial hearing. (1997, June 30). *Columbia Basin Herald,* p. 3.
Kimbrough, H. (1997a, August 11). Loukaitis trial starts this week in seattle. *Columbia Basin Herald,* pp. 1, 3.
Kimbrough, H. (1997b, August 28). He talked of killing. *Columbia Basin Herald,* pp. 1, 7.
Kimbrough, H. (1997c, August 29). Widower, police testify. *Columbia Basin Herald,* pp. 1, 3.
Kimbrough, H. (1997d, June 11). Judge moves hintz lawsuit against school. *Columbia Basin Herald,* pp. 1, 8.
Kimbrough, H. (1997e, September 8). Judge denies request for reduced charges: Motions ask for reduced kidnapping charges. *Columbia Basin Herald,* pp. 1, 3.
Kimbrough, H. (1997f, September 9). Psychiatrist: Loukaitis in 'delusional trance'. *Columbia Basin Herald,* pp. 1, 5.
Kimbrough, H. (1997g, September 10). Psychiatrist paints landscape of barry's mind. *Columbia Basin Herald,* pp. 1, 8.
Kimbrough, H. (1997h, September 11). Psychiatrist cross-examined, defense rests. *Columbia Basin Herald,* p. 1.
Kimbrough, H. (1997i, September 12). Psychologist: Barry was angry, not bipolar. *Columbia Basin Herald,* pp. 1, 3.
Kimbrough, H. (1997j, September 17). Last witness called; testimony ends. *Columbia Basin Herald,* pp. 1, 3.
Kimbrough, H. (1997k, September 18). Jury gets 70 pages of instructions. *Columbia Basin Herald,* pp. 1, 3.
Kimbrough, H. (1997l, September 19). The jury's out. *Columbia Basin Herald,* pp. 1, 3.
Letters. (1996a, February 7). *Columbia Basin Herald,* p. 6.
Letters. (1996b, June 13). *Columbia Basin Herald,* p. 4.
Letters to the editor. (1996a, February 5). *Columbia Basin Herald,* p. 8.
Letters to the editor. (1996b, February 8). *Columbia Basin Herald,* pp. 4, 5.
Letters: Private attorney. (1996, June 6). *Columbia Basin Herald,* p. 4.
Loukaitis defense asks for psychiatric witness. (1997, June 16). *Columbia Basin Herald,* p. 3.
Loukaitis trial scheduled for may 12. (1997, January 27). *Columbia Basin Herald,* p. 1.
Loukaitis trial stays in grant county for now. (1996, November 4). *Columbia Basin Herald,* p. 1.
Mental health professionals offer some tips on healing. (1996, February 5). *Columbia Basin Herald,* p. 4.
A message from the vela family in thanks and gratitude. (1996, February 15). *Columbia Basin Herald,* p. 7.
Miller, R. (1997, February 4). Velas family sues, hopes for answers. *Columbia Basin Herald,* pp. 1, 3.
Mlsd offers counseling services for students, staff. (1996, December 9). *Columbia Basin Herald,* pp. 1, 3.
Natalie hintz released from hospital. (1996, March 15). *Columbia Basin Herald.*
Poems entered into record at loukaitis hearing. (1996, April 19). *Columbia Basin Herald,* p. 7.
Powell, M. (1997a, August 29). Testifying is part of the healing process. *Columbia Basin Herald,* pp. 1, 3.
Powell, M. (1997b, February 3). Looking back on a year of grief, healing. *Columbia Basin Herald,* pp. 1, 3.
Powell, M. (1996a, February 5). Students, teachers, staff return to school today. *Columbia Basin Herald,* pp. 1, 3.
Powell, M. (1996b, February 5). School officials examine security. *Columbia Basin Herald,* p. 5.
Powell, M. (1996c, February 6). Back to school. *Columbia Basin Herald,* pp. 1, 3.
Powell, M. (1996d, February 8). Community pulls together in aftermath. *Columbia Basin Herald,* pp. 1, 3.
Powell, M. (1996e, February 8). Getting the story: Us versus them. *Columbia Basin Herald,* p. 4.
Powell, M. (1996f, February 12). Community prays for healing. *Columbia Basin Herald,* pp. 1, 3.
Powell, M. (1996g, February 23). Task force begins safety discussion. *Columbia Basin Herald,* pp. 1, 3.
Powell, M. (1996h, June 4). Safe schools group makes room for students' opinions. *Columbia Basin Herald,* pp. 1, 3.

Powell, M. (1996i, June 25). Committee comes up with discipline policy. *Columbia Basin Herald*, pp. 1, 3.

Powell, M. (1996j, March 1). Natalie hintz returns home. *Columbia Basin Herald*, pp. 1, 3.

Powell, M. (1996k, March 4). Swarm of journalists follow natalie's return. *Columbia Basin Herald*, p. 1.

Powell, M. (1996l, March 6). Task force begins effort to make safer schools, community. *Columbia Basin Herald*, pp. 1, 3.

Powell, M. (1996m, March 14). Hintz undergoes surgery at samaritan. *Columbia Basin Herald*, p. 1.

Powell, M. (1996n, March 19). Safe schools task force ges specific. *Columbia Basin Herald*, pp. 1, 3.

Powell, M. (1996o, May 14). Hintz family to file claim. *Columbia Basin Herald*, pp. 1, 3.

Powell, M. (1996p, May 17). School: "the district has done nothing wrong and will vigorously defend this claim". *Columbia Basin Herald*, pp. 1, 3.

Powell, M. (1996q, November 19). School board unveils proposed student dress policy. *Columbia Basin Herald*, pp. 1, 3.

Powell, M. (1996r, September 10). Study: Most parents oppose school uniforms. *Columbia Basin Herald*, pp. 1, 3.

Powell, M. (1996s, September 10). Safe schools committee ends formal meetings. *Columbia Basin Herald*, pp. 1, 3.

Relief: The verdict might help people put the tregedy behind them. (1997, September 25). *Columbia Basin Herald*, pp. 1, 3.

Schools facilitator chosen. (1996, May 14). *Columbia Basin Herald*, pp. 1, 3.

Sear, M. (1996a, February 5). List of recent youth violence cases. *Columbia Basin Herald*, p. 7.

Sear, M. (1996b, February 6). A community remembers. *Columbia Basin Herald*, p. 3.

Sear, M. (1996c, March 7). Eight bands to perform at day long frontier benefit. *Columbia Basin Herald*, p. 1.

Some religious thoughts. (1996, February 5). *Columbia Basin Herald*, p. 6.

Sperline recused. (1996, August 8). *Columbia Basin Herald*, p. 1.

Teacher's slaying leaves friends in shock. (1996, February 5). *Columbia Basin Herald*, p. 7.

What can we do? (1996, February 8). *Columbia Basin Herald*, p. 4.

Spokesman Review (13)

Coddington, B. (1996, February 4). Boy describes classroom scene. *The Spokesman Review*, p. A1.

Foster, T. (1996, February 18). 'the terror becomes worse than the reality': In aftermath of school shooting, school grapple with 'why'. *The Spokesman Review*, p. A1.

Harris, B. (1996a, April 10). School killings all too familiar; moses lake horror parallels plot of novel found in suspect's room. *Spokesman Review*, p. 1.

Harris, B. (1996b, April 17). Witnesses say loukaitis vowed to kill; prosecution tries to show premeditation in rampage. *Spokesman Review*, p. 1.

Harris, B. (1996c, April 18). 'how many.Were shot?' boy's murder confession played at emotional evidence hearing. *Spokesman Review*, p. 1.

Harris, B. (1996d, April 19). Teen has mental disorder, expert says, but judge rules testimony from psychiatrist who interviewed loukaitis will be sealed. *Spokesman Review*, p. 1.

Mapes, L. V. (1997a, September 9). Loukaitis' mom tells court about suicidal moods defense portrays teen as disturbed by parents' broken marriage. *Spokesman Review*, p. 1.

Mapes, L. V. (1997b, September 10). Loukaitis delusional, expert says teen was in a trance when he went on rampage, says psychiatrist. *Spokesman Review*, p. 1.

Mapes, L. V. (1997c, September 12). Therapist says loukaitis sane teen in touch with reatlity at time of killings, pyschologist testifies. *Spokesman Review*, p. 1.

Martin, J., Coddington, B., & Sitaramiah, G. (1996, February 3). Student kills 3 in school rampage: 14 year old opens fire in moses lake classroom, leaving teacher and two students dead, another injured. *The Spokesman Review*, p. A1.

Miller, W. (1996a, September 25). Psychiatrist says loukaitis snapped before rampage testimony supports defense contention that accused killer was psychotic. *Spokesman Review*, p. 1.

Miller, W. (1996b, September 26). Prosecutor: Loukaitis is faking attacks defense witnesses that depression behind shootings. *Spokesman Review*, p. 1.

Miller, W. (1996c, September 27). 'cold fury' in loukaitis scared dad; father says he was horrified by change after shootings. *Spokesman Review*, p. 1.

The New York Times (1)

Egan, T. (1998, June 13). Common traits seen among students turned killers. *The New York Times*.

The Seattle Times (47)

Adult-trial hearing delayed. (1996, April 20). *The Seattle Times*.

Anderson, P. (1997a, October 11). 9 years. *The Seattle Times*.

Anderson, P. (1997b, October 11). Loukaitis gets two life terms plus 205 years - 'i feel the guilty of being alive,' says survivor of attack that killed three. *The Seattle Times*.

Anderson, P. (1997c, September 8). Loukaitis' mother says she told her son of plan to kill herself. *The Seattle Times*.

Associated Press. (1996a, April 10). School attack linked to book plot - moses lake student, king character similar, police say. *The Seattle Times*.

Associated Press. (1996b, April 18). Moses lake boy tells of killing three at school. *The Seattle Times*.

Associated Press. (1996c, April 18). On tape, moses lake boy talks about school rampage. *The Seattle Times*.

Associated Press. (1997a, August 9). Insanity plea expert to help in case. *The Seattle Times*.

Associated Press. (1996d, August 9). Judge steps aside in moses lake trial. *The Seattle Times*.

Associated Press. (1997b, August 15). Insanity to be issue in triple slaying trial - jury pool to be asked mental illness views. *The Seattle Times*.

Associated Press. (1996e, December 25). Teen faces king co. Trial in moses lake slayings. *The Seattle Times*.

Associated Press. (1996f, February 21). Murder trial judges to be reviewed. *The Seattle Times*.

Associated Press. (1996g, July 31). Both sides want judge recused from moses lake shooting case. *The Seattle Times*.

Associated Press. (1996h, November 1). Kidnapping charges filed in moses lake case. *The Seattle Times*.

Associated Press. (1996i, November 23). Moses lake teen refuses trial delay. *The Seattle Times*.

Book, deaths share similarities. (1996, April 11). *The Seattle Times*.

Brown, C. E. (1997a, August 26). Teenager recounts shooting rampage - four jurors replaced for variety of reasons. *The Seattle Times*.

Brown, C. E. (1997b, September 4). Tape played at teen's murder trial. *The Seattle Times*.

Family files claim in shootings. (1996, May 15). *The Seattle Times*.

Fitten, R. K. (1997a, August 24). Trial to begin for teen charged in triple slaying. *The Seattle Times*.

Fitten, R. K. (1997b, September 9). Loukaitis jurors hear parents, see pearl jam video - mother, father testify in trial of teen son. *The Seattle Times*.

Fitten, R. K. (1997c, September 11). Loukaitis' godlike notions described. *The Seattle Times*.

Fitten, R. K. (1997d, September 12). Loukaitis sane, psychologist insists - prosecution expert rejects insanity in school killings. *The Seattle Times*.

Fitten, R. K. (1997e, September 19). Loukaitis murder case in hands of jurors - moses lake teen awaits verdict. *The Seattle Times*.

Fitten, R. K. (1997f, September 24). Moses lake teen guilty in 3 murders - jury rejects notion loukaitis insane. *The Seattle Times*.

Fitten, R. K., & Santana, A. (1997, September 25). Teen's trial a no win case - loukaitis' attorney calls for new kind of verdict: Guilty but mentally ill. *The Seattle Times*.

Gun victim's arm improving. (1996, May 26). *The Seattle Times*.

Hearing delayed for suspect in moses lake shooting deaths. (1996, August 27). *The Seattle Times*.

Injured girl back in hospital. (1996, March 13). *The Seattle Times*.

Kidnapping charges added in moses lake murder case. (1996, November 1). *The Seattle Times*.

Loukaitis trial resumes today. (1997, September 2). *The Seattle Times*.

Moses lake girl goes home. (1996, March 18). *The Seattle Times*.

Moses lake schools sued. (1996, October 21). *The Seattle Times*.

Moses lake shooting trial is postponed until august. (1997, March 10). *The Seattle Times*.

Moses lake trial to be open. (1996, July 3). *The Seattle Times*.

Moses lake trial will be open. (1996, March 5). *The Seattle Times*.

No delay in Moses Lake hearing. (1996, March 12). *The Seattle Times*.

Request for new trial denied. (1999, November 18). *The Seattle Times*.

Rock and crime - trying to pin crime on music blatantly ignores the facts. (1997, September 15). *The Seattle Times*.

Searcey, D. (1998, April 1). Educators looking for ways to reduce violence in schools - one suggestion is to punish instigators. *The Seattle Times*.

Searcey, D. (1999, January 19). Democrats lay out plans to improve school safety, reduce threat of violence - other education goals outlined by party. *The Seattle Times*.

Shooting survivor going home. (1996, March 1). *The Seattle Times*.

Shooting victim's family refiles suit against killer, district. (1999, February 10). *The Seattle Times*.

Third lawsuit in slaying of 3. (1997, May 31). *The Seattle Times*.

Tizon, A. (1997, February 23). Scarred by killings, moses lake asks: "what has this town become?" *The Seattle Times*.

Trial date set in triple slaying. (1996, October 9). *The Seattle Times*.

Vandals hit home of teen charged in school slayings. (1996, May 10). *The Seattle Times*.

MICHAEL CARNEAL (Case 10)

Books:

Harding, D., Mehta, J., & Newman, K. (2003). No exit: Mental illness, marginality, and school violence in West Paducah, Kentucky. In M. H. Moore, C. V. Petrie, A. A. Braga & B. L. McLaughlin (Eds.), *Deadly lessons: Understanding lethal school violence: Case studies of school violence committee* (pp. 132-162). Washington, DC: National Academy of Science.

Newspapers and Magazines:

Harper's Magazine (1)

Phillips, J. A. (1999, November). Home after dark. *Harper's Magazine*.

New York Times (2)

Glaberson, W. (2000a, August 4). Finding futility in trying to lay blame in killings. *New York Times*, pp. A1, A17.

Glaberson, W. (2000b, July 25). When grief wanted a hero, truth didn't get in the way. *New York Times*, pp. A1, A22.

Newsweek (1)

Pederson, D. (1999, May 10). Lessons from paducah. *Newsweek*, *133*, 35.

The Cincinatti Enquirer (1)

Gutierrez, K. S. (2002, September 14). Michael carneal: Torment of a teen killer. *The Cincinatti Enquirer*.

The Cincinatti Post (1)

Kreimer, P. (1998, February 21). Move ahead, says young paducah hero. *The Cincinatti Post*.

The Courier Journal (14)

Adams, J. (1997a, December 2). Three students killed, 5 wounded in shooting. *The Courier Journal*, p. 1A.

Adams, J. (1997b, December 7). An unexplained life. *The Courier Journal*, p. 1A.

Adams, J. (1998a, December 7). After the tragedies. *The Courier Journal*.

Adams, J. (1998b, December 18). His essays depict him as friendless, low in self-esteem. *The Courier Journal*, p. 1A.

Adams, J., & Malone, J. (1997, December16). Signs of trouble preceeded shooting. *The Courier Journal*, p. 1A.

Adams, J., & Malone, J. (1999, March 18). Outsider's destructive behavior spiraled into violence. *The Courier Journal*, p. 17A.

Cross, A. (2000, August 16). Victim of shootings at paducah school stirs emotions of delegates. *The Courier Journal*.

Malone, J. (2000a, April 6). Carneal's motives remain a mystery. *The Courier Journal*.

Malone, J. (2000b, April 7). Media suit in carneal slayings dismissed. *The Courier Journal*.

Malone, J. (1998a, December 17). The sentencing of michael carneal. *The Courier Journal*, p. 15A.

Malone, J. (1998b, December 18). Computer yields themes of death and violence. *The Courier Journal*, p. 13A.

Malone, J. (1998c, June 24). Carneal wanted to feel powerful, two mental health experts report. *The Courier Journal*, p. 5A.

Malone, J. (1998d, June 24). Carneal to plead guilty in school killings. *The Courier Journal*, p. 1A.

Wolfson, A. (2002, September 13). Paducah school shooter talks about case, says he's sorry. *The Courier Journal*.

The Kentucky Post (2)

Associated Press. (2001, May 3). Carneal faces transfer to a prison for adults. *The Kentucky Post*.

Associated Press. (2002, September 12). 'i was leaving everything behind'. *The Kentucky Post*.

The Paducah Sun (338)

The 911 call. (1997, December 4). *The Paducah Sun*, p. 14.

Apt response. (1997, December 4). *The Paducah Sun*, p. 4.

Associated Press. (1998a, April 12). In death, nicole hadley gives life. *The Paducah Sun*, p. 9.

Associated Press. (1998b, April 28). Classes resume in wake of shooting. *The Paducah Sun*, p. 5.

Associated Press. (1997a, December 7). 'dairies' not direct link to killings: Experts. *The Paducah Sun*, p. 2.

Associated Press. (1997b, December 17). Pearl high students sending message of unity to heath. *The Paducah Sun*, p. 12.

Associated Press. (1997c, December 17). Changes in carneal's behavior went largely unnoticed. *The Paducah Sun*, p. 12.

Associated Press. (1997d, December 18). Organ donation links two families. *The Paducah Sun*, p. 5.

Associated Press. (1997e, December 20). Pennsylvania mom grateful to hadleys. *The Paducah Sun*, p. 12.

Associated Press. (2000a, July 14). Shadoan dismisses carneal's parents from heath suit. *The Paducah Sun*.

Associated Press. (2000b, July 26). Strong says his role in heath shootings may be exaggerated. *The Paducah Sun*.

Associated Press. (1998c, March 11). Attorney discusses heath suit. *The Paducah Sun*, pp. 1, 12.

Associated Press. (1999a, March 19). Investigators made mistakes in carneal case: Newspaper. *The Paducah Sun*, p. 5.

Associated Press. (1998d, March 26). Teacher slain in arkansas hailed as hero. *The Paducah Sun*, p. 2.

Associated Press. (1998e, March 31). Arkansas law lets juveniles have guns. *The Paducah Sun*, p. 12.

Associated Press. (1998f, March 31). Heath parents write arkansas families. *The Paducah Sun*, p. 12.

Associated Press. (1998g, May 11). United effort helps heath heal. *The Paducah Sun*, pp. 1, 12.

Associated Press. (1998h, May 22). No. 3: In texas. *The Paducah Sun*, p. 16.

Associated Press. (1999b, October 5). Teen faces charges after school shooting. *The Paducah Sun*, p. 10.

Associated Press. (1999c, October 5). Schools report 4,000 assaults. *The Paducah Sun*, pp. 1, 10.

Associated Press. (1998i, October 7). Steger thankful trial avoided for carneal. *The Paducah Sun*, p. 10.

Bailey, S. (1997, December 2). 'anywhere, anytime,' expert says. *The Paducah Sun*, p. 10.

Bartleman, B. (1999, April 1). Carneal gun likely to stay in evidence. *The Paducah Sun*,, pp. 1, 14.

Bartleman, B. (1999, April 2). Hines says nace will get 5 rifles back taken by carneal. *The Paducah Sun*, p. 3.

Bartleman, B. (1999, April 8). Mccraken courthouse shuffles again. *The Paducah Sun*, p. 6.

Bartleman, B. (1999, April 9). Breen says heath case against media will be landmark. *The Paducah Sun*, pp. 1, 6.

Bartleman, B. (1999, April 13). Heath parents hope suit teaches hollywood. *The Paducah Sun*, pp. 1, 2.

Bartleman, B. (1999, April 15). Heath parents sue more students, teachers. *The Paducah Sun*, pp. 1, 14.

Bartleman, B. (1999f, April 20). Breen: Heath suit's appeals should go to supreme court. *The Paducah Sun*, p. 3.

Bartleman, B. (1999g, April 24). In columbine's shadow, heath graduate grieves. *The Paducah Sun*, pp. 1, 6.

Bartleman, B. (1999h, April 24). Haggling between lawyers extending heath proceedings. *The Paducah Sun*, p. 3.

Bartleman, B. (1998a, August 4). Large jury pool summoned for criminal cases. *The Paducah Sun*, pp. 1, 10.

Bartleman, B. (1998b, August 4). No 'deep pockets' likely in carneal civil case. *The Paducah Sun*, pp. 1, 10.

Bartleman, B. (1998c, August 19). Second report on carneal: No mental problems. *The Paducah Sun*, pp. 1, 16.

Bartleman, B. (1998d, August 20). Supreme court rule urged in heath gag order hearing. *The Paducah Sun*, pp. 1, 14.

Bartleman, B. (1998e, August 26). Hearing delayed; publicity worries eased. *The Paducah Sun*, pp. 1,14.

Bartleman, B. (1998f, August 26). Taxpayers shell out $60,000 for carneal. *The Paducah Sun*, pp. 1, 14.

Bartleman, B. (1998g, August 29). Carneal's family subpoenaed by state. *The Paducah Sun*, pp. 1, 3.

Bartleman, B. (1997a, Decembe 10). Five heath victims being interviewed today. *The Paducah Sun*, p. 1.

Bartleman, B. (1997b, Decembe 12). Legal what-ifs surrounding carneal's future. *The Paducah Sun*, pp. 1, 11.

Bartleman, B. (1998h, December 1). 'a nation was moved.' by shootings. *The Paducah Sun*, pp. 1, 10.

Bartleman, B. (1997c, December 2). Teen unable to explain his deadly attack. *The Paducah Sun*, pp. 1, 9.

Bartleman, B. (1997d, December 2). Families, students console each other in shooting wake. *The Paducah Sun*, p. 9.

Bartleman, B. (1998i, December 3). Heath's next chapter. *The Paducah Sun*, pp. 1, 2.

Bartleman, B. (1997e, December 3). School security tightened. *The Paducah Sun*, p. 1.

Bartleman, B. (1997f, December 3). Minister rejects reports of atheism. *The Paducah Sun*, pp. 1, 14.

Bartleman, B. (1997g, December 4). Shooting may be tied to film: Kaltenbach. *The Paducah Sun*, pp. 1, 15.

Bartleman, B. (1997h, December 4). Items from box in carneal room studied for clues. *The Paducah Sun*, pp. 1, 15.

Bartleman, B. (1997i, December 5). Scene from dream in movie shares eerie link with reality. *The Paducah Sun*, pp. 1, 2.

Bartleman, B. (1997j, December 5). Suspect adds little in 2 new interviews. *The Paducah Sun*, pp. 1, 12.

Bartleman, B. (1998j, December 6). Heath civil suit creates immediate questions. *The Paducah Sun*, pp. 1, 14.

Bartleman, B. (1997k, December 7). Augustus interviews more teens. *The Paducah Sun*, pp. 1, 2.

Bartleman, B. (1997l, December 7). Clinton calls for violence prevention. *The Paducah Sun*, pp. 1, 3.

Bartleman, B. (1997m, December 7). Three slain girls' lives left paducah a better place. *The Paducah Sun*, p. 2.

Bartleman, B. (1997n, December 8). No more heath arrests, sheriff predicts. *The Paducah Sun*, p. 1.

Bartleman, B. (1997o, December 9). Counselors available tonight. *The Paducah Sun*, pp. 1, 14.

Bartleman, B. (1997p, December 9). Grand jury may get carneal case friday. *The Paducah Sun*, pp. 1, 14.

Bartleman, B. (1997q, December 11). 14-year old to be tried as an adult. *The Paducah Sun*, pp. 1, 10.

Bartleman, B. (1997r, December 13). Carneal adopts new routine at juvenile center. *The Paducah Sun*, pp. 1, 12.

Bartleman, B. (1998k, December 17). Carneal devised own plot after discussions with friends. *The Paducah Sun*, pp. 1, 16.

Bartleman, B. (1998l, December 17). Emotion-charged statements precede carneal sentencing. *The Paducah Sun*, pp. 1, 12.

Bartleman, B. (1998m, December 17). Investigation pushed hard to link others, came away empty. *The Paducah Sun*, pp. 1, 16.

Bartleman, B. (1998n, December 17). Carneal told second, inconsistent story of takeover plan. *The Paducah Sun*, p. 15.

Bartleman, B. (1998o, December 19). Hines likely to remove himself from carneal civil case if asked. *The Paducah Sun*, pp. 1, 12.

Bartleman, B. (1999i, February 11). Supreme court rejects motion; shadoan to stay on heath case. *The Paducah Sun*, pp. 1, 16.

Bartleman, B. (2003, February 13). Heath litigation gets final dismissal. *The Paducah Sun*.

Bartleman, B. (2001, February 23). Bankruptcy filed against carneal in bid for insurance. *The Paducah Sun*.

Bartleman, B. (1999j, February 27). Defendants fault breen in heath case. *The Paducah Sun*, pp. 1, 12.

Bartleman, B. (1998p, January 3). Newsmakers, events that made headlines last. *The Paducah Sun*, p. 2.

Bartleman, B. (1998q, January 4). Events of 1997 will have big impact on the year to come. *The Paducah Sun*, p. 2.

Bartleman, B. (1999k, January 12). Shadoan: Expect fast decisions in carneal suit. *The Paducah Sun*, pp. 1, 2.

Bartleman, B. (1999l, January 13). Attorney agrees to dismiss 11 teachers from heath suit. *The Paducah Sun*, pp. 1, 12.

Bartleman, B. (1998r, January 15). Carneal back today for arrainment. *The Paducah Sun*, pp. 1, 16.

Bartleman, B. (1998s, January 16). Competency possible defense in carneal case. *The Paducah Sun*, pp. 1, 12.

Bartleman, B. (1999m, January 20). Breen to get bills for legal fees. *The Paducah Sun*, pp. 1, 12.

Bartleman, B. (1998t, January 21). House approves heath prayer bill. *The Paducah Sun*, pp. 1, 12.

Bartleman, B. (1999n, January 28). Man files to get back in carneal case. *The Paducah Sun*, p. 5.

Bartleman, B. (1998u, July 10). Jailer: Carneal move not needed. *The Paducah Sun*, pp. 1, 12.

Bartleman, B. (2000a, July 15). Carneal liable in shooting. *The Paducah Sun*.

Bartleman, B. (2000b, July 16). Carneal trial may not be held. *The Paducah Sun*.

Bartleman, B. (1999o, July 20). Judge: Heath suit faces 'barriers' of legal precedent. *The Paducah Sun*, pp. 1, 9.

Bartleman, B. (1998v, July 22). Lawyers for victims wants carneal gag order lifted. *The Paducah Sun*, pp. 1, 14.

Bartleman, B. (2000c, July 28). Defense upset with breen's motions. *The Paducah Sun*.

Bartleman, B. (1998w, July 28). Kaltenbach says carneal's mental illness disputed. *The Paducah Sun*, pp. 1, 10.

Bartleman, B. (2000d, July 29). Jury won't see all arneal exhibits. *The Paducah Sun*.

Bartleman, B. (1998x, July 1998). Carneal ordered moved from Owensboro. *The Paducah Sun*, pp. 1, 14.

Bartleman, B. (2000e, June 1). Shadoan sets friday date for decisionon carneals. *The Paducah Sun*.

Bartleman, B. (2000f, June 2). Breen wants judge off heath case. *The Paducah Sun*.

Bartleman, B. (2000g, June 3). Carneal's condition worsens, could delay heath civil trial. *The Paducah Sun*.

Bartleman, B. (1998y, June 3). Carneal wrote of 'event in hall' in march. *The Paducah Sun*, pp. 1, 12.

Bartleman, B. (1998z, June 4). Links to carneal friends forcus on inquiry. *The Paducah Sun*, pp. 1, 14.

Bartleman, B. (1999p, June 5). Shadoan gets 2nd heath lawsuit. *The Paducah Sun*, pp. 1, 12.

Bartleman, B. (1998{, June 5). Grand jury 'worthwhile': Kaltenbach. *The Paducah Sun*, pp. 1, 12.

Bartleman, B. (1999q, June 12). Breen asks judge to reduce 'high' fees. *The Paducah Sun*, p. 3.

Bartleman, B. (2000h, June 13). Shadoan sets deadline for court to dismiss him. *The Paducah Sun*.

Bartleman, B. (1999r, June 15). Tentative date set for carneal suit. *The Paducah Sun*, pp. 1, 12.

Bartleman, B. (1998|, June 17). Psychiatrist seeks input on carneal. *The Paducah Sun*, pp. 1, 16.

Bartleman, B. (1998}, June 20). Further testing for carneal. *The Paducah Sun*, pp. 1, 12.

Bartleman, B. (1998~, June 24). The profile. *The Paducah Sun*, pp. 1, 14.

Bartleman, B. (1998 , June 24). The plea. *The Paducah Sun*, pp. 1,14.

Bartleman, B. (1998€, June 24). Motives of families' attorney questioned by kaltenbach. *The Paducah Sun*, p. 2.

Bartleman, B. (1998∞, June 24). Carneal mental plea plan boils over. *The Paducah Sun*, pp. 1, 14.

Bartleman, B. (1998,, June 26). Gay implication spurred teasing: Carneal. *The Paducah Sun*, pp. 1, 14.

Bartleman, B. (2000i, June 29). Parents say heath judge unethical. *The Paducah Sun*.

Bartleman, B. (1999s, March 6). Judge drops school workers from heath suit. *The Paducah Sun*, pp. 1, 10.

Bartleman, B. (1999t, March 27). Judge to drop 5 heath students from suit. *The Paducah Sun*, p. 1.

Bartleman, B. (1999u, March 30). Shadoan: Heath suit filed within deadline. *The Paducah Sun*, p. 1.

Bartleman, B. (1999v, March 31). Fate of guns in heath case still undecided. *The Paducah Sun*, pp. 1, 13.

Bartleman, B. (1999w, May 7). Shadoan orders carneal's school records for review. *The Paducah Sun*, p. 8.

Bartleman, B. (1999x, May 8). Carneals: No signs son was troubled. *The Paducah Sun*, pp. 1, 11.

Bartleman, B. (2000j, May 10). Judge delays dismissals in heath suit. *The Paducah Sun*.

Bartleman, B. (1999y, May 11). Breen on recieving end of suit this time. *The Paducah Sun*, pp. 1, 10.

Bartleman, B. (1999z, May 16). Parents: Carneal a different person. *The Paducah Sun*, pp. 1, 10.

Bartleman, B. (2000k, May 23). Students dismissed in heath case. *The Paducah Sun*.

Bartleman, B. (1999{, May 25). Carneals liable for son's acts, breen says. *The Paducah Sun*, pp. 1, 10.

Bartleman, B. (1999|, November 9). Heath parents set figure in suit: $120 million. *The Paducah Sun*, pp. 1, 12.

Bartleman, B. (1999}, November 20). Heath appeal must start at lower level, court rules. *The Paducah Sun*, pp. 1, 14.

Bartleman, B. (1998f, October 1). Trial or no trial? *The Paducah Sun*, pp. 1, 16.

Bartleman, B. (1998,,, October 2). Carneal's conditional plea opposed by kaltenbach. *The Paducah Sun*, pp. 1, 14.

Bartleman, B. (1998..., October 3). Kaltenbach seeks to bar input to carneal's doctor's. *The Paducah Sun*, pp. 1, 14.

Bartleman, B. (1998†, October 4). The victims. *The Paducah Sun*, p. 9.

Bartleman, B. (1998‡, October 4). The scene. *The Paducah Sun*, pp. 1, 9.

Bartleman, B. (1998^, October 4). The suspect. *The Paducah Sun*, pp. 1, 9.

Bartleman, B. (1998‰, October 5). Tight control set at carneal trial. *The Paducah Sun*, pp. 1, 11.

Bartleman, B. (1998?, October 5). Attorneys have followed similar paths. *The Paducah Sun*, pp. 1, 11.

Bartleman, B. (1998‹, October 6). Kaltenbach praises carneal family for reaching plea. *The Paducah Sun*, p. 2.

Bartleman, B. (1998Œ, October 6). Stage set for final act dec. 16. *The Paducah Sun*, pp. 1, 10.

Bartleman, B. (1998?, October 17). Carneal civil case deadline april 19. *The Paducah Sun*, p. 1.

Bartleman, B. (1999~, September 5). Movie may have inspired carneal. *The Paducah Sun*, pp. 1, 14.

Bartleman, B. (1998?, September 9). Live televised carneal trial may be sought. *The Paducah Sun*, pp. 1, 16.

Bartleman, B. (1998?, September 10). Motion seeks carneal delay into next year. *The Paducah Sun*, p. 1.

Bartleman, B. (1998∏, September 11). Carneal delay motion angers girls' families. *The Paducah Sun*, p. 1.

Bartleman, B. (1998', September 12). Kaltenbach opposes carneal delay motion. *The Paducah Sun*, pp. 1, 6.

Bartleman, B. (1998', September 13). Carneal continuance tough decision for judge. *The Paducah Sun*, pp. 1, 14.

Bartleman, B. (1998", September 16). Carneal in fulton awaiting trial. *The Paducah Sun*, pp. 1, 12.

Bartleman, B. (1998", September 18). Tv camera may put carneal on comcast. *The Paducah Sun*, pp. 1, 12.

Bartleman, B. (1998•, September 22). Carneal may have taken guns earlier. *The Paducah Sun*, p. 5.

Bartleman, B. (1998–, September 23). Kaltenbach: Carneal earlier tried to disturb prayer circle. *The Paducah Sun*, p. 2.

Bartleman, B. (1998—, September 27). Hines to reconsider carneal tv coverage. *The Paducah Sun*, pp. 1, 6.

Bartleman, B. (1998?, September 27). 183 members of jury pool already excused. *The Paducah Sun*, pp. 1, 6.

Bartleman, B. (1998™, September 27). Potential carneal jurors vary widely. *The Paducah Sun*, p. 7.

Bartleman, B. (1998‰, September 30). Hines bars cameras at carneal trial. *The Paducah Sun*, pp. 1, 14.

Bartleman, B., & Zambroski, J. (1998, January 1). Carneal search deepens. *The Paducah Sun*, pp. 1, 16.

Bill bond's statement. (1998, October 6). *The Paducah Sun*, p. 2.

Bond, B. (1998, May 17). Time of healing. *The Paducah Sun*, p. 4.

Bradley, C. D. (1998, June 17). 'second family' honors kayce steger's memory. *The Paducah Sun*, p. 9.

Breed, A. G. (1997, December 7). Carneal's pastor selects sermon on repentance. *The Paducah Sun*, p. 2.

Breed, A. G. (1998a, March 26). Portraits of jonesboro suspects muddled. *The Paducah Sun*, pp. 1, 12.

Breed, A. G. (1998b, March 27). Facing the fear. *The Paducah Sun*, pp. 1, 14.

Bridis, T. (1997, December 4). Community, school offering forgiveness. *The Paducah Sun*, pp. 1,14.

Bridis, T. (1998, March 22). Heath lawsuit to fuel questions on value of life. *The Paducah Sun*, pp. 1, 14.

Brockenborough, P. (1998, April 12). 1995 warning of school violence sad precurser of future. *The Paducah Sun*, p. 2.

Carneal 'sorry'; jenkins can't help. (2000, April 7). *The Paducah Sun*.

Chapman's album includes heath song. (1999, June 14). *The Paducah Sun*, p. 2.

Chapman's heath benefit tickets on sale april 23. (1998, April 12). *The Paducah Sun*, p. 3.

Clarified ruling. (1998, August 28). *The Paducah Sun*, p. 1.

Corneal's attorneys' statement. (1998, October 6). *The Paducah Sun*, p. 2.

Decision to donate hadley organsaids 4 patients. (1997, December 4). *The Paducah Sun*, p. 14.

The defendants. (1999, April 13). *The Paducah Sun*, p. 1.

Defendants and students. (1998, December 3). *The Paducah Sun*, p. 2.

Families' statement. (1998, October 6). *The Paducah Sun*, p. 1.

Firm and fair. (1999, January 14). *The Paducah Sun*, p. 4.

Flawed program. (1998, September 13). *The Paducah Sun*, p. 4.

Foust, B. (1998a, December). Teachers preparing defense. *The Paducah Sun*, pp. 1, 2.

Foust, B. (1997a, December 3). Pearl staff reaches out to counterparts at heath. *The Paducah Sun*, p. 8.

Foust, B. (1997b, December 4). Close ties brought heath tragedy home to concord elementary. *The Paducah Sun*, p. 18.

Foust, B. (1997c, December 6). Nicole hadley laid to rest in peaceful, secluded plot. *The Paducah Sun*, p. 3.

Foust, B. (1998b, December 17). Families, victims tell carneal, court of thier pain, losses. *The Paducah Sun*, p. 14.

Foust, B. (1998c, October 6). Heath, families relieved ordeal seems over. *The Paducah Sun*, pp. 1, 10.

Fraser, D. (2000a, April 1). Breen vows to shadoan: 'i'll go down swinging'. *The Paducah Sun*.

Fraser, D. (2000b, April 7). Heath video suit rejected. *The Paducah Sun*.

Fraser, D. (1998a, April 21). Monument to slain heath high school students dedicated. *The Paducah Sun*, p. 5.

Fraser, D. (1999a, April 24). Scares signal tension at lone oak, reidland. *The Paducah Sun*, pp. 1, 6.

Fraser, D. (1999b, August 5). Jenkins plans walk for diploma. *The Paducah Sun*, pp. 1, 9.

Fraser, D. (1997a, December 2). Tributes to heath students mingle tears and prayers. *The Paducah Sun*, p. 11.

Fraser, D. (1997b, December 2). Certification of teen-ager expected at dec. 10 hearing. *The Paducah Sun*, p. 10.

Fraser, D. (1997c, December 12). Strength comes from faith. *The Paducah Sun*, pp. 1, 16.

Fraser, D. (1997d, December 12). Do not let wheelchair set limitations: Hogancamp. *The Paducah Sun*, pp. 1, 16.

Fraser, D. (1998b, February 26). Hearings clog court calendar. *The Paducah Sun*, pp. 1, 12.

Fraser, D. (1999c, January 8). Hines indicates decision to exit heath civil lawsuit. *The Paducah Sun*, p. 5.

Fraser, D. (1999d, January 16). Heath victims' families want shadoan removed. *The Paducah Sun*, p. 5.

Fraser, D. (1999e, January 21). Shadoan keeping heath lawsuit. *The Paducah Sun*, pp. 1, 14.

Fraser, D. (1998c, March 19). Heath suit expected by april 6. *The Paducah Sun*, p. 6.

Fraser, D. (1998d, March 25). Hadley hurts for jonesboro families. *The Paducah Sun*, pp. 1, 14.

Fraser, D. (1998e, March 25). Bad memories, shock overcome heath residents. *The Paducah Sun*, pp. 1, 5.

Fraser, D. (1998f, March 25). Some draw inspiration from heath. *The Paducah Sun*, pp. 1, 14.

Fraser, D. (1998g, March 26). Jonesboro slayings hit heath parents hard. *The Paducah Sun*, p. 2.

Fraser, D. (1998h, March 26). Jonesboro, paducah share more than tragedy. *The Paducah Sun*, pp. 1, 12.

Fraser, D. (1999f, May 5). A way to help missy walk. *The Paducah Sun*, pp. 1, 16.

Fraser, D. (1998i, May 17). Tougher sentence sought for carneal. *The Paducah Sun*, pp. 1, 14.

Fraser, D. (1999g, May 20). Parents face murder charge. *The Paducah Sun*, pp. 1, 14.

Fraser, D. (1999h, May 23). Jenkins plans stay at california clinic. *The Paducah Sun*, pp. 1, 16.

Fraser, D. (1998j, May 29). Suspect had gun at school before dec. 1. *The Paducah Sun*, pp. 1, 12.

Fraser, D. (1998k, May 30). Heath case to feel grand jury weight. *The Paducah Sun*, p. 1.

Fraser, D. (1999i, November 25). Missy to walk to class monday. *The Paducah Sun*, pp. 1, 16.

Fraser, D. (1999j, November 30). Missy turns attention to future. *The Paducah Sun*, pp. 1, 12.

Fraser, D. (1998l, October 6). Hines relieved media 'vultures' leaving. *The Paducah Sun*, p. 2.

Fraser, D. (1999k, September 16). Missy takes 1st steps to walking. *The Paducah Sun*, pp. 1, 7.

Harrison, K. (1997, December 11). 'missy' jenkins determined to be happy, to walk again. *The Paducah Sun*, pp. 1, 10.

Heath band to march in silence. (1997, December 5). *The Paducah Sun*, p. 12.

Heath lawsuit transferred to daniels. (1999, January 9). *The Paducah Sun*, p. 6.

Heath memories. (1997, December 6). *The Paducah Sun*, p. 4.

Heath shooting. (2002, April 20). *The Paducah Sun*.

Heath shooting. (1997, December 2). *The Paducah Sun*, p. 4.

Hughes, J. (1998, June 4). Pearl shooting suspect's mom died gruesome death:Expert. *The Paducah Sun*, p. 14.

Hughes, J. (1999, May 19). Legislators hear heath student's school violence fears. *The Paducah Sun*, p. 6.

Inventory taken from the bedroom of michael carneal. (1997, December 4). *The Paducah Sun*, p. 15.

Jenkins fund transferred to citizens. (1997, December 13). *The Paducah Sun*, p. 7.

Jenkins trust fund set up. (1997, December 8). *The Paducah Sun*, p. 3.

Jenkins, schaberg gain $3,500 each from benefit. (1998, February 4). *The Paducah Sun*, p. 10.

Joint services scheduled friday. (1997, December 3). *The Paducah Sun*, p. 13.

Kinsey, A. (1997a, December 2). Heath community's security shaken. *The Paducah Sun*, p. 10.

Kinsey, A. (1997b, December 3). Heath band will march in memory of classmates. *The Paducah Sun*, p. 9.

Kinsey, A. (1997c, December 4). Michealson asks stores to close as tribute. *The Paducah Sun*, p. 14.

Kinsey, A. (1997d, December 6). Mother nature pauses as jessica james laid to rest. *The Paducah Sun*, p. 4.

Kinsey, A. (1997e, December 7). Silent parade salutes mixes pride, grief. *The Paducah Sun*, pp. 1, 2.

Kocher, G. (1998, March 31). Frankfort school students impressed by heath speakers. *The Paducah Sun*, pp. 1, 12.

Landini, L. (1998a, April 10). Missy's home. *The Paducah Sun*, pp. 1, 12.

Landini, L. (1999a, August 5). Heath's first days focus on the curriculum of life. *The Paducah Sun*, pp. 1, 9.

Landini, L. (1998b, August 13). Heath quilt moves to school to grow. *The Paducah Sun*, p. 6.

Landini, L. (1998c, December 1). A year later, families finding a new balance. *The Paducah Sun*, pp. 1, 10.

Landini, L. (1998d, December 2). Heath spends day like any other. *The Paducah Sun*, pp. 1, 16.

Landini, L. (1997a, December 3). Quick work on all fronts credited with saving some lives. *The Paducah Sun*, p. 9.

Landini, L. (1997b, December 3). Combined service friday at 1 p.M. *The Paducah Sun*, p. 15.

Landini, L. (1997c, December 6). Solemn notes of 'taps' bid farewell to kayce steger. *The Paducah Sun*, p. 3.

Landini, L. (1997d, December 23). Angel pins aid healing. *The Paducah Sun*, pp. 1, 14.

Landini, L. (1997e, December 24). Troupe organizes heath benefit for jenkins, schaberg. *The Paducah Sun*, p. 2.

Landini, L. (1998e, February 11). Therapy provides road test for new van. *The Paducah Sun*, pp. 1, 14.

Landini, L. (1998f, January 15). Life just series of victories that missy jenkins savors. *The Paducah Sun*, pp. 1, 16.

Landini, L. (1998g, March 26). Jonesboro shootings prove troubling for missy jenkins. *The Paducah Sun*, p. 2.

Landini, L. (1998h, May 10). Heath concert message of hope. *The Paducah Sun*, pp. 1, 14.

Landini, L. (1998i, May 14). Run/walk honors organ donors. *The Paducah Sun*, p. 1.

Landini, L. (1999b, May 20). Chapman testifies on school violence in d.C. *The Paducah Sun*, pp. 1, 14.

Larken, K. (1997, December 4). Farewell notes to adorn caskets. *The Paducah Sun*, p. 1.

The lessons. (1999, August 5). *The Paducah Sun*, p. 9.

Letters from public. (1997, December 6). *The Paducah Sun*, pp. 2, 3.

Levinson, A. (1998, March 27). States lowering age for 'adults'. *The Paducah Sun*, pp. 1, 14.

Lieb, D. A. (1998, March 26). Grandfather: Suspect says he 'fired some shots'. *The Paducah Sun*, pp. 1, 12.

Main points of second and third. (1998, December 17). *The Paducah Sun*, pp. 10, 11.

Medics' work comforted mother. (1997, December 4). *The Paducah Sun*, p. 15.

Missy jenkins named one of the most fascinating women of 1998. (1998, December 11). *The Paducah Sun*, p. 1.

Monument honors slain heath students. (1998, April 18). *The Paducah Sun*, p. 1.

Moving on. (2000, August 6). *The Paducah Sun*.

No simple answer. (1997, December 5). *The Paducah Sun*, p. 4.

Oliver, J. (1998a, December 3). Sheriff: No proof of a conspiracy. *The Paducah Sun*, pp. 1, 2.

Oliver, J. (1998b, December 17). Families comment after carneal sentencing. *The Paducah Sun*, p. 12.

Oliver, J. (1999, February 2). Carneals should testify sooner, latest motion contends. *The Paducah Sun*, p. 5.

Oliver, J. (1998c, October 6). Plea relieves lead investigator of emotionally-draining job. *The Paducah Sun*, p. 2.

Other victims visited. (1997, December 11). *The Paducah Sun*, p. 10.

Parents' statement. (1998, March 7). *The Paducah Sun*, pp. 1, 2.

Patterson, J. (1998, April 22). Gospel singers tune up to benefit heath victims. *The Paducah Sun*, pp. 1, 16.

Paulson, S. K. (1999, April 23). Sheriff: Killer may have had help. *The Paducah Sun*, pp. 1, 14.

Paxton, J. (1999, April 18). Heath lawsuits out of hand. *The Paducah Sun*, p. 4.

Paxton, J. (1997, December 7). Time now to heal, move forward. *The Paducah Sun*, p. 4.

Political hype. (1998, October 17). *The Paducah Sun*, p. 4.

Price, J. (1998, March 25). Cousins face hearing today in shootings. *The Paducah Sun*, pp. 1, 14.

Prichard, J. (1998a, November 29). Parents of victims of heath shooting still in great pain. *The Paducah Sun*, pp. 1, 15.

Prichard, J. (1998b, November 29). Shooting prompted new security policies. *The Paducah Sun*, p. 15.

The prosecutor's staement. (1998, October 6). *The Paducah Sun*, p. 2.

Protected right. (1998, July 29). *The Paducah Sun*, p. 4.

Psychiatrists complete two days of talking to michael carneal. (1998, May 12). *The Paducah Sun*, p. 7.

Quote. (1997, December 8). *The Paducah Sun*, p. 6.

Quotes of note. (1999, August 9). *The Paducah Sun*, p. 4.

Sanders, M. (1997a, December 3). 'it's time we take our school back and overcome what fears we have'. *The Paducah Sun*, p. 9.

Sanders, M. (1997b, December 3). Expressions of hope, forgiveness overwhelm heath high campus. *The Paducah Sun*, pp. 1, 14.

Sanders, M. (1998, May 16). Heath grasps chapman's healing hand. *The Paducah Sun*, pp. 1, 12.

Schaberg, S. (1998, April 27). In a moment, life changed; light shines in the darkness. *The Paducah Sun*, p. 4.

School panic. (1999, May 6). *The Paducah Sun*, p. 4.

School safety. (1998, August 16). *The Paducah Sun*, p. 4.

School safety. (1997, December 16). *The Paducah Sun*, p. 4.

Sense of relief. (1998, October 6). *The Paducah Sun*, p. 4.

Shaky claims. (1998). *The Paducah Sun*, p. 4.

Shooting anniversary to be low key. (1999, November 28). *The Paducah Sun*, p. 10.

Shooting pains. (1998, April 18). *The Paducah Sun*, p. 4.

Steger responds to teacher's death. (1998, April 28). *The Paducah Sun*, p. 5.

Stick to issues. (1999, February 20). *The Paducah Sun*, p. 4.

Texeria, E. (1997, December 15). Time to address youth violence in america. *The Paducah Sun*, p. 4.

Text of michael carneal's first. (1998, December 17). *The Paducah Sun*, pp. 10, 11.

Text of president clinton's radio address. (1997, December 7). *The Paducah Sun*, p. 3.

Thomas, D. (1999, April 24). Prosecutor postulates about school violence. *The Paducah Sun*, pp. 1, 6.

Three shootings turn a school day deadly. (1998, May 22). *The Paducah Sun*, pp. 1, 16.

Thrower, A. (1999a, April 23). Heath advice preceded carnage. *The Paducah Sun*, pp. 1, 14.

Thrower, A. (2000a, August 5). Judge reviews heath lawsuit. *The Paducah Sun*.

Thrower, A. (1999b, December 2). Shooting anniversary a day to grieve, a day for comfort at heath. *The Paducah Sun*, pp. 1, 16.

Thrower, A. (2001, March 7). Carneal sentencing moved up to june 1. *The Paducah Sun*.

Thrower, A. (2000b, May 24). Bond: Now is the time to walk away. *The Paducah Sun*.

Thrower, A. (1999c, November 28). Officers get credit for safe students. *The Paducah Sun*, pp. 1, 10.

Thrower, A. (1999d, November 28). Galloway extra set of eyes, ears at heath. *The Paducah Sun*, pp. 1, 10.

Thrower, A. (1999e, November 28). Schools also use less-visible safety measures. *The Paducah Sun*, pp. 1, 10.

Thrower, A. (1999f, November 30). Friends have stood by her from start. *The Paducah Sun*, pp. 1, 12.

Thrower, A. (2000c, September 12). Report gives hope on heath suit. *The Paducah Sun*.

Thrower, M. (1998, October 16). Mystery of michael carneal lingers. *The Paducah Sun*, p. 4.

Viewpoints. (1997, December 7). *The Paducah Sun*, p. 4.

Week of caring. (1997, December 7). *The Paducah Sun*, p. 4.

Wells, D. (1997a, December 3). Area's schools, churches extend support to heath victims, families. *The Paducah Sun*, p. 8.

Wells, D. (1997b, December 4). Area businesses accommodate invasion by national media. *The Paducah Sun*, p. 15.

Wells, D. (1998, January 5). Outreach service focuses on healing heath's pains. *The Paducah Sun*, pp. 1, 5.

What the investigation indicates. (1998, December 17). *The Paducah Sun*, p. 1.

Whose fault? (1999, April 14). *The Paducah Sun*, p. 4.

Why sue, wilson wonders. (1998, December 3). *The Paducah Sun*, pp. 1, 2.

Witnesses tapped for carneal court case. (1998, August 13). *The Paducah Sun*, p. 6.

Wohlleb, J. (1997a). Mccracken school safety panel begins exploring ideas. *The Paducah Sun*, p. 12.

Wohlleb, J. (1998a, April 3). Schools plan crackdown on threats. *The Paducah Sun*, pp. 1,12.

Wohlleb, J. (1998b, April 10). Former paducahan's child offers scholarship for heath. *The Paducah Sun*, p. 5.

Wohlleb, J. (1998c, April 21). School board's action targets verbal threats. *The Paducah Sun*, pp. 1, 12.

Wohlleb, J. (1998d, April 24). Security guards to finish year in county schools. *The Paducah Sun*, pp. 1, 10.

Wohlleb, J. (1997b, December 2). Principal bond tells media 'i still believe in heath'. *The Paducah Sun*, p. 11.

Wohlleb, J. (1997c, December 2). Talking about the tragedy may be best therapy, official advises. *The Paducah Sun*, p. 11.

Wohlleb, J. (1997d, December 3). Parents join effort for healing. *The Paducah Sun*, pp. 1, 18.

Wohlleb, J. (1997e, December 3). Mccracken school officials ponder changes in security. *The Paducah Sun*, p. 8.

Wohlleb, J. (1997f, December 4). School panel to examine safety options. *The Paducah Sun*, pp. 1,18.

Wohlleb, J. (1997g, December 15). North carolina project sets standard. *The Paducah Sun*, pp. 1, 12.

Wohlleb, J. (1998e, February 25). Memorial garden to honor heath victims. *The Paducah Sun*, pp. 1, 14.

Wohlleb, J. (1998f, January 13). New tributes arrive daily to aid healing for heath students. *The Paducah Sun*, pp. 1, 8.

Wohlleb, J. (1998g, March 18). Heath dedication includes chapman. *The Paducah Sun*, p. 2.

Wohlleb, J. (1998h, May 15). Hundreds view tribute of love at heath high. *The Paducah Sun*, pp. 1, 12.

Wohlleb, J. (1998i, May 15). Families launch anit-violence campaign. *The Paducah Sun*, pp. 1, 12.

Wolfson, A. (2002, September 13). Carneal says he's no monster. *The Paducah Sun*.

Zambroski, J. (1998a, April 19). Eagles give $20,000 to jenkins; 'dateline' to air segment friday. *The Paducah Sun*, p. 15.

Zambroski, J. (1997a, December 2). Witnesses stunned by shootings. *The Paducah Sun*, p. 10.

Zambroski, J. (1997b, December 3). More tears, prayers begin healing process at heath. *The Paducah Sun*, p. 8.

Zambroski, J. (1997c, December 3). Strong's heroism meant more lives saved, bond says. *The Paducah Sun*, pp. 9, 15.

Zambroski, J. (1997d, December 3). Professionals work with students, teachers in shooting aftermath. *The Paducah Sun*, p. 8.

Zambroski, J. (1997e, December 4). Security - the practical, the desirable. *The Paducah Sun*, pp. 1, 14.

Zambroski, J. (1997f, December 4). Classmate's web page honors victims. *The Paducah Sun*, p. 14.

Zambroski, J. (1997g, December 5). Paducah begins goodbyes. *The Paducah Sun*, pp. 1, 12.

Zambroski, J. (1997h, December 6). Families share final moments with world. *The Paducah Sun*, pp. 1, 2.

Zambroski, J. (1997i, December 7). Christian youth evangelist coming to paducah revivial. *The Paducah Sun*, pp. 1, 2.

Zambroski, J. (1997j, December 11). Carneal appearance creates media circus. *The Paducah Sun*, pp. 1, 18.

Zambroski, J. (1997k, December 11). Counselors see link between paducah, oklahoma city. *The Paducah Sun*, p. 10.

Zambroski, J. (1997l, December 14). Breakfast funds help gun victim. *The Paducah Sun*, pp. 1, 14.

Zambroski, J. (1998b, January 9). FBI to search files in carneal's computer. *The Paducah Sun*, pp. 1, 16.

Zambroski, J. (1998c, January 16). Arraignment emotional for families. *The Paducah Sun*, pp. 1, 12.

Zambroski, J. (1998d, March 5). Papers detail state's case against carneal. *The Paducah Sun*, pp. 1, 12.

Zambroski, J. (1998e, March 7). Heath victims' families uniting to plan lawsuit. *The Paducah Sun*, pp. 1, 2.

Zambroski, J. (1998f, March 7). Carneal defense to focus on mental illness at trial. *The Paducah Sun*, pp. 1, 12.

Zambroski, J. (1998g, March 27). Heath boy's threats bring suspension. *The Paducah Sun*, pp. 1, 2.

Zambroski, J., and Bartleman, Bill. (1997m, December 3). Sheriff calls 4 detectives into probe. *The Paducah Sun*, pp. 1, 15.

Zambroski, J., and Wohlleb, Jennifer. (1997n, December 2). Thanksgiving day theft fuels seconds of horror. *The Paducah Sun*, pp. 1, 9.

Time (1)

Grace, J. (1997, December 15). When silence fell. *Time, 150,* 25.

Today's Christian Woman (1)

Jenkins, M., & Gupton, K. L. (1998, September/October). Finding forgiveness. *Today's Christian Woman*.

U.S. News and World Report (2)

Blank, J. (1998, October 12). The kid no one noticed. *U.S. News and World Report, 125,* 27-30.

Blank, J., & Cohen, W. (1997, December 15). Prayer circle murders. *U.S. News and World Report, 123,* 24-28.

MITCHELL JOHNSON, AND ANDREW GOLDEN (Case 11)

Books:

Fox, C., Roth, W. D., & Newman, K. (2003). A deadly partnership: Lethal violence in an arkansas middle school. In M. H. Moore, C. V. Petrie, A. A. Braga & B. L. McLaughlin (Eds.), *Deadly lessons: Understanding lethal school violence: Case studies of school violence committee* (pp. 132-162). Washington, DC: National Academy of Science.

Newspapers and Magazines:

Arkansas Democrat Gazette (165)

Announce fire drills beforehand, officials suggest to schools. (1998, April 2). *Arkansas Democrat Gazette*.

Bowers, R. (1998a, August 13). In wee hours, 2 killers flown to youth compound. *Arkansas Democrat Gazette*.

Bowers, R. (1998b, August 14). State gets guard bill of $6,000 for flying 2 boys to youth lockup. *Arkansas Democrat Gazette*.

Brooks, J. (1998, August 19). Sharing information could avert more jonesboros, officers say. *Arkansas Democrat Gazette*.

Caillouet, L. S. (1998a, April 5). Shootings discussed on Internet. *Arkansas Democrat Gazette*.

Caillouet, L. S. (1998b, March 25). Bullets fly on campus: Fourth case in 6 months. *Arkansas Democrat Gazette*.

Caillouet, L. S. (1998c, March 25). Experts speculate on motives. *Arkansas Democrat Gazette*.

Caldwell, E. (1999, April 8). Huckabee signs measure to put harsher sentences on youths guilty of murder. *Arkansas Democrat Gazette*.

Clergy schedules 'healing' service. (1998, March 29). *Arkansas Democrat Gazette*.

Cofer, B. (1998a, April 7). Lawyer says boy held in ambush molested as kid. *Arkansas Democrat Gazette*.

Cofer, B. (1998b, April 9). Tv comments 'hurt', boy's mother says. *Arkansas Democrat Gazette*.

Cofer, B. (1998c, April 9). Ambush-case lawyer linked to debts, charge involving girl. *Arkansas Democrat Gazette*.

Cofer, B. (1998d, April 10). Each victim in shooting to get $7,500. *Arkansas Democrat Gazette*.

Cofer, B. (1998e, August 11). Journalists bring back bad memories for jonesboro residents. *Arkansas Democrat Gazette*.

Cofer, B. (1999, March 21). Beyond westside: Rash of school shootings across U.S. Mars '97-'98. *Arkansas Democrat Gazette*.

Cofer, B. (1998f, March 29). Jonesboro's jolt strikes tender nerve in paducah. *Arkansas Democrat Gazette*.

Cofer, B., & Heard, K. (1998a, August 9). Husband of slain teacher says 'oldest of these 2' shot her. *Arkansas Democrat Gazette*.

Cofer, B., & Heard, K. (1998b, August 10). Westside students, kin livng nightmare as hearing nears. *Arkansas Democrat Gazette*.

Cofer, B., & Heard, K. (1999, March 21). Families go on but can't forget. *Arkansas Democrat Gazette*.

Cofer, B., & Waite, M. (1998, August 12). Father vows to get convicted boy out of state. *Arkansas Democrat Gazette*.

Davis, S. (1998a, August 12). Death toll 11 students, 1 teacher in nation's recent school shootings. *Arkansas Democrat Gazette*.

Davis, S. (1998b, March 25). Two camoflage-clad boys arrested in schoolyard shootings. *Arkansas Democrat Gazette*.

Davis, S., & Porter, J. (1998, March 26). Illness faked, the weapons were gathered. *Arkansas Democrat Gazette*.

Davis, S., & Satter, L. (1998, March 29). Differing views depict character od suspect, 11. *Arkansas Democrat Gazette*.

Davis, S., & Uyttebrouck, O. (1998, March 27). Boys held over in killings. *Arkansas Democrat Gazette*.

Dungan, T., & Meisel, J. (1998, March 29). In 3 services, teary towns extol slain teacher, 2 girls. *Arkansas Democrat Gazette*.

Dungan, T., Meisel, J., & Heard, K. (1998, March 30). Pastors console residents with prayer. *Arkansas Democrat Gazette*.

Egan, T. (1998, June 15). Patterns emerging in attacks at schools. *Arkansas Democrat Gazette*.

Everett, K. (1998a, March 27). Boys' jailmate also charged in gun death. *Arkansas Democrat Gazette*.

Everett, K. (1998b, March 27). Everywhere, white ribbons flutter as a sign of support. *Arkansas Democrat Gazette*.

Frank, A. R. (1999, August 11). School expulsions for guns drop 8%. *Arkansas Democrat Gazette*.

Fullerton, J. (1998a, July 9). Clinton evokes Jonesboro, urges new lid on guns. *Arkansas Democrat Gazette*.

Fullerton, J. (1998b, March 26). Find way to deter violence in schools, clinton tells Reno. *Arkansas Democrat Gazette*.

Fullerton, J. (1998c, March 27). Justice department eyes charging 2 arkansas boys. *Arkansas Democrat Gazette*.

Fullerton, J. (1998d, March 28). Shooting suspects may yet face federal charges. *Arkansas Democrat Gazette*.

Fullerton, J. (1998e, March 29). Clinton exhorts nation to remedy violence in schools. *Arkansas Democrat Gazette*.

Fullerton, J. (1998f, March 31). In videotape, President prods Jonesboro to 'pray for peace and healing'. *Arkansas Democrat Gazette*.

Gay, L. (1998, March 29). Data show crime down in schools. *Arkansas Democrat Gazette*.

George, E. (1999, June 11). Counties' leaders ok state control for youth lockup. *Arkansas Democrat Gazette*.

Girl shot in ambush released by hospital. (1998, April 5). *Arkansas Democrat Gazette*.

Harris, P. (1998, August 11). Victims' relatives sue, blame boys, parents, gun makers. *Arkansas Democrat Gazette*.

Heard, K. (1999a, April 8). School shooters swiped guns from unlocked rack. *Arkansas Democrat Gazette*.

Heard, K. (1998a, April 8). Westside students returning to rigors; counselors pleased. *Arkansas Democrat Gazette*.

Heard, K. (1998b, April 14). Forum: Media covering shootings biased, rude. *Arkansas Democrat Gazette*.

Heard, K. (1999b, April 22). Counselors help students in Jonesboro; police patrol. *Arkansas Democrat Gazette*.

Heard, K. (1999c, August 5). School shooter sorry, laments 'won't go to prom,' pen pal says. *Arkansas Democrat Gazette*.

Heard, K. (1998c, August 9). No 18 and out if teens convicted, Huckabee vows. *Arkansas Democrat Gazette*.

Heard, K. (1998d, August 10). Fence along edge of woods among school safety moves. *Arkansas Democrat Gazette*.

Heard, K. (1998e, August 11). Jonesboro ambush suspects to face hearing. *Arkansas Democrat Gazette*.

Heard, K. (1999d, August 11). County asks judge to reconsider jonesboro ruling. *Arkansas Democrat Gazette*.

Heard, K. (1998f, August 12). Boys convicted of murdering 5. *Arkansas Democrat Gazette*.

Heard, K. (1998g, August 12). Victims' kin face killers, pour out bitterness. *Arkansas Democrat Gazette*.

Heard, K. (1998h, August 13). Judge in shootings at westside school to rule on restitution. *Arkansas Democrat Gazette*.

Heard, K. (1998i, July 9). Ambush suspect's mom: Law to hold parents responsible good idea. *Arkansas Democrat Gazette*.

Heard, K. (1998j, July 11). House to hear families' views on shootings. *Arkansas Democrat Gazette*.

Heard, K. (1998k, July 11). Mother will call before birthday, son's 'trial' in jonesboro shootings. *Arkansas Democrat Gazette*.

Heard, K. (1998l, July 15). Toughen juvenile laws, slain teacher's husband says. *Arkansas Democrat Gazette*.

Heard, K. (1998m, July 16). Juvenile justice changes coming, legislators vow. *Arkansas Democrat Gazette*.

Heard, K. (1998n, July 22). Westside killing suspects mistreated? *Arkansas Democrat Gazette*.

Heard, K. (1999e, July 27). Public defenders agency to pay for jonesboro shooters civil case. *Arkansas Democrat Gazette*.

Heard, K. (1999f, June 6). Killer's essay haunts westside teacher. *Arkansas Democrat Gazette*.

Heard, K. (1998o, June 10). Memphis seminar: Snoop so kids won't shoot. *Arkansas Democrat Gazette*.

Heard, K. (1998p, June 16). Teen ambush suspect in jonesboro shootings loved rap music, teacher says. *Arkansas Democrat Gazette*.

Heard, K. (1998q, June 18). Westside pupil's former attorney accuses new defenders, prosecutors of misconduct. *Arkansas Democrat Gazette*.

Heard, K. (1998r, June 20). Texans won't take two held in jonesboro shootings. *Arkansas Democrat Gazette*.

Heard, K. (1998s, June 26). Judge issues gag order in jonesboro schoolyard ambush case. *Arkansas Democrat Gazette*.

Heard, K. (1999g, March 21). Services, beels, prayers willmark anniversary of 5 deaths. *Arkansas Democrat Gazette*.

Heard, K. (1999h, March 21). Shooter's mom sees son jailed, innocence lost. *Arkansas Democrat Gazette*.

Heard, K. (1999i, March 24). Jonesboro remembers 5 victims of violence. *Arkansas Democrat Gazette*.

Heard, K. (1999j, March 25). 400 attend memorial to school shooting victims. *Arkansas Democrat Gazette*.

Heard, K. (1999k, March 27). Shooter's anger at teacher drove school ambush, reports suggest. *Arkansas Democrat Gazette*.

Heard, K. (1998t, March 28). Suspect sought lord's help weeks ago, woman says. *Arkansas Democrat Gazette*.

Heard, K. (1998u, March 28). Teacher's students, friends recall her laughter, love for kids. *Arkansas Democrat Gazette*.

Heard, K. (2000, May 10). Gun maker, grandfather dropped from school shooting suit. *Arkansas Democrat Gazette*.

Heard, K. (1999l, May 12). Kin of westside victims press for passage of gun legislation. *Arkansas Democrat Gazette*.

Heard, K. (1998v, May 18). Anger remains after shootings in schoolyard. *Arkansas Democrat Gazette*.

Heard, K. (1998w, May 18). Kids' poems reflect grief, anger at shootings. *Arkansas Democrat Gazette*.

Heard, K. (1998x, May 18). School shooting suspects adjusting to jail routine. *Arkansas Democrat Gazette*.

Heard, K. (1998y, May 22). Shooting evokes memories at jonesboro. *Arkansas Democrat Gazette*.

Heard, K. (1999m, May 22). Senate approval of gun bill lauded. *Arkansas Democrat Gazette*.

Heard, K. (1998z, November 21). Funds for shooting victims given to jonesboro families. *Arkansas Democrat Gazette*.

Heard, K. (1999n, October 15). Panel says defense of boys not state's job. *Arkansas Democrat Gazette*.

Heard, K. (1998{, September 1). Westside fund used for dinner, to hire officer. *Arkansas Democrat Gazette*.

Heard, K. (1998|, September 5). Jonesboro school shooter, 12, plans to appeal guilty ruling. *Arkansas Democrat Gazette*.

Heard, K. (1998}, September 12). Crisis fund to seek help from judge. *Arkansas Democrat Gazette*.

Heard, K., Everett, K., Blomeley, S., & Uyttebrouck, O. (1998, March 25). "i never dreamed it would happen here'. *Arkansas Democrat Gazette*.

Howe, P. (1999a, July 1). Westside survivor has her say. *Arkansas Democrat Gazette*.

Howe, P. (1999b, March 25). Capitol hill remembers westside five with proclamation. *Arkansas Democrat Gazette*.

Jonesboro casualties. (1998, March 27). *Arkansas Democrat Gazette*.

Killings prompt call for review of youth laws. (1998, March 26). *Arkansas Democrat Gazette*.

Kordsmeier, J. (1998a, August 5). Bush to speak at award ceremony for 'heroic' slain westside teacher. *Arkansas Democrat Gazette*.

Kordsmeier, J. (1998b, July 11). Judge wants youths kept in jail longer. *Arkansas Democrat Gazette*.

Lemons, T. (1998a, June 18). Victim's mom in d.C. To push for gun control. *Arkansas Democrat Gazette*.

Lemons, T. (1998b, March 26). Juvenile crime bill may get new look. *Arkansas Democrat Gazette*.

McFarland, E. (1999, March 11). Panel ok's child sentencing bill. *Arkansas Democrat Gazette*.

McFarland, E. (1998, March 29). What age qualifies for adult punishment. *Arkansas Democrat Gazette*.

Meant to shoot over heads, 'scare them,' mitchell says. (1998, August 12). *Arkansas Democrat Gazette*.

Meisel, J. (1998a, April 17). Attorney for boy in jonesboro case gets the boot, cries foul. *Arkansas Democrat Gazette*.

Meisel, J. (1998b, April 26). Shooting puts schools on crisis alert. *Arkansas Democrat Gazette*.

Meisel, J. (1998c, March 29). Some border states tougher on charging teens as adults. *Arkansas Democrat Gazette*.

Moritz, R. (2000a, June 9). Boy merited insanity plea, justices told. *Arkansas Democrat Gazette*.

Moritz, R. (2000b, June 23). Boy shooter may be due new hearing. *Arkansas Democrat Gazette*.

Moritz, R. (2000c, June 24). Shooter, 13, to seek rehearing on high court's insanity ruling. *Arkansas Democrat Gazette*.

Moritz, R. (1999, October 21). State seeks out killer boys' civil suit. *Arkansas Democrat Gazette*.

O'Neal, R. (1998a, April 2). Huckabee absent to fulfill promise to family, aide says. *Arkansas Democrat Gazette*.

O'Neal, R. (1998b, June 3). Not exploiting shootings, author huckabee says. *Arkansas Democrat Gazette*.

O'Neal, R. (1998c, June 4). Books on kids, killing angers victims' kin. *Arkansas Democrat Gazette*.

O'Neal, R. (1999, March 23). State flags to fly at half-staff tomark westside shootings. *Arkansas Democrat Gazette*.

O'Neal, R. (1998d, March 27). 25 chosen to review state laws on juveniles. *Arkansas Democrat Gazette*.

Oman, N. E. (1998, March 26). Nation to train its eyes on state's juvenile justice system. *Arkansas Democrat Gazette*.

Oman, N. E. (1999, September 24). School killer's mental file open for attorney general. *Arkansas Democrat Gazette*.

Peters, D. (1998, April 9). With status as juveniles, mitchell, drew could cash in on their stories. *Arkansas Democrat Gazette*.

Pierce, R. (1998a, April 2). Go slow on juvenile justice legislation, experts tell panel. *Arkansas Democrat Gazette*.

Pierce, R. (1998b, April 3). Juvenile justice still hot topic for legislators. *Arkansas Democrat Gazette*.

Pierce, R. (1998c, April 23). Juvenile justice panel meets, gets outline of tasks. *Arkansas Democrat Gazette*.

Pierce, R. (1999a, February 18). State could keep killer kids in pen for life under bill. *Arkansas Democrat Gazette*.

Pierce, R. (1999b, March 21). Few bill to tighten youth justice enter, clear state legislature. *Arkansas Democrat Gazette*.

Pierce, R. (1998d, March 25). Huckabee cites 'chilling effect' of slayings, bids state to pray. *Arkansas Democrat Gazette*.

Police play tape of frantic 911 calls for help. (1998, March 27). *Arkansas Democrat Gazette*.

Porter, J. (1998, March 31). State 15th in youth killings, was 4th in '94, study says. *Arkansas Democrat Gazette*.

Roth, S. (1999, June 18). Hutchinson additions to juvenile justice bill pass in two house votes. *Arkansas Democrat Gazette*.

Roth, S. (1998, March 27). Solace, demands to cut firearm availability on lawmakers' lips. *Arkansas Democrat Gazette*.

Satter, L. (1999a, June 9). Violence eroding rights of students, its feared. *Arkansas Democrat Gazette*.

Satter, L. (1999b, September 23). Westside shooter returns to court to face federal charges. *Arkansas Democrat Gazette*.

Satter, L., & Heard, K. (1999, September 4). Second westside killer appears in u.S.Court. *Arkansas Democrat Gazette*.

Shameer, D. (1998a, March 25). Sixth-grader wonders, 'why wasn't it me?' *Arkansas Democrat Gazette*.

Shameer, D. (1998b, March 27). 43 of 251 students absent on first day back after tuesday's shooting. *Arkansas Democrat Gazette*.

Shameer, D. (1998c, March 28). Orders for flowers pour in. *Arkansas Democrat Gazette*.

Shameer, D., Werner, E., & Slivka, J. (1998, March 26). Shocked school copes also with media tumult. *Arkansas Democrat Gazette*.

Shooting victims. (1998, March 25). *Arkansas Democrat Gazette*.

Simmons, B. (1998a, April 26). Get tough on youth crime, polled Arkansans say. *Arkansas Democrat Gazette*.

Simmons, B. (1998b, May 30). Huckabee opens book with gunfire. *Arkansas Democrat Gazette*.

Slivka, J. (1998a, March 27). Community begins saying goodbye to the five slain. *Arkansas Democrat Gazette*.

Slivka, J. (1998b, March 28). The funerals start: Two girls laid to rest. *Arkansas Democrat Gazette*.

Still hospitalized. (1998, March 28). *Arkansas Democrat Gazette*.

Stumpe, J. (1998a, August 12). Other judges allow minors' insanity defense. *Arkansas Democrat Gazette*.

Stumpe, J. (1998b, March 25). Kids waited on slope, shot, officials say. *Arkansas Democrat Gazette*.

The Associated Press. (1998a, April 1). Older suspect in shootings accused of molesting, 2 say. *Arkansas Democrat Gazette*.

The Associated Press. (1998b, April 1). Ammunition clip used at Jonesboro in Congress' sights. *Arkansas Democrat Gazette*.

The Associated Press. (1998c, April 3). Casings found at ambush site came from rifles. *Arkansas Democrat Gazette*.

The Associated Press. (1998d, April 6). Jonesboro ambush plan was 11-year-old's, mother of 13-year-old says. *Arkansas Democrat Gazette*.

The Associated Press. (1998e, April 10). Johnson revises sex-abuse tale. *Arkansas Democrat Gazette*.

The Associated Press. (1998f, April 10). Songwriter turns feelings on shootings into music; profits to fund scholarships. *Arkansas Democrat Gazette*.

The Associated Press. (1998g, April 27). Judge in schoolyard shootings decides to open case to public. *Arkansas Democrat Gazette*.

The Associated Press. (2000, April 28). Westside killers back in court. *Arkansas Democrat Gazette*.

The Associated Press. (1998h, March 29). Scotland town looks to Jonesboro, mourns all over again. *Arkansas Democrat Gazette*.

The Associated Press. (1998i, March 29). 51% in poll favor trying boys as adults. *Arkansas Democrat Gazette*.

The Associated Press. (1998j, March 29). Divorce file shows parents fought over mitchell, brother. *Arkansas Democrat Gazette*.

The Associated Press. (1998k, March 30). Lawmakers debate tougher juvenile punishment. *Arkansas Democrat Gazette*.

The Associated Press. (1998l, March 30). Girl hurt in shooting says suspect was trouble. *Arkansas Democrat Gazette*.

The Associated Press. (1998m, September 1). Johnson's, Golden's parents want suit against them dropped. *Arkansas Democrat Gazette*.

Waite, M. (1998a, April 1). Minute of silence puts children, future on mind of nation. *Arkansas Democrat Gazette*.

Waite, M. (1998b, April 5). Teacher saw boy, 11, as 'friend'. *Arkansas Democrat Gazette*.

Waite, M. (1998c, August 11). Talk of shooting rare as school set to reopen. *Arkansas Democrat Gazette*.

Waite, M. (1998d, August 12). Day 'is like a storm' passing for families of victims, and boys. *Arkansas Democrat Gazette*.

Waite, M. (1998e, March 31). Westside students back in class; memorial service today for slain. *Arkansas Democrat Gazette*.

Waite, M., & Cofer, B. (1998, April 1). 9,000 mourn, seek strength in jonesboro. *Arkansas Democrat Gazette*.

Weapons, ammunition. (1998, March 28). *Arkansas Democrat Gazette*.

Werner, E. (1998a, April 9). Tragedy at Jonesboro draws checkbook journalists. *Arkansas Democrat Gazette*.

Werner, E. (1999, March 21). Close-knit town hopes life before loss returns. *Arkansas Democrat Gazette*.

Werner, E. (1998b, March 29). 'innocence is gone' but life goes on in tiny, quiet bono. *Arkansas Democrat Gazette*.

Werner, E., & Slivka, J. (1998, March 27). Town reels from shootings. *Arkansas Democrat Gazette*.

Whiteley, M. (1998a, March 27). Boys locked up, but for how long? *Arkansas Democrat Gazette*.

Whiteley, M. (1998b, March 28). Police detail arsenal 2 boys carried. *Arkansas Democrat Gazette*.

Whiteley, M., & O'Neal, R. (1998, March 26). Huckabee to create task force to revise juvenile justice code. *Arkansas Democrat Gazette*.

Denver Post   (1)

Bragg, R. (1998, August 12). Boys guilty of school slayings. *Denver Post*, p. A2.

The Courier Journal   (8)

Adams, J. (1998, December 6). School shooters sent many warnings: They brought guns to school, talked of violence. *The Courier Journal*.

Adams, J., Hall, C. R., Malone, J., & Riley, R. (1998, December 6). In search of why: Warning signs. *The Courier Journal*.

Hall, C. R. (1998a, December 6). Our schools' lost innocence: Shooting sprees desecrate the little red schoolhouse. *The Courier Journal*.

Hall, C. R. (1998b, December 6). Our school's lost innocence: Is violent pop culture holding kids hostage? *The Courier Journal*.

Malone, J. (1998, December 7). 3 paducah families ask: Why, michael? Victims' families say knowing more is vital for healing. *The Courier Journal*.

Malone, J., Riley, R., Hall, C. R., & Adams, J. (1998a, December 6). Who, what, where, when: Facts and memories. *The Courier Journal*.

Malone, J., Riley, R., Hall, C. R., & Adams, J. (1998b, December 7). After the tragedies: Who's got a good cause and who's cashing in? *The Courier Journal*.

Malone, J., Riley, R., Hall, C. R., & Adams, J. (1998c, December 8). How the other shooters' mindsets compare to luke woodham's. *The Courier Journal*.

The New York Times (8)

Allen, M. (1998, March 27). Bloodshed in a schoolyard: The media; shielding young suspects is no longer automatic. *The New York Times*.

Ayres Jr., B. D. (1998, March 26). Bloodshed in a schoolyard: The teacher; stunned residents find solace in act of heroism. *The New York Times*.

Bragg, R. (1998a, March 25). 5 are killed at school; boys 11 and 13, are held. *The New York Times*.

Bragg, R. (1998b, March 27). Bloodshed in schoolyard: The impact; determined to find healing in a good and decent place. *The New York Times*.

Goodman, W. (1998, March 26). Bloodshed in a schoolyard: The coverage - critics notebook; little news fails to slows tv reports. *The New York Times*.

Kifner, J., Bragg, R., Johnson, D., & Verhovek, S. H. (1998). From wild talk and friendship to five deaths in a schoolyard. *The New York Times*.

Lewin, L. (1998, March 26). Bloodshed in a schoolyard: The reasons; experts note access to guns lack of ties to adults. *The New York Times*.

Verhovek, S. H. (1998, March 27). Bloodshed in a schoolyard: The overview; in arkansas jail, one boy cries and the other studies the bible. *The New York Times*.

The Register Guard (1)

Dietz, D. (1998, March 25). Returning to thurston won't be easy. *The Register Guard*.

U.S. News and World Reports (1)

Blank, J., Vest, J., Parker, S., Witkin, G., & Walsh, K. T. (1998, April 6). The children of jonesboro. *U.S. News and World Reports*.

KIP KINKEL (Case 12)

Frontline (6)

Kirk, M., & Boyer, P. J. (2000a). The killer at thurston high; an interview with kristin kinkel. *Frontline* Retrieved October 7, 2004, from www.pbs.org/wgbh/pages/frontline/shows/kinkel/kip/kristin.html

Kirk, M., & Boyer, P. J. (2000b). The killer at thurston high; 111 years without parole. *Frontline* Retrieved October 7, 2004, from www.pbs.org/wgbh/pages/frontline/shows/kinkel/trial/

Kirk, M., & Boyer, P. J. (2000c). The killer at thurston high; kip's writings & statements. *Frontline* Retrieved October 7, 2004, from www.pbs.org/wgbh/pages/frontline/shows/kinkel/kip/writings.html

Kirk, M., & Boyer, P. J. (2000d). The killer at thurston high; transcript of kip kinkel's confession. *Frontline* Retrieved October 7, 2004, from www.pbs.org/wgbh/pages/frontline/shows/kinkel/etc/confesst.html

Kirk, M., & Boyer, P. J. (2000e). The killer at thurston high; chronology: Kip kinkel's life and events leading up to the horror of may 20-21, 1998. *Frontline* Retrieved October 7, 2004, from www.pbs.org/wgbh/pages/frontline/shows/kinkel/kip/cron.html

Kirk, M., & Boyer, P. J. (2000f). The killer at thurston high: Program transcript. *Frontline* Retrieved November 6, 2004, from http://www.pbs.org/wgbh/pages/frontline/shows/kinkel/etc/script.html

The Register Guard (183)

911 transcript. (1998, May 24). *The Register Guard.*

After the shooting: Important facts, events and a call for solutions. (1998, May 24). *The Register Guard.*

Associated Press. (1998a, June 9). Ryker family praised at NRA convention. *The Register Guard.*

Associated Press. (1998b, May 24). President links shootings to kids' exposure to violence. *The Register Guard.*

Bacon, L. (1998a, May 23). Somber mood settles on local schools. *The Register Guard.*

Bacon, L. (1998b, May 25). Jonesboro back to normal? Not yet. *The Register Guard.*

Beebe, E. (1998, May 24). Churches extend helping hand. *The Register Guard.*

Berney, J. (1998, June 1). Chalktalk: Find community solutions, not quick fix. *The Register Guard.*

Bigham, V. (1998, May 26). Poem for faith kinkel. *The Register Guard.*

Bishoff, D. (1998a, June 1). Don bishoff: Violent videos have impact. *The Register Guard.*

Bishoff, D. (1998b, June 3). Don bishoff: Readers debate violence issue. *The Register Guard.*

Bishoff, D. (1998c, June 10). Don bishoff: Good sense or censorship? *The Register Guard.*

Bishoff, D. (1998d, May 22). Don bishoff: When children fall to gunfire, rational explanations fails us. *The Register Guard.*

Bishoff, D. (1998e, May 25). Don bishoff: We must act, not just react. *The Register Guard.*

Bishoff, D. (1998f, May 27). Don bishoff: Thurston coach sees the bad, but stays focused on the good. *The Register Guard.*

Bishoff, D. (1998g, May 29). Don bishoff: Mental triage much needed. *The Register Guard.*

Bishop, B. (1998a, August 8). Judge puts hold on kinkel papers. *The Register Guard.*

Bishop, B. (1998b, December 16). Kinkel's attorney's want trial relocated. *The Register Guard.*

Bishop, B. (1998c, December 17). Lawyers argue searches illegal. *The Register Guard.*

Bishop, B. (1998d, December 20). Potential defense for kinkel emerges. *The Register Guard.*

Bishop, B. (1998e, December 24). Kinkel admitted killings. *The Register Guard.*

Bishop, B. (1998f, June 17). Kinkel faces range of charges in indictment. *The Register Guard.*

Bishop, B. (1998g, June 17). Kinkel arraigned as victims watch. *The Register Guard.*

Bishop, B. (1998h, May 25). Kinkels recalled as caring, committed. *The Register Guard.*

Bishop, B. (1998i, May 25). Shooting victims continue to improve. *The Register Guard.*

Bishop, B. (1998j, May 26). Students return to school seeking healing, courage. *The Register Guard.*

Bishop, B. (1998k, May 26). Chief seeks solutions far and wide. *The Register Guard.*

Bishop, B., & Mortenson, E. (1998, October 2). Unsealed documents give glimpse into killings. *The Register Guard.*

Bjornstad, R. (1998a, June 1). Gathering 'good start' to recovery. *The Register Guard.*

Bjornstad, R. (1998b, June 3). Speakers cast about for answer to violence. *The Register Guard.*

Bjornstad, R. (1998c, June 10). Springfield park district boosts kids' activities. *The Register Guard.*

Bjornstad, R. (1998d, May 23). Community gathers in healing. *The Register Guard.*

Bjornstad, R. (1998e, May 24). Boy's father reached out to stranger. *The Register Guard.*

Bjornstad, R. (1998f, May 26). Visits bring home reality of death. *The Register Guard.*

Bjornstad, R. (1998g, May 27). Boy's kindness, antics remembered. *The Register Guard.*

Boyd, J. (1998, May 22). School districts mobilize crisis teams. *The Register Guard.*

Bulletin: Thurston high shooter kills one. (1998, May 21). *The Register Guard.*

Buri, S. (1998a, May 22). Community faces blitz from media. *The Register Guard.*

Buri, S. (1998b, May 23). Some weary of media's presence. *The Register Guard.*

Buri, S. (1998c, May 28). Businesses offer compassion, aid. *The Register Guard.*

Buri, S. (1998d, May 29). 'thank god they're gone'. *The Register Guard.*

Capital conversations:Many factors can turn kids toward crime. (1998, June 1). *The Register Guard.*

Community members comment. (1998, May 23). *The Register Guard.*

Contributions to victim fund reach $33,000. (1998, May 27). *The Register Guard*.

Countdown to tragedy. (1998, June 14). *The Register Guard*.

DeSilver, D. (1998a, June 2). Gun control the answer to violence in many nations. *The Register Guard*.

DeSilver, D. (1998b, May 23). Weapons at schools a rarity in state. *The Register Guard*.

Dietz, D. (1998a, August 6). Bills target violence by youths. *The Register Guard*.

Dietz, D. (1998b, July 5). Schools struggling to keep guns away. *The Register Guard*.

Dietz, D. (1998c, June 6). Tragedy dogs thurston's graduation. *The Register Guard*.

Dietz, D. (1998d, June 29). Police taped re-enactment. *The Register Guard*.

Dietz, D. (1998e, May 23). Parents shoulder agony of life and death choice. *The Register Guard*.

Dietz, D. (1998f, May 24). Shooting plants new fears in kids' minds. *The Register Guard*.

Dietz, D. (1998g, May 25). Returning to thurston won't be easy. *The Register Guard*.

Dietz, D. (1998h, May 27). Grief, fear lurk in the hallways. *The Register Guard*.

Dietz, D. (1998i, May 30). Tragedy is personal to student journalists. *The Register Guard*.

Dietz, D., & Foster, A. (1998, May 31). Links to the heart: Treasures big and small spill from thurston's fence. *The Register Guard*.

Dietz, D., Neville, P., & Mortenson, E. (1998, June 14). Love against the odds: A kinkel family portrait. *The Register Guard*.

Drescher, M. (1998, May 24). Killing of teacher stuns adult student. *The Register Guard*.

Esteve, H. (1998a, June 11). President will visit springfield. *The Register Guard*.

Esteve, H. (1998b, May 22). Shootings add fuel to debate on gun control. *The Register Guard*.

Esteve, H. (1998c, May 23). Assault renews debate on crime prevention. *The Register Guard*.

Esteve, H. (1998d, May 31). Epidemic or overreaction: Observers agree that the thurston shootings aren't likely to result in significantly stricter gun laws in oregon. *The Register Guard*.

Foster, A. (1998a, May 22). Gathering spots helps students cope. *The Register Guard*.

Foster, A. (1998b, May 23). Public's 20-20 hindsight frustrates police. *The Register Guard*.

Foster, A. (1998c, May 31). Sidestreets: Let's not forget that sometimes kids are just kids. *The Register Guard*.

Graduates ready to leave, but not to forget thurston. (1998, June 7). *The Register Guard*.

Grievous violence unusual at area schools. (1998, May 22, 1998). *The Register Guard*.

Hartman, J. (1998a, June 13). Shooting probe proving costly. *The Register Guard*.

Hartman, J. (1998b, May 23). Boy charged as adult on 4 counts of murder. *The Register Guard*.

Hartman, J. (1998c, May 27). Rescuers wrestled with private fears. *The Register Guard*.

Hartman, J. (1998d, May 29). Officers sorting truth from rumors. *The Register Guard*.

Hartman, J. (1998e, May 30). Ribbons tie hopes to sorrow. *The Register Guard*.

Hartman, J., & Foster, A. (1998, May 26). Family, friends, mourn ben walker. *The Register Guard*.

Harvey, T. (1998, May 27). Resilient students hold the keys to change. *The Register Guard*.

Harwood, J. (1998a, May 22). Painful news raises a host of questions. *The Register Guard*.

Harwood, J. (1998b, May 23). Counselors' goal is getting kids to share feelings. *The Register Guard*.

Harwood, J. (1998c, May 23). Floral tributes make thurston fence a shrine to tragedy, hope. *The Register Guard*.

Harwood, J. (1998d, May 24). Grabbing gun just 'instinct'. *The Register Guard*.

A heartening response: Tragedy shows community at its best. (1998, May 27). *The Register Guard*.

Hospital releases shooting victim case. (1998, June 5). *The Register Guard*.

How to help, how to get help. (1998, May 24). *The Register Guard*.

Kayfes, D. (1998, May 31). Write on: Family's guns not that easy to destroy. *The Register Guard*.

Keefer, B. (1998a, May 22). Real-life disaster claims fantasy-loving student. *The Register Guard*.

Keefer, B. (1998b, May 31). Potentially deadly youngsters not common. *The Register Guard*.

Kidd, J. (1998a, May 22). Heroes: Jake ryker and 3 other boys are credited with disarming the shooter, preventing him from taking more lives. *The Register Guard*.

Kidd, J. (1998b, May 23). Teen-agers' bravery earns praise amid the anguish. *The Register Guard*.

Kinkel defense gets more time to prepare. (1998, October 14). *The Register Guard*.

Kitzhaber reacts with prevention ideas. (1998, May 30). *The Register Guard.*

Kristin kinkel's statement. (1998, May 27). *The Register Guard.*

Local churches respond to tragedy. (1998, May 24). *The Register Guard.*

McCowan, K. (1998a, June 2). Karen mccowan: Ribbon drive aiming high. *The Register Guard.*

McCowan, K. (1998b, June 4). Karen mccowan: Doctors lobby against guns. *The Register Guard.*

McCowan, K. (1998c, May 22). Karen mccowan: Reducing access to firearms one way to stop the slaughter. *The Register Guard.*

McCowan, K. (1998d, May 23). Karen mccowan: 'system' failed thurston teens. *The Register Guard.*

McCowan, K. (1998e, May 26). Karen mccowan: Let analysis begin within. *The Register Guard.*

McCowan, K. (1998f, May 28). Karen mccowan: Now we listen to cries for help. *The Register Guard.*

McCowan, K. (1998g, May 30). Karen mccowan: Teachers put lives on line. *The Register Guard.*

McDermott, T. (1998, May 25). Could northwest be losing its cool? *The Register Guard.*

A message from jonesboro; community events; how to cope. (1998, May 26). *The Register Guard.*

Molaski, S. (1998, May 25). Birth to three: Rewards of anger control worth the work. *The Register Guard.*

Mortenson, E. (1998a, August 31). Kinkel marks birthday with transfer to jail. *The Register Guard.*

Mortenson, E. (1998b, December 16). Sister to appear on national tv. *The Register Guard.*

Mortenson, E. (1998c, December 17). Sister expresses support for kinkel. *The Register Guard.*

Mortenson, E. (1998d, July 5). Insanity defense no smooth legal path. *The Register Guard.*

Mortenson, E. (1998e, July 19). Kinkel headed to county jail soon. *The Register Guard.*

Mortenson, E. (1998f, July 28). Warrant records for kinkel case will be unsealed. *The Register Guard.*

Mortenson, E. (1998g, June 4). Putting away the heartache: Thurston students dismantle memorial. *The Register Guard.*

Mortenson, E. (1998h, June 7). Sidestreets: Senior citizens convey insight, grief for thurston students. *The Register Guard.*

Mortenson, E. (1998i, May 22). Tragedy hits home: Shootings in springfield. *The Register Guard.*

Mortenson, E. (1998j, May 23). School, law officers defend decision to release kinkel. *The Register Guard.*

Mortenson, E. (1998k, May 23). Panel deciding how to allocate thurston funds. *The Register Guard.*

Mortenson, E. (1998l, May 24). Mending fence links broken hearts. *The Register Guard.*

Mortenson, E. (1998m, May 24). Teacher sees lesson in shooting. *The Register Guard.*

Mortenson, E. (1998n, May 27). Where innocence slumped to the floor. *The Register Guard.*

Mortenson, E. (1998o, May 28). Smile, touch give teresa's family and friends hope. *The Register Guard.*

Mortenson, E. (1998p, May 29). Minister hopes tragedy will bring about action. *The Register Guard.*

Mortenson, E. (1998q, May 30). Kitzhaber: Help, not blame, useful. *The Register Guard.*

Mortenson, E. (1998r, October 3). Records track kinkel detention. *The Register Guard.*

Mortenson, E. (1998s, October 22). Kinkel appears a model prisoner. *The Register Guard.*

Mosley, J. (1998a, June 4). Neighbors of bill kinkel's mom gather to pray. *The Register Guard.*

Mosley, J. (1998b, June 11). Ryker's dad fears gun backlash. *The Register Guard.*

Mosley, J. (1998c, May 22). Kinkels: Neighbors and friends paint a picture of a level-headed family whose son had a fascination with guns. *The Register Guard.*

Mosley, J. (1998d, May 23). Kinkel's father abhorred guns, friends insist. *The Register Guard.*

Mosley, J. (1998e, May 24). Humble hero took his chance: "i saw her shot and said, 'that's enough'." *The Register Guard.*

Mosley, J. (1998f, May 24). Aftermath: Young suspect is under a suicide watch, and his principal defends the school. *The Register Guard.*

Mosley, J. (1998g, May 26). Kristin kinkel remains in seclusion while tending to her murdered parents affairs. *The Register Guard.*

Mosley, J. (1998h, May 27). Venue, sanity expected to be key issues. *The Register Guard.*

Mosley, J. (1998i, May 28). Teachers' memorial service friday. *The Register Guard.*

Mosley, J. (1998j, May 29). Victim on his feet after ordeal. *The Register Guard.*

Mosley, J. (1998k, May 30). Kinkels inspire 'joy, remembrance'. *The Register Guard.*

Neville, P. (1998a, June 3). Communities reach for security, solace. *The Register Guard.*

Neville, P. (1998b, June 16). Criminologist discerns pattern in violent teens. *The Register Guard.*

Neville, P. (1998c, May 27). Young hero back, briefly, at thurston. *The Register Guard.*

Robertson, L. (1998a, June 5). City workers donate days off to dawna nickolauson. *The Register Guard.*

Robertson, L. (1998b, May 23). Crews' training, parental feelings collided. *The Register Guard.*

Robertson, L. (1998c, May 23). Team effort saves lives of students. *The Register Guard.*

Robertson, L. (1998d, May 27). Colleagues, students feel 'empty space'. *The Register Guard.*

Robertson, L. (1998e, May 27). Experts: Let kids talk about feelings. *The Register Guard.*

Robertson, L. (1998f, May 28). Vigils bring connection, hope. *The Register Guard.*

Robertson, L. (1998g, May 29). Governor wants strict gun policy. *The Register Guard.*

Robertson, L. (1998h, May 30). Law allows detention of youths in gun cases. *The Register Guard.*

Robertson, L., and Dietz, Diane. (1998i, May 22). Bullets didn't discriminate among shooting victims. *The Register Guard.*

The search for solutions. (1998, June 1). *The Register Guard.*

Shannon, T. (1998a, June 1). Study: Suicide, drugs trouble teens. *The Register Guard.*

Shannon, T. (1998b, June 4). Police reveal brave act of another wounded student. *The Register Guard.*

Shannon, T. (1998c, May 22). Sure violence cure? Lock schools down. *The Register Guard.*

Shannon, T. (1998d, May 28). Stuffed animals pour in as reply to needs of kids. *The Register Guard.*

Shannon, T. (1998e, May 29). Song a gift of healing offered to victims. *The Register Guard.*

Shannon, T. (1998f, May 31). Group gains 71 firearms during gun turn-in. *The Register Guard.*

Shannon, T. (1998g, May 31). Quilters plan a keepsake for thurston. *The Register Guard.*

Shared tragedy unites gathering. (1998, June 10). *The Register Guard.*

Sheldon journalist has new perspective on safety of schools. (1998, May 30). *The Register Guard.*

Sixth student added to hero fund. (1998, June 5). *The Register Guard.*

Suggestions offered. (1998, May 26). *The Register Guard.*

Swanson, C. (1998, June 8). Shooting victim shows marked improvement. *The Register Guard.*

Teens: Vent on violence. (1998, May 25). *The Register Guard.*

'they would want us to teach our children. Right and wrong'. (1998, May 29). *The Register Guard.*

Trying to help: Recollections of the kinkels. (1998, June 14). *The Register Guard.*

Victims' status; how to give and get help. (1998, May 26). *The Register Guard.*

Victims' status; kinkel service; community events; benefit concerts. (1998, May 28). *The Register Guard.*

Warning signs start at age 2. (1998, May 31). *The Register Guard.*

We can't hide from social violence. (1998, May 23). *The Register Guard.*

Welch, B. (1998, May 24). Sidestreets: Split by river and attitudes, two cities unite for healing. *The Register Guard.*

What they said. (1998, May 22). *The Register Guard.*

What visitors left behind. (1998, May 31). *The Register Guard.*

Williams, K. (1998a, May 31). State looks at solutions to violence in schools. *The Register Guard.*

Williams, K. (1998b, May 31). For the complex challenges of today's families, schools may still be the last best chance. *The Register Guard.*

Wright, J. (1998a, June 1). Crowd extols 'spirit of god'. *The Register Guard.*

Wright, J. (1998b, June 11). Teen's recovery an amazing case. *The Register Guard.*

Wright, J. (1998c, May 22). Jonesboro still recovering after shooting. *The Register Guard.*

Wright, J. (1998d, May 22). Little protection at closed campus. *The Register Guard.*

Wright, J. (1998e, May 24). Warning signs clear, need heeding. *The Register Guard.*

Wright, J. (1998f, May 25). Congregations pray, hear message of hope, compassion. *The Register Guard.*

Wright, J. (1998g, May 26). Children taught to kill, author says. *The Register Guard*.
Wright, J. (1998h, May 28). Surgical advances kept students alive. *The Register Guard*.
Wright, J. (1998i, May 29). Helping youth key, mayor says. *The Register Guard*.
Wright, J., & Hartman, J. (1998, May 28). Suspect's dad sought national guard help. *The Register Guard*.

CHAPTER 1

MEDIA SOURCES

Evening Tribune (11)
Cook, J. (1979, January 30). It felt 'like an electric shock'. *The Evening Tribune*, pp. B-3.
Cook, J., & Gilmore, J. (1979, January 30). School reopens;'Life must go on'. *The Evening Tribune*, pp. A-1, A-6.
Cook, J., & Theskin, J. (1979, January 29). 'No, no, don't tell me that he's dead'. *The Evening Tribune*, pp. A-1, A-8.
Durham, J. (1979, January 30). Secrecy cloaks girl sniper. *The Evening Tribune*, pp. A-1, A-6.
Gerchen, M. (1979, January 30). Psychiatrist sees rise in kids' crimes here. *The Evening Tribune*, pp. B-1, B-3.
Gerchen, M. (1979, January 30). Why did SWAT stand by? 'No present danger'. *The Evening Tribune*, pp. B-1.
Gilmore, J. (1979, January 30). Victims die trying to help. *The Evening Tribune*, pp. B-1.
Grambau, H. (1979, January 30). Brenda Spencer: 'Nice' or frightening? *The Evening Tribune*, pp. B-1, B-3.
Saldana, F. (1979, January 30). 'I was just buying time'. *The Evening Tribune*, pp. A-6.
Stevens, G., & Weigand, S. (1979, January 29). Brenda's Reason; 'I hate Monday's'. *The Evening Tribune*, pp. A-1, A-9.
Welles, D. (1979, January 30). 'Shakes' come later in emergency. *The Evening Tribune*, pp. B-3.

New York Times (2)
Hollie, P. G. (1979, January 31). Coast sniper vowed she would 'do something big'. *The New York Times*, pp. A-13.
San Diego girl slays 2 with rifle and wounds 9 on school grounds. (1979, January 30). *The New York Times*, pp. A-10.

SignOnSandiego.com (1)
Branscomb, L. W. (2001). *A fatal day in 1979*. The Union-Tribune Publishing Company. Retrieved July 12, 2002, from the World Wide Web: www.signonsandiego.com/news/metro/santana/20010309-9999_1n9spencer.html

San Diego Tribune (1)
McLaren, J. (1989, January 18). Stockton slaughter recalls '79 schoolyard horror here. *The San Diego Tribune*, pp. A-8.

San Diego Union (14)
Brenda Spencer given neurological tests. (1979, March 21). *The San Diego Union*, pp. B-2.
Cannon, C. M. (1979, March 29). Emergency appeal says Spencer has epilepsy. *The San Diego Union*, pp. B-1, B-6.
Cannon, C. M. (1979, January 30). The schoolyard: Horror to some, show for others. *The San Diego Union*, pp. A-1, A-8.
Cannon, C. M. (1979, January 31). Sniper suspect, 16, may be tried as adult. *The San Diego Union*, pp. A1, A-4.
City school flags at half-staff. (1979, January 30). *The San Diego Union*, pp. A-9.
Cubbison, G. (1979, January 30). Police negotiator was instrumental in ending crisis at San Carlos. *The San Diego Union*, pp. A-9.
Goleman, D. (1990, January 16). After the horror: More children than ever witnessing brutal violence - and they need help. *The San Diego Union*, pp. D-1.
Judge schedules diagnostic studies prior to sentencing Brenda Spencer. (1979, December 1). *The San Diego Union*, pp. B-4.
Lopez, M. (1979, January 30). Drastically changing moods marked life of teen-age sniping suspect. *The San Diego Union*, pp. A-1, A-8.
Scarr, L. (1979, April 12). Epilepsy - caused violence extremely rare, 3 specialists report. *The San Diego Union*, pp. B-3.
Scott-Blair, M. (1979, January 30). Slain schoolmen knew of danger; Aide describes scenes of horror. *The San Diego Union*, pp. A-9.

Sniper victims indentified. (1979, January 30). *The San Diego Union*, pp. A-9.

Standefer, J. (1979, January 31). Reactions to sniper hint youths' potential for violence. *The San Diego Union*, pp. B-1, B-5.

Standefer, J. (1979, January 30). Sniper attack leaves 2 dead, 9 hurt in schoolyard; girl, 16, surrenders: Youngsters scramble for their lives in hail of rifle fire. *The San Diego Union*, pp. A-1, A-8, A-9.

San Diego Union-Tribune (4)

Gaines, J. (1994, December 17). On cruelty to children and animals. *The San Diego Union-Tribune*, pp. B-1.

Krueger, A. (1993, January 22). No parole for sniper who hated Mondays: She killed 2, wounded 9 in '79 San Carlos spree. *The San Diego Union-Tribune*, pp. B-1.

Schoolyard killer Spencer delays hearing. (1998, January 21). *The San Diego Union-Tribune*, pp. B-8.

Wolf, L. (1998, March 26). Sniper victims recall '79 tragedy here. *The San Diego Union-Tribune*, pp. A-1.

SCHOLARLY SOURCES

American Psychiatric Association. (2000). *Diagnostic and statistical manual of mental disorders (DSM-IV-TR)* (IV ed.). Washington, DC: American Psychiatric Association.

APA. (2000). *Diagnostic and statistical manual of mental disorders*. Washington, DC: American Psychiatric Association.

Bowlby. (1982). *Attachment & Loss: Loss and Depression* (Vol. III). New York City: Basic Books.

Chu, J. A., & Dill, D. L. (1990). Dissociative Symptoms in Relation to Childhood Physical and Sexual Abuse. *American Journal of Psychiatry, 147*(7), 887-892.

Damasio, H., Grabowski, T., Frank, R., Galaburda, A. M., & Damasio, A. R. (2004). The return of Phineas Gage: Clues about the brain from the skull of a famous person. In J. T. Cacioppo & G. Berntson (Eds.), *Social Neuroscience: Key Readings*. Brighton, UK: Psychology Press.

Harwood, V. (2005). *Diagnosing 'Disorderly' Children: Critical Perspectives on a Global Phenomenon*. Florence, Kentucky: Routledge.

Herman, J., & Hirschman, L. (1977). Father-daughter incest. *Signs: Journal of women in Culture and Society, 2*(4), 735-756.

Hoffman, A. (1971/2002). *Steal this book*. New York: Four Walls Eight Windows.

Kuhn, T. S. (1962). *The Structure of Scientific Revolutions* Chicago: University of Chicago.

Larkins, G. (1971). Law and order: The policeman is our friend—off the "pig". *Social Education, 35*(5), 503-506.

Lewis, D. O. (1998). *Guilty by reason of insanity*. New York: Random House.

Lewis, D. O., Moy, E., Jackson, L. D., Aaronson, R., Ritvo, U., Settu, S., et al. (1985). Biopsychosocial characteristics of children who later murder: A prospective study. *American Journal of Psychiatry, 142*(10), 1161-1166.

Lewis, D. O., Pincus, J. H., & Bard, B. (1988). Neuropsychiatric, psychoeducational, and family characteristics of fourteen juveniles condemned to death in the United States. *American Journal of Psychiatry, 145*, 584-589.

Lewis, D. O., Yeager, C. A., Swica, Y., Pincus, J. H., & Lewis, M. (1997). Objective Documentation of Child Abuse and Dissociation in 12 Murderers With Dissociative Identity Disorder. *154*(12), 1703-1710.

McLean, L. (2004). Childhood sexual abuse and adult psychiatric diagnosis : Current views and clinical implications. *Psychiatry, 15*(2), 29-34.

Newman, K. S., Fox, C., Harding, D. J., Mehta, J., & Roth, W. (2004). *Rampage: the social roots of school shootings*. New York: Basic Books.

Newsreel Film Collective, & Black Panther Party (Writer) (1968). Off the Pig. USA.

O'Toole, M. E. (2000). *The School Shooter: A threat assessment perspective*. Quantico, VA: FBI, National Center for the Analysis of Violent Crime.

Pincus, J. H. (2001). *Base instincts; What makes killers kill*. New York: W.W. Norton & Co. .

Raine, A. R. (2002). The role of prefrontal deficits, low autonomic arousal, and early health factors in the development of antisocial and aggressive behavior in children. *Journal of child psychology & psychiatry & allied disciplines, 43*(4), 417-435.

Raine, A. R., Lencz, T., Bihrle, S., LaCasse, L., & Colletti, P. (2000). Reduced prefrontal gray matter volume and reduced autonomic activity in antisocial personality disorder. *Archive of General Psychology, 57*, 119-127.

Raine, A. R., Meloy, J. R., Bihrle, S., Stoddard, J., LaCasse, L., & Buchsbaum, M. S. (1998). Reduced prefrontal and increased subcortical brain functioning assessed using positron emission tomography in predatory and affective murderers. *Behavioral Science and the Law, 16*(3), 319-332.

Talvi, S. (1999, August 17). Criminal Procedure. *Mother Jones*.

Treimen, D. (1986). Epilepsy and violence: medical and legal issues. *Epilepsia, 27*(Suppl 2), S77-104.

Vossekuil, B., Fein, R., Reddy, M., Borum, R., & Modzeleski, W. (2002). *The final report and findings of the safe school initiative: Implications for the prevention of school attacks in the United States*. Washington, DC: U.S. Department of Education, Office of Elementary and Secondary Education, Safe and Drug Free Schools Program; and U.S. Secret Service, Nation Threat Assessment Center.

CHAPTER 2

MEDIA SOURCES

Berkshire Eagle   (49)

Bahlman, D. R. (1998, July 23). Wayne Lo is denied new trial. *The Berkshire Eagle*, pp. 1, 4.

Black, M. (1992, December 19). Reaction of high school students to killings at Simon's Rock worry some in community. *The Berkshire Eagle*, pp. 4.

Black, M. (1992, December 16). Suspect bigot, senior says. *The Berkshire Eagle*, pp. 5.

Butler, M. G. (1992, December 18). Downing says investigators applying "full-court press". *The Berkshire Eagle*, pp. 7.

Butler, M. G. (1992, December 16). Pittsfield store sold the SKS assault rifle. *The Berkshire Eagle*, pp. 1, 4.

Daley, L. (1992, December 20). Counselors: Teens show signs of holiday stress. *The Berkshire Eagle*, pp. 5.

Drohan, G. (1992, December 23). Rampage echoed Williams shooting. *The Berkshire Eagle*, pp. 1, 7.

Etkind, S. (1994, January 6). 16 jurors picked from pool of 100 to hear Lo case. *The Berkshire Eagle*, pp. 1B.

Etkind, S. (1994, January 29). Defense rests without calling Lo to stand. *Berkshire Eagle*, pp. 1, 4.

Etkind, S. (1994, January 22). Defense: Lo fired in grip of delusion. *Berkshire Eagle*, pp. 1, 4.

Etkind, S. (1994, January 27). Doctor: Lo said God ordered him to punish sinners. *Berkshire Eagle*, pp. 1, 4.

Etkind, S. (1994, January 8). For the defense... *Berkshire Eagle*, pp. 1, 8.

Etkind, S. (1994, January 21). Inmate says Lo tod him 'he didn't feel nothing'. *Berkshire Eagle*, pp. 1, 4.

Etkind, S. (1994, January 8). Jurors view Simon's Rock. *Berkshire Eagle*, pp. 1, 8.

Etkind, S. (1994, January 26). Lo called schizophrenic, sensitive lover of guns. *Berkshire Eagle*, pp. 1, 4.

Etkind, S. (1994, January 25). Lo's father: God told him 'to do a job'. *Berkshire Eagle*, pp. 1, 4.

Etkind, S. (1994, January 28). Lo's mother takes stand for defense. *Berkshire Eagle*, pp. 1, 4.

Etkind, S. (1994, January 15). Officer says Lo reported rampage. *Berkshire Eagle*, pp. 1, 6.

Etkind, S. (1994, January 11). Prosecutor: Lo plotted killings for nine months. *The Berkshire Eagle*, pp. 1, 4.

Etkind, S. (1994, January 8). The prosecutors: More than a job. *Berkshire Eagle*, pp. 8.

Etkind, S. (1994, January 13). Shooting victims recount a night of terror. *Berkshire Eagle*, pp. 1, 6.

Etkind, S. (1994, January 20). Student says Lo's goal was to kill many people. *Berkshire Eagle*, pp. 1, 4.

Etkind, S. (1994, February 4). Wayne Lo guilty; Sentenced to life without parole. *The Berkshire Eagle*, pp. 1, 4.

For Lo, buying assault rifle piece of cake. (1992, December 17). *The Berkshire Eagle*, pp. 1, 4.

Gentile, D. (1992, December 20). College's silence irks faculty, alumni. *Berkshire Eagle*, pp. 5.

Gentile, D. (1992, December 20). College's silence irks faculty, alumni. *Berkshire Eagle*, pp. B5.

Gentile, D. (1992, December 19). Did campus gunman telegraph act? Expert says no. *The Berkshire Eagle*, pp. 1, 4.

Gentile, D. (1992, December 19). Did campus gunman telegraph act? Expert says no. *Berkshire Eagle*, pp. A1, A4.

Gentile, D. (1992, December 18). The night all hell broke loose on campus. *The Berkshire Eagle*, pp. 1, 8.

Gentile, D. (1992). The night all hell broke out on campus. *The Berkshire Eagle*.

Gentile, D. (1994, February 4). Defense couldn't sell insanity plea to jury. *The Berkshire Eagle*, pp. 1, 4.

Gentile, D. (1994, February 4). For survivors, verdict brings sense of closure. *The Berkshire Eagle*, pp. 1, 4.

Gentile, D. (1995, October 25). Dean's inaction challenged in Lo rampage. *The Berkshire Eagle*, pp. 1, 4.

Gold, G. (1992, December 16). The day after, stunned college, town wonder why. *The Berkshire Eagle*, pp. 5.

Lahr, E. G. (1992, December 16). Back in Montana they liked Wayne Lo. *The Berkshire Eagle*, pp. 5.

Lahr, E. G. (1992, December 16). College community mourns two "sparks". *The Berkshire Eagle*, pp. 1, 5.

Lahr, E. G. (1992, December 16). "Hold on," she told him, "there's a guy with a gun". *The Berkshire Eagle*, pp. 1, 4.

Lahr, E. G. (1994, January 14). Lo victims: Shock, brave jokes. *Berkshire Eagle*, pp. 1, 4.

Pratt, A. (1992, December 17). At Simon's Rock, question is: Why? *The Berkshire Eagle*, pp. 1, 4.

Pratt, A. (1992, December 22). Beavers gains, faces long recovery. *The Berkshire Eagle*, pp. B1, B5.

Pratt, A. (1992). College outlines the steps it took. *Berkshire Eagle*, pp. B5.

Pratt, A. (1992, December 17). The day "our world collapsed". *The Berkshire Eagle*, pp. 1, 4.

Pratt, A. (1992, December 18). Friends bid a fond farewell. *The Berkshire Eagle*, pp. 1, 6.

Pratt, A. (1992, December 22). One week after rampage, Barrington still in shock. *The Berkshire Eagle*, pp. 1, 5.

Pratt, A. (1992, December 16). Student goes on rampage. *The Berkshire Eagle*, pp. 1, 4.

Pratt, A. (1992, December 18). Students say Lo talked of rampage. *The Berkshire Eagle*, pp. 1, 6.

Pratt, A. (1992, December 17). What happened and when; Barrington police on scene within minutes of first shot. *The Berkshire Eagle*, pp. 4.

Pratt, A. (1992, December 23). Wounded student plans to return to Simon's Rock. *The Berkshire Eagle*, pp. 1, 4.

Silwa, C. (1992, December 18). Other states' gun laws to be viewed by Mass. *The Berkshire Eagle*, pp. 7.

Berkshire Record (1)

McChesney, S. (2002, Desember 13). Simon's Rock College - a decade later. *Berkshire Record*, pp. 1, 4.

Billings Gazette (33)

Appeal to be heard in college campus shooting spree. (1998, May 4). *Billings Gazette*, pp. 1C.

Billings teenager opens fire on Massachusets campus 2 killed, 4 wounded. (1992, December 16). *Billings Gazette*, pp. 1A.

Billings youth denies charges in campus shootings. (1993, January 6). *Billings Gazette*, pp. 9A.

College killer's defender says client was psychotic. (1994, January 22). *Billings Gazette*, pp. 2C.

Ehli, N. (1992, December 16). Shocked family, friends recall youth as a talented violinist. *Billings Gazette*, pp. 1A.

Expert says Lo is 'on vacation'. (1994, January 30). *Billings Gazette*, pp. 8C.

Experts: Lo knew attack was wrong. (1994, February 1). *Billings Gazette*, pp. 9A.

Father: Lo had 'different soul inside'. (1994, January 25). *Billings Gazette*, pp. 1B.

Friends of Lo receive counseling. (1992, December 18). *Billings Gazette*, pp. 1C.

Husband heard shots, wife's scream on the phone. (1992, December 17). *Billings Gazette*, pp. 11A.

Insanity plea possible for Lo. (1993, March 4). *Billings Gazette*, pp. 7A.

Jurors weigh Lo verdict in campus slayings. (1994, February 2). *Billings Gazette*, pp. 4C.

Jury selection to start in college shootings. (1994, January 5). *Billings Gazette*, pp. 3C.

Kennedy speaks at Simon's Rock. (1993, May 16). *Billings Gazette*, pp. 2A.

Life in prison: Billings student opened fire on college campus. (1994, February 4). *Billings Gazette*, pp. 1A.

Lo called 911 after shootings. (1994, January 14). *Billings Gazette*, pp. 4C.
Lo 'calm, coherent' before shooting. (1992, December 25). *Billings Gazette*, pp. 1C.
Lo jury deliberates. (1994, February 3). *Billings Gazette*, pp. 2C.
Lo liked weapons, hated father, friends say at trial. (1994, January 26). *Billings Gazette*, pp. 8C.
Long trial expected for Billings teenager. (1994, January 6). *Billings Gazette*, pp. 3C.
Loophole in Massachusets gun law let Lo buy rifle. (1992, December 22). *Billings Gazette*, pp. 5C.
Lo's attorneys prepare insanity defense in shooting. (1993, May 12). *Billings Gazette*, pp. 6C.
Lo's friend testified about 'Last Supper'. (1994, January 13). *Billings Gazette*, pp. 5C.
Lo's last exam gave cryptic warning. (1994, January 12). *Billings Gazette*, pp. 4C.
Mother: Jailed Lo is 'empty'. (1994, January 28). *Billings Gazette*, pp. 4C.
Murder suspect left note and drawing. (1993, August 14). *Billings Gazette*, pp. 4B.
Prosecutor: Lo 'cold, brutal'. (1994, January 11). *Billings Gazette*, pp. 9A.
Psychiatrist: Lo was acting for God. (1994, January 27). *Billings Gazette*, pp. 4C.
School looks for answers to shooting. (1992, December 17). *Billings Gazette*, pp. 1A.
Search in killing spree challenged. (1993, August 4). *Billings Gazette*, pp. 1B.
Student's lawyers ask for change of venue. (1993, August 13). *Billings Gazette*, pp. 3C.
Tynan, T. (1992, December 26). Delivery to Lo not stopped. *Billings Gazette*, pp. 1C.
Wayne Lo case: Opening statements expected in Monday. (1994, January 8). *Billings Gazette*, pp. 1B.

Boston Globe (29)

Carton, B. (1994, January 12). Trial watch this week, real-life courtroom dramas put "L.A. Law" to shame. Lorena Bobbitt. *Boston Globe*, pp. 57.
Extension given in college slaying case. (1993, March 31). *Boston Globe*, pp. 29.
Flint, A. (1992, December 16). Alternative college was born in the 1960's. *Boston Globe*, pp. 39.
Galen C. Gibson, 18 was Simon Rock freshman. (1992, December 18). *Boston Globe*, pp. 71.
Gorov, L., & Roche, B. J. (1992, December 16). Wayne Lo showed his world two personalities. *Boston Globe*, pp. 38.
Gun proposals shelved by town. (1994, May 25). *Boston Globe*, pp. 83.
Higgins, R. (2001, April 19). Working past grief father honors slain son in battle against gun violence. *Boston Globe*, pp. B1.
Hohler, B. (1994, March 29). Curb on plea of insanity is let stand Supreme Court action retains Montana law that limits use. *Boston Globe*, pp. 1.
Hohler, B. (1994, May 26). Trade renewal for China seen in next 2 days. *Boston Globe*, pp. 2.
Jury being chosen in murder trial. (1994, January 6). *Boston Globe*, pp. 29.
Jury tours scene of college killings. (1994, January 8). *Boston Globe*, pp. 19.
Krupa, G. (1993, December 20). Cheap imports flood weapon market. *Boston Globe*, pp. 1.
Lahr, E. G. (1997, December 10). College said to settle two suits from '92 shootings. *Boston Globe*, pp. D19.
Laidler, J. (1992, December 20). Gloucester student is laid to rest 500 gather to remember intelligence, spirit of college slaying victim. *Boston Globe*, pp. 62.
Locy, T. (1993, April 8). Witnesses disagree on limiting gun buys. *Boston Globe*, pp. 30.
McGrory, B. (1992, December 25). At Simon's Rock, officials recall the day of killings. *Boston Globe*, pp. 37.
McGrory, B. (1992, December 19). Injured students to return to school where 2 men slain. *Boston Globe*, pp. 14.
McGrory, B. (1992, December 17). Questions abound on rampage weapon purchase, ammo mailing eyed. *Boston Globe*, pp. 37.
Murder made easy. (1992, December 17). *Boston Globe*, pp. 18.
Murphy, S. P. (1992, December 16). Buying weapon was easy. *Boston Globe*, pp. 1.
New trial sought in campus killings. (1998, May 5). *Boston Globe*, pp. B4.
No verdict yet in Wayne Lo case. (1994, February 3). *Boston Globe*, pp. 64.
Saunders, M. (1992, December 17). Sick of it all: An emblem for anger, or just a band? *Boston Globe*, pp. 78.
SJC upholds murder conviction. (1998, July 23). *Boston Globe*, pp. C6.
State toyed with weapons ban. (2000, December 31). *Boston Globe*, pp. D6.
Tong, B. Q. M. (1992, December 22). Suspicious mailings worrisome on campus. *Boston Globe*, pp. 25.
Trial move sought in campus killings. (1993, July 29). *Boston Globe*, pp. 34.
Victim's kin sue Simon's Rock. (1994, March 3). *Boston Globe*, pp. 25.

Wong, D. S. (1993, December 16). Panel OK's gun control bills. *Boston Globe*, pp. 82.

Scholarly and Other Sources

"Zach". (2007). Official Wayne Lo Store/ Wayne Lo/ Interview. from http://www.skidloshop .com/2.html

A.P.A. (2000). *Diagnostic and statistical manual of mental disorders (DSM-IV-TR)* (IV ed.). Washington, DC: American Psychiatric Association.

Coulter, A. (2003, July 10). We'll let you know when you're being censored. *Jewish World Review*.

Erikson, E. H. (1968). *Identity: Youth and Crisis*. New York: Norton.

Freud, A. (1967). *The Ego and the Mechanisms of Defense*. Madison, CT: Intl Universities Pr Inc.

Glaberson, W. (2000a, April 12). Man and his son's slayer unite to ask why. *New York Times*.

Glaberson, W. (2000b, April 12). Man and his son's slayer unite to ask why. *New York Times*, pp. A1, A28.

Linder, J. (2001). The Trial of John Hinckley Jr. Retrieved Jan. 4, 2007, from http://www.law .umkc.edu/faculty/projects/ftrials/hinckley/hinckleyaccount.html

Lo, W. (2007). Cho-Lo/ SkidLoBlogs. *MySpace.Com* Retrieved June 4, 2007, from http://pro- file.myspace.com/index.cfm?fuseaction=user.viewprofile&friendID=165364300

Morrissey, M. (1997). The invisible minority: counselling Asian-Americans. *Counseling Today*.

Pincus, J. H. (2001). *Base instincts; What makes killers kill*. New York: W.W. Norton & Co. .

Random House Unabridged Dictionary. (2006). New York: Random House.

Reagan, R. (1984, Feb. 23). Remarks at a Meeting With Asian and Pacific-American Leaders. from http://www.reagan.utexas.edu/archives/speeches/1984/22384a.htm

Smith, C., & Thornberry, T. P. (1995). The relationship between childhood maltreatment and adolescent involvement in delinquency. *Criminology, 33*, 451-481.

Insanity Defense Reform Act of 1984, Title 18, U.S. Code, Section 17 C.F.R. (1984).

Van IJzendorn, M. H. (1992). Intergeneration transmission of parenting: A review of studies in nonlinical populations. *Developmental Review, 12*, 76-99.

Widom, C. S. (1989). The cycle of violence. *Science, 244*(4901), 160-166.

Widom, C. S. (2001, February). An update on the "cycle of violence." *Research in Brief,* 1-8.

Yen, R. J. (2000). Racial stereotyping of Asians and Asian-Americans and its effect on crim- inal justice: a reflection on the Wayne Lo case. *Asian Law Journal, 7*(1), 1-28.

Zingraff, M. T., Leiter, J., Myers, K. A., & Johnsen, M. C. (1993). Child maltreatment and youthful problem behavior *Criminology, 31*, 173-202.

CHAPTER 3

MEDIA SOURCES

Books:
Bellini, J. (2001). *Child's Prey*. New York: Pinnacle.

Newspapers:
Advocate (39)
Accessory trial sites offered. (1998, July 31). *Advocate*, p. 5.

Attorneys ask venue change in pearl high shooting case. (1998, February 11). *Advocate*, p. 3.

Brown, T. R. (1998, July 23). Teens' conspiracy charges dropped. *Advocate*, p. 5.

Class time extended an hour for days lost after schooting. (1998, January 11). *Advocate*, p. 5.

Conflict resolution part of curriculum. (1998, August 9). *Advocate*, p. 9.

Conspiracy suspect reported plot to kill before pearl school shooting. (1998, June 22). *Advocate*, p. 3.

Elliott Jr., J. (2003, November 28). Supreme court denies school killer's request. *Advocate*, p. 2.

Hardwell, S. (1997, December 2). Conspiracy suspect jailed again in miss. *Advocate*, p. 4.

Hardwell, S. (1998, January 31). Suspect in murder conspiracy ordered back to jail in miss. *Advocate*, p. 5.

Holland, G. (1998a, November 12). Prosecutors expand case against teen in pearl high shooting. *Advocate*, p. 12.

Holland, G. (1998b, October 1). Pearl marks anniversary of school shooting case. *Advocate*, p. 4.

Holland, G. (1997a, October 21). Grand jury indicts teen-ager in death of mom, classmates. *Advocate*, p. 5.

Holland, G. (1997b, October 31). Teen arraigned in conspiracy. Pearl fears halloween violence. *Advocate*, p. 8.

Hughes, J. (1998a, February 24). Trial set april 27 for slaying suspect. Miss. Criminal case moving unusually fast. *Advocate*, p. 17.

Hughes, J. (1998b, June 6). School shooting suspect, 17, convicted of killing mother. *Advocate*, p. 5.

Hughes, J. (1998c, June 9). Prosecutors reject deal in woodham murder trial. *Advocate*, p. 3.

Hughes, J. (1998d, June 10). Opening statements set today in mississippi school shootings. *Advocate*, p. 13.

Hughes, J. (1998e, June 11). Students: Routine became terror when teen-ager started shooting. *Advocate*, p. 7.

Hughes, J. (1998f, June 12). Defendant admits gunning down 9 pearl classmates. *Advocate*, p. 13.

Hughes, J. (1998g, June 13). Miss. Teen convicted of slaying two at school. *Advocate*, p. 2.

Hughes, J. (1998h, June 14). Victim's family says verdict deserved in school slayings. *Advocate*, p. 7.

Luke woodham enters miss. Prison system. (1998, June 16). *Advocate*, p. 2.

Man pleads guilty in school shootings role. (2000, February 9). *Advocate*, p. 5.

Message of unity sent to ky. School. (1997, December 18). *Advocate*, p. 5.

Moment of silence marks rampage anniversary. (1998, September 19). *Advocate*, p. 15.

Payne, P. (2000, February 12). Alleged mastermind in miss. School shootings sentenced. *Advocate*, p. 9.

Pearl high trials facing booked-up courthouse. (1998, August 2). *Advocate*, p. 5.

Pearl officials offer west paducah aid. (1997, December 4). *Advocate*, p. 6.

Pearl shooting figure wants new judge. (1999, February 2). *Advocate*, p. 5.

Prosecutor wants shooting-case defendent jailed. (1998, January 15). *Advocate*, p. 7.

School shooter loses appeal in mom's murder. (2001, December 1). *Advocate*, p. 6.

School shooting suspect's lawyers want jurors polled. (1998, January 11). *Advocate*, p. 5.

Second bond hearing asked in pearl high shooting case. (1998, February 25). *Advocate*, p. 5.

Teen says accusation in killings devastating despite innocence. (1998, December 24). *Advocate*, p. 10.

Trial delayed for teen charged in miss. High shooting. (1998, October 12). *Advocate*, p. 4.

Trial in miss. School slayings delayed. (1998, February 7). *Advocate*, p. 9.

Trial in school slayings may be delayed months. (1999, January 30). *Advocate*, p. 3.

Two pearl high conspiracy suspects to graduate. (1998, May 25). *Advocate*, p. 3.

Ward, S. (2004, January 22). Woman praises officials in handling of alleged plot. *Advocate*, p. 1.

Associated Press (2)

Associated Press. (2000a, February 11). Miss. Shooter's friend sentenced. *Associated Press*.

Associated Press. (2000b, March 15). Lawyer: Gunman's rights trampled. *Associated Press*.

Boston Globe (1)

Holland, G. (1997, October 2). Miss. Teen stabs mother; 2 more at school, police say. *Boston Globe*, p. A3.

Clarion Ledger (65)

Ammerman, J. (1997, October 2). Officials: More security still not a preventative. *Clarion Ledger*, p. 13.

Berry, P. (1997, October 8). Woodham's lawyers say arrests could impact their defense. *Clarion Ledger*, p. 6.

Floyd, N. L. (1997, October 2). School plans counseling for pupils, staff. *Clarion Ledger*.

Friedeman, M. (1997, October 10). Did halloween have role on lives of those linked with pearl slayings? *Clarion Ledger*.

Graham, C. (1997, October 2). Church services provide comfort for teens, adults. *Clarion Ledger*.

Graham, C., & Berry, P. (1997, October 8). Rumors of cults, heavy drugs not new in pearl, clergy say. *Clarion Ledger*, p. 7.

Harden, C. (1997a, October 2). City is known for cohesiveness, not crime. *Clarion Ledger*, p. 11.

Harden, C. (1997b, October 2). Sinking realization may be that no one is immune. *Clarion Ledger*, p. 11.

Harden, C. (1997c, October 3). Parents express fears, concerns at board meeting. *Clarion Ledger*, p. 9.

Harden, C. (1997d, October 5). Pearl high to slowly ease back into studies. *Clarion Ledger*.
Hayden, C. (1997a, October 2). Security issues edge to forefront after shooting. *Clarion Ledger*, p. 13.
Hayden, C. (1997b, October 3). Adult having gun at school called legal. *Clarion Ledger*, p. 9.
John, B. (1997a, November 13). Woodham showed no remorse in interview, pearl mayor says. *Clarion Ledger*, pp. 1, 13.
John, B. (1997b, October 2). Tragedy compared to earlier rampages. *Clarion Ledger*, p. 12.
John, B. (1997c, October 3). Slain teen known for her forgiving nature. *Clarion Ledger*, pp. 1, 8.
John, B. (1997d, October 11). Accused teen's father says he 'never had doubt' about son. *Clarion Ledger*, pp. 1, 11.
John, B. (1997e, October 12). Teen told police about group. *Clarion Ledger*, pp. 1, 16.
John, B. (1997f, October 12). Victim's father dispels rumors; wants christy's life remembered. *Clarion Ledger*, pp. 1, 16.
John, B. (1997g, October 15). Pearl suspect linked to cult. *Clarion Ledger*, pp. 1, 5.
John, B., & Rossilli, M. (1997, October 8). Teens linked to rampage. *Clarion Ledger*, pp. 1, 6.
Kanengiser, A. (1997a, October 2). High school shooting spree too close to home. *Clarion Ledger*, p. 13.
Kanengiser, A. (1997b, October 3). Pastors console grieving teachers, staff. *Clarion Ledger*, p. 8.
Kanengiser, A. (1997c, October 3). Students mourn, seek diversions. *Clarion Ledger*, p. 8.
Kanengiser, A. (1997d, October 7). Police, pastors greet pearl students. *Clarion Ledger*, pp. 1, 7.
Kanengiser, A. (1997e, October 8). School still on; some fear more violence. *Clarion Ledger*, p. 7.
Kanengiser, A., & King, J. F. (1997, October 2). 2 dead, 7 hurt in shooting at pearl high; student held. *Clarion Ledger*, pp. 1, 16.
Kanengiser, A. (1998, February). Sledge says he faced fear, hatred after arrest. *Calrion Ledger*, pp. 1, 8.
King, J. F. (1997a, October 2). 70 officers respond to shooting call. *Clarion Ledger*, p. 13.
King, J. F. (1997b, October 3). 'why?' official asked suspect. *Clarion Ledger*, pp. 1, 8.
King, J. F. (1997c, October 3). Wounded students recall chilling moments. *Clarion Ledger*, p. 8.
King, J. F. (1997d, October 16). Manifesto curses humanity accused's lifelong suffering. *Clarion Ledger*, pp. 1, 9.
Lindsay, A., & John, B. (1997, October 8). News baffles neighbors, friends of 6. *Clarion Ledger*, pp. 1, 6.
Lindsay, V. (1997a, October 2). Emotional students recall near misses. *Clarion Ledger*, p. 11.
Lindsay, V. (1997b, October 2). Tragedy delays state-required pearl schools testing. *Clarion Ledger*, p. 11.
Lindsay, V., Graham, C., Shaw, C., & Fisher, G. S. (1997, October 2). Student 'scared to go back'. *Clarion Ledger*, p. 12.
Mitchell, J. (1997, October 8). Experts draw link from philosopher to alleged group. *Clarion Ledger*, p. 6.
Patrick, S. (1997, October 2). Grieved, concerned roll up sleeves to donate blood. *Clarion Ledger*, p. 12.
Pearl police chief, da won't disclose details. (1997, October 8). *Clarion Ledger*, p. 6.
Pearl shooting: Tragedy gives vital lesson nationwide. (1997, October 3). *Clarion Ledger*, p. 14.
Pearl tragedy. (1997, October 2). *Clarion Ledger*, p. 14.
Pettus, G. (1997a, October 2). Waves of well wishers wait outside emergency rooms. *Clarion Ledger*.
Pettus, G. (1997b, October 2). Jackson tv stations mobilize to cover nation's 'top story'. *Clarion Ledger*, p. 11.
Plohetski, T. (1997, October 3). Internet site offers chance to comment. *Clarion Ledger*, p. 9.
Rossilli, M. (2000, February 8). Cult like conspiracy claim closes with 2 convictions. *Clarion Ledger*, pp. 1, 6.
Rossilli, M. (1998, July 31). Dismissals sought in pearl cases. *Clarion Ledger*, pp. 1, 6.
Rossilli, M. (1997a, November 13). Lawyers filmed woodham for tv. *Clarion Ledger*, pp. 1, 13.
Rossilli, M. (1997b, November 26). Pearl high conspiracy suspect free on bond. *Clarion Ledger*, pp. 1, 9.
Rossilli, M. (1997c, October 2). Clear headed heros acted instinctively. *Clarion Ledger*, p. 11.
Rossilli, M. (1997d, October 3). Rampage suspect pleads not guilty. *Clarion Ledger*, pp. 1, 9.
Rossilli, M. (1997e, October 7). Prosecutor: Confession legal. *Clarion Ledger*, pp. 1, 7.
Rossilli, M. (1997f, October 8). Injured pearl high student took bullet allegedly intended for son of mayor. *Clarion Ledger*, pp. 1, 6.

Rossilli, M. (1997g, October 11). Mother calls son's conspiracy arrest 2nd tragedy. *Clarion Ledger*, pp. 1, 11.

Rossilli, M. (1997h, October 16). Attorneys fence over prosecutor's case. *Clarion Ledger*, pp. 1, 9.

Rossilli, M. (1997i, October 29). Pearl 'game' led to slayings, woodham friend says. *Clarion Ledger*, pp. 1, 7.

Rossilli, M., & Kanengiser, A. (1997a, October 2). Several see 'hero' wield his own gun. *Clarion Ledger*, p. 11.

Rossilli, M., & Kanengiser, A. (1997b, October 3). Friend of alleged shooter decries societal pressures, disrupts vigil. *Clarion Ledger*, p. 9.

Rossilli, M., & King, J. F. (1997a, October 11). 2nd pearl suspect freed. *Clarion Ledger*, pp. 1, 11.

Rossilli, M., & King, J. F. (1997b, October 15). Longtime friend testifies boyette prayed to satan, admired hitler. *Clarion Ledger*, pp. 1, 5.

Smith, S., & Spencer, B. (1997, October 2). Pearl-northwest rankin football game postponed. *Clarion Ledger*, p. 13.

Wagster, E. (1997a, October 2). Students transported to city hospitals according to injuries, officials say. *Clarion Ledger*.

Wagster, E. (1997b, October 2). Teen prose may signal early angst. *Clarion Legder*, p. 13.

Wagster, E. (1997, October 8). Events put media focus on pearl. *Clarion Ledger*, p. 6.

Warren, K. (1997, October 2). Incident reminds editor of life's thin thread. *Clarion Ledger*, p. 12.

Watkins, B. (1997, October 8). Traumatized pearl takes 2nd blow. *Clarion Ledger*, p. 7.

Works of art linked to violence in past. (1997, October 8). *Clarion Ledger*, p. 6.

Zimmer, J. (1997, October 2). Alleged gunman described as 'intelligent', 'picked on'. *Clarion Ledger*, pp. 1, 16.

New York Times (5)

Bragg, R. (1998, June 3). School slaying suspect on trial in mother's death. *New York Times*, p. A12.

Sack, K. (1997, October 9). Southern town stunned by arrests in murder plot. *New York Times*, p. A16.

Teen-ager accused of killing says he got demons' orders. (1998, June 5). *New York Times*, p. A17.

Teen-agers charged with plotting to kill in satanic campaign. (1997, October 17). *New York Times*, p. A33.

Youth sentenced to life in killing of his mother. (1998, June 6). *New York Times*, p. A12.

Newsweek (1)

Begley, S., & Rogers, A. (1998, July 13). You're ok, i'm terrific: 'self-esteem' backfires. *Newsweek*, *131*, 69.

People (1)

Hewitt, B., & Harmes, J. (1997, November 3). The avenger. *People*, *48*, 116-121.

Rankin County News (10)

Bowers, M. (1998, July 17). Woodham guilty second time. *Rankin County News*.

Bowers, M. (1997, October 1). Three killed in pearl. *Rankin County News*, pp. 1, 2.

Hill, T. (1998a, August). Prosecutor plays confession. *Rankin County News*, p. 3.

Hill, T. (1998b, January 14). Attorneys file motions. *Rankin County News*.

Hill, T. (1998c, January 14). Security continues at pearl high school. *Rankin County News*.

Hill, T. (1997a, October 1). Student charged in triple murder. *Rankin County News*, pp. 1, 2.

Hill, T. (1997b, October 8). Six teens charged with conspiracy in murders. *Rankin County News*, p. 1.

Hill, T. (1997c, October 8). Pearl high assistant principal tells of arrest of murder suspect. *Rankin County News*, p. 1.

Hill, T. (1997d, October 8). Students, faculty work to recover from tragedy. *Rankin County News*, p. 2.

Pearl parents only: Seminar on the occult. (1997, November 5). *Rankin County News*, p. 3.

The Commercial Appeal (1)

Elliott Jr., J. (2003, November 28). School shooter's request denied - court sees no new information from wodham in mom's slaying. *The Commercial Appeal*, p. 7.

The Daily Mississippian (1)

Salter, S. (1998, June 3). Pearl high killer deserves justice. *The Daily Mississippian*.

Time South Pacific (1)
Cloud, J., & Grace, J. (1998, July 8). Of arms and the body. *Time South Pacific*, 38-41.

SCHOLARLY AND OTHER REFERENCES
A.P.A. (2000). *Diagnostic and statistical manual of mental disorders (DSM-IV-TR)* (IV ed.). Washington, DC: American Psychiatric Association.
Athens, L. H. (1992). *The creation of dangerous violent criminals*. Urbana & Chicago: University of Illinois Press.
Bernard, B. (1998). *Fostering Resiliency in Kids: Protective Factors in the Family, School, and Community*. Minneapolis, MN: National Resilience Resource Center, University of Minnesota.
Byrd, R. S. (2005). School Failure Assessment, Intervention, and Prevention in Primary Pediatric Care. *Pediatrics in Review, 26*(7), 233-243.
Coloroso, B. (2003). *The bully, the bullied, and the bystander* New York: Harper Collins.
Durkheim, E. (1897/ 1952). *Suicide: A Study in Sociology*. London: Routledge. .
Garbarino, J. (1999). *Lost boys; Why our sons turn violent and how we can save them*. New York: The Free Press.
Garbarino, J., Kostelny, K., & Dubrow, N. (1998). *No Place to Be a Child: Growing Up in a War Zone*. San Francisco: Josey-Bass.
Goluboff, B. (Writer) (1995). The Basketball Diaries [Film]. In L. Heller & J. B. Manulis (Producer). U.S.A.
Harrison, K. (1998). *The Kiss*. New York: Harper Perennial.
Herman, J., & Hirschman, L. (1977). Father-daughter incest. *Signs: Journal of women in Culture and Society, 2*(4), 735-756.
King, S. (1977). *Rage*. New York: Signet.
Lavey, A. S. (1969). *Satanic Bible*. New York: Avon.
Lewis, D. O. (1998). *Guilty by reason of insanity*. New York: Random House.
Looper, K. J., & Paris, J. (2000). What dimensions underlie cluster B personality disorders? *Comprehensive Psychiatry, 41*(6), 432-437.
Maslow, A. (1987). *Motivation and Personality*: Harper & row.
New York Times Reporting and Research Staff. (2000, April 13). A closer look at rampage killings. *New York Times*.
Newman, K. S., Fox, C., Harding, D. J., Mehta, J., & Roth, W. (2004). *Rampage: the social roots of school shootings*. New York: Basic Books.
Olweus, D. (1993). *Bullying at school*. Oxford, UK: Blackwell Publishers Inc.
Pellington, M. (Writer) (1992). Jeremy [Music Video]. In C. Chris (Producer): Epic Records.
Pincus, J. H. (2001). *Base instincts; What makes killers kill*. New York: W.W. Norton & Co. .
Simon. (1980). *Necronomicon*. New York: Avon.
Twemlow, S. W., Sacco, F. C., & Williams, P. (1996). A clinical and interactionist perspective on bully-victim-bystander relationship. *Bulletin of the Menninger Clini, 60*(3), 296-313.

CHAPTER 4
MEDIA SOURCES

Books:
Bellini, J. (2001). *Child's Prey*. New York: Pinnacle.

Newspapers:
Advocate (39)
Accessory trial sites offered. (1998, July 31). *Advocate*, p. 5.
Attorneys ask venue change in pearl high shooting case. (1998, February 11). *Advocate*, p. 3.
Brown, T. R. (1998, July 23). Teens' conspiracy charges dropped. *Advocate*, p. 5.
Class time extended an hour for days lost after schooting. (1998, January 11). *Advocate*, p. 5.
Conflict resolution part of curriculum. (1998, August 9). *Advocate*, p. 9.
Conspiracy suspect reported plot to kill before pearl school shooting. (1998, June 22). *Advocate*, p. 3.
Elliott Jr., J. (2003, November 28). Supreme court denies school killer's request. *Advocate*, p. 2.
Hardwell, S. (1997, December 2). Conspiracy suspect jailed again in miss. *Advocate*, p. 4.
Hardwell, S. (1998, January 31). Suspect in murder conspiracy ordered back to jail in miss. *Advocate*, p. 5.
Holland, G. (1998a, November 12). Prosecutors expand case against teen in pearl high shooting. *Advocate*, p. 12.

Holland, G. (1998b, October 1). Pearl marks anniversary of school shooting case. *Advocate*, p. 4.

Holland, G. (1997a, October 21). Grand jury indicts teen-ager in death of mom, classmates. *Advocate*, p. 5.

Holland, G. (1997b, October 31). Teen arraigned in conspiracy. Pearl fears halloween violence. *Advocate*, p. 8.

Hughes, J. (1998a, February 24). Trial set april 27 for slaying suspect. Miss. Criminal case moving unusually fast. *Advocate*, p. 17.

Hughes, J. (1998b, June 6). School shooting suspect, 17, convicted of killing mother. *Advocate*, p. 5.

Hughes, J. (1998c, June 9). Prosecutors reject deal in woodham murder trial. *Advocate*, p. 3.

Hughes, J. (1998d, June 10). Opening statements set today in mississippi school shootings. *Advocate*, p. 13.

Hughes, J. (1998e, June 11). Students: Routine became terror when teen-ager started shooting. *Advocate*, p. 7.

Hughes, J. (1998f, June 12). Defendant admits gunning down 9 pearl classmates. *Advocate*, p. 13.

Hughes, J. (1998g, June 13). Miss. Teen convicted of slaying two at school. *Advocate*, p. 2.

Hughes, J. (1998h, June 14). Victim's family says verdict deserved in school slayings. *Advocate*, p. 7.

Luke woodham enters miss. Prison system. (1998, June 16). *Advocate*, p. 2.

Man pleads guilty in school shootings role. (2000, February 9). *Advocate*, p. 5.

Message of unity sent to ky. School. (1997, December 18). *Advocate*, p. 5.

Moment of silence marks rampage anniversary. (1998, September 19). *Advocate*, p. 15.

Payne, P. (2000, February 12). Alleged mastermind in miss. School shootings sentenced. *Advocate*, p. 9.

Pearl high trials facing booked-up courthouse. (1998, August 2). *Advocate*, p. 5.

Pearl officials offer west paducah aid. (1997, December 4). *Advocate*, p. 6.

Pearl shooting figure wants new judge. (1999, February 2). *Advocate*, p. 5.

Prosecutor wants shooting-case defendent jailed. (1998, January 15). *Advocate*, p. 7.

School shooter loses appeal in mom's murder. (2001, December 1). *Advocate*, p. 6.

School shooting suspect's lawyers want jurors polled. (1998, January 11). *Advocate*, p. 5.

Second bond hearing asked in pearl high shooting case. (1998, February 25). *Advocate*, p. 5.

Teen says accusation in killings devastating despite innocence. (1998, December 24). *Advocate*, p. 10.

Trial delayed for teen charged in miss. High shooting. (1998, October 12). *Advocate*, p. 4.

Trial in miss. School slayings delayed. (1998, February 7). *Advocate*, p. 9.

Trial in school slayings may be delayed months. (1999, January 30). *Advocate*, p. 3.

Two pearl high conspiracy suspects to graduate. (1998, May 25). *Advocate*, p. 3.

Ward, S. (2004, January 22). Woman praises officials in handling of alleged plot. *Advocate*, p. 1.

Associated Press (2)

Associated Press. (2000a, February 11). Miss. Shooter's friend sentenced. *Associated Press*.

Associated Press. (2000b, March 15). Lawyer: Gunman's rights trampled. *Associated Press*.

Boston Globe (1)

Holland, G. (1997, October 2). Miss. Teen stabs mother; 2 more at school, police say. *Boston Globe*, p. A3.

Clarion Ledger (65)

Ammerman, J. (1997, October 2). Officials: More security still not a preventative. *Clarion Ledger*, p. 13.

Berry, P. (1997, October 8). Woodham's lawyers say arrests could impact their defense. *Clarion Ledger*, p. 6.

Floyd, N. L. (1997, October 2). School plans counseling for pupils, staff. *Clarion Ledger*.

Friedeman, M. (1997, October 10). Did halloween have role on lives of those linked with pearl slayings? *Clarion Ledger*.

Graham, C. (1997, October 2). Church services provide comfort for teens, adults. *Clarion Ledger*.

Graham, C., & Berry, P. (1997, October 8). Rumors of cults, heavy drugs not new in pearl, clergy say. *Clarion Ledger*, p. 7.

Harden, C. (1997a, October 2). City is known for cohesiveness, not crime. *Clarion Ledger*, p. 11.

Harden, C. (1997b, October 2). Sinking realization may be that no one is immune. *Clarion Ledger*, p. 11.

Harden, C. (1997c, October 3). Parents express fears, concerns at board meeting. *Clarion Ledger*, p. 9.

Harden, C. (1997d, October 5). Pearl high to slowly ease back into studies. *Clarion Ledger*.

Hayden, C. (1997a, October 2). Security issues edge to forefront after shooting. *Clarion Ledger*, p. 13.

Hayden, C. (1997b, October 3). Adult having gun at school called legal. *Clarion Ledger*, p. 9.

John, B. (1997a, November 13). Woodham showed no remorse in interview, pearl mayor says. *Clarion Ledger*, pp. 1, 13.

John, B. (1997b, October 2). Tragedy compared to earlier rampages. *Clarion Ledger*, p. 12.

John, B. (1997c, October 3). Slain teen known for her forgiving nature. *Clarion Ledger*, pp. 1, 8.

John, B. (1997d, October 11). Accused teen's father says he 'never had doubt' about son. *Clarion Ledger*, pp. 1, 11.

John, B. (1997e, October 12). Teen told police about group. *Clarion Ledger*, pp. 1, 16.

John, B. (1997f, October 12). Victim's father dispels rumors; wants christy's life remembered. *Clarion Ledger*, pp. 1, 16.

John, B. (1997g, October 15). Pearl suspect linked to cult. *Clarion Ledger*, pp. 1, 5.

John, B., & Rossilli, M. (1997, October 8). Teens linked to rampage. *Clarion Ledger*, pp. 1, 6.

Kanengiser, A. (1997a, October 2). High school shooting spree too close to home. *Clarion Ledger*, p. 13.

Kanengiser, A. (1997b, October 3). Pastors console grieving teachers, staff. *Clarion Ledger*, p. 8.

Kanengiser, A. (1997c, October 3). Students mourn, seek diversions. *Clarion Ledger*, p. 8.

Kanengiser, A. (1997d, October 7). Police, pastors greet pearl students. *Clarion Ledger*, pp. 1, 7.

Kanengiser, A. (1997e, October 8). School still on; some fear more violence. *Clarion Ledger*, p. 7.

Kanengiser, A., & King, J. F. (1997, October 2). 2 dead, 7 hurt in shooting at pearl high; student held. *Clarion Ledger*, pp. 1, 16.

Kanengiser, A. (1998, February). Sledge says he faced fear, hatred after arrest. *Calrion Ledger*, pp. 1, 8.

King, J. F. (1997a, October 2). 70 officers respond to shooting call. *Clarion Ledger*, p. 13.

King, J. F. (1997b, October 3). 'why?' official asked suspect. *Clarion Ledger*, pp. 1, 8.

King, J. F. (1997c, October 3). Wounded students recall chilling moments. *Clarion Ledger*, p. 8.

King, J. F. (1997d, October 16). Manifesto curses humanity accused's lifelong suffering. *Clarion Ledger*, pp. 1, 9.

Lindsay, A., & John, B. (1997, October 8). News baffles neighbors, friends of 6. *Clarion Ledger*, pp. 1, 6.

Lindsay, V. (1997a, October 2). Emotional students recall near misses. *Clarion Ledger*, p. 11.

Lindsay, V. (1997b, October 2). Tragedy delays state-required pearl schools testing. *Clarion Ledger*, p. 11.

Lindsay, V., Graham, C., Shaw, C., & Fisher, G. S. (1997, October 2). Student 'scared to go back'. *Clarion Ledger*, p. 12.

Mitchell, J. (1997, October 8). Experts draw link from philosopher to alleged group. *Clarion Ledger*, p. 6.

Patrick, S. (1997, October 2). Grieved, concerned roll up sleeves to donate blood. *Clarion Ledger*, p. 12.

Pearl police chief, da won't disclose details. (1997, October 8). *Clarion Ledger*, p. 6.

Pearl shooting: Tragedy gives vital lesson nationwide. (1997, October 3). *Clarion Ledger*, p. 14.

Pearl tragedy. (1997, October 2). *Clarion Ledger*, p. 14.

Pettus, G. (1997a, October 2). Waves of well wishers wait outside emergency rooms. *Clarion Ledger*.

Pettus, G. (1997b, October 2). Jackson tv stations mobilize to cover nation's 'top story'. *Clarion Ledger*, p. 11.

Plohetski, T. (1997, October 3). Internet site offers chance to comment. *Clarion Ledger*, p. 9.

Rossilli, M. (2000, February 8). Cult like conspiracy claim closes with 2 convictions. *Clarion Ledger*, pp. 1, 6.

Rossilli, M. (1998, July 31). Dismissals sought in pearl cases. *Clarion Ledger*, pp. 1, 6.

Rossilli, M. (1997a, November 13). Lawyers filmed woodham for tv. *Clarion Ledger*, pp. 1, 13.

Rossilli, M. (1997b, November 26). Pearl high conspiracy suspect free on bond. *Clarion Ledger*, pp. 1, 9.

Rossilli, M. (1997c, October 2). Clear headed heros acted instinctively. *Clarion Ledger*, p. 11.

Rossilli, M. (1997d, October 3). Rampage suspect pleads not guilty. *Clarion Ledger*, pp. 1, 9.

Rossilli, M. (1997e, October 7). Prosecutor: Confession legal. *Clarion Ledger*, pp. 1, 7.

Rossilli, M. (1997f, October 8). Injured pearl high student took bullet allegedly intended for son of mayor. *Clarion Ledger*, pp. 1, 6.

Rossilli, M. (1997g, October 11). Mother calls son's conspiracy arrest 2nd tragedy. *Clarion Ledger*, pp. 1, 11.

Rossilli, M. (1997h, October 16). Attorneys fence over prosecutor's case. *Clarion Ledger*, pp. 1, 9.

Rossilli, M. (1997i, October 29). Pearl 'game' led to slayings, woodham friend says. *Clarion Ledger*, pp. 1, 7.

Rossilli, M., & Kanengiser, A. (1997a, October 2). Several see 'hero' wield his own gun. *Clarion Ledger*, p. 11.

Rossilli, M., & Kanengiser, A. (1997b, October 3). Friend of alleged shooter decries societal pressures, disrupts vigil. *Clarion Ledger*, p. 9.

Rossilli, M., & King, J. F. (1997a, October 11). 2nd pearl suspect freed. *Clarion Ledger*, pp. 1, 11.

Rossilli, M., & King, J. F. (1997b, October 15). Longtime friend testifies boyette prayed to satan, admired hitler. *Clarion Ledger*, pp. 1, 5.

Smith, S., & Spencer, B. (1997, October 2). Pearl-northwest rankin football game postponed. *Clarion Ledger*, p. 13.

Wagster, E. (1997a, October 2). Students transported to city hospitals according to injuries, officials say. *Clarion Ledger*.

Wagster, E. (1997b, October 2). Teen prose may signal early angst. *Clarion Legder*, p. 13.

Wagster, E. (1997, October 8). Events put media focus on pearl. *Clarion Ledger*, p. 6.

Warren, K. (1997, October 2). Incident reminds editor of life's thin thread. *Clarion Ledger*, p. 12.

Watkins, B. (1997, October 8). Traumatized pearl takes 2nd blow. *Clarion Ledger*, p. 7.

Works of art linked to violence in past. (1997, October 8). *Clarion Ledger*, p. 6.

Zimmer, J. (1997, October 2). Alleged gunman described as 'intelligent', 'picked on'. *Clarion Ledger*, pp. 1, 16.

New York Times (5)

Bragg, R. (1998, June 3). School slaying suspect on trial in mother's death. *New York Times*, p. A12.

Sack, K. (1997, October 9). Southern town stunned by arrests in murder plot. *New York Times*, p. A16.

Teen-ager accused of killing says he got demons' orders. (1998, June 5). *New York Times*, p. A17.

Teen-agers charged with plotting to kill in satanic campaign. (1997, October 17). *New York Times*, p. A33.

Youth sentenced to life in killing of his mother. (1998, June 6). *New York Times*, p. A12.

Newsweek (1)

Begley, S., & Rogers, A. (1998, July 13). You're ok, i'm terrific: 'self-esteem' backfires. *Newsweek*, *131*, 69.

People (1)

Hewitt, B., & Harmes, J. (1997, November 3). The avenger. *People*, *48*, 116-121.

Rankin County News (10)

Bowers, M. (1998, July 17). Woodham guilty second time. *Rankin County News*.

Bowers, M. (1997, October 1). Three killed in pearl. *Rankin County News*, pp. 1, 2.

Hill, T. (1998a, August). Prosecutor plays confession. *Rankin County News*, p. 3.

Hill, T. (1998b, January 14). Attorneys file motions. *Rankin County News*.

Hill, T. (1998c, January 14). Security continues at pearl high school. *Rankin County News*.

Hill, T. (1997a, October 1). Student charged in triple murder. *Rankin County News*, pp. 1, 2.

Hill, T. (1997b, October 8). Six teens charged with conspiracy in murders. *Rankin County News*, p. 1.

Hill, T. (1997c, October 8). Pearl high assistant principal tells of arrest of murder suspect. *Rankin County News*, p. 1.

Hill, T. (1997d, October 8). Students, faculty work to recover from tragedy. *Rankin County News*, p. 2.

Pearl parents only: Seminar on the occult. (1997, November 5). *Rankin County News*, p. 3.

The Commercial Appeal (1)

Elliott Jr., J. (2003, November 28). School shooter's request denied - court sees no new information from wodham in mom's slaying. *The Commercial Appeal*, p. 7.

The Daily Mississippian (1)
Salter, S. (1998, June 3). Pearl high killer deserves justice. *The Daily Mississippian*.
Time South Pacific (1)
Cloud, J., & Grace, J. (1998, July 8). Of arms and the body. *Time South Pacific*, 38-41.

SCHOLARLY AND OTHER REFERENCES
A.P.A. (2000). *Diagnostic and statistical manual of mental disorders (DSM-IV-TR)* (IV ed.). Washington, DC: American Psychiatric Association.
Athens, L. H. (1992). *The creation of dangerous violent criminals*. Urbana & Chicago: University of Illinois Press.
Bernard, B. (1998). *Fostering Resiliency in Kids: Protective Factors in the Family, School, and Community*. Minneapolis, MN: National Resilience Resource Center, University of Minnesota.
Byrd, R. S. (2005). School Failure Assessment, Intervention, and Prevention in Primary Pediatric Care. *Pediatrics in Review, 26*(7), 233-243.
Coloroso, B. (2003). *The bully, the bullied, and the bystander* New York: Harper Collins.
Durkheim, E. (1897/ 1952). *Suicide: A Study in Sociology*. London: Routledge. .
Garbarino, J. (1999). *Lost boys; Why our sons turn violent and how we can save them*. New York: The Free Press.
Garbarino, J., Kostelny, K., & Dubrow, N. (1998). *No Place to Be a Child: Growing Up in a War Zone*. San Francisco: Josey-Bass.
Goluboff, B. (Writer) (1995). The Basketball Diaries [Film]. In L. Heller & J. B. Manulis (Producer). U.S.A.
Harrison, K. (1998). *The Kiss*. New York: Harper Perennial.
Herman, J., & Hirschman, L. (1977). Father-daughter incest. *Signs: Journal of women in Culture and Society, 2*(4), 735-756.
King, S. (1977). *Rage*. New York: Signet.
Lavey, A. S. (1969). *Satanic Bible*. New York: Avon.
Lewis, D. O. (1998). *Guilty by reason of insanity*. New York: Random House.
Looper, K. J., & Paris, J. (2000). What dimensions underlie cluster B personality disorders? *Comprehensive Psychiatry, 41*(6), 432-437.
Maslow, A. (1987). *Motivation and Personality*: Harper & row.
New York Times Reporting and Research Staff. (2000, April 13). A closer look at rampage killings. *New York Times*.
Newman, K. S., Fox, C., Harding, D. J., Mehta, J., & Roth, W. (2004). *Rampage: the social roots of school shootings*. New York: Basic Books.
Olweus, D. (1993). *Bullying at school*. Oxford, UK: Blackwell Publishers Inc.
Pellington, M. (Writer) (1992). Jeremy [Music Video]. In C. Chris (Producer): Epic Records.
Pincus, J. H. (2001). *Base instincts; What makes killers kill*. New York: W.W. Norton & Co. .
Simon. (1980). *Necronomicon*. New York: Avon.
Twemlow, S. W., Sacco, F. C., & Williams, P. (1996). A clinical and interactionist perspective on bully-victim-bystander relationship. *Bulletin of the Menninger Clini, 60*(3), 296-313.

CHAPTER 5

REFERENCES
ABC News (Writer) (1999). Nate Dykeman Interview [Television], *Good Morning America*. USA.
Anton, M., & Ryckman, L. (1999, May 2). In hindsight, signs to killings obvious. *Rocky Mountain news*.
Bartels, L. (2004, May 17). Columbine parents outraged. *Rocky Mountain News*, p. 5A.
Bartels, L., & Crowder, C. (1999, August 22). Fatal Friendship. *Rocky Mountain News*.
Bowlby. (1982). *Attachment & Loss* (Vol. III. Loss: Sadness and depression). New York City: Basic Books.
Breggin, P. (1995). *Talking back to po Prozac*. New York: St. Martin's Press.
Breggin, P. (April 30, 1999). Eric Harris was taking Luvox (a Prozac-like drug) at the time of the Littleton murders. *Psychiatric drug facts* Retrieved Sept 3, 2007, from http://www.breggin.com/luvox.html
Brooks, D. (2004, May 15). Columbine: Parents of a Killer. *New York Times*.
Brown, B., & Merritt, R. (2002). *No easy answers; The truth behind the death at Columbine*. New York City: Lantern Books

Carnahan, A. (1999, May 1). Girl turned down Harris for prom date. *Rocky Mountain News*.

Coccio, B. (Writer) (2003). Zero Day [DVD]. U.S.: Homevision.

Coloroso, B. (2003). *The bully, the bullied, and the bystander* New York: Harper Collins.

Crowder, C. (1999, June 21). Harrises didn't see a monster in their midst friends believe that family taught kids right and wrong, respect for others. *Rocky Mountain News*, p. 5A.

Erickson, W. H. (2001). *The report of Governor Bill Owens' Columbine review commission*. Denver: Office of the Governor.

Faulkner, A. H., & Cranston, K. (1998). Correlates of same-sex sexual behavior in a random sample of Massachusetts high school students. *American Journal of Public Health, 88*(2), 262-266.

Fergusson, D. (1999). Is Sexual Orientation Related to Mental Health Problems and Suicidality in Young People? *Archives of General Psychiatry, 56*(10), 876-880.

Freud, A. (1936). Identification with the aggressor. In *The ego and the mechanisms of defense: The writings of Anna Freud* (Revised edition (June 1967) ed., Vol. 2, pp. 109-121). Madison, CT: International Universities Press.

Galoway. (1999). *Autopsy Report - Dylan Klebold*. Littleton, CO: Jefferson County Sheriff's Office.

Garbarino, J. (1999). *Lost boys; Why our sons turn violent and how we can save them*. New York: The Free press.

Garbarino, J., & Bedard, C. (2001). *Parents under siege*. New York: The Free Press.

Garofalo, R., & Wolf, C. (1998). The Association Between Health Risk Behaviors and Sexual Orientation Among a School-based Sample of Adolescents. *Pediatrics, 101*(5), 895-902.

Gibbs, N., & Roche, T. (1999, December 20). The Columbine tapes. *Time Magazine*.

Glick, P. C. (1993). The impact of geographic mobility on individuals and families. In B. H. Settles, D. E. Hanks III & M. B. Sussman (Eds.), *Families on the move: migration, immigration, emigration, and mobility*. Binghampton, NY: Haworth Press.

Goldwasser, J. W. (2007). Can a Jewish child be baptized in a Catholic church? *Ask the Reform Rabbi*. Retrieved August 15, 2007, from http://judaism.about.com/od/asktherabbi/a/ask_reform.htm

Grollman, E. A. (1971). *Suicide*. Boston: Beacon Press.

Harris, E., & Klebold, D. (1998). Hit men for hire. Littleton, CO: Unpublished manuscript.

Heckerling, A. (Writer) (1982). Fast times at Ridgemont High [Film]. In I. Azoff (Producer). USA.

Hershberger, S. L., & Pilkington, N. W. (1997). Predictors of suicide attempts among gay, lesbian, and bisexual youth. *Journal of Adolescent Research, 12*(4), 477-497.

Hutton, J. B., Roberst, T. G., Walker, J., & Zuniga, J. (1987). Ratings of severity of life events by ninth grade students. *Psychology in the Schools, 24*, 63-68.

JCSO. (1999a). Dylan Bennet Klebold [CD-ROM]. Boulder, CO: Quality Data Systems, Inc.

JCSO. (1999b, May 17). Evidence; Columbine High School; 99-7625; Associates. Retrieved May 22, 2005, from http://columbine-research.info/p10601-10700.pdf

JCSO. (1999c). *JC-001-016023 Charles Mansion Essay, by Klebold, 11-3-98(Hand numbered 10351)* Boulder, CO: JCSO.

JCSO. (2003). 1997 Documents [CD-ROM and web-based materials]: Author/ Quality Data Systems Inc.

Leppek, C. (1999, April 30). Dylan Klebold led life of religious contradictions. *Intermountain Jewish News*.

Lindsay, S. (2000, June 24). Duran gets prison term. *Rocky Mountain News*.

Pooley, E. (1999, May 10). Portrait of a deadly bond. *Time Magazine*.

Raviv, A., Keinan, G., Abazon, Y., & Raviv, A. (1990). Moving as a stressful life event for adolescents. *Journal of Community Psychology, 18*(2), 130-140.

The Robyn Anderson Bill, Colorado House of Representatives(2000).

Russakoff, D., Goldstein, A., & Achenbach, J. (2006, May 2). Shooter's neighbors had little hint. *Washington Post*, p. A1.

Sanchez, A. (1998a). *Juvenile Diversion Program; Needs assessment; Dylan Klebold*. Golden, CO: Office of the district attorney, first judicial district.

Sanchez, A. (1998b). *Juvenile Diversion Program; Needs assessment; Eric Harris*. Golden, CO: Office of the district attorney, first judicial district.

Savidge, M., Zewe, C., & Associated Press. (1999, April 27). Report: Harris and friends tried to buy machine gun. Retrieved June 30, 2005, from http://www.cnn.com/US/9904/27/school.shooting.02/

Shepard, C. (1999a). Columbine shooter Eric Harris's webpages. *A Columbine Site*, from http://www.acolumbinesite.com/ericpage.html

Shepard, C. (1999b). Dylan Bennet Klebold. *A Columbine Site*, from http://acolumbinesite.com/dylan.html

Tarentino, Q., Veloz, D., & Stone, O. (1994). Natural Born Killers. USA.

Wenzel, F. (1999, April 22). Father of 1 Gunman Grew up near Toledo. *Toledo Blade*, p. 12.

Wood, D., Halfon, N., Scarlata, D., Newacheck, P., & Nessim, S. (1993). Impact of family relocation on children's growth, development, school function and behavior. *Journal of the American Medical Association, 720*, 1334-1338.

CHAPTER 6

REFERENCES

American Atheists. (1999, April 30). Out of control? Columbine religious services outrage minority faiths, spur accusations of proselytizing. Retrieved June 13, 2005, from http://www.atheists.org/flash.line/colo7.htm

Associated Press. (1999, September 27). Fathers of Columbine victims cut memorial tree for gunmen's families. Retrieved October 8, 1999, from http://www.cnn.com/US/9909/27/memorialtree/index.html

Associated Press. (2002, March 5). Columbine lawsuit against makers of video games, movies thrown out. Retrieved June 15, 2005, from http://www.freedomforum.org/templates/document.asp?documentID=15820

Bartels, L., & Imse, A. (1999, April 22). Friendly faces hid kid killers. *Rocky Mountain News*.

Belkin, L. (1999, October 31). Parents blaming parents. *New York Times Sunday Magazine*.

Bernall, M. (1999). *She said yes; the unlikely martyrdom of Cassie Bernall*. North Farmington, PA: The Plough Publishing House.

Bilchik, S. (2000). *Kids and guns*. Washington, DC: U.S. Department of Justice.

Boulder News Staff. (1999, April 22). Guns and legislature. *Boulder News*, p. 1A.

Brown, B., & Merritt, R. (2002). *No easy answers; The truth behind the death at Columbine*. New York City: Lantern Books

CBS News. (2001). Most Columbine lawsuits dismissed. Retrieved June 6, 2005, from http://www.cbsnews.com/stories/2001/11/27/national/main319250.shtml

Columbine Memorial Committee. (2004). Columbine Memorial. Retrieved June 21, 2005, from http://www.columbinememorial.org/overview.html

Denton, J. S., Segovia, A., & Filkins, J. A. (2006). Practical pathology of gunshot wounds. Σ *Archive of Pathological Laboratory Medicine, 130*, 1283-1289.

Dwyer, K., Osher, D., & Warger, C. (1998). *Early Warning, Timely Response; A Guide to Safe Schools*. Washington, DC: U.S.Department of Education.

Erickson, W. H. (2001). *The report of Governor Bill Owens' Columbine review commission*. Denver: Office of the Governor.

Fish, S. (1999, May 2). Gun control strife. *The Daily Camera*, p. 1A.

Galloway, B. (1999). *Autopsy Report - Dylan Klebold*. Golden, CO: Jefferson County Coroner's Office.

Gay, L. (1999, June 15). GOP tinkers further with gun legislation; Irate democrats call it the latest attempt to kill gun provisions. *The Daily Camera*, p. 1A.

Hilliard, C. (1999, April 22). Leaders scrap gun bills. *Boulder news*, p. 1A.

JCSO. (1999a). Evidence; Columbine High School; 99-7625; Library Injured; Austin Eubanks Retrieved June 9, 2005, from http://www.boulderdailycamera.com/shooting/report/p001-100.pdf

JCSO. (1999b). Evidence; Columbine High School; 99-7625; Library Injured; Patricia Nielson Retrieved June 9, 2005, from http://www.boulderdailycamera.com/shooting/report/p001-100.pdf

JCSO. (1999c). Hallway Events - Part 2 [CD-ROM]. Boulder, CO: Quality Data Systems, Inc.

JCSO. (1999d). Narrative Time Line of Events 12:00 noon to 5:00 pm [CD-ROM]. Boulder, CO: Quality Data Systems, Inc.

Kalvert, S. (Writer) (1995). Basketball Diaries. In I. Pictures (Producer). USA: New Line Cinema.

Kasindorf, M. (1999, April 26). At memorial, powerful words and a message of redemption 65,000 attend outdoor service. *USA Today*, p. 03. A.

Kick, R. (2002). Witnesses to a massacre: Other participants in Columbine. In R. Kick (Ed.), *Everything you know is wrong*. NY: MJF Books.

Kuntz, T. (1999, May 23). How carnage in our hallways scarred us, and made us better people. *New York Times*.

Lowe, P. (2000, February 14). Columbine was packed with bombs Killers had 95 devices, officials say. *Denver Post*, pp. A-01.

McGowan, D. (2001). Anatomy of a school shooting. In R. Kick (Ed.), *You are being lied to*. NY: The Disinformation Company, Ltd.

Merriam-Webster online dictionary. (2005). Retrieved June 11, 2005, from http://www.m-w.com/cgi-bin/dictionary?book=Dictionary&va=columbine

Roemer, E., Litz, B. T., Orsillo, S. M., Elhlich, P. J., & Freidman, M. J. (1998). Increases in Retrospective Accounts of War-Zone Exposure Over Time: The Role of PTSD Symptom Severity. *Journal of Traumatic Stress, 11*(3), 597-605.

Salazar, K., *Attorney General*, Goodbee, F. M., *Deputy Attorney General*, & Langfield, M., *Senior Assistant Attorney General*. (2004). *Grand Jury Report: Investigation of Missing Guerra Files* Denver: District Court, City and County of Denver Colorado.

Scanlon, B. (1999, April 21 (?)). Dave Sanders alerted lunchroom and than warned others before being fatally wounded. *The Daily Camera*, p. 1A (?).

Schwarz, E. D., Kowalski, J. M., & McNally, R. J. (2005). Malignant memories: Post traumatic changes in memory in adults after a school-shooting. *Journal of Traumatic Stress, 6*(4), 545-553.

Southwick, S. M., Morgan, C. A., Nicolau, A. L., & Charney, D. S. (1997). Consistency of memory for combat-related traumatic events in veterans of Operation Desert Storm. *American Journal of Psychiatry, 154*(2), 173-177.

Today show (Writer) (2000). In T. Touchet (Producer).

Vogt, K. (1999, April 30). Isaiah Shoels funeral is final farewell. *The Daily Camer (Associated Press)*, p. 1 A.

CHAPTER 7

REFERENCES

Blauvelt, P. D. (1999). *Making schools safe for students: Creating a proactive school safety plan*. Thousand Oaks, CA: Corwin press, Inc.

Brown, D. R. (1999, August 17). Safety plan a must for each school district updating policies for dealing with emergencies. *Journal Star*, p. A 1.

Butterfield, F. (2001, March 8). Tips by students result in arrests at 5 schools. *New York Times*, p. 20.

Centers for Disease Control. (2001). National Vital Statistics Report. *49*(8).

Cumming, D. (1999, July 3). Honing safety plans tops school's agenda summer work: new state law, recent shootings ratchet up more dramatic security measures. *The Atlanta Journal*, p. G: 1.

Dwyer, K., Osher, D., & Warger, C. (1998). *Early warning, timely response: A guide to safe schools*. Washington, DC: U.S. Department of Education.

Dwyer, K., Osher, D., & Warger, C. (1998). *Early Warning, Timely Response; A Guide to Safe Schools*. Washington, DC: U.S.Department of Education.

Dwyer, K. P., Osher, D., & Warger, C. (1998). *Early warning, timely response: A guide to safe schools*. Washington, DC: U.S. Department of Education.

Fein, R., Vossekuil, B., Pollack, W. S., Borum, R., Modzeleski, W., & Reddy, M. (2002). *Threat assessment in schools: A guide to managing threatening situations and ti creating safe school climates*. Washington, DC: U.S. Department of Education, Office of Elementary and Secondary Education, Safe and Drug Free Schools Program; and U.S. Secret Service, Nation Threat Assessment Center.

Ferdinand, P. (2001, December 27). Shaken but unharmed, Mass. school says, 'The system worked.' *Washington Post*, p. 3.

Franklyn, B. A. (1964a, December 6). Rifle unit split over gun curbs. *New York Times*, pp. 1, 29.

Franklyn, B. A. (1964b, December 6). Rifle unit split over gun curbs. *New York Times*, p. 1.

Goodall, H. (2008). Students Don't Sign Up for Text Alerts, Colleges Find [Electronic Version]. *The Wired Campus: Education technology news from around the Web*, Feb. 29. Retrieved March 6, 2008 from http://chronicle.com/wiredcampus/article/2787/students-dont-sign-up-for-text-alerts-colleges-find.

The Robyn Anderson Bill, HB-1242 C.F.R. (2000).

Gun Control Alliance. (2005). Facts and Fifures. Retrieved October 12, 2005, from http://www.gca .org.za/facts/briefs/23.htm

Holmes, R., & Holmes, S. (1996). *Profiling violent crimes: An investigative tool.* Thousand Oaks, CA: Sage.

Kline, M., Schnfeld, D. J., & Lichtenstein, R. (1995). Benefits and challenges of school-based crisis response teams. *The Journal of School Health, 65*(7), 245.

Kupersanin, E. (2002, June 21). FBI expert says school shooters always give hints about plans. *Psychiatric News*, p. 2.

Liepe-Levinson, K., & Levinson, M. H. (2005). A general semantics approach to school-age bullying. *Concord, 1*(64), 267-273.

Linenthal, E. T. (1998). Memory, memorial, and the Oklahoma City bombing. *The Chronicle of Higher Education, 45*(11), B4, B5.

MattMaxwellMedia. (2008). Connected, Parts I & II. Abilene, TX: Abilene Christian University.

Norman, M. B. (2001, December 18). Chronology of Getman Case. *Star-Gazette.*

O'Toole, M. E. (2000). *The School Shooter: A threat assessment perspective.* Quantico, VA: FBI, National Center for the Analysis of Violent Crime.

Olweus, D. (1973). *Hackkycklingar och översittare. Forskning om skolmobbning.* Stockholm: Almqvist & Wicksell.

Olweus, D. (1978). *Aggression in the school. Bullies and whipping boys.* Washington, DC: Hemisphere Press (Wiley).

Olweus, D. (1986). *Mobbning—vad vi vet och vad vi kan göra.* Stockholm: Liber.

Olweus, D. (1993a). *Bullying at school.* Oxford, UK: Blackwell Publishers Inc.

Olweus, D. (1993b). Victimization by peers: Antecedents and long term outcomes. In K. H. Rubin & J. B. Asendorf (Eds.), *Social withdrawal, inhibition and shyness in childhood.* Hillsdale, NJ: Erlbaum.

Przygoda, M. J. (2000, October 19). Gurnee safety plan could be model for county. *Daily Herald*, p. 4.

SAFE Colorado. (2000). Welcome to SAFE Colorado.   Retrieved April 19, 2000, from www.safecolorado.org

Semple, J., Robert B. (1966, August 3). President asserts Texas shooting points up needs for a law. *New York Times*, pp. 1, 21.

Simmons, R., & Phimister, R. A. (2003). *Odd Girl Out.* San Diego: Harvest Books.

Vossekuil, B., Fein, R., Reddy, M., Borum, R., & Modzeleski, W. (2002). *The final report and findings of the safe school initiative: Implications for the prevention of school attacks in the United States.* Washington, DC: U.S. Department of Education, Office of Elementary and Secondary Education, Safe and Drug Free Schools Program; and U.S. Secret Service, Nation Threat Assessment Center.

Vossekuil, B., Reddy, M., & Fein, R. (2000). *An interim report on the prevention of targeted violence in schools.* Washington, DC: U.S. Secret service National Threat Assessment Center

U.S. Dept. of Education

National Institute of Justice.

Wiseman, R. (2002). *Queen Bees & Wannabees.* New York: Crown.

INDEX

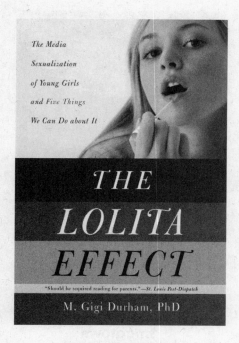

ALSO AVAILABLE FROM THE OVERLOOK PRESS

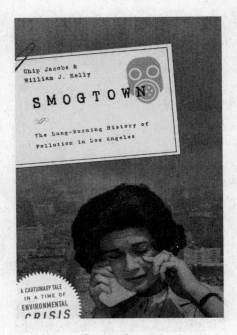

Smogtown
Chip Jacobs & William J. Kelly

"This book is just amazing, a gripping story well told, with the requisite plucky scientists..., hapless politicians, and a nebulous biochemical villain who just will not be stopped."
—*Booklist* (starred)

"In this tale of underhanded deals, gritty politics, community organizing and burgeoning environmentalism, the corruption is plentiful and the subplots replete with intrigue… A zany and provocative cultural history." —*Kirkus Reviews*

THE OVERLOOK PRESS • NEW YORK • WWW.OVERLOOKPRESS.COM